Commonwealth Games and Sports Tourism

Commonwealth Games and Sports Tourism

Global and National Perspectives

Rattandeep Singh

KANISHKA PUBLISHERS, DISTRIBUTORS
NEW DELHI-110 002

KANISHKA PUBLISHERS, DISTRIBUTORS
4697/5-21A, Ansari Road, Daryaganj
New Delhi-110 002
Phones : 2327 0497, 2328 8285
Fax : 011-2328 8285
e-mail: kanishka_publishing@yahoo.co.in

First Published 2010

ISBN 978-81-8457-222-3

PRINTED IN INDIA

Published by Madan Sachdeva for Kanishka Publishers, Distributors, 4697/5-21A, Ansari Road, Daryaganj, New Delhi-110 002; Typeset by Manas Enterprises, Delhi, and Printed at Rajdhani Printers, Delhi.

Preface

The book under discussion deals with the subject area of sports tourism with special reference to Commonwealth Games. Both global and national perspectives are provided herein highlighting the upcoming New Delhi Commonwealth Games. This book gives an introductory overview of Commonwealth Games, Tourism and Sports Tourism. Case Study of Jamaica's New Tourism Strategy is done. An indepth analysis of Commonwealth of Nations is conducted. Also a select review of multi-sport events and types of sports are highlighted. Statistics related to Commonwealth Games with special focus on 2004 Youth Games are given. Similarly, a detailed case study is done for 2006 Commonwealth Games events, ceremonies and festivals. The upcoming 2010 Commonwealth Games in Delhi has been discussed in detail, both in traditional and modern terms. The legacy of Delhi City for hosting the Commonwealth Games, its participants and tourists, has been outlines in detail. Other programmes, mascot, logos and role of organizing committee have been described. Sports schedule and all kinds of related venues have been highlighted. The responsible factors having various impacts on tourism and tourism related institutions have been discussed in detail. As a full-fledged case study, Australia's draft national sports tourism strategy has been presented. The book also contains relevant appendices, acronyms, glossary of terms, bibliography and index. The book is timely and serves the purpose of a reference book.

Rattandeep Singh

Contents

Preface v

1. **Introduction to Commonwealth Games, Tourism and Sports Tourism** 1
   - An Introductory Overview of Commonwealth Games
   - Commonwealth Games England
   - Commonwealth Youth Games
   - Commonwealth Youth Games, 2000
   - Commonwealth Games Federation
   - Tourism: An Introduction
   - Sports Tourism: An Introductory Overview
   - Case Study: Jamaica's New Tourism Strategy

2. **Commonwealth of Nations: In-depth Analysis** 25
   - Towards Understanding Commonwealth of Nations

3. **Multi-Sport Events and Types of Sports: A Select Review** 41
   - Multi-Sport Events: An Introduction
   - Sports: An Introductory Overview
   - Track and Field Athletics
   - Powerlifting
   - Tennis
   - Swimming
   - Squash
   - Hockey
   - Fencing

4. **Statistics Related to Commonwealth Games with Special Focus on 2004 Youth Games** 160
   - Commonwealth Games Statistics (1911—2006)
   - 2004 Commonwealth Youth Games

5. **Case Study: 2006 Commonwealth Games Event, Ceremony and Festival** 172

- 2006 Commonwealth Games
- Opening Ceremony
- Events
- Operation Acolyte
- Festival Melbourne

6. **India at the Commonwealth Games: An Analysis** 205

- Sports History of India
- India at the 2006 Commonwealth Games
- Commonwealth Business Club India
- Impact of Commonwealth Games 2010 on India

7. **2010 Commonwealth Games in Delhi: A Brief Overview** 213

- 2010 Commonwealth Games: An Introduction
- XIX Commonwealth Games at Delhi: A Brief Overview
- Commonwealth Games Movement
- Queen's Baton 2010 Delhi
- Tradition
- Queen's Baton Relay Facts
- Queen's Baton Relay 2010 Delhi
- International Sector
- 2010 New Delhi Commonwealth Games

8. **Legacy of Delhi City for Hosting Commonwealth Games Participants and Tourists** 237

- An Overview of Commonwealth 2010
- Legacy of Delhi
- City Make-Over
- City Infrastructure
- XIX Commonwealth Games 2010 Delhi
- Bed and Breakfast
- Hotel Fact Sheet
- Accommodation Manual

9. **Other Programmes, Mascot, Logos and Organising Committee for XIXth Commonwealth Games** 267

- Volunteer Programme
- Shera—The Mascot
- Commonwealth Games 2010 Official Logos
- Key Stakeholders
- CGF
- Organising Committee Commonwealth Games 2010 Delhi
- Key Objectives
- Business Partners

10. **Sports, Competition and Non-Competition Venues for XIXth CWG: A Detailed Account** 279

- Introduction
- Commonwealth Games 2010 Schedule
- Competition Schedule
- Para-Sports
- Sports Personnels
- Competition Venues
- Non-Competition Venues

11. **Commonwealth Games, Tourism and India: Factors, Impacts and Institutions** 288

- Commonwealth Tourism 2010
- Impact of Commonwealth Games on Tourism
- 2010 Commonwealth Games and India Tourism Industry
- ASSOCHAM's Viewpoint
- Delhi and the 2010 Commonwealth Games
- Commonwealth Games 2010 in Delhi and Tourism Industry
- India Tourism all Set for the Commonwealth Games
- Share in Tourist Arrivals
- India to Boost Tourism Using Commonwealth Games
- Appeal for Looking through the Eyes of Tourists
- Planned Roadshows to Attract Tourists
- Impact of Commonwealth Games 'Tourism Boom'
- Transport Industry as an Integral Part of Tourism
- Sports and Adventure Tourism in India

- Case Study: Himachal Tourism to Offer Commonwealth Games Package
- An Overview of Tourism Related Preparations for XIX CWG in India

12. Draft National Sports Tourism Strategy: A Case of Australia 316

- Sports Tourism: An Overview of Australian Initiatives
- Draft National Sports Tourism Strategy: A Case Study of Australia
- Opportunities for Australia at the International, National and Regional Levels
- Industry Coordination
- Education and Training
- Regulatory Issues
- Research and Data Collection
- Evaluation of Events
- Implementation
- Development Process Strategy
- Summary of Focus Group Outcomes
- Discussion of Definitions
- International Case Studies

Appendix Sports Related Terms, Acronyms and Definitions 366

Glossary 390

Bibliography 404

Index 414

1

Introduction to Commonwealth Games, Tourism and Sports Tourism

AN INTRODUCTORY OVERVIEW OF COMMONWEALTH GAMES

The Commonwealth Games is a multinational, multi-sport event. Held every four years, it involves the elite athletes of the Commonwealth of Nations. Attendance at the Commonwealth Games is typically around 5,000 athletes. The Commonwealth Games Federation (CGF) is the organisation that is responsible for the direction and control of the Commonwealth Games.

The first such event, then known as the British Empire Games, was held in 1930 in Hamilton, Ontario, Canada. The name changed to British Empire and Commonwealth Games in 1954, to British Commonwealth Games in 1970 and assumed the current name of the Commonwealth Games in 1978. As well as many Olympic sports, the Games also include some sports that are played mainly in Commonwealth countries, such as lawn bowls, rugby sevens and netball.

There are currently 53 members of the Commonwealth of Nations, and 71 teams participate in the Games. The four constituent countries of the United Kingdom — England, Scotland, Wales and Northern Ireland — send separate teams to the Commonwealth Games (unlike at the Olympic Games, where the United Kingdom sends a single team), and individual teams are also sent from the British Crown dependencies — Guernsey, Jersey and the Isle of Man — and many of the British overseas territories. The Australian external territory of Norfolk Island also sends its own team, as do the Cook Islands and Niue, two states in free association with New Zealand.

Only six teams have attended every Commonwealth Games: Australia, Canada, England, New Zealand, Scotland and Wales. Australia has been the highest scoring team for ten games, England for seven and Canada for one.

In the 1930 games, women competed in Swimming and Diving only. From 1934, women also competed in some Athletics events.

The next edition will be held in 2010 in Delhi, India. In 2014 the Games will be held in Glasgow, Scotland.

Origins

A sporting competition bringing together the members of the British Empire was first proposed by the Reverend Astley Cooper in 1891 when he wrote an article in *The Times* suggesting a "Pan-Britannic-Pan-Anglican Contest and Festival every four years as a means of increasing the goodwill and good understanding of the British Empire".

In 1911, the Festival of the Empire was held in London to celebrate the coronation of King George V. As part of the festival an Inter-Empire Championships was held in which teams from Australia, Canada, South Africa and the United Kingdom competed in events such as boxing, wrestling, swimming and athletics.

In 1928, Melville Marks Robinson of Canada was asked to organise the first ever British Empire Games. These were held in Hamilton, Ontario two years later.

Opening Ceremony Traditions

- From 1930 through 1950, the parade of nations was led by a single flagbearer carrying the Union Flag, symbolising Britain's leading role in the British Empire.
- Since 1958, there has been a relay of athletes carrying a baton from Buckingham Palace to the Opening Ceremony. This baton has within it the Queen's Message of Greeting to the athletes. The baton's final bearer is usually a famous sporting personage of the host nation.
- All other nations' march in English alphabetical order, except that the first nation marching in the Parade of

Athletes is the host nation of the previous games, and the host nation of the current games marches last. In 2006 countries marched in alphabetical order in geographical regions.

- Three national flags fly from the stadium on the poles that are used for medal ceremonies: Previous host nation, Current host nation, Next host nation.
- The military is more active in the Opening Ceremony than in the Olympic Games. This is to honour the British Military traditions of the Old Empire.

Boycotts

The Commonwealth Games, like the Olympic Games, has also suffered from political boycotts. Nigeria boycotted the 1978 Games in protest of New Zealand's sporting contacts with apartheid-era South Africa, and 32 of 59 nations from Africa, Asia, and the Caribbean boycotted the 1986 Commonwealth Games due to the Thatcher government's attitude towards South African sporting contacts. Boycotts were also threatened in 1974, 1982, and 1990 because of South Africa.

Editions

British Empire Games

- 1930 games - Hamilton, Ontario, Canada
- 1934 games - London, England, United Kingdom
- 1938 games - Sydney, New South Wales, Australia
- 1950 games - Auckland, New Zealand

British Empire and Commonwealth Games

- 1954 games - Vancouver, British Columbia, Canada
- 1958 games - Cardiff, Wales, United Kingdom
- 1962 games - Perth, Western Australia, Australia
- 1966 games - Kingston, Jamaica

British Commonwealth Games

- 1970 games - Edinburgh, Scotland, United Kingdom
- 1974 games - Christchurch, New Zealand

Commonwealth Games

- 1978 games - Edmonton, Alberta, Canada
- 1982 games - Brisbane, Queensland, Australia
- 1986 games - Edinburgh, Scotland, United Kingdom
- 1990 games - Auckland, New Zealand
- 1994 games - Victoria, British Columbia, Canada
- 1998 games - Kuala Lumpur, Malaysia
- 2002 games - Manchester, England, United Kingdom
- 2006 games - Melbourne, Victoria, Australia
- 2010 games - Delhi, India
- 2014 games - Glasgow, Scotland, United Kingdom
- 2018 games - To Be Determined by 2011

Approved Sports

There are a total of 31 sports (with two multi-disciplinary sports) and a further 7 para-sports which are approved by the Commonwealth Games Federation. They are categorised into three types. Core sports must be included on each programme. A number of optional sports may be picked by the host nation, which may include some team sports such as basketball. Recognised sports are sports which have been approved by the CGF but which are deemed to need expansion; host nations may not pick these sports for their programme until the CGF's requirements are fulfilled.

Sport	*Type*	*Years*
Archery	Optional	1982, 2010
Athletics	Core	1930–present
Badminton	Core	1966–present
Basketball	Optional	2006
Billiards	Recognised	Never
Boxing	Core	1930–present
Canoeing	Recognised	Never
Cycling	Optional	1934–present
Diving	Optional	1930–present
Fencing	Recognised	1950–1970
Golf	Recognised	Never
Gymnastics (Artistic and Rhythmic)	Optional	1978, 1990–present
Handball	Recognised	Never
Field Hockey	Core	1998–present

(Contd.)

Sport	*Type*	*Years*
Judo	Optional	1990, 2002, 2014
Lawn bowls	Core	1930–present (except 1966)
Life saving	Recognised	Never
Netball	Core	1998–present
Rowing	Recognised	1930, 1938–62, 1986
Rugby sevens	Core	1998–present
Sailing	Recognised	Never
Shooting	Optional	1966, 1974–present
Softball	Recognised	Never
Squash	Core	1998–present
Swimming	Core	1930–present
Synchronized swimming	Optional	1986, 2006
Table tennis	Optional	2002–present
Tennis	Optional	2010
Tenpin bowling	Recognised	1998
Triathlon	Optional	2002, 2006, 2014
Volleyball	Recognised	Never
Water polo	Recognised	1950
Weightlifting	Core	1950–present
Wrestling	Optional	1930–present (except 1990 and 1998)

Numbers of Athletes, Sports and Nations

This list shows the total number of athletes, male and female, the number of sports they were selected to compete in, and the number of nations (including dependencies) competing.

Year	*Athletes*	*Male*	*Female*	*Sports*	*Events*	*Officials*	*Nations*
2000	4500			16[2]	247		71
2002	3863			17[3]			72
1998	3638			15			70
1994	2669			12			63
1990	2073			10	205		55
1986	1660			10	165		27
1982	1580			12	140		45
1978	1475			11	126		47
1974	1276	977	299	10	121	372	38
1970	1744[1]			10	121		42

(Contd.)

Year	Athletes	Male	Female	Sports	Events	Officials	Nations
1966	1316[1]			10	110		34
1962	863			9		178	35
1958	1122			9		228	35
1954	662			9		127	24
1950	590	495	95	9			12
1938	464			7		43	15
1934	500			6			17
1930	400			6			11

[1]Total including athletes and officials. [2]Includes 4 team sports. [3]Includes 3 team sports.

List of Nations/Dependencies to compete

Nations/Dependencies that have competed

- Aden 1962
- Anguilla 1982, 1998-
- Antigua and Barbuda 1966-1970, 1978, 1994-
- Australia 1930-
- Bahamas 1954-1970, 1978-1982, 1990-
- Bangladesh 1978, 1990-
- Barbados 1954-1966, 1970-1982, 1990-
- Belize 1978, 1994-
- Bermuda 1930-1938, 1954-1982, 1990-
- Botswana 1974, 1982-
- British Guiana 1930-1938, 1954-1962
- British Honduras 1962-1966
- British Virgin Islands 1990-
- Brunei Darussalam 1958, 1990-
- Cameroon 1998-
- Canada 1930-
- Cayman Islands 1978-
- Ceylon 1938-1950, 1958- 1970
- Cook Islands 1974-1978, 1986-
- Cyprus 1978-1982, 1990-
- Dominica 1958-1962, 1970, 1994-
- England 1930-
- Falkland Islands 1982-
- Fiji 1938, 1954-1986, 1998-2006
- The Gambia 1970-1982, 1990-
- Ghana 1958-1982, 1990-
- Gibraltar 1958-
- Gold Coast 1954
- Grenada 1970-1974, 1994-
- Guernsey 1970-
- Guyana 1966-1970, 1978-1982, 1990-
- Hong Kong 1934, 1954- 1962, 1970-1994
- India 1934-1938, 1954-1958, 1966-1982, 1990-

(Contd.)

- Ireland 1930
- Irish Free State 1934
- Isle of Man 1958-
- Jamaica 1934, 1954-1982, 1990-
- Jersey 1958-
- Kenya 1954-1982, 1990-
- Kiribati 1998-
- Lesotho 1974-
- Malawi 970-
- Malaya 1950, 1958-1962
- Malaysia 1966-1982, 1990-
- Maldives 1986-
- Malta 1958-1962, 1970, 1982-
- Mauritius 1958, 1966-1982, 1990-
- Montserrat 1994-
- Mozambique 1998-
- Namibia 1994-
- Nauru 1990-
- Newfoundland 1930-1934
- New Zealand 1930-
- Nigeria 1950-1958, 1966-1974, 1982, 1990-1994, 2002-
- Niue 2002-
- Norfolk Island 1986
- North Borneo 1958-1962
- Northern Ireland 1934-1938, 1954-
- Northern Rhodesia 1954
- Pakistan 1954-1970, 1990-
- Papua New Guinea 1962-1982, 1990-
- Rhodesia 1934-1950
- Rhodesia and Nyasaland 1958-1962
- Saint Helena 1982, 1998-
- Saint Kitts and Nevis (Saint Christopher-Nevis-Anguilla 1978), 1990-
- Saint Lucia 1962, 1970, 1978, 1994-
- Saint Vincent and the Grenadines 1958, 1966-1978, 1994-
- Samoa *and Western Samoa* 1974-
- Scotland 1930-
- Seychelles 1990-
- Sierra Leone 1966-1970, 1978, 1990-
- Singapore 1958-
- Solomon Islands 1982, 1990-
- South Africa 1930-1958, 1994-
- South Arabia 1966
- Southern Rhodesia 1954
- Sri Lanka 1974-1982, 1990-
- Swaziland 1970-
- Tanganyika 1962
- Tanzania 1966-1982, 1990-
- Tonga 1974, 1982, 1990-
- Trinidad and Tobago 1934-1982, 1990-
- Turks and Caicos Islands 1978, 1998-
- Tuvalu 1998-
- Uganda 1954-1982, 1990-
- Vanuatu 1982-
- Wales 1930-
- Zambia 1970-1982, 1990-
- Zimbabwe 1982, 1990-2002

Commonwealth Nations/Dependencies yet to send Teams

Very few Commonwealth dependencies and nations have yet to take part.

- Tokelau is expected to take part in the 2010 Games in Delhi.

- The Turkish Republic of Northern Cyprus have made applications to the CGF to send teams.
- The Pitcairn Islands' tiny population (50 as of July 2009) would appear to prevent the overseas territory from competing. For the same reason Saint Helena's territories of Ascension Island and Tristan da Cunha are unlikely to ever send separate teams.
- Other states and territories with native populations within the Commonwealth that may be eligible include Christmas Island, the Cocos (Keeling) Islands and Rodrigues.
- It is also conceivable that any future members of the Commonwealth such as applicants Rwanda and Yemen may participate in future games.

All Time Medal Table

Rank	*Nation*	*Gold*	*Silver*	*Bronze*	*Total*
1.	Australia	643	556	508	1707[1]
2.	England	579	553	563	1695
3.	Canada	374	402	412	1188
4.	New Zealand	124	168	238	525
5.	India	104	90	72	266
6.	South Africa	92	92	96	280
7.	Scotland	82	94	153	329
8.	Kenya	59	47	56	162
9.	Wales	47	71	96	214
10.	Jamaica	40	30	35	105
11.	Nigeria	37	48	57	142
12.	Malaysia/Malaya	36	48	51	135
13.	Pakistan	21	17	16	54
14.	Northern Ireland	17	23	38	78
15.	Sri Lanka/Ceylon	16	19	19	54
16.	Ghana	15	17	187	50
17.	Singapore	13	9	18	40
18.	Uganda	10	12	17	39
19.	Nauru	9	6	11	26
20.	Cameroon	9	5	7	21
21.	Cyprus	9	5	6	20
22.	Trinidad and Tobago	8	13	17	38

(Contd.)

Rank	Nation	Gold	Silver	Bronze	Total
23.	Bahamas	8	9	9	26
24.	Tanzania	6	6	9	21
25.	Hong Kong	5	2	7	14
26.	Zimbabwe/Southern Rhodesia	3	6	12	21
27.	Zambia	3	5	14	22
28.	Fiji	3	4	5	12
29.	Namibia	3	2	7	12
30.	Guyana/British Guiana	2	5	6	13
31.	Papua New Guinea	2	4	2	8
32.	Barbados	2	3	4	9
33.	Isle of Man	2	1	4	7
34.	Mozambique	2	1	1	4
35.	Bangladesh	2	1	0	3
36.	Mauritius	1	4	3	8
37.	Northern Rhodesia	1	2	4	7
38.	Bermuda	1	2	2	5
39.	Lesotho	1	1	1	3
40.	Jersey	1	0	3	4
41.	Saint Vincent and the Grenadines	1	0	1	2
42.	Saint Kitts and Nevis	1	0	0	1
43.	Botswana	0	3	4	7
44.	Guernsey	0	3	2	5
45.	Rhodesia and Nyasaland	0	2	5	7
46.	Seychelles	0	2	3	5
47.	Samoa	0	1	3	4
47.	Swaziland	0	1	3	4
49.	Rhodesia	0	1	2	3
50.	Grenada	0	1	0	1
51.	Malawi	0	0	3	3
52.	Malta	0	0	2	2
53.	Cayman Islands	0	0	1	1
53.	Gambia	0	0	1	1
53.	Norfolk Island	0	0	1	1
53.	Saint Lucia	0	0	1	1
53.	Tonga	0	0	1	1

[1] Total here lower than total on country page Australia at the Commonwealth Games.

List of Sports at the Commonwealth Games

The current regulations state that a minimum of ten and no more than fifteen sports must be included in a Commonwealth Games schedule. There is a list of core sports, which must be included, and a further list of approved sports from which the host nation may choose to include. The host nation may also apply for the inclusion of other team sports to the CGF General Assembly, as the Melbourne organising committee did with basketball for the 2006 Games.

The current core sports consist of athletics, aquatics (swimming, diving and synchronised swimming), lawn bowls, netball (for women) and rugby sevens (for men). These will all remain core sports until at least the 2014 Commonwealth Games.

The approved list of sports also includes archery, badminton, billiards and snooker, boxing, canoeing, cycling, fencing, gymnastics, judo, rowing, sailing, shooting, squash, table tennis, tennis, ten-pin bowling, triathlon, weightlifting, and wrestling. Some of these are often included in the programme, while others, like billiards and sailing, have not yet been included.

In 2002, the CGF introduced the David Dixon Award for the outstanding athlete of the Games.

There is also a requirement to include some events for Elite Athletes with a Disability (EAD). This was introduced in the 2002 Games.

On 18th November 2006, tennis and archery were added to the list of disciplines for the 2010 Games in New Delhi, bringing the total number of sports to 17. Billiards and snooker were considered but not accepted.

Sports currently included

The years, in brackets, show when the sports have appeared at the games.

- Aquatics (1930-)
- Swimming
- Synchronised swimming
- Diving
- Athletics (men: 1930-, women: 1934-)
- Badminton (1966-)
- Basketball (2006-)
- Boxing (1930-)
- Cycling (1934-)

- Gymnastics (1978, 1990-)
- Rhythmic gymnastics (1994-1998, 2006-)
- Field hockey (1998-)
- Lawn bowls (1930-1962, 1972-)
- Netball (1998-)
- Rugby sevens (1998-)
- Shooting (1966, 1974-)
- Squash (1998-)
- Table tennis (2002-)
- Triathlon (2002-)
- Weightlifting (1950-)
- Events for Athletes with a Disability (2002-)
- Athletics
- Swimming
- Table tennis
- Powerlifting
- Events on Hiatus
- Archery (1982 probably 2010)
- Cricket (1998)
- Fencing (1950-1970)
- Freestyle wrestling (1930-1986, 1994, 2002, back in 2010)
- Judo (1990, 2002)
- Rowing (1930, 1938-1962, 1986) (may be held in 2014)
- Ten-pin bowling (1998)
- Events which have not yet been held
- Karate
- Tennis
- Orienteering
- Snooker
- Yachting
- Taekwondo
- Water Polo
- Lifesaving
- Football

Delhi's Pact for Commonwealth Games: A Case Study

New Delhi: Commonwealth Games 2010 hosts Delhi Tuesday entered into an agreement for strategic alliance with the past hosts of the event—Melbourne. Lord Mayor of Melbourne John So and Chief Minister Shiela Dikshit signed the Delhi-Melbourne Strategic

City Alliance Programme, which will focus on sharing experiences in the preparations and management of the event. "The two cities will also promote development of sports, exchange of sporting knowledge, business relating to sports and tourism and cultural activities," a Delhi Government official here said. Speaking on this occasion, the Chief Minister described the agreement as the beginning of a friendship between the two prominent cities.

"Melbourne is a beautifully managed city, which hosted the last edition of the Commonwealth Games meticulously in 2006." The agreement provides for the establishment of a joint working group. The group, having equal representation from both the cities, will develop an action plan for promotion of sports, economic activities, sports medicine, and tourism between the two cities. Exchange of information and expertise for hosting the Commonwealth Games will be the prime focus for the first three years of the Delhi-Melbourne Strategic City Alliance Programme (IANS).

COMMONWEALTH GAMES ENGLAND

Commonwealth Games England is the organisation responsible for all matters relating to the Commonwealth Games in England. Membership of the Games Council consists of representatives of 26 sports in the Commonwealth Games programme from which the host city selects up to 17 sports for each Games. The Officers are elected by the Council and hold office for 4 years, their work will be supported by four salaried staff. The current President is Dame Kelly Holmes, who won her first international Gold medal at the 1994 Commonwealth Games, in Victoria, Canada.

CGE is a member of the Commonwealth Games Federation who have overall responsibility for the direction and control of the Commonwealth Games.

England has competed in every Games since the first Empire Games in 1930, one of only six countries to do so. The others are Australia, Canada, New Zealand, Scotland, and Wales.

After the 2006 Commonwealth Games, England was second in the All-time tally of medals, with an overall total of 1695 medals (579 Gold, 553 Silver and 563 Bronze). Australia has been the highest scoring team for ten games, England for seven and Canada for one.

Host Nation

England has hosted the Games twice:

1934 British Empire Games - London, England
2002 Commonwealth Games - Manchester, England

How it Helps English Competitors

CGE has been a beneficiary of Sport England funding towards the costs of the preparation of Team England since 1994. This has enabled the CGCE to run extensive management, training and educational programmes, ensuring that competitors and officials alike are fully prepared to meet the challenges ahead.

Funds

The raising of funds for the Team's participation in the Games themselves is the sole responsibility of the CGCE and is raised through sponsorship and fund-raising activities. Donations from Commerce and Industry as well as the general public towards the team's costs are always most gratefully received. Without this ongoing support Team England would not be able to participate in the Games.

England at the Commonwealth Games

- England at the 1998 Commonwealth Games
- England at the 2002 Commonwealth Games
- England at the 2006 Commonwealth Games

COMMONWEALTH YOUTH GAMES

The Commonwealth Youth Games are a small-scale version of the Commonwealth Games, designed for children and young people.

The inaugural Commonwealth Youth Games were held in Edinburgh, Scotland, in 2000, and the second in Bendigo, Victoria, Australia, in 2004.

The third Games took place in Pune, India, in 2008, and were viewed in part as a test event for the 2010 main Commonwealth Games. The fourth Games are scheduled to take place in Douglas, Isle of Man, in 2011. From 2011 onwards the Games will revert to a four-yearly cycle. The hosting of the 2015 Commonwealth Youth Games has been awarded to Apia, Samoa. Wrexham in Wales has so far expressed an interest in hosting the 2019 Commonwealth Youth Games.

In the latest edition of the Games, in Pune, hosts India topped the gold medal tally with 33 gold, followed by Australia and England with 24 and 18 respectively.

COMMONWEALTH YOUTH GAMES, 2000

The 2000 Commonwealth Youth Games were held in August 2000, in the Scottish capital of Edinburgh.

Sports

The following sports were included in the 2000 games:

- Athletics
- Fencing
- Hockey (women)
- Squash
- Swimming
- Tennis
- Weightlifting.

Medal Count

This is the full table of the medal count of these Games. These rankings sort by the number of gold medals earned by a country. The number of silvers is taken into consideration next and then the number of bronze. If, after the above, countries are still tied, equal ranking is given and they are listed alphabetically. This follows the system used by the IOC, IAAF and BBC.

Rank	*Nation*	*Gold*	*Silver*	*Bronze*	*Total*
1.	England	36	41	18	95
2.	Australia	36	27	23	86
3.	Nauru	17	1	0	18
4.	South Africa	13	25	28	66
5.	New Zealand	6	0	0	6
6.	Scotland (host)	3	7	22	32
7.	Malaysia	1	3	5	9
8.	Canada	1	2	1	4
9.	Wales	0	5	3	8
10.	Northern Ireland	0	1	0	1
		113	112	100	325

COMMONWEALTH GAMES FEDERATION

At the heart of the CGF's work is the will to dynamically promote and celebrate a unique, friendly, world class Games. The Commonwealth is an association of independent sovereign states spread over every continent and ocean. From Africa to Asia, the Pacific shores to the Caribbean, the Commonwealth's 2 billion people make up 30 per cent of the world's population and are of many faiths, races, languages, cultures and traditions. The Commonwealth Games is a unique, world class, multi-sports event which is held once every four years. It is often referred to as the 'Friendly Games'. The Commonwealth Games Federation (CGF) is the organisation that is responsible for the direction and control of the Commonwealth Games. As a means of improving society and the general well-being of the people of the Commonwealth, the CGF also encourages and assists education via sport development and physical recreation. Underlying every decision made by the CGF are three core values: HUMANITY - EQUALITY - DESTINY. These values help to inspire and unite millions of people and symbolise the broad mandate of the CGF within the Commonwealth.

TOURISM: AN INTRODUCTION

Tourism is travel for recreational or leisure purposes. The World Tourism Organization defines tourists as people who "travel to and stay in places outside their usual environment for not more than one consecutive year for leisure, business and other purposes not related to the exercise of an activity remunerated from within the place visited". Tourism has become a popular global leisure activity. In 2007, there were over 903 million international tourist arrivals, with a growth of 6.6 per cent as compared to 2006. International tourist receipts were USD 856 billion in 2007. Despite the uncertainties in the global economy, arrivals grew at around 5 per cent during the first four months of 2008, almost a similar growth than the same period in 2007. Tourism is vital for many countries such as Egypt, Iran, Thailand and many island nations such as Fiji, due to the large intake of money for businesses with their goods and services and the opportunity for employment in the service industries associated with tourism. These service industries include transportation services such as cruise ships and taxis, accommodation such as hotels and entertainment venues, and other hospitality industry services such as resorts. As the heritors of Ancient Persian culture, Iranians are among the world nations that are known globally for their warm and appreciatable manner of hospitality as well as French and Chinese people. It is said that the people of these three countries receive their guests in the best possibile situations.

Hunziker and Krapf, in 1941, defined tourism as "the sum of the phenomena and relationships arising from the travel and stay of non-residents, insofar as they do not lead to permanent residence and are not connected with any earning activity." In 1976, the Tourism Society of England defined it as "Tourism is the temporary, short-term movement of people to destination outside the places where they normally live and work and their activities during the stay at each destination. It includes movements for all purposes." In 1981, International Association of Scientific Experts in Tourism defined Tourism in terms of particular activities selected by choice and undertaken outside the home environment. The United Nations classified three forms of tourism in 1994 in its Recommendations on Tourism Statistics: Domestic tourism, which involves residents of the given country travelling only within this country; Inbound tourism, involving non-residents travelling in the given country; and Outbound tourism, involving residents travelling in another country. The UN also derived different categories of tourism by combining the 3 basic forms of tourism: Internal tourism, which comprises domestic tourism and inbound tourism; National tourism, which comprises domestic tourism and outbound tourism; and International tourism, which consists of inbound tourism and outbound tourism. Intrabound tourism is a term coined by the Korea Tourism Organization and widely accepted in Korea. Intrabound tourism differs from domestic tourism in that the former encompasses policymaking and implementation of national tourism policies. Recently, the tourism industry has shifted from the promotion of inbound tourism to the promotion of intrabound tourism because many countries are experiencing tough competition for inbound tourists. Some national policymakers have shifted their priority to the promotion of intrabound tourism to contribute to the local economy. Examples of such campaigns include "See America" in the United States,

"Malaysia Truly Asia" in Malaysia, "Get Going Canada" in Canada, "Wow Philippines" in the Philippines, "Uniquely Singapore" in Singapore, "100 per cent Pure New Zealand" in New Zealand, "Amazing Thailand" in Thailand and "Incredible India" in India.

Most Visited Countries

The World Tourism Organization reports the following ten countries as the most visited in 2007 by number of international travellers. When compared to 2006, Ukraine and Turkey entered the top ten list, surpassing Russia, Austria and Mexico. Most of the top visited countries continue to be on the European continent.

Rank	*Country*	*UNWTO Regional Market*	*International Tourist Arrivals (2007)*	*International Tourist Arrivals (2006)*
1.	France	Europe	81.9 million	79.1 million
2.	Spain	Europe	59.2 million	58.5 million
3.	United States	North America	56.0 million	51.1 million
4.	China	Asia	54.7 million	49.6 million
5.	Italy	Europe	43.7 million	41.1 million
6.	United Kingdom	Europe	30.7 million	30.7 million
7.	Germany	Europe	24.4 million	23.6 million
8.	Ukraine	Europe	23.1 million	18.9 million
9.	Turkey	Europe	22.2 million	18.9 million
10.	Mexico	North America	21.4 million	21.4 million

International tourist receipts were USD 856 billion in 2007 (Euro 625 billion), up from USD 742 billion (Euro 879 billion), in 2006. When the export value of International passenger travel receipts is accounted for, total receipts in 2007 reached a record of USD 1.02 trillion. The World Tourism Organization reports the 10 countries (shown in table 1.1) S1 as the top ten tourism earners for the year 2007. It is noticeable that most of them are on the European continent, but the United States continues to be the top earner.

International Tourism Top Spenders

The World Tourism Organization reports the following 10 countries as the top ten biggest spenders on international tourism for the year 2007. For the fifth year in a row, German tourists continue as the top spenders. A study by Dresdner Bank study forecasts that for 2008 Germans and Europeans in general will continue to be the top spenders because of the strength of the Euro against the US dollar, with strong demand for the US in favour of other destinations.

Rank	*Country*	*UNWTO Regional Market*	*International Tourism Expenditures (2007)*	*International Tourism Expenditures (2006)*
1.	Germany	Eurpoe	$82.9 billion	$73.9 billion
2.	United States	North America	$76.2 billion	$72.1 billion
3.	United Kingdom	Europe	$72.3 billion	$63.1 billion
4.	France	Europe	$36.7 billion	$31.2 billion
5.	China	Asia	$29.8 billion	$24.3 billion
6.	Italy	Europe	$27.3 billion	$23.1 billion
7.	Japan	Asia	$26.5 billion	$26.9 billion
8.	Canada	North America	$24.8 billion	$20.5 billion
9.	Russia	Europe	$22.3 billion	$18.2 billion
10.	South Korea	Asia	$20.9 billion	$18.9 billion

Table 1.1: Analysis of the International Tourism Receipts

Rank	*Country*	*UNWTO Regional Market*	*International Tourism Receipts (2007)*	*International Tourism Receipts (2006)*
1.	United States	North America	$96.7 billion	$85.7 billion
2.	Spain	Europe	$57.8 billion	$51.1 billion
3.	France	Europe	$54.2 billion	$46.3 billion
4.	Italy	Europe	$42.7 billion	$38.1 billion
5.	China	Asia	$41.9 billion	$33.9 billion
6.	United Kingdom	Europe	$37.6 billion	$33.7 billion
7.	Germany	Europe	$36.0 billion	$32.8 billion
8.	Australia	Oceania	$22.2 billion	$17.8 billion
9.	Austria	Europe	$18.9 billion	$16.6 billion
10.	Turkey	Europe	$18.5 billion	$16.9 billion

SPORTS TOURISM: AN INTRODUCTORY OVERVIEW

There are many different definitions of sports tourism, from those involving travel for the purpose of participating in competitive sports, to those involving more leisure or adventure sporting activities. Thus, the extent of sports tourism varies quite a bit. Sports tourism involves people travelling to participate or to observe sports. These activities may include people competing in an international event, such as the Olympics, or simply sitting amongst the audience watching the World Cup match. Inevitably, following sports tourism, there will be consequential impacts. These may be classified under economic impacts, socio-cultural impacts, health impacts and environmental impacts.

The increasing and important impact sport has in economic terms required a more multi disciplinary approach. The economic sector of sport has transformed itself in the last decade from a traditional Spectators-Subsidies-Sponsors-Local (SSSL)-model to a more global Media-Corporations-Merchandising-Markets or MCCM-model. The new sport model has executed forms of vertical integration in the industry and has created synergisms as an outcome of the relations between business and sport. Some of the economic developments are—Broadcasting rights, merchandising, sponsoring, organising of mega sporting events, multiplication effect of organising a sport event, the mobile leisure society, sport tourism, sport and the impact on health, the public-private cooperation in building of sporting infrastructures, the betting industry, raising market share of sporting goods, shoes and clothing. The British Tourism Authority claims that 20 per cent of the tourist trips are for the prime purpose of sport participation, and 50 per cent of the tourist trips include among other purposes sport participation. The data was also validated by 1998 Canadian Travel Survey which set an evaluation of 37 per cent of the domestic trips for sport oriented activities. In the year 2007 the first search engine for sports tourism activities was set.

- *Land Use:* The use of land is necessary to sports tourism. Sports take up space. Some of these sports may even require facilities to be specially built. For instance, golf will definitely require land to be allocated to build its course. Singaporeans who want to experience golf in a bigger and more fulfilling golf course, may seek to travel to nearby Malaysia instead, and this is a form of land use for Malaysia resulting from sports tourism.

- *Cultural Exchanges*: It is certain that cultural exchanges will take place whenever people of different cultural backgrounds meet. Sports tourists will nevertheless learn about the culture of the country they visit when they arrive at their destination, although their main purpose of travel is to participant in sports, or to observe sports (but not for cultural purposes).
- *Preservation of Traditions:* Once-dying traditions can also be 'revived' through sports tourism. The need to display these traditions to tourists will bring these traditions 'back to life'. Showcasing traditional food, traditional costumes, culture and ethnics will not only enrich these sports tourists' experience to the country, but also help preserve the traditions, instead of letting them gradually disappear from this world.
- *National Identity*: The national pride and prestige one feels when a mega event is held in his country is perpetual. It is a proud feeling to know that your country is able to hold an international event, because it will be broadcast worldwide, and therefore known to the rest of the world.

"In Germany "national pride" ("Nationalstolz") is often associated with the former Nazi regime. Strong displays of national pride are therefore considered poor taste by many Germans. There is an ongoing public debate about the issue of German patriotism. The World Cup in 2006, held in Germany, saw a wave of patriotism sweep of the country in a manner not seen for many years. Although many were hesitant to show such blatant support as the hanging of the national flag from windows, as the team progressed through the tournament, so too did the level of support across the nation. By the time the semi-final against Italy came around, the level of national pride and unity was at its highest throughout the tournament, and the hosting of the World Cup is seen to have been a great success for Germany as a nation."

- *Violence:* This usually occurs among the spectators who are unsatisfied with the announced results. The spectators/ audiences usually from the losing side will create fights with the other side. Violence is one of the negative impacts that cam arise from sports tourism. It is an unhealthy scene as this can sour the relationship between two counterparts. Violence in sports tourism does not only happen among countries, but also within one country itself.

There are various health impacts involved when looking at Sports Tourism, they are:

- Physiological impacts
- Psychological impacts, and
- Social health impacts.
  - *Physiological Impacts*: People are generally interested and motivated to play sports when participating in Sports Tourism. Many people all over the world travel to Hawaii to surf as it is a popular destination for big waves. The physiological impact of Sports Tourism can be seen in athletes who are actively involved, going overseas to compete with other people. These athletes typically have a good physique as it is naturally normal for them to want to improve and train to be better. They lead a lifestyle which centres on their health and physical well-being.
  - *Psychological Impacts:* Sports allow for the mind to relax when done for recreation. People who engage in Sports Tourism in a non-competitive environment typically use it as an opportunity to get away and re-charge

    Sports also cause the brain to secrete endorphins, which prevents stress and strengthens the body against pain. At the same time, it makes people increase their self-confidence and boosts their self-esteem.
  - *Social Health Impacts:* The health risks involved in Sports Tourism applies to both the athletes and fans. They might train too hard to compete, risking injuries. Also, one needs time to adapt to another country and

this may sometimes be difficult, sometimes even causing sickness. For example, jet lag.

Similarly, because of the internal time difference, fans all over the world purposely stay up to watch games, and this leads to an irregular sleeping pattern. Cases of fans falling ill during these periods are common, with increased consumption of junk food combined with late nights.

- *Environmental Impacts:* The environmental impacts of sports tourism are classified as negative impacts. It consists of pollution and depletion.
- *Pollution:* Pollution can occur in terms of air, land, water and sound. Air pollution happens basically due to the emission of harmful gases from vehicles. For example during major world games such as the Olympics and World Cup, there will be more vehicles than usual thus increasing the amount of air pollution. Sound pollution occurs due to the noise made by the spectators. As for land pollution, it usually occurs in natural habitats. For instance, sports like mountain climbing pollute the land as the equipment's use can destroy the natural surroundings. Apart from that, littering caused by the masses also contributes to land pollution.
- *Depletion:* In this case, it refers to depletion of resources. For a sports events to be held (which is the main reason for sports tourism), many resources are required.

CASE STUDY: JAMAICA'S NEW TOURISM STRATEGY

New Delhi: Close on the heels of world's fastest human athlete Usain Bolt's dream runs at the Beijing Olympics, his native Jamaica has unveiled a new tourism strategy to strengthen its position online to target discerning 21st century travellers, including hi-end visitors from India. "At the most basic level, the new VisitJamaica.com is an improved means to communicate with and educate travellers about the diversity and culture of Jamaica," the island's tourism director Basil Smith said Wednesday as he and

Tourism Minister Edmund Bartlett globally launched, via a live webcast, the refurbished site. "Sure, we're hoping to cash in on Bolt's tremendous performance at Beijing," Rajiv Nangia, who represents the Jamaica Tourism Board (JTB) in India, told IANS here. Bolt won golds in the 100 metres, 200 metres and the 4 × 100 metres relay at the Olympics, setting new world records in all three events—the first athlete to do so in a single Games since Carl Lewis in 1984. His performance has sparked new interest worldwide in the Caribbean, which is otherwise known for its calypso music and the West Indies' cricket team. The West Indies, of which Jamaica is one of the largest islands, had hosted the 2007 cricket World Cup.

"Jamaica is a new destination for discerning and high-end Indian travellers. Last year, 1,008 Indian tourists visited Jamaica, which was a 100 per cent ramp up over the previous year. We hope to raise this to between 2,000 and 5,000 by 2009," Nangia added. "The refurbished website will definitely help in this as it has an inbuilt booking facility for travellers who may want to make their plans independent of a travel agent if they wish to," Nangia pointed out, adding that the site also has additional features to enable the travel trade better market for the Caribbean nation. The website features a fresh look with a focus on Jamaica's tourism product offerings that go from the "roadside" to the "ritzy". Catering to the needs of the modern and technically savvy global traveller, the website offers a stimulated interactive online experience of the country's diverse attractions, accommodation and indulgences, which many visitors seek before they arrive.

The website is also powered with key features including improved functionality, updated content, quicker response time, GPS tracking of favourite spots and Google Maps. According to Smith, the new site "will be a medium to reach the travel industry and influencers around the world and to maintain Jamaica's position as the premier Caribbean tourism destination". Visitors to the site will be able to explore what Jamaica offers through an engaging experience featuring the country's people, culture, art, music, cuisine, history, attractions and diverse range of accommodation. Greeted with an upbeat version of universal calypso hit "One Love", visitors will be invited to use the "slider" function to navigate through Jamaica's "ritzy" to "roadside" offerings through a flash experience, moving images and videos.

Visitors can also "flip" each image over to learn more and save their favourites in a personalised trip planning page called "My Jamaica". Founded in 1955, the Jamaica Tourist Board is the nation's national tourism agency based in capital Kingston. The JTB was declared the Caribbean's Leading Tourist and Convention Bureau by the World Travel Awards (WTA) for 2006 and 2007, while Jamaica earned the WTA's vote as the World's Leading Cruise Destination, the Caribbean's Leading Destination and the Caribbean's Leading Cruise Destination (IANS).

2

Commonwealth of Nations: In-depth Analysis

TOWARDS UNDERSTANDING COMMONWEALTH OF NATIONS

The Commonwealth of Nations, often referred to as the Commonwealth and previously as the British Commonwealth, is an intergovernmental organisation of fifty-three independent member states. Most of them were formerly part of the British Empire. They co-operate within a framework of common values and goals as outlined in the Singapore Declaration. These include the promotion of democracy, human rights, good governance, the rule of law, individual liberty, egalitarianism, free trade, multilateralism and world peace.

The Commonwealth traces its origins to the Statute of Westminster 1931. It is not a political union, but an intergovernmental organisation through which countries with diverse social, political and economic backgrounds are regarded as equal in status. Its activities are carried out through the permanent Commonwealth Secretariat, headed by the Secretary-General; biennial Meetings between Commonwealth Heads of Government; and the Commonwealth Foundation, which facilitates activities of non-governmental organisations in the so-called 'Commonwealth Family'. The symbol of this free association is the Head of the Commonwealth, which is a ceremonial position currently held by Queen Elizabeth II.

Elizabeth II is also the monarch, separately, of sixteen members of the Commonwealth, known as the Commonwealth realms. As each realm is an independent kingdom, the Queen, as monarch, holds a distinct title for each, though, by a Meeting of

Commonwealth Prime Ministers in 1952, all include the style *Head of the Commonwealth* at the end; for example: Elizabeth the Second, by the Grace of God, Queen of Australia and of Her other Realms and Territories, Head of the Commonwealth. Beyond the realms, the majority of the members of the Commonwealth have separate heads of state: thirty-two members are republics, and five members have distinct monarchs: the Sultan of Brunei; the King of Lesotho; the Yang di-Pertuan Agong (or King) of Malaysia; the King of Swaziland; and the King of Tonga.

History

Origins

The Commonwealth is the successor of the British Empire. In 1884, while visiting Australia, Lord Rosebery described the changing British Empire, as some of its colonies became more independent, as the "Commonwealth of Nations."

Conferences of British and colonial Prime Ministers had occurred periodically since 1887, leading to the creation of the Imperial Conferences in 1911. The formal organisation of the Commonwealth developed from the Imperial Conferences, where the independence of the self-governing colonies and especially of dominions was recognised. The Irish Oath of Allegiance, agreed in 1921, included the Irish Free State's adherence to and membership of the group of nations forming the British Commonwealth of Nations. In the Balfour Declaration at the Imperial Conference in 1926, Britain and its dominions agreed that they were equal in status, in no way subordinate one to another in any aspect of their domestic or external affairs, though united by common allegiance to the Crown, and freely associated as members of the British Commonwealth of Nations. This relationship was eventually formalised by the Statute of Westminster in 1931. The word "British" was dropped when the modern Commonwealth of Nations was formed in April 1949, after the London Declaration.

Remaining Members gain Independence

After World War II, the British Empire was gradually dismantled to just 14 remaining 'British overseas territories', still held by the United Kingdom of Great Britain and Northern Ireland today, partly owing to the rise of independence movements in the subject territories and partly owing to both the British Government's straitened circumstances resulting from the cost of the war and a progressive domestic movement to decolonise. In 1949, the word "British" was dropped from the title of the Commonwealth to reflect its changing nature. Burma (a.k.a. Myanmar, 1948), and Aden (1967) are the only former colonies not to have joined the Commonwealth upon post-war independence. Among the former British protectorates and mandates, those which never became members of the Commonwealth are Egypt (independent in 1922), Iraq (1932), Transjordan (1946), Palestine (most of which became the state of Israel in 1948), Sudan (1956), British Somaliland (which became part of Somalia, 1960), Kuwait (1961), Bahrain (1971), Oman (1971), Qatar (1971), and the United Arab Emirates (1971).

Members with Heads of State other than the British Sovereign

The issue of countries with constitutional structures not based on a shared Crown, but which wished to remain members of the Commonwealth, came to a head in 1948 with the passage of the Republic of Ireland Act 1948 in which Ireland renounced the sovereignty of the Crown and thus left the Commonwealth. However, the Ireland Act 1949 passed by the Parliament of Westminster gave citizens of the Republic of Ireland a status similar to that of citizens of the Commonwealth in UK law. The issue was resolved in April 1949 at a Commonwealth prime ministers' meeting in London. Under this London Declaration, India agreed that, when it became a republic, in January 1950, it would accept the British Sovereign as a 'symbol of the free association of its independent member nations and, as such, Head of the Commonwealth'.

The other Commonwealth countries in turn recognised India's continuing membership of the association. At Pakistan's insistence, India was not regarded as an exceptional case and it was assumed that other states would be accorded the same treatment as India.

The London Declaration is often seen as marking the beginning of the modern Commonwealth. Following India's precedent, other nations became republics, or constitutional monarchies with monarchs different from that of the United Kingdom, while some countries retained the same monarch as the United Kingdom, but their monarchies developed differently and soon became fully independent of the British monarchy. The monarch of each

Commonwealth realm, whilst the same person is regarded as a separate legal personality for each realm.

New Commonwealth

As the Commonwealth grew, Britain and the pre-1945 dominions (a term formally dropped in the 1940s) became informally known as the "Old Commonwealth", particularly since the 1960s when some of them disagreed with poorer, African and Asian (or New Commonwealth) members about various issues at Commonwealth Heads of Government meetings. Accusations that the old, "White" Commonwealth had different interests from African Commonwealth nations in particular, and charges of racism and colonialism, arose during heated debates about Rhodesia in the 1960s and 1970s, the imposition of sanctions against apartheid-era South Africa in the 1980s and, more recently, about whether to press for democratic reforms in Nigeria and then Zimbabwe.

The term *New Commonwealth* is also used in the United Kingdom (especially in the 1960s and 1970s) to refer to recently decolonised countries, which are predominantly non-white and developing. It was often used in debates about immigration from these countries.

Membership

Membership Criteria

The criteria for membership of the Commonwealth of Nations have developed over time from a series of separate documents. The Statute of Westminster 1931, as the fundamental founding document of the organisation, laid out that membership required dominionhood. The 1949 London Declaration ended this, allowing republican and indigenous monarchic members on the condition that they recognised the British monarch as the 'Head of the Commonwealth'. In the wake of the wave of decolonisation in the 1960s, these constitutional principles were augmented by political, economic, and social principles. The first of these was set out in 1961, when it was decided that respect for racial equality would be a requisite of membership, leading directly to the withdrawal of South Africa's re-application (which they were required to make under the formula of the London Declaration upon becoming a republic). The fourteen points of the 1971 Singapore Declaration dedicated all members to the principles of world peace, liberty, human rights, equality, and free trade.

These criteria were unenforceable for two decades, until, in 1991, the Harare Declaration was issued, dedicating the leaders to applying the Singapore principles to the completion of decolonisation, the end of the Cold War, and the fall of Apartheid in South Africa. The mechanisms by which these principles would be applied were created, and the manner clarified by the 1995 Millbrook Commonwealth Action Programme, which created the Commonwealth Ministerial Action Group (CMAG), which has the power to rule on whether members meet the requirements for membership under the Harare Declaration. Also in 1995, an Inter-Governmental Group was created to finalise and codify the full requirements for membership. Upon reporting in 1997, as adopted under the Edinburgh Declaration, the Inter-Governmental Group ruled that any future members would have to have a direct constitutional link with an existing member.

In addition to this new rule, the former rules were consolidated into a single document. These requirements, which remain the same today, are that members must: accept and comply with the Harare principles, be fully sovereign states, recognise the monarch of the Commonwealth realms as the Head of the Commonwealth, accept the English language as the means of Commonwealth communication, and respect the wishes of the general population *vis-à-vis* Commonwealth membership. These requirements had undergone review, and a report on potential amendments was presented by the Committee on Commonwealth Membership to the Commonwealth Heads of Government Meeting 2007. New members will not be admitted at the 2007 CHOGM, with 2009 set as the earliest date of entry.

Members

The Commonwealth comprises fifty-three of the world's countries, across all six inhabited continents. The members have a combined population of 2.1 billion people, almost a third of the world population, of which 1.17 billion live in India and 94 per cent live in Asia and Africa combined. After India, the next largest Commonwealth countries by population are Pakistan (176 million),

Bangladesh (156 million), Nigeria (154 million), the United Kingdom (61 million) and South Africa (49 million). Tuvalu is the smallest member, with only 12,000 people.

The land area of the Commonwealth nations is about 31,500,000 km^2 (12,200,000 sq mi), or about 21 per cent of the total world land area. The three largest Commonwealth nations by area are Canada at 10,000,000 km^2 (3,900,000 sq mi), Australia at 7,700,000 km^2 (2,970,000 sq mi), and India at 3,300,000 km^2 (1,270,000 sq mi). The Commonwealth members have a combined gross domestic product (measured in purchasing power parity) of $10.6 trillion, 66 per cent of which is accounted for by the four largest economies: India ($3.3 trillion), the United Kingdom ($2.3 trillion), Canada ($1.3 trillion), and Australia ($800 billion).

The status of 'Member in Arrears' is used to denote those that are in arrears in paying subscription dues to the Commonwealth. The status was originally known as 'special membership', but was renamed on the Committee on Commonwealth Membership's recommendation. Currently, there is one Member in Arrears: Nauru. Nauru joined as a special member, but was a full member from 1 May 1999 to January 2006, when it reverted.

New members must 'as a general rule' have a direct constitutional link to an existing member. In most cases, the existing member is the United Kingdom, but some have links to other countries, either exclusively or more directly (e.g. Samoa to New Zealand, Papua New Guinea to Australia, and Namibia to South Africa). There is only one member of the present Commonwealth that has never had any constitutional link to the British Empire or a Commonwealth member; Mozambique, a former Portuguese colony, was admitted in 1995 on the back of the triumphal re-admission of South Africa and Mozambique's first democratic elections, held in 1994. Mozambique's entry was controversial, leading to the Edinburgh Declaration and the current membership guidelines.

Applicants

Rwanda (since 2003), Sudan, Algeria, Madagascar and Yemen have applied to join the Commonwealth, and there was some interest expressed by Israel (being formerly administered by the United Kingdom) and the Palestinian National Authority. In 2006 the Commonwealth of Nations secretary-general said Israel and Palestine could join the Commonwealth.

Other eligible applicants could come from any of the remaining inhabited British overseas territories, Crown dependencies, Australian external territories and Associated States of New Zealand if any become fully independent. Many such jurisdictions are already directly represented within the Commonwealth, particularly through the Commonwealth Family.

France secretly considered membership in the 1950s, under the leadership of Prime Minister Guy Mollet. In the context of nationalisation of the Suez Canal, colonial unrest, and increasing tensions between British-backed Jordan and French-backed Israel, Mollet saw a union between Britain and France as a possible solution. A British Government document of the time reported "That the French would welcome a common citizenship arrangement on the Irish basis". The request was turned down by the British Prime Minister Anthony Eden, along with a request for Commonwealth membership, and a year later France signed the Treaty of Rome with West Germany and the other founding nations of the Common Market, later to become the EU.

Suspension

In recent years, the Commonwealth has suspended several members "from the Councils of the Commonwealth" for "serious or persistent violations" of the Harare Declaration, particularly in abrogating their responsibility to have democratic government. This is done by the Commonwealth Ministerial Action Group (CMAG), which meets regularly to address potential breaches of the Harare Declaration. Suspended members are not represented at meetings of Commonwealth leaders and ministers, although they remain members of the organisation. Currently, there is one suspended member: Fiji

Nigeria was suspended between 11 November 1995 and 29 May 1999, following its execution of Ken Saro-Wiwa on the eve of the 1995 CHOGM. Pakistan was the second country to be suspended, on 18 October 1999 following a military coup by Pervez Musharraf. The Commonwealth's longest suspension came to an end on 22 May 2004, with the readmittance of Pakistan, following the restoration of the country's constitution. Pakistan was suspended for a second time, far more briefly, for six months from 22 November 2007, when Musharraf called a state of emergency. Zimbabwe was suspended in 2002 over concerns with the electoral and land reform policies of Robert Mugabe's ZANU-PF government, before Zimbabwe withdrew from the organisation in 2003.

Fiji, which was not a member of the Commonwealth between 1987 and 1997 as a result of a pair of coups *d'état*, has also been suspended twice, with the first suspension being imposed from 6 June 2000 to 20 December 2001 after another coup. Fiji has been suspended once again, since 8 December 2006, following the most recent coup, this suspension only applying to membership on the Councils of the Commonwealth. After failing to meet a Commonwealth deadline for setting national elections by 2010, Fiji was "fully suspended" on 1 September 2009. The Secretary-General of the Commonwealth, Kamalesh Sharma, confirmed that full suspension meant that Fiji would be excluded from Commonwealth meetings, sporting events, and the technical assistance programme (with an exception for assistance in re-establishing democracy). Sharma also stated that Fiji would remain a member of the Commonwealth during its suspension, but would be excluded from emblematic representation by the secretariat.

Termination of Membership

As membership is purely voluntary, member governments can choose at any time to leave the Commonwealth. Pakistan left on 30 January 1972 in protest at the Commonwealth's recognition of breakaway Bangladesh, but rejoined on 2 August 1989. Zimbabwe left in 2003 when the Commonwealth heads of government refused to lift the country's suspension on the grounds of alleged human rights violations and deliberate misgovernment.

Although heads of government have the power to suspend member states from active participation, the Commonwealth has no provision for the expulsion of members. Until 2007, Commonwealth realms that became republics automatically ceased to be members, until (like India in 1950) they obtained the permission of other members to remain in the organisation. This policy has been changed, so if any current Commonwealth realms were to become republics, they would not have to go through this process. The Irish Free State left the Commonwealth when it declared itself a republic, on 18 April 1949, after passing the Republic of Ireland Act 1948; because it preceded India's London Declaration, remaining in the Commonwealth was not an option.

South Africa was prevented from continuing as a member after it became a republic in 1961, due to hostility from many members, particularly those in Africa and Asia as well as Canada, to its policy of apartheid. The South African government withdrew its application to remain in the organisation as a republic when it became clear at the 1961 Meeting of Commonwealth Prime Ministers that any such application would be rejected. South Africa was re-admitted to the Commonwealth in 1994, following the end of apartheid earlier that same year.

The declaration of a republic in Fiji in 1987, after military coups designed to deny Indo-Fijians political power there, was not accompanied by an application to remain. Commonwealth membership was held to have lapsed until 1997, after discriminatory provisions in the republican constitution were repealed and reapplication for membership made.

Objectives and Activities

The Commonwealth's objectives were first outlined in the 1971 Singapore Declaration, which committed the Commonwealth to the institution of world peace; promotion of representative democracy and individual liberty; the pursuit of equality and opposition to racism; the fight against poverty, ignorance, and disease; and free trade. To these were added opposition to discrimination on the basis of gender by the Lusaka Declaration of 1979 (which mostly concerned racism), and environmental sustainability by the Langkawi Declaration of 1989. These objectives were reinforced by the Harare Declaration in 1991.

The Commonwealth's current highest-priority aims are on the promotion of democracy and development, as outlined in the 2003 Aso Rock Declaration, which built on those in Singapore and Harare and clarified their terms of reference, stating: "We are committed to democracy, good governance, human rights, gender equality, and a more equitable sharing of the benefits of globalisation." The Commonwealth website lists its areas of work as: Democracy, Economics, Education, Gender, Governance, Human Rights, Law, Small States, Sport, Sustainability, and Youth.

The Commonwealth has long been distinctive as an international forum where highly developed economies (such as the United Kingdom, Australia, Canada, Singapore, and New

Zealand) and many of the world's poorer countries seek to reach agreement by consensus. This aim has sometimes been difficult to achieve, as when disagreements over Rhodesia in the late 1960s and 1970s and over apartheid in South Africa in the 1980s led to a cooling of relations between the United Kingdom and African members.

Through a separate voluntary fund, Commonwealth governments support the Commonwealth Youth Programme, a division of the Secretariat with offices in Gulu (Uganda), Lusaka (Zambia), Chandigarh (India), Georgetown (Guyana) and Honiara (Solomon Islands).

Structure

Head of the Commonwealth

Under the formula of the London Declaration, Queen Elizabeth II is the Head of the Commonwealth, a title that is currently annexed to that of British monarchy. However, when the monarch dies, the successor to the crown does not automatically become Head of the Commonwealth. The position is symbolic: representing the free association of independent members. Sixteen members of the Commonwealth, known as Commonwealth realms, recognise the Queen as their head of state. The majority of members, thirty-one, are republics, and a further five have monarchs of different royal houses.

Commonwealth Heads of Government Meeting

The main decision-making forum of the organisation is the biennial Commonwealth Heads of Government Meeting (CHOGM), where Commonwealth Heads of Government, including (amongst others) Prime Ministers and Presidents, assemble for several days to discuss matters of mutual interest. CHOGM is the successor to the Meetings of Commonwealth Prime Ministers and earlier Imperial Conferences and Colonial Conferences dating back to 1887. There are also regular meetings of finance ministers, law ministers, health ministers, etc. Members in Arrears, as Special Members before them, are not invited to send representatives to either ministerial meetings or CHOGMs.

The head of government hosting the Head of Government Meeting is called the Commonwealth Chairperson-in-Office, and retains the position until the following CHOGM. The Chairperson-in-Office is often granted authority.

Commonwealth Secretariat

The Commonwealth Secretariat, established in 1965, is the main intergovernmental agency of the Commonwealth, facilitating consultation and cooperation among member governments and countries. It is responsible to member governments collectively. The Commonwealth of Nations is represented in the United Nations General Assembly by the Secretariat, as an observer.

Based in London, the Secretariat organises Commonwealth summits, meetings of ministers, consultative meetings and technical discussions; it assists policy development and provides policy advice, and facilitates multilateral communication among the member governments. It also provides technical assistance to help governments in the social and economic development of their countries and in support of the Commonwealth's fundamental political values.

The Secretariat is headed by the Commonwealth Secretary-General who is elected by Commonwealth Heads of Government for no more than two four-year terms. The Secretary-General and two Deputy Secretaries-General direct the divisions of the Secretariat. The present Secretary-General is Kamalesh Sharma, from India, who took office on 1 April 2008, succeeding Don McKinnon of New Zealand (2000–08). The first Secretary-General was Arnold Smith of Canada (1965–75), followed by Sir Shridath Ramphal of Guyana (1975–90).

Commonwealth Family

Commonwealth countries share many links outside government, with over a hundred Commonwealth-wide non-governmental organisations, notably for sport, culture, education and charity. The Association of Commonwealth Universities is an important vehicle for academic links, particularly through scholarships, principally the Commonwealth Scholarship, for students to study in universities in other Commonwealth countries. There are also many non-official associations that bring together individuals who work within the spheres of law and government, such as the Commonwealth Lawyers Association and the Commonwealth Parliamentary Association.

Commonwealth Foundation

The Commonwealth Foundation is an intergovernmental organisation, resourced by and reporting to Commonwealth governments, and guided by Commonwealth values and priorities. Its mandate is to strengthen civil society in the achievement of Commonwealth priorities: democracy and good governance, respect for human rights and gender equality, poverty eradication and sustainable, people-centred development, and to promote arts and culture.

The Foundation was established by the Heads of Government in 1965. Admittance is open to all members of the Commonwealth and (as of December 2008) stands at 46 governments out of the 53 member countries. Associate Membership, which is open to associated states or overseas territories of member governments, has been granted to Gibraltar. The year 2005 saw celebrations for the Foundation's 40th Anniversary. The Foundation is headquartered in Marlborough House, Pall Mall, London. Regular liaison and cooperation between the Secretariat and the Foundation is in place.

The Foundation continues to serve the broad purposes for which it was established as written in the Memorandum of Understanding:

The Foundation's vision is of a Commonwealth where citizens are able to give voice to their aspirations, identify their own solutions and fulfill their role in society. It is a Commonwealth where citizens, individually and collectively, express themselves for the public good at local, national and international levels by facing global challenges, building strong communities and promoting the rights of all citizens. It is a Commonwealth where civil society organisations realise their full potential, engaging with both government and the private sector in the shared enterprise of transformation of nation-building and international cooperation.

The Commonwealth Foundation's mission is to strengthen civil society organisations across the Commonwealth by promoting democracy, advancing sustainable development and fostering inter-cultural understanding.

Commonwealth Games

A multi-sport championship called the Commonwealth Games is held every four years; the most recent having been held in

Melbourne, Australia, in 2006, and the next due to be held in New Delhi, India, in 2010. As well as the usual athletic disciplines, as at the Summer Olympic Games, the Games include sports particularly popular in the Commonwealth, such as bowls, netball, and rugby sevens. Starting in 1930, the Games were founded on the Olympic model of amateurism, but were deliberately designed to be, as they are still renowned for being, 'the Friendly Games', with the goal of promoting relations between Commonwealth countries and celebrating their shared sporting and cultural heritage.

The Games are the Commonwealth's most visible activity, and interest in the operation of the Commonwealth increases greatly when the Games are held. There is controversy over whether the Games, and sport generally, should be involved in the Commonwealth's wider political concerns. The 1977 Gleneagles Agreement was signed to commit Commonwealth countries to combat Apartheid through discouraging sporting contact with South Africa (which was not then a member), whilst the 1986 Games were boycotted by most African, Asian, and Caribbean countries for failure of other countries to enforce the Gleneagles Agreement.

Commonwealth of Learning

The Commonwealth of Learning (COL) is an intergovernmental organisation created by the Heads of Government to encourage the development and sharing of open learning/distance education knowledge, resources and technologies. COL is helping developing nations improve access to quality education and training.

Commonwealth Business Council

The Commonwealth Business Council (CBC) was formed at 1997 CHOGM. The aim was to utilise the global network of the Commonwealth more effectively for the promotion of global trade and investment for shared prosperity.

The CBC acts as a bridge for co-operation between business and government, concentrating efforts on these specific areas enhancing trade, facilitating ICT for Development, mobilising investment, promoting corporate citizenship, and Public Private

Partnerships. The CBC has a dedicated team, CBC Technologies, based in London and is focused on the international technology and global services industry throughout the Commonwealth.

Culture

Mostly due to their history of British rule, many Commonwealth nations possess certain identifiable traditions and customs that are elements of a shared Commonwealth culture. Examples include common sports such as cricket and rugby, driving on the left, the Westminster system of parliamentary democracy, common law, and the use of British rather than American spelling conventions (see English in the Commonwealth of Nations). None of these is universal amongst, nor exclusive to, the Commonwealth; but are more commonly found within its members than elsewhere.

Sport

Due to the legacy of British colonial rule, many Commonwealth nations play similar sports that are considered quintessentially 'Commonwealth' in character, including cricket, both codes of rugby, and netball. This has led to the development of friendly national rivalries between the main sporting nations that have often defined their relations with each another. Indeed, said rivalries provided a constant in their relationships, even as the Empire transformed into the Commonwealth: preserving close ties. Externally, playing these sports is seen to be a sign of sharing a certain Commonwealth culture; the adoption of cricket at schools in Rwanda is seen as symbolic of the country's move towards Commonwealth membership.

Besides the Commonwealth Games, a number of other sporting competitions are organised on a Commonwealth basis, through championship tournaments such as the Commonwealth Judo Championships, Commonwealth Rowing Championships, Commonwealth Sailing Championships, and Commonwealth Shooting Championships. Boxing has long maintained Commonwealth titles, administered by the Commonwealth Boxing Council, for the best boxers in the Commonwealth.

Literature

The shared history of British presence has also produced a substantial body of writing in many languages, known as Commonwealth Literature. There is an Association for Commonwealth Literature and Language Studies, with nine chapters worldwide and an international conference is held every three years.

In 1987, the Commonwealth Foundation established the Commonwealth Writers Prize 'to encourage and reward the upsurge of new Commonwealth fiction and ensure that works of merit reach a wider audience outside their country of origin'. Caryl Phillips won the Commonwealth Writers Prize 2004 for *A Distant Shore*. Mark Haddon won the Commonwealth Writers' Prize 2004 Best First Book prize worth £3,000 for *The Curious Incident of the Dog in the Night-time*.

Although not affiliated with the Commonwealth in an official manner, the prestigious Man Booker Prize is awarded annually to an author from a Commonwealth country or the Republic of Ireland. This honour is one of the highest in literature.

Symbols

The Commonwealth has adopted a number of symbols that represent the association of its members. Elizabeth II holds the position of Head of the Commonwealth as a symbol of the Commonwealth's free association, dating back to the London Declaration, issued in 28 April 1949. The English language is recognised as a symbol of the members' heritage; as well as being considered a symbol of the Commonwealth, recognition of it as 'the means of Commonwealth communication' is a prerequisite for Commonwealth membership.

The flag of the Commonwealth consists of the symbol of the Commonwealth Secretariat, represented by a gold globe surrounded by emanating 'rays', on a dark blue field; it was designed for the second CHOGM, in 1973, and officially adopted on 26 March 1976. 1976 also saw the organisation agree to a common date on which to commemorate Commonwealth Day, the second Monday in March, having developed separately on different dates from pre-existing 'Empire Day' celebrations.

Similar Organisations

In recent years the Commonwealth model has inspired similar initiatives on the part of France, Spain and Portugal and their respective ex-colonies, and in the former case, other sympathetic governments: the *Organisation Internationale de la Francophonie* (International Organisation of Francophone Countries), the *Comunidad Iberoamericana de Naciones* (Organization of Ibero-American States) and the *Comunidade dos Países de Língua Portuguesa* (Community of Portuguese Language Countries). The Arab League, an association similar to the Commonwealth, was founded in 1945 and whose members and observers (except observer state India) use Arabic as an official language.

The Commonwealth Conversation

A public consultation on the future of the Commonwealth was launched in July 2009. The Commonwealth Conversation is independently managed by The Royal Commonwealth Society.

3

Multi-Sport Events and Types of Sports: A Select Review

MULTI-SPORT EVENTS: AN INTRODUCTION

A multi-sport event is an organised sporting event, often held over multiple days, and featuring competition in many different sports between organised teams of athletes from (mostly) nation-states. The first major, modern, multi-sport event of international significance was the modern Olympic Games.

Many regional multi-sport events have since been founded, modelled after the Olympics. Most have the same basic structure. Games are held over the course of several days in and around a "host city," which changes for each competition. Countries send national teams to each competition, consisting of individual athletes and teams that compete in a wide variety of sports. Athletes or teams are awarded gold, silver, or bronze medals for first, second, and third place respectively. The games are generally held every four years, though some are annual competitions.

Olympics

The first modern multi-sport event organised were the Olympic Games, organised by the International Olympic Committee (est. 1894) for the first time in 1896 in Athens, Greece. After some badly organised celebrations (1900, 1904), the Olympics became very popular. The number of sports, initially only a few, is still growing.

Other Events

At the beginning of the 20th century, another multi-sport event, the Nordic Games were first held. These Games were held in Scandinavia, and the sports conducted were winter sports such as cross country skiing and speed skating. The Nordic Games were last held in 1926, after which the 1924 Winter Sports Week in Chamonix was declared the first Olympic Winter Games.

In the 1920s, all kinds of other multi-sport events were set up. These were usually directed for a selected group of athletes, rather than everybody, which was - basically - the case with the Olympic Games. The Soviets organised the first Spartakiad in 1920, a communist alternative to the 'bourgeois' Olympic Games, and in 1922 the University Olympia was organised in Italy, the forerunner of the World University Games, meant for students only. Regional Games were another kind of multi-sport event that was established, such as the Far Eastern Championship Games or the Central American and Caribbean Games.

Central Audiences

Since the establishment of the Olympics, most serial multi-sport events have been organised for specific audiences and participating countries or communities:

- regional, such as the East Asian Games and the South American Games
- political, such as the Spartakiad and the GANEFO
- historic or historicultural roots, such as the Commonwealth Games (for members of the Commonwealth of Nations) and the Jeux de la Francophonie (for members of La Francophonie)
- ethnocultural or ethnoreligious, such as the Pan-Armenian Games (for ethnic communities of Armenians both in Armenia and in other countries) and the Maccabiah Games (for communities of Jews of both ethnic and religious origins)
- religious, such as the Islamic Solidarity Games and the previously mentioned Maccabiah Games
- occupational, such as the Military World Games, the World Police and Fire Games and the Universiade

- physical structure, such as the Paralympics, the Deaflympics and the Special Olympics World Games
- human age, such as the World Masters Games, Commonwealth Youth Games and the Senior Olympics
- gender and sexual orientation, such as the Women's Islamic Games and the Gay Games.

List of Major International Competitions

The Olympic Games are still the largest multi-sport event in the world in terms of worldwide interest and importance (though no longer in participation), but several others also have significance.

Worldwide Events

Multi-sports Events for non-Olympic Sports

- World Games, held first in 1981, stage many sports (though not all) that are not Olympic sports. The World Games is therefore sometimes also unofficially called *Olympics for non-Olympic sports*. (They cannot be called "Olympic" games without infringing on the Olympic committees' trademarks.)
- World Mind Sports Games, first held in 2008 for games of skill (e.g. chess, go, etc.)
- The X Games and Winter X Games, which highlight extreme action sports.

By Occupation

- World University Games (also called Universiade), held first in 1923, for students at universities worldwide
- Military World Games, held first in 1995, for military athletes from over 100 countries
- World Police and Fire Games, begun in 1985, for law enforcement officers and firefighters worldwide; third only to the World Masters Games and Summer Olympics in number of participants.

By Organisation and Language

- Commonwealth Games, held first in 1930 (although similar games in 1911) for all nations from the Commonwealth of Nations
- Commonwealth Youth Games, began in 2000
- Francophone Games, held first in 1989, for nations that speak French
- Lusophony Games, begun in 2006, for Portuguese-speaking countries
- Islamic Solidarity Games, first held in 2005, for all nations from the Organisation of the Islamic Conference
- Women's Islamic Games, began in 1993.

By Political and Historical Allegiance

- Bolivarian Games, began in 1938, for countries liberated by Simón Bolívar
- Games of the Small States of Europe held first in 1985, for eight small states in Europe
- Games of the New Emerging Forces, held first in 1963 in Jakarta, Indonesia, for the so-called "emerging nations" (mainly newly independent socialist states)
- Goodwill Games, held first in 1986, held as an alternative after the boycotted Olympics of 1980 and 1984
- Spartakiad, a defunct event involving athletes from the Soviet Union.

By Ethnicity

- Maccabiah Games, first held in 1932, for Jewish athletes worldwide
- Pan Arab Games, held first in 1953, for Arabic nations
- Pan-Armenian Games, began in 1999.

Other

- Gay Games and World OutGames held first in 1982 and 2006, for the worldwide gay community
- World Masters Games, first held in 1985, for mature athletes. Most participants of any multi-sport event, with approximately twice as many competitors as the Summer Olympics.

Regional Events

- All-Africa Games, held first in 1965, for all African nations
- Pan American Games, held first in 1951, for all nations of the Americas
- South American Games, began in 1978
- Arafura Games, held first in 1991 and hosted in the Oceania region
- Asian Games, held first in 1951, for all Asian nations
- Southeast Asian Games, held first in 1959, for nations in Southeast Asia
- East Asian Games, for nations in East Asia
- West Asian Games, for nations in West Asia
- Central Asian Games, for nations in Central Asia
- South Asian Games, for nations in South Asia
- European Youth Olympic Festival (EYOF), for youth athletes from Europe, began in 1991 (summer) and 1993 (winter)
- Mediterranean Games, held first in 1951, for all nations bordering the Mediterranean Sea
- South Pacific Games, held first in 1963 for countries around the South Pacific.

Disability

Other Games are intended for handicapped or disabled athletes. The International Silent Games, held in Paris in 1924, were the first Games for deaf athletes. The Stoke Mandeville Wheelchair Games, incepted in 1948 in England, were the first Games for wheelchair athletes. In 1960, the first Paralympic Games were held, connected with the Olympic Games. The Special Olympics World Games, for athletes with intellectual disabilities, were first held in 1968.

SPORTS: AN INTRODUCTORY OVERVIEW

Sports is an activity that is governed by a set of rules or customs and often engaged in competitively. Sports commonly refer to activities where the physical capabilities of the competitor are the sole or primary determiner of the outcome (winning or losing), but the term is also used to include activities such as mind sports (a common name for some card games and board games with little to no element of chance) and motor sports where mental acuity or equipment quality are major factors. Etymology — "Sports" comes from the old French *desport* meaning "leisure."

The entertainment aspect of sports, together with the spread of mass media and increased leisure time, has led to professionalism in sports. This has resulted in some conflict, where the paycheck can be seen as more important than recreational aspects, or where the sports are changed simply to make them more profitable and popular, thereby losing certain valued traditions. The entertainment aspect also means that sportsmen and women are often elevated to celebrity status.

At times, sports and politics can have a large amount of influence on each other. When apartheid was the official policy in South Africa, many sports people, particularly in rugby union, adopted the conscientious approach that they should not appear in competitive sports there. Some feel this was an effective contribution to the eventual demolition of the policy of apartheid, others feel that it may have prolonged and reinforced its worst effects. The 1936 Summer Olympics held in Berlin was an illustration, perhaps best recognised in retrospect, where an ideology was developing which used the event to strengthen its spread through propaganda. In the history of Ireland, Gaelic sports were connected with cultural nationalism. Until the mid 20th century a person could have been banned from playing Gaelic football, hurling, or other sports administered by the Gaelic Athletic Association (GAA) if she/he played or supported association football, or other games seen to be of British origin. Until recently the GAA continued to ban the playing of soccer and rugby union at Gaelic venues. This ban is still enforced, but has been modified to allow football and rugby be played in Croke Park while Lansdowne Road (both in Dublin) is being redeveloped. Until recently, under Rule 21, the GAA also banned members of the British security forces and members of the RUC from playing Gaelic games, but the advent of the Good Friday Agreement in 1998 led to the eventual removal of the ban. Nationalism is often evident in the pursuit of sports, or in its reporting: people compete in national teams, or commentators and audiences can adopt a partisan view. On occasion, such tensions can lead to violent confrontation among players or spectators within and beyond the sporting venue. These trends are seen by many as contrary to the fundamental ethos of sports being carried on for its own sake and for the enjoyment of its participants.

Gymnastics

Sports have many affinities with art. Ice skating and Tai chi, and Dancesport for example, are sports that come close to artistic spectacles in themselves. Similarly, there are other activities that have elements of sport and art in their execution, such as artistic gymnastics, Bodybuilding, Free running, performance art, professional wrestling, Yoga, bossaball, dressage, culinary arts, marching band, drum corps, etc. Perhaps the best example is Bull-fighting, which in Spain is reported in the arts pages of newspapers. The fact that art is so close to sports in some situations is probably related to the nature of sports. The definition of "sports" above put forward the idea of an activity pursued not just for the usual purposes, for example, running not simply to get places, but running for its own sake, running as well as we can. This is similar to a common view of aesthetic value, which is seen as something over and above the strictly functional value coming from an object's normal use. So an aesthetically pleasing car is one which doesn't just get from A to B, but which impresses us with its grace, poise, and charisma. In the same way, a sporting performance such as jumping doesn't just impress us as being an effective way to avoid obstacles or to get across streams. It impresses us because of the ability, skill, and style which is shown. Art and sports were probably more clearly linked at the time of Ancient Greece, when gymnastics and calisthenics invoked admiration and aesthetic appreciation for the physical build, prowess and 'arete' displayed by participants. The modern term 'art' as skill, is related to this ancient Greek term 'arete'. The closeness of art and sport in these times was revealed by the nature of the Olympic Games which, as we have seen, were celebrations of both sporting and artistic achievements, poetry, sculpture and architecture.

Sports Technology

Technology has an important role in sports, whether applied to an athlete's health, the athlete's technique, or equipment's characteristics. *Equipment* as sports have grown more competitive, the need for better equipment has arisen. Golf clubs, football helmets, baseball bats, soccer balls, hockey skates, and other equipment have all seen considerable changes when new technologies have been applied. *Health* ranging from nutrition to the treatment of injuries, as the knowledge of the human body has deepened over time, an athlete's potential has been increased. Athletes are now able to play to an older age, recover more quickly from injuries, and train more effectively than previous generations of athletes. *Instruction* advancing technology created new opportunities for research into sports. It is now possible to analyse aspects of sports that were previously out of the reach of comprehension. Being able to use motion capture to capture an athlete's movement, or advanced computer simulations to model physical scenarios has greatly increased an athlete's ability to understand what they are doing and how they can improve themselves.

In British English, sporting activities are commonly denoted by the collective noun "sport". In American English, "sports" is more used. In all English dialects, "sports" is the term used for more than one specific sport. For example, "football and swimming are my favourite sports", would sound natural to all English speakers, whereas "I enjoy sport" would sound less natural than "I enjoy sports" to North Americans. The term "sport" is sometimes extended to encompass all competitive activities, regardless of the level of physical activity. Both games of skill and motor sport exhibit many of the characteristics of physical sports, such as skill, sportsmanship, and at the highest levels, even professional sponsorship associated with physical sports. Air sports, billiards, bridge, chess, motorcycle racing, and powerboating are all recognised as sports by the International Olympic Committee with their world governing bodies represented in the Association of the IOC Recognised International Sports Federations.

Spectator Sport

As well as being a form of recreation for the participants, much sport is played in front of an audience. Most professional sport is played in a 'theatre' of some kind; be it a stadium, arena, golf course, race track, or the open road, with provision for the (often paying) public. Large television or radio audiences are also commonly attracted, with rival broadcasters bidding large amounts of money for the 'rights' to show certain fixtures. Association football's FIFA World Cup attracts a global television audience of hundreds of millions; the 2006 Final alone attracted an estimated worldwide audience of well over 700 million. In the United States, the championship game of the NFL, the Super Bowl, has become one of the most watched television broadcasts of the year. Super Bowl Sunday is a *de facto* national holiday in America; the viewership being so great that in 2007 advertising space was reported as being sold at US$2.6m for a 30 second slot.

Winter Sports

A winter sport is a sport commonly played during winter. As a formal term, it refers to a sport played on snow or ice, but informally can refer to sports played in winter that are also played year-round like basketball. The main winter sports are ice hockey and figure skating, sledding events such as luge, skeleton, and bobsleigh, skiing (Alpine and Nordic) and snowboarding. Other common winter sports include snow-blading, monoskiing, skwal and tobogganing.

List of Winter Sports

(*a*) *Ice Skating*
- (*i*) Sports with asterisks denotes that it is included in the Olympics, as accurate as the 2006 Turin Olympics
- (*ii*) Figure skating
- (*iii*) Short-track speed skating
- (*iv*) Speed skating
- (*v*) Synchronised skating
- (*vi*) Xtreme Ice Skating- A sport more closely related to Extreme Inline Skating.

(*b*) *Snowboarding*
- (*i*) Freestyle snowboarding
- (*ii*) Alpine snowboarding
- (*iii*) Boardercross
- (*iv*) Slalom.

(*c*) *Skiing*

Sports in which skis are used on snow

(*i*) Alpine skiing
(*ii*) Biathlon
(*iii*) Cross country skiing
(*iv*) Firngleiten
(*v*) Freestyle skiing
(*vi*) Newschool skiing
(*vii*) Nordic combined
(*viii*) Ski archery
(*ix*) Skiboarding
(*x*) Skibob
(*xi*) Skijoring
(*xii*) Ski jumping
(*xiii*) Snowshoe
(*xiv*) Speed skiing
(*xv*) Telemark skiing

(*d*) *Sledding*

Sports that use sleds going down ice tracks or pulled by something

(*i*) Ice Blocking
(*ii*) Bobsleigh
(*iii*) Luge
(*iv*) Skeleton
(*v*) Wok racing
(*vi*) Dogsled racing.

(*e*) *Team Sports*

Sports that involve teams, played on ice

(*i*) Bandy
(*ii*) Broomball
(*iii*) Curling
(*iv*) Ice hockey
(*v*) Ice stock sport
(*vi*) Ringette
(*vii*) Sledge hockey—(Winter Para-Olympic Sport)
(*viii*) Snowball Association—(Last one standing).

(*f*) *Recreational Sports*

Some 'sports' are competed (or simply enjoyed) on a more casual basis, often by children

(*i*) Ice boating or Ice sailing

(*ii*) Tobogganing
(*iii*) Snowball fight
(*iv*) Building snowmen
(*v*) Shinny
(*vi*) Ice swimming
(*vii*) Ice fishing.

(*g*) *Famous Winter Sport Resort Regions*

(*i*) Andes
(*ii*) Rocky Mountains
(*iii*) Alps
(*iv*) Snowy Mountains
(*v*) Karkonosze Mountains/Sudeten mountains
(*vi*) Lapland
(*vii*) Appalachian Mountains
(*viii*) Carpathian Mountains
(*ix*) Balkan Mountains
(*x*) Swiss Alps.

Towards Listing of Sports in General

The following is a list of sports, divided by category. There are many more sports to be added. This system has a disadvantage because some sports may fit in more than one category. Soccer is currently the most watched and played sport in the world.

Physical Sports by Family

Aquatics

Ball Sports

(*i*) Underwater football
(*ii*) Underwater rugby
(*iii*) Water polo

Competitive Swimming

(*i*) Backstroke
(*ii*) Breaststroke
(*iii*) Butterfly stroke
(*iv*) Freestyle swimming
(*v*) Individual Medley
(*vi*) Synchronised swimming

Diving

(*i*) Diving

Underwater Hockey

(*i*) Underwater hockey

Underwater Diving

(*i*) Free-diving
(*ii*) Scuba Diving
(*iii*) Snorkeling

Archery

(*i*) Clout archery
(*ii*) Field archery
(*iii*) Flight archery
(*iv*) Kyudo
(*v*) Popinjay (sport)
(*vi*) Target archery

Auto Racing

(*i*) Autocross
(*ii*) Autograss
(*iii*) Banger racing
(*iv*) Board track racing
(*v*) Demolition derby
(*vi*) Dirt speedway racing
(*vii*) Dirt track racing
(*viii*) Drag racing
(*ix*) Drifting
(*x*) Folkrace
(*xi*) Hillclimbing
(*xii*) Ice racing
(*xiii*) Kart racing
(*xiv*) Legends car racing
(*xv*) Midget car racing
(*xvi*) Off-road racing
(*xvii*) Open wheel racing
(*xviii*) Production car racing
(*xix*) Rallycross
(*xx*) Rallying
(*xxi*) Road racing
(*xxii*) Short track motor racing
(*xxiii*) Slalom
(*xxiv*) Sports car racing

(*xxv*) Sprint car racing
(*xxvi*) Sprinting
(*xxvii*) Street racing
(*xxviii*) Time Attack
(*xxix*) Touring car racing
(*xxx*) Truck racing

Bat-and-ball

(*i*) Baseball
(*ii*) Brännboll
(*iii*) Cricket
(*iv*) Test cricket
(*v*) First-class cricket
(*vi*) Blind cricket
(*vii*) Catchy Shubby
(*viii*) Club cricket
(*ix*) French cricket
(*x*) Gilli-danda
(*xi*) Kilikiti
(*xii*) One Day International
(*xiii*) Kwik cricket
(*xiv*) List A cricket
(*xv*) Pro 40
(*xvi*) Limited overs cricket
(*xvii*) Short form cricket
(*xviii*) Single Wicket
(*xix*) Twenty20
(*xx*) Lapta
(*xxi*) Oina
(*xxii*) Old Cat
(*xxiii*) Pesäpallo
(*xxiv*) Podex
(*xxv*) Rounders
(*xxvi*) Softball
(*xxvii*) T-Ball

Boardsports

Sports that are played with some sort of board as the primary equipment

(*i*) Bodyboarding
(*ii*) Riverboarding
(*iii*) Mountainboarding

(*iv*) Kite landboarding
(*v*) Skateboarding
(*vi*) Freeboarding
(*vii*) Longboarding
(*viii*) Streetboarding
(*ix*) Skysurfing
(*x*) Streetluge.
(*xi*) Snowboarding
(*xii*) Sandboarding.
(*xiii*) Snowkiting
(*xiv*) Surfing
(*xv*) Kitesurfing
(*xvi*) Skimboarding
(*xvii*) Wakeboarding
(*xviii*) Kneeboarding
(*xix*) Windsurfing

Bowling

(*i*) Bocce
(*ii*) Boccia
(*iii*) Boule lyonnaise
(*iv*) Bowls
(*v*) Curling
(*vi*) Duckpin bowling
(*vii*) Five-pin bowling
(*viii*) Klootschieten
(*ix*) Lawn bowls
(*x*) Pétanque
(*xi*) Skittles (sport)
(*xii*) Ten-pin bowling
(*xiii*) Varpa

Catch Games

(*i*) Curby
(*ii*) Dodgeball
(*iii*) Ga-ga
(*iv*) Prisoner Ball
(*v*) Snowball fight
(*vi*) Yukigassen

Climbing

(*i*) Bouldering
(*ii*) Canyoning

(*iii*) Mountaineering
(*iv*) Rope climbing

Cycling

(*i*) Cycling sports using bicycles or unicycles.

Bicycle

(*i*) Artistic cycling
(*ii*) BMX racing
(*iii*) Bobrun cycling
(*iv*) Cyclo-cross
(*v*) Mountain bicycling
(*vi*) Road bicycle racing
(*vii*) Track cycling
(*viii*) FMX or foot motocross

Skibob

(*i*) Skibobbing

Unicycle

(*i*) Mountain unicycling
(*ii*) Unicycle trials

Combat Sports

Combat sport is a competitive contact sport where two combatants fight against each other using certain rules of engagement.

Grappling

(*i*) Aikido
(*ii*) Aiki-jujutsu
(*iii*) Brazilian Jiu-Jitsu
(*iv*) Catch wrestling
(*v*) Glima
(*vi*) Judo
(*vii*) Jujutsu
(*viii*) Kinomichi
(*ix*) Kurash
(*x*) Malla-yuddha
(*xi*) Mongolian wrestling
(*xii*) Pehlwani
(*xiii*) Sambo
(*xiv*) Shuai Jiao
(*xv*) Ssireum
(*xvi*) Sumo

(*xvii*) Varzesh-e Pahlavani
(*xviii*) Wrestling
(*xix*) Yaðlý Güreþ

Skirmish

(*i*) Baseball
(ii) Airsoft
(iii) Laser tag
(iv) Paintball

Weapons

(*i*) Battôjutsu
(*ii*) Eskrima
(*iii*) Egyptian stick fencing
(*iv*) Fencing
(*v*) Gatka
(*vi*) Haidong Gumdo
(*vii*) Hojôjutsu
(*viii*) Iaidô
(*ix*) Iaijutsu
(*x*) Jôdô
(*xi*) Jogo do Pau
(*xii*) Jûkendô
(*xiii*) Juttejutsu
(*xiv*) Kendo
(*xv*) Kenjutsu
(*xvi*) Kyûdô
(*xvii*) Kyûjutsu
(*xviii*) Modern Arnis
(*xix*) Naginatajutsu
(*xx*) Okinawan kobudô
(*xxi*) Shurikenjutsu
(*xxii*) Silambam
(*xxiii*) Sôjutsu

Striking

(*i*) Bâjíquán
(*ii*) Boxing
(*iii*) Bokator
(*iv*) Capoeira
(*v*) Fujian White Crane
(*vi*) Karate
(*vii*) Kenpô

(*viii*) Kickboxing
(*ix*) Lethwei
(*x*) Muay Thai
(*xi*) Pradal Serey
(*xii*) San shou
(*xiii*) Savate
(*xiv*) Shaolin kung fu
(*xv*) Sikaran
(*xvi*) Silat
(*xvii*) Spanish Punching Derby
(*xviii*) Subak
(*xix*) Taekkyeon
(*xx*) Taekwondo
(*xxi*) Taido
(*xxii*) Wing Chun
(*xxiii*) Wing Tsun
(*xxiv*) Zui Quan

Mixed or hybrid

(*i*) Baguazhang
(*ii*) Bando
(*iii*) Bartitsu
(*iv*) Bujinkan
(*v*) Hapkido
(*vi*) Hwa Rang Do
(*vii*) Jeet Kune Do
(*viii*) Kajukenbo
(*ix*) Kalarippayattu
(*x*) Krav Maga
(*xi*) Kuk Sool Won
(*xii*) MCMAP
(*xiii*) Northern Praying Mantis
(*xiv*) Ninjutsu
(*xv*) Pankration
(*xvi*) Pencak Silat
(*xvii*) Sanshou
(*xviii*) Shidokan
(*xix*) Shoot boxing
(*xx*) Shootfighting
(*xxi*) Shorinji Kempo
(*xxii*) Systema

(*xxiii*) Tai chi chuan
(*xxiv*) Vajra Mushti
(*xxv*) Vovinam
(*xxvi*) Xingyiquan

Cue Sports

(*i*) Carom billiards
- Three-cushion
- Five-pins
- Balkline and straight rail
- Cushion caroms
- Four-ball (yotsudama)
- Artistic billiards

(*ii*) Novuss

(*iii*) Pocket billiards (pool)
- Eight-ball (and Blackball)
- Nine-ball
- Straight pool (14.1 continuous)
- One-pocket
- Three-ball
- Seven-ball
- Ten-ball
- Rotation
- Baseball pocket billiards
- Cribbage (pool)
- Bank pool
- Artistic pool
- Trick shot competition
- Speed pool
- Bowlliards
- Chicago
- Kelly pool
- Cutthroat
- Killer
- Russian pyramid

(*iv*) Snooker
- Snooker plus

(*v*) Hybrid carom—pocket games
- English billiards
- Bottle pool
- Cowboy

(*vi*) Obstacle variations
- Bagatelle
- Bar billiards
- Bumper pool

Dance

(*i*) Ballet
(*ii*) Ballroom dance
(*iii*) Breakdance
(*iv*) Irish dance
(*v*) Latin dance
(*vi*) Salsa
(*vii*) Tap dance
(*viii*) Hip-hop
(*ix*) Cheerleading
(*x*) Majorette

Equine Sports

Sports using a horse

(*i*) Barrel Racing
(*ii*) Cross Country
(*iii*) Dressage
(*iv*) English Pleasure
(*v*) Equitation
(*vi*) Equestrian vaulting
(*vii*) Harness racing
(*viii*) Horse racing
(*ix*) Hunter
(*x*) Reining
(*xi*) Rodeo
(*xii*) Show Jumping
(*xiii*) Steeplechase
(*xiv*) Western Pleasure

Fishing

(*i*) Angling
(*ii*) Big-game fishing
(*iii*) Casting
(*iv*) Noodling
(*v*) Sport fishing
(*vi*) Surf fishing
- Rock fishing

Flying Disc Sports

(*i*) Disc dog
(*ii*) Disc golf
(*iii*) Dodge disc
(*iv*) Durango boot
(*v*) Double disc court
(*vi*) Flutterguts
(*vii*) Freestyle
(*viii*) Fricket, (AKA disc cricket, cups, suzy sticks or crispy wickets)
(*ix*) Friskee
(*x*) Goaltimate
(*xi*) Guts
(*xii*) Hot box
(*xiii*) Ringo
(*xiv*) Ultimate (sport)

Flying Sports

Airplane

(*i*) Aerobatics
(*ii*) Air racing

Ballooning

(*i*) Cluster ballooning
(*ii*) Hopper ballooning

Football Family

(*i*) Association Football
- Five-a-side football

(*ii*) Australian Football
(*iii*) Gaelic football
(*iv*) Gridiron football
- American Football
- Canadian Football
- Arena Football

(*v*) Rugby Football
- Rugby League
- Rugby Union

(*vi*) Wheelchair rugby
(*vii*) Footvolley

Gymnastics

(*i*) Artistic gymnastics
- Balance Beam

- Floor
- High Bar
- Parallel Bars
- Pommel Horse
- Still Rings
- Uneven Bars
- Vault

(*ii*) Cheerleading
(*iii*) Majorette
(*iv*) Competitive rope jumping
(*v*) Juggling
(*vi*) Rhythmic gymnastics
(*vii*) Sports acrobatics
(*viii*) Tricking
(*ix*) Trampolining
(*x*) Trapeze

- Flying trapeze
- Static trapeze

Handball Family

Handball games often have similarities to racquet or catch games

(*i*) American handball
(*ii*) Basketball
(*iii*) European handball
(*iv*) Field handball
(*v*) Fistball
(*vi*) Fives

- Eton Fives
- Rugby Fives

(*vii*) Frisian handball
(*viii*) Four square
(*ix*) Gaelic handball
(*x*) Goalball
(*xi*) Jeu de paume
(*xii*) Korfball
(*xiii*) Netball
(*xiv*) Palla
(*xv*) Tchoukball
(*xvi*) Valencian pilota

(*xvii*) Volleyball
(*xviii*) Volutobol
(*xix*) Water polo

Hockey Family

(*i*) Bandy
(*ii*) Broomball
(*iii*) Field hockey
- Indoor field hockey

(*iv*) Floorball
(*v*) Hurling (The ball can be handled so Hurling is on the periphery of the 'hockey family').
(*vi*) Ice hockey: (1) Ringette
(*vii*) Knotty
(*viii*) Roller hockey
- Inline hockey
- Road hockey
- Roller hockey (Quad)

(*ix*) Shinty
(*x*) Underwater hockey

Hunting

Sometimes considered blood sports
(*i*) Beagling
(*ii*) Big game hunting
(*iii*) Deer hunting
(*iv*) Fox hunting
(*v*) Hare coursing
(*vi*) Wolf hunting

Kite Sports

(*i*) Kite buggy
(*ii*) Kite fighting
(*iii*) Kite landboarding
(*iv*) Kitesurfing
(*v*) Snow kiting
(*vi*) Sport kite (Stunt kite)

Mixed Discipline

(*i*) Biathlon
(*ii*) Decathlon

(*iii*) Modern pentathlon
(*iv*) Pentathlon
(*v*) Triathlon

Motorboat Racing

(*i*) Drag boat racing
(*ii*) F1 Powerboat racing
(*iii*) Hydroplane racing
(*iv*) Jet sprint boat racing
(*v*) Offshore powerboat racing

Motorcycle Racing

(*i*) Auto race
(*ii*) Board track racing
(*iii*) Cross-country rally
(*iv*) Endurance racing
(*v*) Enduro
(*vi*) Grand prix motorcycle racing
(*vii*) Grass track
(*viii*) Hill climb
(*ix*) Ice racing
(*x*) Indoor short track
(*xi*) Motocross
(*xii*) Motorcycle drag racing
(*xiii*) Motorcycle speedway
(*xiv*) Road racing
(*xv*) Superbike racing
(*xvi*) Supercross
(*xvii*) Supermoto
(*xviii*) Supersport racing
(*xix*) Superside
(*xx*) Track racing
(*xxi*) TT racing

Orienteering Family

(*i*) Amateur Radio Direction Finding
(*ii*) Geo caching
(*iii*) Orienteering

Paddle Sports

Canoeing

(*i*) Canoeing
(*ii*) Outrigger canoeing

Kayaking

(*i*) Creeking
(*ii*) Flyak
(*iii*) Freeboating
(*iv*) Royaking
(*v*) Sea kayaking
(*vi*) Squirt boating
(*vii*) Surf kayaking
(*viii*) Whitewater kayaking

Rafting

(*i*) Rafting
(*ii*) White water rafting

Rowing

(*i*) Coastal and ocean rowing
- Surfboat

(*ii*) Dragon boat racing
(*iii*) Double scull
(*iv*) Quad four
(*v*) Single scull
(*vi*) Straight four

Parachuting

(*i*) BASE jumping
(*ii*) Paragliding
(*iii*) Parasailing
(*iv*) Sky diving
(*v*) Skysurfing
(*vi*) Wingsuit flying
(*vii*) Hang gliding

Polo

(*i*) Bicycle polo
(*ii*) Canoe polo
(*iii*) Elephant polo

(*iv*) Equine polo
(*v*) Segway polo
(*vi*) Yak polo

Racquet (or racket) Sports

Sports where a player uses a racquet (or racket) to hit a ball or other objects.

(*i*) Badminton
(*ii*) Ball badminton
(*iii*) Bilbocatch
(*iv*) Frontenis
(*v*) Jai-Alai
(*vi*) Matkot
(*vii*) Paddleball
(*viii*) Pelota mixteca
(*ix*) Pickleball
(*x*) Platform tennis
(*xi*) Pington
(*xii*) Racquetball
(*xiii*) Racquets
(*xiv*) Racketlon
(*xv*) Rapid ball
(*xvi*) Real tennis
(*xvii*) Soft tennis
(*xviii*) Speedball
(*xix*) Speedminton
(*xx*) Squash
(*xxi*) Squash tennis
(*xxii*) Stické
(*xxiii*) Table tennis, recognised by IOC in 1981
(*xxiv*) Tennis
(*xxv*) Xare

Radiosports

Sports using a radio:

(*i*) Amateur Radio Direction Finding
(*ii*) Radiosport/Contesting
(*iii*) High Speed Telegraphy

Remote Control

(*i*) Model Aerobatics

(*ii*) RC racing
(*iii*) Robot combat

Running

(*i*) Endurance
- Cross-country running
- Half marathon
- Marathon
- Ultramarathon

(*ii*) Sprint
(*iii*) Hurdles

Sled Sports

(*i*) Sledding
(*ii*) Bobsleigh
(*iii*) Luge
(*iv*) Skeleton
(*v*) Toboggan

Shooting Sports

Ports using a firearm:
(*i*) Clay pigeon shooting
(*ii*) Field target
(*iii*) Fullbore target rifle

Sport Stacking

(*i*) Sport stacking

Street Stunts

(*i*) Free running
(*ii*) Tricking
(*iii*) Freestyle football

Tag Games

(*i*) British bulldogs (American Eagle)
(*ii*) Hana Ichi Monme
(*iii*) Hide and seek
(*iv*) Kabaddi
(*v*) Kho kho

(*vi*) Red rover
(*vii*) Tag

Walking

(*i*) Hiking
(*ii*) Race walking

Weightlifting

(*i*) Clean and jerk
(*ii*) Snatch

Mind Sports by Family

Requiring little or no physical exertion or agility mind sports are often not considered true sports. Some mind sports are recognised by sporting federations. The following list is intended to represent anything that is likely to be referred to as a mind sport, not to argue their validity as sports.

Card Games
Speedcubing
(*i*) Speedcubing
Strategy Board Games
(*ii*) Chess
(*iii*) Checkers
(*iv*) Chinese Checkers
(*v*) Draughts
(*vi*) Go
(*vii*) Go-Moku
(*viii*) Jacquet
(*ix*) Mancala
(*x*) Mahjong (Taipei)
(*xi*) Sogo (Score four)
(*xii*) Stratego

By Other

Air Sports
(*i*) Aerobatics
(*ii*) Ballooning

(*iii*) BASE jumping
(*iv*) Hang gliding
(*v*) Paragliding
(*vi*) Wingsuit flying
(*vii*) Sky diving
(*viii*) Bungee jumping
(*ix*) Parasailing

Animal Sports

(*i*) Angling
(*ii*) Bull riding
(*iii*) Bull fighting
(*iv*) Dog sports
(*v*) Camel racing
(*vi*) Elephant polo
(*vii*) Ferret legging
(*viii*) Hamster racing
(*ix*) Pigeon sport
(*x*) Sport fishing
(*xi*) Surf fishing
(*xii*) Hunting
(*xiii*) Horse racing
(*xiv*) Steeplechase
(*xv*) Equestrianism
(*xvi*) Thoroughbred racing
(*xvii*) Western Pleasure
(*xviii*) Harness racing
(*xix*) Pato
(*xx*) Polo
(*xxi*) Chilean rodeo
(*xxii*) Buzkashi
(*xxiii*) Dressage
(*xxiv*) Hunter-jumpers
(*xxv*) Combined training
(*xxvi*) Equestrian vaulting
(*xxvii*) Rodeo
(*xxviii*) Rattlesnake Round-Up

Athletics (track and field)

(*i*) Cross-country
(*ii*) Jumping
- Triple jump

- Long jump
- High jump
- Pole vault

(*iii*) Throwing
- Discus
- Hammer throw
- Javelin
- Atlatl
- Shot put

(*iv*) Race walking

Electronic Sports

Sports played using electronic devices

(*i*) Combat robot
(*ii*) Radio-control vehicles
(*iii*) Geo caching
(*iv*) Amateur Radio Direction Finding
(*v*) Contesting
(*vi*) High Speed Telegraphy

Endurance Sports

(*i*) Cycling
(*ii*) Running
(*iii*) Ultramarathon
(*iv*) Swimming
(*v*) Triathlon
(*vi*) Orienteering
(*vii*) Decathlon
(*viii*) Inline speed skating
(*ix*) Rowing
(*x*) Wheelchair racing
(*xi*) Wood chopping
(*xii*) Razza racing
(*xiii*) Cross-country skiing

Miscellaneous

(*i*) Baton twirling
(*ii*) Boomerang throw
(*iii*) Bungee jumping

(*iv*) Competitive eating
(*v*) Egg and spoon race
(*vi*) Footbag (hacky sack)
(*vii*) Haggis hurling
(*viii*) Lumberjack
(*ix*) Mattress jumping
(*x*) Tetherball
(*xi*) Three-legged race
(*xii*) Sack race
(*xiii*) Soap shoes
(*xiv*) Speed typing
(*xv*) Patball
(*xvi*) Wallball

Motorsport

Skating Sports

(*i*) Aggressive skating
(*ii*) Artistic roller skating
(*iii*) Bandy
(*iv*) Bobrun skating
(*v*) Ice hockey
(*vi*) Ice skating
(*vii*) Inline speed skating
(*viii*) Inline hockey
(*ix*) Figure skating
(*x*) Ringette
(*xi*) Rinkball
(*xii*) Rink hockey
(*xiii*) Skateboarding
(*xiv*) Freestyle slalom skating
(*xv*) Roller derby
(*xvi*) Roller hockey
(*xvii*) Roller skating
(*xviii*) Roller speed skating
(*xix*) Short track speed skating
(*xx*) Skater hockey
(*xxi*) Speed skating
(*xxii*) Synchronised skating

Snow Sports

(*i*) Skiing

(*ii*) Snowball Association
(*iii*) Snowboarding:
- Boardercross
- Freestyle snowboarding

(*iv*) Snowkiting
(*v*) Snowshoeing

Strength Sports

Sports mainly based on sheer power

(*i*) Arm wrestling
(*ii*) Thumb wrestling
(*iii*) Bodybuilding
(*iv*) Powerlifting
(*v*) Toe wrestling
(*vi*) Tug-o-war
(*vii*) Zourkhaneh
(*viii*) Weightlifting
(*ix*) Wife carrying

Tables Sports

(*i*) Air hockey
(*ii*) Backgammon
(*iii*) Card games
(*iv*) Chess
(*v*) Chinese Checkers
(*vi*) Connect Four
(*vii*) Cue sports
- Carom billiards
  - Three-cushion
  - Five-pins
  - Balkline and straight rail
  - Cushion caroms
  - Four-ball (yotsudama)
  - Artistic billiards
  - Several other variants
- Pocket billiards (pool)
  - Eight-ball (and Blackball)
  - Nine-ball
  - Straight pool (14.1 continuous)
  - One-pocket
  - Three-ball
  - Seven-ball

- Ten-ball
- Rotation
- Baseball pocket billiards
- Cribbage (pool)
- Bank pool
- Artistic pool
- Trick shot competition
- Speed pool
- Bowlliards
- Chicago
- Kelly pool
- Cutthroat
- Killer
- Russian pyramid
- Many other variants

- Snooker
  - Snooker plus
- Hybrid carom—pocket games
  - English billiards
  - Bottle pool
  - Cowboy
- Obstacle variations
  - Bagatelle
  - Bar billiards
  - Bumper pool
  - many other (generally obsolete) variants

(*viii*) Draughts (checker)
(*ix*) Dominoes
(*x*) Go
(*xi*) Go-Moku
(*xii*) Jacquet
(*xiii*) Mancala
(*xiv*) Mahjong (Taipei)
(*xv*) Reversi (Othello)
(*xvi*) Shogi
(*xvii*) Scrabble (and variants)
(*xviii*) Speedcubing
(*xix*) Stratego
(*xx*) Table football
(*xxi*) Table Tennis (Ping Pong)

(*xxii*) Table hockey
(*xxiii*) Xiangqi

Target Sports

Sports where the main objective is to hit a certain target.

(*i*) Archery
(*ii*) Kyûdô
(*iii*) Duckpin bowling
(*iv*) Atlatl
(*v*) Five-pin bowling
(*vi*) Billiards
(*vii*) Bar billiards
(*viii*) Bowls
(*ix*) Bowling pin shooting
(*x*) Carambole billiard
(*xi*) Candlepin bowling
(*xii*) Pool
(*xiii*) Snooker
(*xiv*) Bocce
(*xv*) Boccia
(*xvi*) Boules
(*xvii*) Calva
(*xviii*) Croquet
(*xix*) Curling
(*xx*) Darts
(*xxi*) Gateball
(*xxii*) Disc golf
(*xxiii*) Speed golf
(*xxiv*) Golfcross
(*xxv*) Horseshoes (horseshoe throwing)
(*xxvi*) Knife throwing
(*xxvii*) Laser tag
(*xxviii*) Lawn bowls
(*xxix*) Marbles
(*xxx*) Matball
(*xxxi*) Pall mall
(*xxxii*) Petanque
(*xxxiii*) Paintball
(*xxxiv*) Shooting
(*xxxv*) Skittles

(*xxxvi*) Ten-pin bowling
(*xxxvii*) Trugo
(*xxxviii*) Skittles
(*xxxix*) Skee ball
(*xl*) Pitch and putt

Team Sports

Sports that involve teams

(*i*) American football
(*ii*) Kilikiti
(*iii*) Association Football (soccer)
(*iv*) Australian rules football
(*v*) Ball hockey
(*vi*) Bandy
(*vii*) Baseball
(*viii*) Basketball
(*ix*) Beach handball
(*x*) Beach soccer
(*xi*) Beach rugby
(*xii*) Beach volleyball
(*xiii*) Bossaball
(*xiv*) Box/indoor lacrosse
(*xv*) Bowling
(*xvi*) Basque pelota
(*xvii*) Broomball
(*xviii*) Camogie
(*xix*) Canadian football
(*xx*) Cricket
(*xxi*) Curling
(*xxii*) Dodgeball
(*xxiii*) Eton wall game
(*xxiv*) Field hockey
(*xxv*) Fistball
(*xxvi*) Floorball
(*xxvii*) Cubbies
(*xxviii*) Footballtennis
(*xxix*) Footvolley
(*xxx*) Frisian handball
(*xxxi*) Futsal
(*xxxii*) Gaelic football
(*xxxiii*) Gaelic handball

(*xxxiv*) Gateball
(*xxxv*) Goalball
(*xxxvi*) Handball
(*xxxvii*) Harrow football
(*xxxviii*) Hoover ball
(*xxxix*) Hornussen
(*xl*) Horseshoe
(*xli*) Hurling
(*xlii*) Indoor soccer
(*xliii*) Ice hockey
(*xliv*) Inline hockey
(*xlv*) Kabaddi
(*xlvi*) Kickball
(*xlvii*) Korfball
(*xlviii*) Lacrosse
(*xlix*) Mesoamerican ballgame
(*l*) Marching band
(*li*) Netball
(*lii*) Oina
(*liii*) Paintball
(*liv*) Pesäpallo
(*lv*) Petanque
(*lvi*) Polo
(*lvii*) Polocrosse
(*lviii*) Ringette
(*lix*) Rinkball
(*lx*) Road hockey
(*lxi*) Roller hockey (Rink hockey)
(*lxii*) Rounders
(*lxiii*) Rowing
(*lxiv*) Royal Shrovetide Football
(*lxv*) Rugby football
(*lxvi*) Rugby league
(*lxvii*) Rugby union
(*lxviii*) Sepak Takraw
(*lxix*) Shinty
(*lxx*) Skater hockey
(*lxxi*) Skittles
(*lxxii*) Slamball
(*lxxiii*) Softball

(*lxxiv*) Surfboat
(*lxxv*) Motorcycle speedway
(*lxxvi*) Speedball
(*lxxvii*) Spongee polo
(*lxxviii*) Tennis polo
(*lxxix*) Tennis
(*lxxx*) Tchoukball
(*lxxxi*) Test cricket
(*lxxxii*) Throwball
(*lxxxiii*) Ultimate football
(*lxxxiv*) Ultimate (Ultimate frisbee)
(*lxxxv*) Underwater football
(*lxxxvi*) Underwater hockey
(*lxxxvii*) Underwater rugby
(*lxxxviii*) Volleyball
(*lxxxix*) Viperball
(*xc*) Wallyball
(*xci*) Water polo
(*xcii*) Wheelchair basketball
(*xciii*) Wheelchair tennis
(*xciv*) Wheelchair rugby
(*xcv*) Wiffle ball
(*xcvi*) Rugby sevens
(*xcvii*) Six-man football
(*xcviii*) Flag football
(*xcix*) Touch football
(*c*) Twenty 20
(*ci*) Prisoner ball

Wind Sports

Sport which uses wind:
(*i*) Iceboating
(*ii*) Land sailing
(*iii*) Windsurfing
(*iv*) Kitesurfing
(*v*) Kite buggy
(*vi*) Kite fighting
(*vii*) Kite flying
(*viii*) Sailing
(*ix*) Flysailing

TRACK AND FIELD ATHLETICS

Track and field athletics is a collection of sports events that involve running, throwing, jumping and walking. Organised athletics are traced back to the Ancient Olympic Games from 776 BC, and most modern events are conducted by the member clubs of the International Association of Athletics Federations. The athletics meeting forms the backbone of the modern Summer Olympics, and other leading international meetings include the IAAF World Championships and World Indoor Championships.

Etymology

The sport is commonly known as athletics in most of the world or track and field in the United States and Canada. The name "athletics" is derived from the Greek word *"athlos"*, meaning "contest."

History

The original and only event at the first Olympics in 776 BC was a stadium-length foot race or "stade", run on a track.

There were several other "games" held in Europe in the classical era:

- Panhellenic Games:
    - *The Pythian Games* (founded 527 BC) held in Delphi every four years
    - *The Nemean Games* (founded 516 BC) held in Argolid every two years
    - *The Isthmian Games* (founded 523 BC) held on the Isthmus of Corinth every two years
- *The Roman Games* – Arising from Etruscan rather than purely Greek roots, the Roman Games deemphasised footraces and throwing. Instead, the Greek sports of chariot racing and wrestling, as well as the Etruscan sport of gladiatorial combat, took centre stage.
- *The Tailteann Games* (claimed foundation 1829 BC) – held near modern Telltown in Ireland, this thirty-day meeting included foot races and stone-throwing events.

Other peoples, such as the Celts, Teutons and Goths who succeeded the Romans, enjoyed athletic contests. However, these were often related to combat training. In the Middle Ages the sons of noblemen would be trained in running, leaping and wrestling, in addition to riding, jousting and arms-training. Contests between rivals and friends may have been common on both official and unofficial grounds.

Annually, from 1796-1798, L'Olympiade de la République was held in revolutionary France, and is an early forerunner to the modern summer Olympic Games. The premier event of this competition was a footrace, but various ancient Greek disciplines were also on display. The 1796 Olympiade also marks the introduction of the metric system into sport.

In the 19th century the formal organization of the modern events accelerated in France, Germany, and Great Britain in particular. This included the incorporation of regular sports and exercise into school regimes. The Royal Military College, Sandhurst has claimed to be the first to adopt this in 1812 and 1825, but without any supporting evidence. The earliest recorded meeting was organised at Shrewsbury, Shropshire in 1840 by the Royal Shrewsbury School Hunt. There are details of the meeting in a series of letters written 60 years later by C.T. Robinson, who was a pupil there from 1838 to 1841. The Royal Military Academy at Woolwich held an organised competition in 1849, but the first regular series of meetings was held by Exeter College, Oxford from 1850.

Modern athletic events are usually organised around a 400 metre running track on which most of the running events take place. Field events (vaulting, jumping, and throwing) often take place on the infield, inside the track.

Athletics was included in the first modern Olympic Games in 1896 and has formed their backbone ever since. Women were first allowed to participate in track and field events in the 1928 Olympics.

An international governing body, the International Amateur Athletics Federation (IAAF), was founded in 1912; it adopted its current name, the International Association of Athletics Federations, in 2001. The IAAF established separate outdoor World Championships in 1983. There are a number of regional games as well, such as the European Championships, the Pan-American

Games, and the Commonwealth Games. In addition there is a professional Golden League circuit, culminating in the IAAF World Athletics Final, and indoor championships such as the World Indoor Championships. The sport has a very high profile during major championships, especially the Olympics, but otherwise is less popular.

The AAU (Amateur Athletic Union) was the governing body in the United States until it collapsed under pressure from advancing professionalism in the late 1970s. A new governing body called The Athletics Congress (TAC) was formed. It was later renamed USA Track & Field (USATF or USA T&F). An additional, less structured organisation, the Road Runners Club of America (RRCA), also exists in the United States to promote road racing.

In modern times, athletes can receive money for racing, putting an end to the so-called "amateurism" that existed before.

Indoor Athletics

There are two seasons for track and field. There is an indoor season, run during the winter and an outdoor season, run during the spring. Most indoor tracks are 200 metres and consist of four to 8 lanes. There are also some 150 metre indoor tracks, and others as small as 120 metres have been used. Some "oversize tracks" (larger than 200 metres) are popular for American collegiate athletics despite the fact that they are not considered valid for setting indoor records. Often an indoor track will have banked turns to compensate for the tight radius of the turns. The banking can help prevent injuries to the athlete, while also promoting higher speeds.

In an indoor track meet athletes contest the same track events as at an outdoor meet, with the exception of the 100 m and 110 m/100 m hurdles (replaced by the 55 or 60 m sprint and 55 or 60 m hurdles at most levels, or the 55 m sprint and hurdles at the high school level), the 10,000 m run, 3,000 m steeplechase, 400 m hurdles. Indoor meets also have the addition of a 3,000 m run normally at both the collegiate and elite level, instead of the 10,000 m. The 5,000 m is the longest event commonly run indoors, although there are situations where longer distances have been raced. In the mid-20th century, there was a series of "duel" races on Madison Square Garden's indoor track, some of which featured two men racing a marathon (42.2 km). However, this is an extremely rare occurrence, for obvious reasons. On some occasions, there may also be a 500 m race instead of the open 400 m normally found outdoors, and in many college championship races indoors both are contested.

In field events, indoor meets only feature the high jump, pole vault, long jump, triple jump, and shot put (weight throw). Due to space limitations, these events take place on the infield, within the circumferential track. The longer throws of javelin, hammer and discus are added only for outdoor meets, as there is normally not enough space in an indoor stadium to house these events.

Other events unique to indoor meets (especially in North America) are the 300 m, 600 m, 1000 m, and 35 lb (16 kg) weight throw. In some countries, notably Norway, standing long jump and standing high jump are also contested, even in the National Championships.

For multi-event athletes there is the Pentathlon for women (consisting of 60 m hurdles, high jump, shot put, long jump and 800 m) and heptathlon for men (consisting of 60 m, long jump, shot put, high jump, 60 m hurdles, pole vault and 1000 m) indoors.

Outdoor Athletics

The outdoor track and field season usually begins in the spring and lasts through the summer. Most tracks are ovals of 400 metres in circumference. Modern "tartan tracks" or more recently "mondo tracks" are made with a rubberised surface; older tracks were cinder-covered. Tracks normally consist of 6-10 lanes (up to 12 lanes on the 'front' straight) and many include a steeplechase lane with a water pit on one of the turns. This steeplechase pit can be placed either inside or outside the track, making for a tighter turn or a wider turn. It is common that tracks will surround a playing field used for American football, association football (soccer), or lacrosse. This inner field is usually known as the infield and has a surface of either grass or artificial turf.

All field events can be contested on the infield. However the javelin, hammer and discus throws are sometimes contested on fields outside of the track stadium because they take up a large amount of space, the implements may damage the infield, and the implements could end up landing on the track. However, some infields are used specifically for these events, and for the javelin, an athlete may have a longer run-up by starting it on the other side of the track, and crossing when there are no athletes passing.

Events

There are other variations besides the ones listed below, but races of unusual length (e.g. 300 m) are run much less often. The unusual races are typically held during indoor season because of the shorter 200 m indoor track. With the exception of the mile run, races based on imperial distances are rarely run on the track anymore since most tracks have been converted from a quarter mile (402.3 m) to 400 m; almost all record keeping for imperial distances has been discontinued. However, the IAAF record book still includes the mile world record (currently held by Hicham El Guerrouj of Morocco for men and Svetlana Masterkova of Russia for women) because of its worldwide historic significance.

Men and women do not compete against each other, although they may sometimes run in the same races due to time constraints at high school meets. Women generally run the same distances as men although hurdles and steeplechase barriers are lower and the weights of the shot, discus, javelin and hammer are less.

All Comers Track Meets

Track and Field is the most accessible sport for anyone to participate in. It only takes two people to have a race, or one can simply race a stopwatch. In events called *All Comers Track Meets,* anyone who wishes to participate is welcome. All comers meets are usually organised by communities, schools, or sports teams. Some sports teams also use all comers meets for fundraising. Most meets are low cost or free. All comers meets are fairly low-key and merely intended for gaining experience or just practicing for races. There is no exclusion on account of participants' lack of teams or equipment. While races are usually seeded based on the entrant's expected level of ability, the most elite of athletes can and do use these meets for training or practice.

Running and Racewalking Events

Running events conducted on a track (generally 400 metres, except indoors).

Sprints are events up to and including the 400 metres. Events commonly contested are:

- 50 metres (indoors only)
- 55 metres (indoors only)
- 60 metres (indoors only)
- 100 metres
- 200 metres
- 400 metres

Middle Distance Events are events longer than sprints and up to 3000 metres. Events commonly contested are:

- 600 metres (uncommon)
- 800 metres
- 1000 metres (uncommon)
- 1500 metres
- One mile
- 2000 metres (uncommon)
- 3000 metres
- 3000 metres steeplechase

Long Distance Events are events over 3000 metres. Events commonly contested are:

- 5000 metres
- 10000 metres

Hurdles events require the runner to run over evenly spaced barriers during the race. Events commonly contested are:

- 60 metres hurdles (indoors only)
- 100 metres hurdles (women)
- 110 metres hurdles (men)
- 400 metres hurdles

Relay races are events in which four athletes participate as a team, passing a metal baton in between. Events commonly contested are:

- 4 × 100 metres relay
- 4 × 200 metres relay (high school & collegiate)
- 4 × 400 metres relay

- 4 × 800 metres relay

Some events, such as medley relays, are rarely run except at large relay carnivals. Typical medley relays include:

- Sprint Medley Relay (SMR): the four legs are two 200 metre legs, 400 metres, 800 metres; or alternately two 100 metre legs, 200 metres, 400 metres
- Distance Medley Relay (DMR): the four legs are 1200 metres, 400 metres, 800 metres, 1600 metres

Road Races are events conducted on open roads, sometimes finishing on a track. Events commonly contested are:

- 10 km
- 20 km
- Half marathon (21.0975 km)
- Marathon (42.195 km). The marathon is the only common road-racing distance run in major international athletics championships, such as the Olympics.

Racewalking may be contested on either the track or on open roads. Events commonly contested are:

- 10 km
- 20 km
- 50 km

Field Events

Throwing Events

- Discus Throw
- Hammer Throw
- Javelin Throw
- Shot Put

Jumping Events

- High Jump

- Pole Vault
- Long Jump
- Triple Jump

The following events also take place, but are uncommon:

- Standing high jump
- Standing long jump
- Standing triple jump

Multiple-event Competitions

Multiple event competitions include events from both the track (running) and field events.

Pentathlon: the outdoor Pentathlon includes the following five events:

- Long Jump
- Javelin
- 200 metres
- Discus
- 1500 metres

The outdoor Pentathlon was a national championship event in the United States un.il 1978. It is still contested in many places throughout the world, but rarely as a championship event. The Pentathon was also contested in several of the early Olympic Games, notably in the 1912 Olympics which was won by Jim Thorpe, who also won the Decathlon. The event was modelled after the original Greek Olympic Games, in which the Pentathlon was the foremost contest. It consisted of a Long Jump, Javelin, a statia run of approximately 180 metres, Discus, and Greco-Roman style wrestling.

Pentathlon: the indoor Pentathlon includes the following five events:

- High Hurdles (110 metres for men, 100 metres for women)
- Shot Put
- Long Jump
- High Jump
- Middle distance (1500 metres for men, 800 metres for women)

Heptathlon: the Heptathlon includes the following seven events: Outdoors (usually only women)

- 100 metre high hurdles
- High Jump
- Shot Put
- 200 metres
- Long Jump
- Javelin Throw
- 800 metres

Indoors (usually only men):

- 60 metres
- Long Jump
- Shot Put
- High Jump
- 60 metres hurdles
- Pole Vault
- 1000 metres

Decathlon: the Decathlon includes the following ten events:

- 100 metres
- Long Jump
- Shot Put
- High Jump
- 400 metres
- 110 metre high hurdles
- Discus
- Pole Vault
- Javelin
- 1500 metres

Rules

Track Events

The rules of track athletics or of track events in athletics as observed in most international athletics competitions are set by the Competition Rules of the International Association of Athletics Federations (IAAF). The most recent complete set of rules is the

2009 rules that relate only to competitions in 2009. Key rules of track events are those regarding starting, running and finishing.

Starting

The start of a race is marked by a white line 5 cm wide. In all races that are not run in lanes the start line must be curved, so that all the athletes start the same distance from the finish. Starting blocks may be used for all races up to and including 400 m (including the first leg of the 4 × 200 m and 4 × 400 m) and may not be used for any other race. No part of the starting block may overlap the start line or extend into another lane. All races must be started by the report of the starter's gun or approved starting apparatus fired upwards after he or she has ascertained that athletes are steady and in the correct starting position. An athlete may not touch either the start line or the ground in front of it with his hands or his feet when on his marks. At most international competitions the commands of the starter in his own language, in English or in French, shall, in races up to and including 400 m, be "On your marks" and "Set". When all athletes are "set", the gun must be fired, or an approved starting apparatus must be activated. However, if the starter is not satisfied that all is ready to proceed, the athletes may be called out of the blocks and the process started over.

False start: An athlete, after assuming a final set position, may not commence his starting motion until after receiving the report of the gun, or approved starting apparatus. If, in the judgement of the starter or recallers, he does so any earlier, it is considered a false start. It is deemed a false start if, in the judgement of the starter an athlete fails to comply with the commands "on your marks" or "set" as appropriate after a reasonable time; or an athlete after the command "on your marks" disturbs other athletes in the race through sound or otherwise. Any athlete making a false start must be warned.

Running the Race

In all races run in lanes, each athlete must keep within his allocated lane from start to finish. This also applies to any portion of a race run in lanes. If an athlete leaves the track or steps on the line demarking the track, he/she should be disqualified. Also, any athlete who jostles or obstructs another athlete, in a way that impedes his progress, should be disqualified from that event. However, if an athlete is pushed or forced by another person to run outside his lane, and if no material advantage is gained, the athlete should not be disqualified.

The Finish

The finish of a race is marked by a white line 5 cm wide. The athletes must be placed in the order in which any part of their torso (as distinguished from the head, neck, arms, legs, hands or feet) reaches the vertical plane of the nearer edge of the finish line.

Ties between different athletes are resolved as follows: In determining whether there has been a tie in any round for a qualifying position for the next round based on time, a judge (called the chief photo finish judge) must consider the actual time recorded by the athletes to 1/1000th of a second. If the judge decides that there has been a tie, the tying athletes must be placed in the next round or, if that is not practicable, lots must be drawn to determine who must be placed in the next round. In the case of a tie for first place in any final, the referee decides whether it is practicable to arrange for the athletes so tying to compete again. If he decides it is not, the result will stand. Ties in other placings remain.

Track and Field on Coinage

Track and field events have been selected as a main motif in numerous collectors' coins. One of the recent samples is the €10 Greek Running commemorative coin, minted in 2003 to commemorate the 2004 Summer Olympics. In the obverse of the coin, a modern athlete figure appears in the foreground, shown in the starting position, while in the background two ancient runners are carved in a manner that gives the appearance of a coin that is "worn" by time. This scene originally appeared on a black-figure vase of the 6th century BC.

POWERLIFTING

Powerlifting is a strength sport, consisting of three events: the squat, the bench press, and the deadlift.

Powerlifting resembles the sport of olympic weightlifting, as both disciplines involve lifting weights in three attempts. It evolved from a sport known as 'odd lifts' which followed the same 3 attempt format but using a wide variety of events akin to Strongman events. Eventually odd lifts became standardised to the three events (squat, bench, deadlift) and became known as Powerlifting.

Powerlifting meets take place across the world but mostly in the USA, UK and Russia. Powerlifting has been a Paralympic sport since 1984 and is also a World Games sport.

Competition

A powerlifting competition takes place as follows:

> Each competitor is allowed three to four attempts on each lift depending on their standing and the organisation they are lifting in (usually smallest w-class to heaviest). The lifter's best valid attempt on each lift counts toward his competition total. If two or more lifters achieve the same total, the lighter lifter ranks above the heavier lifter.

Competitors are judged against other lifters of the same gender, weight class, and age. This helps to ensure that the accomplishments of lifters like Lamar Gant, who deadlifted five times his own weight, are recognised alongside those of Andy Bolton, the current World Powerlifting Organization deadlift world record holder.

Comparisons of lifters and scores across different weight classes can also be made using handicapping systems such as the Wilks formula.

Events

Powerlifting, in most federations, involves three events: squat, bench press and deadlift. Some variations of this are found at some meets such as "push-pull only" meets where lifters only compete in the bench press and deadlift, with the bench press coming first and the deadlift after. Single lift meets are often held, sometimes alongside a normal 3-lift event. This is most common in the bench press.

At a powerlifting meet the events will follow in order: squat, then bench press, and the deadlift will be the final lift of the meet. If the federation also has an event for strict curls this will normally occur before the squat event.

Rules of each Event

Squat

The lift starts with the lifter standing erect and the bar loaded with weights resting on the lifter's shoulders. At the referee's command the lift begins. The lifter bends his knees and lowers himself into a squatting position with the hips slightly below parallel position. The lifter returns to an erect position. At the referee's command the bar is returned to the rack and the lift is completed.

- After removing the bar from the racks while facing the front of the platform, the lifter may move forward or backward to establish the lifting position. The top of the bar not more than 3 cm below the top of the anterior deltoids. The bar shall be held horizontally across the shoulders with the hands and/or fingers gripping the bar, and the feet flat upon the platform with the knees locked.
- The lifter shall wait in this position for the head referee's signal. The signal will be given as soon as the lifter is set and demonstrates control with the bar properly positioned. The head referee's signal shall consist of a downward movement of the arm and audible command "Squat."
- Upon receiving the head referee's signal, the lifter must bend the knees and lower the body until the top surface of the legs at the hip joint is lower than the top of knees.
- The lifter must recover at will, without double bouncing, to an upright position with the knees locked. The bar may stop, but there must be no downward motion during recovery. As soon as the lifter demonstrates a controlled final position, the head referee will give the signal indicating completion of the lift and to replace the bar.
- The signal to replace the bar will consist of a backward motion of the arm and the audible command "Rack". The

lifter must then make a *bona fide* attempt to return the bar to the racks.

- The lifter shall face the front of the platform, towards the head referee.
- The lifter shall not hold the collars or discs at any time during the performance of the lift. However, the edge of the hands gripping the bar may be in contact with the inner surface of the collar.
- Not more than five and not less than two loaders/spotters shall be on the platform at any time.
- The lifter may enlist the help of spotters in removing the bar from the racks; however, once the bar has cleared the racks, the spotters shall not physically assist the lifter with regards to actually getting into the proper set position. The spotters may assist the lifter to maintain control should the lifter stumble or demonstrate any evident instability.
- The lifter will be allowed only one commencement signal per attempt.
- The lifter may be given an additional attempt at the same weight at the head referee's discretion if failure in an attempt was due to any error by one or more of the spotters.

Causes for Disqualification of a Squat

- Failure to observe the head referee's signals at the commencement or completion of a lift.
- Double bouncing or more than one recovery attempt at the bottom of the lift.
- Failure to assume an upright position with knees locked at the commencement and completion of the lift.
- Movement of the feet laterally, backward or forward that would constitute a step or stumble.
- Failure to bend the knees and lower the body until the surface of the legs at the hip joint is lower than the tops of the knees.
- Any resetting of the feet after the squat signal.
- Contact with the bar by the spotters between the referee's signals.
- Contact of elbows or upper arms with the legs.
- Failure to make a *bona fide* attempt to return the bar to the racks.
- Any intentional dropping or dumping of the bar.

Bench Press

With his or her back resting on the bench, the lifter takes the loaded bar at arm's length. The lifter lowers the bar to the chest. When the bar becomes motionless on the chest, the referee gives a press command. Then the referee will call 'Rack' and the lift is completed as the weight is retuned to the rack.

- The front of the bench must be placed on the platform facing the head referee.
- The lifter must lie backward with shoulders and buttocks in contact with the flat bench surface. The lifter's shoes or toes must be in solid contact with the platform or surface. The position of the head is optional.
- To achieve firm footing, a lifter of any height may use discs or blocks to build up the surface of the platform. Whichever method is chosen, the shoes must be in a solid contact with the surface. If blocks are used, they shall not exceed 45 cm × 45 cm.
- Not more than five and not less than two loaders/spotters shall be in attendance. The lifter may enlist the help of one or more of the designated spotters or enlist a personal spotter in removing the bar from the racks. Only designated spotters may remain on the platform during the lift. The lift off must be to arms length and not down to the chest. A designated spotter, having provided a centre lift off, must immediately clear the area in front of the head referee and move to either side of the bar. If the personal spotter does not immediately leave the platform area and/or in any way distracts or impedes the head referees' responsibilities, the referees may determine that the lift is unacceptable, and be declared "no lift" by the referees and given three red lights.
- The spacing of the hands shall not exceed 81 cm, measured between the forefingers. The bar shall have circumferential machine markings or tape indicating this maximum grip allowance. If the lifter should use an offset or unequal grip on the bar, whereby one hand is placed outside the marking or tape, it is the lifter's responsibility to explain this to the head referee, and allow inspection of the

intended grip prior to making an attempt. If this is not done until the lifter is on the platform for an official attempt, any necessary explanation and/or measurements will be done on the lifter's time for that attempt. The reverse or underhand grip is permitted.

- After receiving the bar at arm's length, the lifter shall lower the bar to the chest and await the head referees' signal.
- The signal shall be an audible command "Press" and given as soon as the bar is motionless on the chest. As long as the bar is not so low that it touches the lifter's belt, it is acceptable.
- The lifter will be allowed only one commencement signal per attempt.
- After the signal to commence the lift has been given, the bar is pressed upward. The bar shall not be allowed to sink into the chest or move downwards prior to the lifter's attempt to press upward. The lifter will press the bar to straight arm's length and hold motionless until the audible command "Rack" is given. Bar may move horizontally and may stop during the ascent, but may not move downward towards the chest.

Causes for Disqualification of a Bench Press

- Failure to observe the referee's signals at the commencement or completion of the lift.
- Any change in the elected position that results in the buttocks breaking contact with the bench or lateral movement of the hands (between the referee's signals). Any excessive movement or change of contact of the feet during the lift proper.
- Bouncing the bar off the chest.
- Allowing the bar to sink into the chest after receiving the referee's signal.
- Pronounced uneven extension of the arms during or at the completion of the lift.
- Any downward motion of the bar during the course of being pressed out.
- Contact with the bar by the spotters between the referee's signals.

- Any contact of the lifter's shoes with the bench or its supports.
- Deliberate contact between the bar and the bar rest uprights during the lift to assist the completion of the press.
- It is the responsibility of the lifter to inform any personally enlisted spotters to leave the platform as soon as the bar is secured at arm's length. Such spotters shall not return to the platform upon completion or failure of the attempt. It is especially important for a spotter providing a centre lift off to leave the platform quickly so as not to impair the head referee's view. Failure of any personal spotters to leave the platform may cause disqualification of the lift.

Deadlift

In the deadlift the athlete grasps the loaded bar which is resting on the platform floor. The powerlifter pulls the weights off the floor and assumes an erect position. The knees must be locked and the shoulders back, with the weight held in the lifters's grip. At the referee's command the bar will be returned to the floor under the control of the lifter.

- The bar must be laid horizontally in front of the lifter's feet, gripped with an optional grip in both hands, and lifted until the lifter is standing erect. The bar may stop but there must be no downward motion of the bar.
- The lifter shall face the front of the platform.
- On completion of the lift, the knees shall be locked in a straight position and the lifter shall be standing erect.
- The head referee's signal shall consist of a downward movement of the arm and the audible command "Down". The signal will not be given until the bar is held motionless and the lifter is in an apparent finished position.
- Any raising of the bar or any deliberate attempt to do so will count as an attempt.

Causes of Disqualification of a Deadlift

- Any downward motion of the bar before it reaches the final position.

- Failure to stand erect.
- Failure to lock the knees straight at the completion of the lift.
- Supporting the bar on the thighs during the performance of the lift. 'Supporting' is defined as a body position adopted by the lifter that could not be maintained without the counterbalance of the weight being lifted.
- Movement of the feet laterally, backward or forward that would constitute a step or stumble.
- Lowering the bar before receiving the head referee's signal.
- Allowing the bar to return to the platform without maintaining control with both hands.

Training

Powerlifting requires specialised training techniques that are focused on strength and explosive power. Traditional training methods dictated low repetitions with maximal weight. These practices are still true today, however training methods have advanced to include emphasis on explosive power. This may be achieved through dynamic exercises which utilise lighter weight and alternating repetition patterns.

A well-known training method is known as the Westside Barbell method developed by Louie Simmons, or the high volume routines developed by Boris Sheiko. Other alternatives exist, notably the Smolov Squat Routine from Russia.

Regulations

Although powerlifting always uses the squat, bench press and deadlift as events, different federations have different rules and different interpretations of the rules, leading to a myriad of variations.

The ADAU and 100 per cent Raw Federation allow no supportive gear to be worn by the lifter while the IPF, AAU, NASA, U.S.A.P.L. and the ADFPF only allow a single-ply tight polyester squat suit, deadlift suit and bench shirt, wraps for knees and wrists, and a belt. Other federations, such as the APF, APA, IPA and WPO, allow opened or closed back bench shirts, multi-ply gear, and a wide array of gear materials such as canvas, denim, polyester etc.

In an IPF bench press, the barbell can go as low as the xiphoid process and no further in the lift, whereas in other federations, the barbell can touch the abdomen. (This shortens the distance in which the barbell is moved and is an advantage to the lifter.)

Although there are various different powerlifting organisations, the International Powerlifting Federation (IPF) is considered the gold standard of powerlifting with regards to the judging of depth and the execution of the various lifts. However, this assertion is hotly debated throughout the powerlifting community.

The IPF routinely conducts random drug tests on its athletes, and is the only organisation to hold competitions on every continent around the world except Antarctica.

The IPF has suspended entire member nations' federations, including the Russian Powerlifting Federation and the Ukrainian Powerlifting Federation, for repeated violations of the IPF's anti-doping policies. However Russia and the Ukraine never served the full 2 year suspension.

TENNIS

Tennis is a sport played between two players (singles) or between two teams of two players each (doubles). Each player uses a strung racquet to strike a hollow rubber ball covered with felt over a net into the opponent's court.

The modern game of tennis originated in the United Kingdom in the late 19th century as "lawn tennis" which has heavy connections to various field/lawn games as well as to the ancient game of *real tennis*. After its creation, tennis spread throughout the upper-class English-speaking population before spreading around the world. Tennis is an Olympic sport and is played at all levels of society at all ages. The sport can be played by anyone who can hold a racket, including people in wheelchairs. In the United States, there is a collegiate circuit organised by the National Collegiate Athletic Association.

The rules of tennis have changed very little since the 1890s Two exceptions are that from 1908 to 1960 the server had to keep one foot on the ground at all times, and then the adoption of the tie-break in the 1970s. A recent addition to professional tennis has been the adoption of electronic review technology coupled with a point challenge system, which allows a player to challenge the line (or chair) umpire's call of a point.

Tennis enjoys millions of recreational players and is also a hugely popular worldwide spectator sport, especially the four Grand Slam tournaments (sometimes referred to as the "majors"): the Australian Open, the French Open, Wimbledon, and the US Open.

History

Tennis as the modern sport can be dated to two separate roots. Between 1859 and 1863, Major Harry Gem and his friend Augurio Perera developed a game that combined elements of rackets and the Basque ball game pelota, which they played on Perera's croquet lawn in Birmingham, United Kingdom. In 1872, along with two local doctors, they founded the world's first tennis club in Leamington Spa. The Courier of July 23, 1884 recorded one of the first tennis tournaments, held in the grounds of Shrubland Hall.

In December 1873, Major Walter Clopton Wingfield designed and patented a similar game—which he called *sphairistike* (from ancient Greek meaning "skill at playing at ball"), and was soon known simply as "sticky"—for the amusement of his guests at a garden party on his estate of Nantclwyd, in Llanelidan, Wales. He likely based his game on the evolving sport of outdoor tennis including real tennis. According to some tennis historians, modern tennis terminology also derives from this period, as Wingfield borrowed both the name and much of the French vocabulary of real tennis and applied them to his new game.

The first championships at Wimbledon in London were played in 1877. The first Championships culminated a significant debate on how to standardise the rules.

In America in 1874 Mary Ewing Outerbridge, a young socialite, returned from Bermuda where she met Major Wingfield. She laid out a tennis court at the Staten Island Cricket Club in New Brighton Staten Island, New York. The exact location of the club was under what is now the Staten Island Ferry terminal. The first American National tournament in 1880 was played there. An Englishman named O.E. Woodhouse won the singles match. There was also a doubles match which was won by a local pair. There were different rules at each club. The ball in Boston was larger than the one normally used in NY. On May 21, 1881, the United States National Lawn Tennis Association (now the United States Tennis Association) was formed to standardise the rules and organise competitions. The U.S. National Men's Singles Championship, now the US Open, was first held in 1881 at Newport, Rhode Island. The U.S. National Women's Singles Championships were first held in 1887. Tennis was also popular in France, where the French Open dates to 1891. Thus, Wimbledon, the US Open, the French Open, and the Australian Open (dating to 1905) became and have remained the most prestigious events in tennis. Together these four events are called the Majors or *Slams* (a term borrowed from bridge rather than baseball).

The comprehensive International Lawn Tennis Federation, now known as the International Tennis Federation, rules promulgated in 1924 have remained remarkably stable in the ensuing eighty years, the one major change being the addition of the *tie-break* system designed by James Van Alen. That same year, tennis withdrew from the Olympics after the 1924 Games but returned 60 years later as a 21- and -under demonstration event in 1984. This reinstatement was credited by the efforts by the then ITF President Philippe Chatrier, ITF General Secretary David Gray and ITF Vice President Pablo Llorens, and support from IOC President Juan Antonio Samaranch. The success of the event was overwhelming and the IOC decided to reintroduce tennis as a full medal sport at Seoul in 1988.

The Davis Cup, an annual competition between men's national teams, dates to 1900. The analogous competition for women's national teams, the Fed Cup, was founded as the Federation Cup in 1963 to celebrate the 50th anniversary of the founding of the ITF.

In 1926, promoter C.C. Pyle established the first professional tennis tour with a group of American and French tennis players playing exhibition matches to paying audiences. The most notable of these early professionals were the American Vinnie Richards and the Frenchwoman Suzanne Lenglen. Once a player *turned pro* he or she could not compete in the major (amateur) tournaments.

In 1968, commercial pressures and rumours of some amateurs taking money under the table led to the abandonment of this distinction, inaugurating the open era, in which all players could compete in all tournaments, and top players were able to make their living from tennis. With the beginning of the open era, the establishment of an international professional tennis circuit, and revenues from the sale of television rights, tennis's popularity has spread worldwide, and the sport has shed its upper/middle-class English-speaking image (although it is acknowledged that this stereotype still exists).

In 1954, Van Alen founded the International Tennis Hall of Fame, a non-profit museum in Newport, Rhode Island. The building contains a large collection of tennis memorabilia as well as a hall of fame honouring prominent members and tennis players from all over the world. Each year, a grass-court tournament and an induction ceremony honouring new Hall of Fame members are hosted on its grounds.

Equipment

Part of the appeal of tennis stems from the simplicity of equipment required for play. Beginners need only a racquet and balls.

Racquets

The tennis racquet comprises a handle and neck joining a roughly circular frame that holds an array of tightly pulled strings. For the first century of the modern game, racquets were of wood and of standard size, and strings were of animal gut. Laminated wood construction yielded more strength in rackets used through most of the 20th century until first metal and then composites of carbon graphite, ceramics, and lighter metals such as titanium were introduced. These stronger materials enabled the production of oversized rackets that yielded yet more power. Meanwhile technology led to the use of synthetic strings that match the feel of gut yet with added durability.

Balls

Tennis balls are of hollow rubber with a felt coating. Traditionally white, the predominant colour was gradually changed to Optic Yellow in the latter part of the twentieth century to allow for improved visibility.

Miscellaneous

Advanced players improve their performance through a number of accoutrements. Vibration dampers may be interlaced in the proximal part of the string array for improved feel. Racket handles may be customised with absorbent materials to improve the players' grip. Players often use sweat bands on their wrists to keep their hands dry as well. Finally, although the game can be played in a variety of shoes, specialised tennis shoes have wide, flat soles for stability and a built-up front structure to avoid excess wear.

Manner of Play

Court

Tennis is played on a rectangular, flat surface, usually grass, clay, a hardcourt of concrete and/or asphalt and occasionally carpet (indoor). The court is 78 feet (23.77 m) long, and its width is 27 feet (8.23 m) for singles matches and 36 ft (10.97 m) for doubles matches. Additional clear space around the court is required in order for players to reach overrun balls. A net is stretched across the full width of the court, parallel with the baselines, dividing it into two equal ends. The net is 3 feet 6 inches (1.07 m) high at the posts and 3 feet (91.4 cm) high in the centre.

The modern tennis court owes its design to Major Walter Clopton Wingfield who, in 1873, patented a court much the same as the current one for his stické tennis (sphairistike). This template was modified in 1875 to the court design that exists today, with markings similar to Wingfield's version, but with the hourglass shape of his court changed to a rectangle.

Lines

The lines that delineate the width of the court are called the baseline (farthest back) and the service line (middle of the court). The short mark in the centre of each baseline is referred to as either the hash mark or the centre mark. The outermost lines that make up the length are called the doubles sidelines. These are the boundaries used when doubles is being played. The lines to the inside of the doubles sidelines are the singles sidelines and are used as boundaries in singles play. The area between a doubles sideline and the nearest singles sideline is called the doubles alley, which is considered playable in doubles play. The line that runs across the centre of a player's side of the court is called the service line because the serve must be delivered into the area between the service line and the net on the receiving side. Despite its name, this is not where a player legally stands when making a serve. The line dividing the service line in two is called the centre line or centre service line. The boxes this centre line creates are called the service boxes; depending on a player's position, he will have to hit the ball into one of these when serving. A ball is out only if none of it has hit the line or the area inside the lines upon its first bounce. All the lines are required to be between 1 and 2 inches (51 mm) in width. The baseline can be up to 4 inches (100 mm) wide if so desired.

Play of a Single Point

The players (or teams) start on opposite sides of the net. One player is designated the *server*, and the opposing player, or in doubles one of the opposing players, is the *receiver*. Service alternates between the two halves of the court. For each point, the server starts behind his baseline, between the centre mark and the sideline. The receiver may start anywhere on their side of the net. When the receiver is ready, the server will serve, although the receiver must play to the pace of the server.

In a legal service, the ball travels over the net (without touching it) and into the diagonally opposite service box. If the ball hits the net but lands in the service box, this is a *let* or *net service*, which is void, and the server gets to retake that serve. The player can serve any number of let services in a point and they are always treated as voids and not as faults. A fault is a serve that is long, wide, or not over the net. There is also a "foot fault", which occurs when a player's foot touches the baseline or an extension of the centre mark before the ball is hit. If the second service is also faulty, this is a *double fault*, and the receiver wins the point. However, if the serve is in, it is considered a legal service.

A legal service starts a *rally*, in which the players alternate hitting the ball across the net. A legal return consists of the player or team hitting the ball exactly once before it has bounced twice or hit any fixtures except the net, provided that it still falls in the server's court. The ball then travels back over the net and bounces in the court on the opposite side. The first player or team to fail to make a legal return loses the point.

Scoring

A tennis match is determined through the best of 3 or 5 *sets*. Typically for both men's and women's matches, the first player to win two sets wins the match. At certain important tennis tournaments for men, including all four Grand Slam tournaments and the final of the Olympic Games, the first man to win three sets wins the match. A set consists of *games*, and games, in turn, consist of *points*.

A game consists of a sequence of points played with the same player serving. A game is won by the first player to have won at least four points in total and at least two points more than the opponent. The running score of each game is described in a manner peculiar to tennis: scores from zero to three points are described as *"love"*, *"fifteen"*, *"thirty"*, and *"forty"* respectively. If at least three points have been scored by each player, and the scores are equal, the score is *"deuce"*. If at least three points have been scored by each side and a player has one more point than his opponent, the score of the game is *"advantage"* for the player in the lead. During informal games, "advantage" can also be called "ad in" or "ad out", depending on whether the serving player or receiving player is ahead, respectively.

In tournament play, the chair umpire calls the point count (e.g., *"fifteen-love"*) after each point. The score of a tennis match during play is always read with the serving player's score first. After a match, the score is always read with the winning player's score first. At the end of a game, the chair umpire also announces the winner of the game and the overall score.

A *game point* occurs in tennis whenever the player who is in the lead in the game needs only one more point to win the game. The terminology is extended to sets (set point), matches (match point), and even championships (championship point). For example, if the player who is serving has a score of 40-love, the player has a triple game point (triple set point, etc.) as the player has three consecutive chances to win the game. Game points, set points, and match points are not part of official scoring and are not announced by the chair umpire in tournament play.

A *break point* occurs if the receiver, not the server, has a game point. Break points are of particular importance because serving is generally advantageous. A receiver who has two (score of 15-40) or three (score of love-40) consecutive chances to win the game has *double break point* or *triple break point*, respectively. As with game, set, and match points, break points are not announced.

A set consists of a sequence of games played with service alternating between games, ending when the count of games won meets certain criteria. Typically, a player wins a set by winning at least six games and at least two games more than the opponent. If one player has won six games and the opponent five, an additional game is played. If the leading player wins that game, the player wins the set 7–5. If the trailing player wins the game, a *tie-break* is played. A tie-break, played under a separate set of rules, allows one player to win one more game and thus the set, to give a final set score of 7–6. Only in the final sets of matches at the Australian Open, the French Open, Wimbledon, the Olympic Games, Davis Cup, and Fed Cup are tie-breaks not played. In these cases, sets are played indefinitely until one player has a two-game lead. A "love" set means that the loser of the set won zero games. In tournament play, the chair umpire announces the winner of the set and the overall score.

In tournament play, the chair umpire announces the end of the match with the well-known phrase "*Game, set, match*" followed by the winning person's or team's name.

Rules Variations

Variations

Name	*Description*
No-ad	The first player or doubles team to win four points wins the game, regardless of whether the player or team is ahead by two points. When the game score reaches three points each, the receiver chooses which side of the court (advantage court or deuce court) the service is to be delivered on the seventh and game-deciding point.
Pro set	Instead of playing multiple sets, players may play one "pro set". A pro set is first to 8 (or 10) games by a margin of two games, instead of first to 6 games. A 12-point tie-break is usually played when the score is 8-8 (or 10-10). These are often played with no-ad scoring.
Match tiebreak	This is sometimes played instead of a third set. This is played like a regular tiebreak, but the winner must win ten points instead of seven. Match tiebreaks are used in the Hopman Cup for mixed doubles, on the ATP and WTA tours for doubles and as a player's choice in USTA league play.

Another, however informal, tennis format is called "Kiwi doubles", "Canadian doubles" or "cut-throat". This involves three players, with one person playing a doubles team. The single player gets to utilise the alleys normally reserved only for a doubles team. Conversely, the doubles team does not use the alleys when executing a shot. The scoring is the same as a regular game. This format is not sanctioned by any official body.

"Australian doubles", another informal and unsanctioned form of tennis, is played with similar rules to the "Kiwi" style, only in this version, players rotate court position after each game. As such, each player plays doubles and singles over the course of a match, with the singles player always serving. Scoring styles vary, but one popular method is to assign a value of 2 points to each game, with the server taking both points if he or she holds serve and the doubles team each taking one if they break serve.

Wheelchair tennis can be played by able-bodied players as well as people who require a wheelchair for mobility. An extra bounce is permitted. This rule makes it possible to have mixed wheelchair and able-bodied matches. It is possible for a doubles team to consist of a wheelchair player and an able-bodied player (referred to as "one-up, one-down"), or for a wheelchair player to play against an able-bodied player. In such cases, the extra bounce is permitted for the wheelchair users only.

Surface

There are four main types of court surface, each different in the speed and bounce of the ball:

Name	*Description*
Clay	Examples are red clay (used at the French Open and many other tournaments, especially in Europe and Latin America) and green clay (an example of which is Har-Tru and used mainly in the U.S.). Clay courts normally have a slower paced ball and a fairly true bounce with more spin.
Hard	Examples are acrylic (e.g. Plexicushion used at the Australian Open, DecoTurf used at the US Open), asphalt, and concrete. Hardcourts typically have a faster-paced ball with a very true bounce.

(*Contd.*)

Name	Description
Grass	Used at Wimbledon. Grass courts usually have a faster-paced ball, and a more erratic bounce. Wimbledon has slowed its courts over the years.
Indoor	Examples are carpet and very rarely, wood. Carpet courts typically have a very fast-paced ball with a true but low bounce.

Officials

In most professional play and some amateur competition, there is an officiating head judge or chair umpire (usually referred to as the umpire), who sits in a raised chair to one side of the court. The umpire has absolute authority to make factual determinations. The umpire may be assisted by line judges, who determine whether the ball has landed within the required part of the court and who also call foot faults. There also may be a net judge who determines whether the ball has touched the net during service. In some tournaments, certain line judges, usually those who would be calling the serve, are replaced by electronic sensors that beep when an out call would have been made. In some tournaments, electric line calls aren't made, but rather are used to assist the linespeople. When a ball lands in a spot where the linesperson isn't sure if the ball was in or out, a noise is made that only linespeople can hear (because they are wearing headsets), and helps them to make the call. In some open-tournament matches, players are allowed to challenge a limited number of close calls by means of electronic review. The US Open, the NASDAQ-100 Open in Key Biscayne, Florida, the US Open Series, and World Team Tennis started using a "challenge" system in 2006 and the Australian Open and Wimbledon introduced the system in 2007. This used the Hawk-Eye system and the rules were similar to those used in the NFL, where a player gets a limited number of opportunities to challenge per match/set. More recently, a player may use unlimited challenges in a set, provided that he or she is not incorrect more than three times. In clay-court matches, such as at the French Open, a call may be questioned by reference to the mark left by the ball's impact on the court surface.

The referee, who is usually located off the court, is the final authority about tennis rules. When called to the court by a player or team captain, the referee may overrule the umpire's decision if the tennis rules were violated (question of law) but may not change the umpire's decision on a question of fact. If, however, the referee is on the court during play, the referee may overrule the umpire's decision.

Ball boys and girls may be employed to retrieve balls, pass them to the players, and hand players their towels. They have no adjudicative role. In rare events (e.g., if they are hurt or if they have caused a hindrance), the umpire may ask them for a statement of what actually happened. The umpire may consider their statements when making a decision. In some leagues, especially junior leagues, players make their own calls, trusting each other to be honest. This is the case for many school and university level matches. The referee or referee's assistant, however, can be called on court at a player's request, and the referee or assistant may change a player's call. In unofficiated matches, a ball is out only if the player entitled to make the call is sure that the ball is out.

Juniors

In tennis, a junior is a player under the age of 18 who is still legally protected by a parent or guardian. Players on the main adult tour who are under 18 must have documents signed by a parent or guardian. These players, however, are still eligible to play in junior tournaments.

The International Tennis Federation (ITF) conducts a junior tour that allows juniors to establish a world ranking and an Association of Tennis Professionals (ATP) or Women's Tennis Association (WTA) ranking. Most juniors who enter the international circuit do so by progressing through ITF, Satellite, Future, and Challenger tournaments before entering the main circuit. The latter three circuits also have adults competing in them. Some juniors, however, such as Australian Lleyton Hewitt and Frenchman Gaël Monfils, have catapulted directly from the junior tour to the ATP tour by dominating the junior scene or by taking advantage of opportunities given to them to participate in professional tournaments.

In 2004, the ITF implemented a new rankings scheme to encourage greater participation in doubles, by combining two rankings (singles and doubles) into one combined tally. Junior tournaments do not offer prize money except for the Grand Slams, which are the most prestigious junior events. Juniors may earn income from tennis by participating in the Future, Satellite, or Challenger tours. Tournaments are broken up into different tiers offering different amounts of ranking points, culminating with Grade A.

Leading juniors are allowed to participate for their nation in the Junior Fed Cup and Davis Cup competitions as well. To succeed in tennis often means having to begin playing at a young age. To facilitate and nurture a junior's growth in tennis, almost all tennis playing nations have developed a junior development system. Juniors develop their play through a range of tournaments on all surfaces, accommodating all different standards of play. Talented juniors may also receive sponsorships from governing bodies or private institutions.

Match Play

A tennis match is intended to be continuous. Because stamina is a relevant factor, arbitrary delays are not permitted. In most cases, service is required to occur no more than 20 seconds after the end of the previous point. This is increased to 90 seconds when the players change ends (after every odd-numbered game), and a 120 second break is permitted between sets. Other than this, breaks are permitted only when forced by events beyond the players' control, such as rain, damaged footwear, damaged racquet, or the need to retrieve an errant ball. Should a player be determined to be stalling repeatedly, the chair umpire may initially give a warning followed by subsequent penalties of "point", "game", and default of the match for the player who is consistently taking longer than the allowed time limit.

In the event of a rain delay, darkness or other external conditions halting play, the match is resumed at a later time, with the same score as at the time of the delay, and the players at the same end of the court when rain halted play, or at the same position (north or south) if play is resumed on a different court.

Balls wear out quickly in serious play and, therefore, in ATP and WTA tournaments, they are changed after every nine games with the first change occurring after only seven games, because the first set of balls is also used for the pre-match warm-up. As a courtesy to the receiver, the server will often signal to the receiver before the first serve of the game in which new balls are used as a reminder that they are using new balls. However, in ITF tournaments like Fed Cup, the balls are changed in a 9-11 style. Continuity of the balls' condition is considered part of the game, so if a re-warm-up is required after an extended break in play (usually due to rain), then the re-warm-up is done using a separate set of balls, and use of the match balls is resumed only when play resumes.

A recent proposed rules change is to allow coaching on court during a match on a limited basis, and this has, in fact, been instituted for WTA Tour events.

Shots

A competent tennis player has eight basic shots in his or her repertoire: the serve, forehand, backhand, volley, half-volley, overhead smash, drop shot, and lob.

Serve

A serve (or, more formally, a "service") in tennis is a shot to start a point. The serve is initiated by tossing the ball into the air and hitting it (usually near the apex of its trajectory) into the diagonally opposite service box without touching the net. The serve may be hit under- or overhand.

Experienced players strive to master the conventional overhand serve to maximise its power and placement. The server may employ different types of serve including flat serve, topspin serve, slice serve, and kick (American twist) serve. A reverse type of spin serve is hit in a manner that spins the ball opposite the natural spin of the server, the spin direction depending upon right- or left-handedness. If the ball is spinning counterclockwise, it will curve right from the hitter's point of view and curve left if spinning clockwise.

Some servers are content to use the serve simply to initiate the point; however, advanced players often try to hit a winning shot with their serve. A winning serve that is not touched by the opponent is called an "ace". If the receiver manages to touch it but fails to successfully return it, it is called a "service winner."

Grips

Players use various grips during play, including the continental, eastern, and western grips. Different grips generally are used for different types of spin and shots.

Forehand

For a right-handed player, the forehand is a stroke that begins on the right side of the body, continues across the body as contact is made with the ball, and ends on the left side of the body. There are various grips for executing the forehand, and their popularity has fluctuated over the years. The most important ones are the *continental*, the *eastern*, the *semi-western*, and the *western*. For a number of years, the small, apparently frail 1920s player Bill Johnston was considered by many to have had the best forehand of all time, a stroke that he hit shoulder-high using a *western* grip. Few top players used the *western* grip after the 1920s, but in the latter part of the 20th century, as shot-making techniques and equipment changed radically, the *western* forehand made a strong comeback and is now used by many modern players. No matter which grip is used, most forehands are generally executed with one hand holding the racquet, but there have been fine players with two-handed forehands. In the 1940s and 50s, the Ecuadorian/American player Pancho Segura used a two-handed forehand to achieve a devastating effect against larger, more powerful players. Currently, France's Fabrice Santoro uses a two-handed forehand. Some females such as Monica Seles and France's Marion Bartoli also use a two-handed forehand.

Backhand

For right-handed players, the backhand is a stroke that begins on the left side of their body, continues across their body as contact is made with the ball, and ends on the right side of their body. It can be executed with either one hand or with both and is generally considered more difficult to master than the forehand. For most of the 20th century, the backhand was performed with one hand, using either an *eastern* or a *continental* grip. The first notable players to use two hands were the 1930s Australians Vivian McGrath and John Bromwich, but they were lonely exceptions. The two-handed grip gained popularity in the 1970s as Björn Borg, Chris Evert, Jimmy Connors, and later Mats Wilander and Andre Agassi used it to great effect, and it is now used by a large number of the world's best players, including Rafael Nadal and Serena Williams. Andy Roddick uses the *extreme western* grip to create massive amounts of top spin. It is difficult to do this and could possibly cause injury if done incorrectly. Two hands give the player more control, while one hand can generate a slice shot, applying backspin on the ball to produce a low trajectory bounce. Reach is also limited with the two-handed shot. The player long considered to have had the best backhand of all time, Don Budge, had a powerful one-handed stroke in the 1930s and 1940s that imparted topspin onto the ball. Ken Rosewall, another player noted for his one-handed backhand, used a very accurate slice backhand through the 1950s and 1960s. A small number of players, notably Monica Seles, use two hands on both the backhand and forehand sides.

Other Shots

A *volley* is made in the air before the ball bounces, generally near the net, and is usually made with a stiff-wristed punching motion to hit the ball into an open area of the opponent's court. The *half volley* is made by hitting the ball on the rise just after it has bounced, once again generally in the vicinity of the net. The *swinging volley* is hit out of the air as the player approaches the net. It is an offensive shot used to take preparation time away from the opponent. From a poor defensive position on the baseline, the *lob* can be used as either an offensive or defensive weapon, hitting the ball high and deep into the opponent's court to either enable the lobber to get into better defensive position or to win the point outright by hitting it over the opponent's head. If the lob is not hit deeply enough into the other court, however, the opponent may then hit an *overhead smash,* a hard, serve-like shot, to try to end the point. Finally, if an opponent is deep in his court, a player may suddenly employ an unexpected *drop shot,* softly tapping the ball just over the net so that the opponent is unable to run in fast enough to retrieve it.

Tournaments

Tournaments are often organised by gender and number of players. Common tournament configurations include men's singles, women's singles, and doubles, where two players play on each side of the net. Tournaments may be arranged for specific age groups, with upper age limits for youth and lower age limits for senior players. Example of this include the Orange Bowl and Les Petits As. There are also tournaments for players with disabilities, such as wheelchair tennis and deaf tennis. In the four Grand Slam tournaments, the singles draws are limited to 128 people for each gender.

Players may also be matched by their skill level. According to how well a person does in sanctioned play, a player is given a rating that is adjusted periodically to maintain competitive matches. For example, the United States Tennis Association administers the National Tennis Rating Programme, which rates players between 1.0 and 7.0 in 1/2 point increments. Average club players under this system would rate 3.0-4.5 while world class players would be 7.0 on this scale.

Grand Slam Tournaments

The four Grand Slam tournaments are considered to be the most prestigious tennis tournaments in the world. They are held annually and include, in chronological order, the Australian Open, the French Open, Wimbledon, and the US Open. Apart from the Olympic Games, Davis Cup, Fed Cup, and Hopman Cup, they are the only tournaments regulated by the International Tennis Federation (ITF). The ITF's national associations, Tennis Australia (Australian Open), the French Tennis Federation (French Open), the United States Tennis Association (US Open), and the All England Lawn Tennis and Croquet Club and Lawn Tennis Association (Wimbledon), are delegated the responsibility to organise these events.

Aside from the historical significance of these events, they also carry larger prize funds than any other tour event and are worth double the number of ranking points to the champion than in the next echelon of tournaments, the Masters 1000 (men) and Premier events (women). Another distinguishing feature is the number of players in the singles draw, 128, more than any other professional tennis tournament. This draw is composed of 32 seeded players, other players ranked in the world's top 100, qualifiers, and players who receive invitations through wild cards. Grand Slam men's tournaments have best-of-five set matches throughout. Grand Slam tournaments are among the small number of events that last two weeks, the others being the BNP Paribas Open in Indian Wells, California and the Sony Ericsson Open in Key Biscayne, Florida. Currently, the Grand Slam tournaments are the only tour events that have mixed doubles contests. Grand Slam tournaments are held in conjunction with wheelchair tennis tournaments (with the exception being Wimbledon, where the grass surface prevents this) and junior tennis competitions. Grand Slam tournaments are often seen as the culmination of a particular season, such as the US Open Series. These tournaments also contain their own idiosyncrasies. For example, players at Wimbledon are required to wear predominantly white, a rule that has motivated certain players, such as Andre Agassi, to skip the tournament. Wimbledon also has its own particular methods for disseminating tickets, often leading tennis fans to follow complex procedures to obtain tickets.

Grand Slam

Period	*Tournament*	*Location*	*Surface*
January	Australian Open	Melbourne	Hard (Plexicushion)
May-June	French Open	Paris	Clay
June-July	Wimbledon	London	Grass
August-September	US Open	New York City	Hard (DecoTurf)

Masters 1000

The ATP World Tour Masters 1000 is a group of nine tournaments that form the second highest echelon in men's tennis. Each event is held annually, and a win at one of these events is currently worth 1000 ranking points. When the Association of Tennis Professionals, led by Hamilton Jordan, began running the men's tour in 1990, the directors designated the top nine tournaments, outside of the Grand Slam events, as "Super Nine" events. These eventually became the Tennis Masters Series. In November at the end of the tennis year, the world's top eight players compete in the ATP World Tour Finals, a tournament with a rotating locale. It is currently held in London, England.

On August 31, 2007 the ATP announced that major changes will take place in 2009. The Masters Series will be renamed to the "Masters 1000", with the addition of the number 1000 referring to the number of ranking points earned by the winner of each tournament. Contrary to earlier plans, the number of tournaments will not be reduced from nine to eight and the Monte Carlo Masters will remain part of the series although, unlike the other events, it will not have a mandatory player commitment. The Hamburg Masters event will be downgraded to a 500 point event. The Madrid Masters will move to May and onto clay courts, and a new tournament in Shanghai will take over Madrid's former indoor

October slot. In 2011 six of the nine "1000" level tournaments will be combined ATP and WTA events.

Current Masters 1000 Tournaments (2009)

Start Month	*Tournament Name*	*City*	*Surface*	*Opening*
March	BNP Paribas Open	Indian Wells	Hard	Outdoors
March	Sony Ericsson Open	Miami[1]	Hard	Outdoors
April	Monte-Carlo Rolex Masters	Monte-Carlo[2]	Clay	Outdoors
April	Internazionali BNL d'Italia	Rome	Clay	Outdoors
May	Mutua Madrileña Masters Madrid	Madrid	Clay	Outdoors
August	Rogers Cup	Montreal, Toronto	Hard	Outdoors
August	Western & Southern Financial Group Masters & Women's Open	Cincinnati[3]	Hard	Outdoors
October	Shanghai Masters 1000 presented by Rolex	Shanghai	Hard	Outdoors
November	BNP Paribas Masters	Paris	Hard	Indoors

[1] Actually in the adjacent suburb of Key Biscayne, Florida.
[2] Actually in the adjacent French commune of Roquebrune-Cap-Martin.
[3] Actually in the suburb of Mason, Ohio.

250 and 500 Series

The International Series for men is split into two categories, both run by the ATP: the 250 Series and 500 Series. Like the Masters 1000, these events offer various amounts of prize money, and some regular International Series events offer larger prize monies than 500 Series tournaments. The Barclays Dubai Tennis Championships offer the largest financial incentive to players, with total prize money of US$1,426,000.

Challenger Tour and Futures Tournaments

The Challenger Tour for men is the lowest level of tournament administered by the ATP. It is composed of roughly 160 events and, as a result, features a more diverse range of countries hosting events. The majority of players use the Challenger Series to work their way up the rankings, including World No. 1s Pete Sampras, Marcelo Ríos, Patrick Rafter, and Gustavo Kuerten. Andre Agassi, between winning Grand Slam titles, plummeted to World No. 141 and used Challenger Series events for match experience and to progress back up the rankings. The Challenger Series offers prize funds of between US$25,000 and US$150,000.

Below the Challenger Series are the Futures Tournaments, the main events on the ITF Men's Circuit. These tournaments also contribute towards a player's ATP rankings points. Futures Tournaments offer prize funds of between US$10,000 and US$15,000; however, futures status is granted only to events offering a total of US$30,000 meaning that two or three tournaments are played. Approximately 400 Futures Tournaments are played each year.

Premier Events

Premier events for women form the most prestigious level of events on the Women's Tennis Association Tour after the Grand Slam tournaments. These events offer the largest rewards in terms of points and prize money. Within the Premier category are Premier Mandatory, Premier 5, and Premier tournaments. The tiering system in women's tennis was introduced in 1988. At the time of its creation, only two tournaments, the Lipton International Players Championships in Florida and the German Open in Berlin, comprised the Tier I category. In 2009, four tournaments are Premier Mandatory, five tournaments are Premier 5, and ten tournaments are Premier.

Players

Professional tennis players enjoy the same relative perks as most top sports personalities: clothing, equipment and endorsements. As an individual sport, like Golf, they are not salaried, but must play and place highly in tournaments to obtain money.

Grand Slam Winners

Male players who have played at least part of their careers during the open era and who have won at least two Grand Slam singles titles are as follows: Roger Federer (15), Pete Sampras (14), Roy Emerson (12), Rod Laver (11), Björn Borg (11), Ken Rosewall (8), Jimmy Connors (8), Ivan Lendl (8), Andre Agassi (8), John Newcombe (7), John McEnroe (7), Mats Wilander (7), Boris Becker (6), Stefan Edberg (6), Rafael Nadal (6), Jim Courier (4), Guillermo Vilas (4), Arthur Ashe (3), Jan Kodeš (3), Gustavo Kuerten (3), Stan Smith (2), Ilie N. stase (2), Johan Kriek (2), Lleyton Hewitt (2), Yevgeny Kafelnikov (2), Patrick Rafter (2), Sergi Bruguera (2), and Marat Safin (2).

Female players who have played at least part of their careers during the open era and who have won at least two Grand Slam singles titles are as follows: Margaret Court (24), Steffi Graf (22), Chris Evert (18), Martina Navrátilová (18), Billie Jean King (12), Serena Williams (11), Monica Seles (9), Justine Henin (7), Evonne Goolagong Cawley (7), Venus Williams (7), Martina Hingis (5), Hana Mandlíková (4), Arantxa Sánchez Vicario (4), Maria Sharapova (3), Virginia Wade (3), Lindsay Davenport (3), Jennifer Capriati (3), Nancy Richey Gunter (2), Tracy Austin (2), Mary Pierce (2), Amélie Mauresmo (2), Svetlana Kuznetsova (2) and Kim Clijsters (2).

Greatest Male Players

Lawn Tennis has churned out more legends than any other sports in history. A frequent topic of discussion among tennis fans and commentators is who was the greatest male singles player of all time. No consensus has ever existed, however. By a large margin, an Associated Press poll in 1950 named Bill Tilden as the greatest player of the first half of the 20th century. From 1920-1930, Tilden won singles titles at Wimbledon three times and the U.S. Championships seven times. In 1938, however, Donald Budge became the first person to win all four Grand Slam singles titles during the same calendar year and won six consecutive Grand Slam singles titles in 1937 and 1938. Tilden called Budge "the finest player 365 days a year that ever lived." And in his 1979 autobiography, Jack Kramer said that, based on consistent play, Budge was the greatest player ever. Some observers, however, also felt that Kramer deserved consideration for the title. Kramer was among the few who dominated amateur and professional tennis during the late 1940s and early 1950s. Tony Trabert has said that of the players he saw before the start of the open era, Kramer was the best male champion. By the latter half of the 1950s and 1960s, Budge and others had added Pancho Gonzales and Lew Hoad to the list of contenders. Budge reportedly believed that Gonzales was the greatest player ever. Gonzales said about Hoad, "When Lew's game was at its peak nobody could touch him. ... I think his game was the best game ever. Better than mine. He was capable of making more shots than anybody. His two volleys were great. His overhead was enormous. He had the most natural tennis mind with the most natural tennis physique."

During the open era, first Rod Laver and then more recently Björn Borg and Pete Sampras were regarded by many of their contemporaries as among the greatest ever. Roger Federer is now considered by many observers to have the most "complete" game in modern tennis. Many experts of tennis, former tennis players and his own tennis peers believe Federer is the greatest player in the history of the game.

Greatest Female Players

Further information: World number one women tennis players, List of WTA number 1 ranked players.

Popular Culture

- David Foster Wallace, an amateur tennis player himself at Urbana High School in Illinois, included tennis in many of his works of nonfiction and fiction including "Tennis Player Michael Joyce's Professional Artistry as a Paradigm of Certain Stuff about Choice, Freedom, Discipline, Joy, Grotesquerie, and Human Completeness," the autobiographical piece "Derivative Sport in Tornado Alley," and *Infinite Jest*, which is partially set at the fictional "Enfield Tennis Academy" in Massachusetts.
- The Royal Tennenbaums (2001) features Richie Tenenbaum (Luke Wilson), a tennis pro who suffers from depression and has a breakdown on court in front of thousands of fans.
- Wimbledon (2004) is a film about a discouraged pro tennis player (Paul Bettany) who meets a young woman on the women's tennis circuit (Kirsten Dunst) who helps him find his drive to go and win Wimbledon.

- In The Squid and the Whale (2005), Joan (Laura Linney) has an affair with her kids' tennis coach, Ivan (William Baldwin). In a symbolic scene, Joan's ex-husband, Bernard (Jeff Daniels), loses a tennis match against Ivan in front of the kids.
- Woody Allen's Match Point (2005) features a love affair between a former tennis pro (Jonathan Rhys Meyers) who falls in love with his best friend's fiance (Scarlett Johansson).
- Confetti (2006) is a mockumentary which sees three couples competing to win the title of "Most Original Wedding of the Year". One competing couple (Meredith MacNeill and Stephen Mangan) are a pair of hyper-competitive professional tennis players holding a tennis-themed wedding.
- There are several tennis video games including Mario Tennis, the TopSpin series, and Wii Sports.

SWIMMING

The aquatic sport of swimming involves competition amongst participants to be the fastest over a given distance under self propulsion. The different events include 25(8&U), 50, 100, 200, breaststroke, backstroke and butterfly, the 25(8&U), 50, 100, 200, 400, 500, 800, 1000, 1500, and 1650 free and the 100, 200, and 400 individual medley (IM, consisting of all strokes). The order of the individual medley is butterfly, backstroke, breaststroke, freestyle. In the 100 IM you swim a 25 (one lap) of each stroke, 200-50 (2 laps) 400-100 (4 laps) of each stroke in the IM. Swimming has been part of the modern Olympic Games since inception in 1896. Along with the other aquatic disciplines of diving, synchronised swimming and water polo, the sport is governed by the Fédération Internationale de Natation (FINA).

History

Competitive swimming in Europe started around 1800, mostly using breaststroke. In 1873 John Arthur Trudgen introduced the trudgen to Western swimming competitions, after copying the front crawl used by Native Americans. Due to a British disregard for splashing, Trudgen employed a scissor kick instead of the front crawl's flutter kick. Swimming was part of the first modern Olympic games in 1896 in Athens. In 1902 Richard Cavill introduced the front crawl to the Western world. In 1908, the world swimming association, Fédération Internationale de Natation (FINA), was formed. Butterfly was developed in the 1930s and was at first a variant of breaststroke, until it was accepted as a separate style in 1952.

Strokes

Butterfly: Butterfly (a.k.a. fly) is a stroke in which the swimmer brings both hands over their head, breathing forward, kick with both feet together in sequence, two kicks per arm stroke. All walls must be touched with two hands at the same time.

Backstroke: Backstroke (a.k.a. back) is a stroke which is similar to the front crawl, except on your back. Kicking by alternating both feet, pulling each arm one at a time, and looking straight up. At walls, flip turns are permitted, and a two-hand touch is not necessary.

Breaststroke: Breaststroke (a.k.a. breast) is a stroke where the swimmer kicks legs out (much like a frog), scoops the water in towards the chest with his or her hands and then thrusts the hands out in front just before the kick is repeated. One underwater "pull-out" is permitted after every wall and each wall requires a two hand (simultaneous) touch.

Freestyle: Freestyle (a.k.a. free) is not a defined stroke as the others are. However, as swimmers are free to choose any stroke they wish, most select the Front Crawl, as it is both the fastest and most efficient. The front crawl is a stroke where the swimmer breathes to the side, kicks by alternating both legs, and pulls with each arm at different times. Flip turns are legal. Many meets also include free relays, in which four team members each swim an equal distance of freestyle; when one member touches the wall, the next can dive off the block.

IM: IM stands for individual medley, and includes, in this order: fly, back, breast, free. Open turns are required in the switch from one stroke to another, but flip turns can be made during back and free. Each stroke must be completed before moving on to the next stroke. 25:100 is the ratio for the amount swam for each stroke.

25 yards stroke to each 100 total. Many meets also include medley relays, in which four team members each swim one stroke. Other IM events are a 200, and 400 which is the same except that in a 200 it is 2 laps of each stroke and 400 is 4 laps of each stroke. In the 200 and 400 IM flip turns are allowed off the wall in backstroke to backstroke and freestyle to freestyle.

Open-turn: An open-turn is a touch and go turn. Fly and breast must touch with two hands, but can push off with one.

Flipturn: In a flipturn, the swimmer swims to the wall, tucks, flip, and pushes off. This is only legal in back and free. A backwards flip is also allowed between Backstroke and Breaststroke in the Individual Medley.

Competition

The goal of competitive swimming is to be have the fastest to complete a given distance. Competitive swimming became popular in the nineteenth century, and comprises 36 individual events – 18 male events and 18 female events; however the IOC only recognises 34 events – 17 male and 17 female events. Swimming is an event at the Summer Olympic Games, where male and female athletes compete in 13 of the recognised events each. Olympic events are held in a 50 metre pool. Competitive swimming's international governing body is FINA (Fédération Internationale de Natation), the International Swimming Federation.

Competition Pools

The majority of competitions are held either in a long course (50 m) or short course (25 m or 25 yd) pool.

Officials

There are several types of officials:

- A starter sends the swimmers off the blocks and may call a false start if a swimmer leaves the block before the starter sends them;
- Finish judges determine the order of finish and make sure the swimmers finish in accordance with the rules (two

hands simultaneously for breaststroke and butterfly, on the back for backstroke, etc.);
- Turn judges check that the swimmers' turns are within rules;
- Stroke judges check the swimmers' strokes;
- Timekeepers time the swimmers' swims;
- The referee takes overall responsibility for running the race and makes the final decisions as to who wins the competition.

If an official catches a swimmer breaking a rule concerning the stroke he or she is swimming, that swimmer is said to be disqualified (commonly referred to as a "DQ") and the swim is not considered valid.

Meet Setup

A meet consists of a number of events classified by age, gender, distance, and stroke. For example, Event 1: Girls 8&U 25 fly. Each event has a certain amount of heats. A heat is a group of people who swim at the same time, yet compete against all entries in that event. Most meets do one stroke at one time. All fly, back, breast, free, IM, and relay. Example: Fly: 25, 50, 100, 200. Back: 25, 50, 100, 200. Breast: 25, 50, 100, 200. Free: 25, 50, 100, 200, 400, 800, 1000, 1500, 1750. IM: 100, 200, 400. Relays: 100, 200, 400, 800. A heat sheet tells a swimmer what he or she will swim, what heat, and what lane. A psych sheet tells the place the swimmer is in before the start of the meet. Larger meets normally cover a three day period: Friday, Saturday, and Sunday. Friday: distance events (400 free and up and the 400 IM). Saturday: Half of the events and, most likely, free relays. Sunday: the remainder of the events and the other relays. In championship meets (state, regionals, district, DII, DI, etc.) and some other meets, preliminaries and finals take place. Other meets, the time you get is the time you stick with. Time trials can also improve your time, but this counts as one of your events.

Swimwear

"*Team colours*" would be referred to as the "team suit and cap."

Suit: The suit covers the skin for modesty. Competitive swimwear seeks to improve upon bare human skin for a speed advantage. For extra speed a swimmer wears a body suit, which has rubber or plastic bumps that break up the water close to the body and provides a small amount of thrust—just barely enough to help a swimmer swim faster.

Swim Cap: A swim cap (a.k.a. cap) keeps the swimmer's hair out of the way to reduce drag. During practice, many female swimmers wear caps with different sayings, patterns or both. *Latex Cap* is made of latex which sticks to anything. If you are having trouble putting on this type of cap or removing it, try putting water on the cap, place your hands on your forehead with your cap between your fingers and forehead, then have someone pull the back of the cap over your head. This is easy to tell by both how it looks, and how it feels. *Silicone Caps* This cap is very stretchy, yet is snug. If you are having trouble putting this cap on, place both hands in the cap, stretch the cap out, place your head down in the front of the cap, and pull it back, over your head, and pull your hands out. Tuck any loose hair back in. *Lycra Cap:* This is a new type of cap that does not pull on your hair like latex caps. However, it is not as snug as silicone.

Goggles: Goggles keep water and chlorine out of swimmer's eyes. New goggles can help those that need glasses. If you have contacts, you should find ones that are a more dependable to prevent protein build-up in your eyes (including starts).

Brands include: Arena, Speedo, TYR, Nike, Dolfin (There are other brands of suits).

Regular Practice and Competition-Swimwear

Men

Men's most used practice swimwear includes speedos (briefs) and jammers.

Women

Women wear one piece suits with different backs for competition, though there are two-piece suits that can be worn to compete as well. Backs vary mainly in strap thickness and geometric design. Most common styles include: racerback, diamondback, butterfly-back. There are also different style lengths: three quarter length (reaches the knees), full body (down to ankles), regular length (shoulders to hips), and bikini style (2 piece).

Drag Suits

Drag suits are used for increasing the resistance against the swimmer in order to help adjust the swimmer to drag. This way when swimmers switch back normal practice suits they swim faster as a result of feeling less resistance. (This is not normally worn during competition.)

Drag Shorts

Drag shorts like drag suits are worn in training and are also used to increase drag so that when taken off in racing it feels easier and you have less resistance. Other forms of drag wear include nylons, and t-shirts; the point is to increase friction in the water to build strength during training, and increase speed once drag items are removed for competition. It is also very common for swimmers to shave areas of exposed skin, to reduce friction in the water. (Drag wear is not normally worn during competition.)

Changes to the Sport

Swimming times have dropped over the years due to better training techniques and to new developments.

The first four Olympics competitions were not held in pools, but in open water (1896 - The Mediterranean, 1900 - The Seine River, 1904 - an artificial lake, 1906 - The Mediterranean). The 1904 Olympics' freestyle race was the only one ever measured at 100 yards, instead of the usual 100 metres. A 100 metre pool was built for the 1908 Olympics and sat in the centre of the main stadium's track and field oval. The 1912 Olympics, held in the Stockholm harbour, marked the beginning of electronic timing.

Male swimmers wore full body suits until the 1940s, which caused more drag in the water than their modern swimwear counterparts did. Competition suits now include engineered fabric and designs to reduce swimmers' drag in the water and prevent athlete fatigue. In addition, over the years, pool designs have lessened the drag. Some design considerations allow for the reduction of swimming resistance, making the pool faster. Namely, proper pool depth, elimination of currents, increased lane width, energy absorbing racing lane lines and gutters, and the use of other innovative hydraulic, acoustic and illumination designs.

The 1924 Summer Olympics were the first to use the standard 50 metre pool with marked lanes. In the freestyle, swimmers originally dived from the pool walls, but diving blocks were incorporated at the 1936 Summer Olympics. The flip turn was developed by the 1950s and goggles were first used in the 1976 Olympics.

There were also changes in the late 20th century in terms of technique. Breaststrokers are now allowed to dip their head completely under water, which allowed for a longer stroke and faster time. However, the breaststrokers must bring their heads up at the completion of each cycle. In addition, a split stroke in the breaststroke start and turns has been added to help speed up the stroke. There have been some other changes added recently as well. Now off the flip turns and starts breaststrokers are allowed 1 butterfly kick to help increase their speed. Backstrokers are now allowed to turn on their stomachs before the wall in order to perform a "flip-turn". Previously, they had to reach and flip backwards this turn is now only used in backstroke to breaststroke in an IM.

Records in Swimming

The foundation of FINA in 1908 signalled the commencement of recording the first official world records in swimming. At that time records could be established in any swimming pool of length not less than 25 yards, and records were also accepted for intermediate distance split times from longer distance events. The Danish swimmer Ranghild Hveger established forty-two records between 1936 and 1942 due to these rules.

Records in events such as 300 yd, 300 m, 1000 yd and 1000 m freestyle, 400 m backstroke, 400 m and 500 m breaststroke were no longer ratified from 1948. A further removal of the 500 yd and 500 m freestyle, 150 m backstroke and 3×100 m medley relay from the record listings occurred in 1952.

In 1952 the national federations of the United States and Japan proposed at the FINA Congress the separation of records achieved in long course and short course pools; however it was four more years for action to come into effect with Congress deciding to retain only records held in 50 m pools as the official world record listings.

By 1969 there were thirty-one events in which FINA recognised official world records – 16 for men, 15 for women – closely resembling the event schedule that was in use at the Olympic Games.

The increase in accuracy and reliability of electronic timing equipment led to the introduction of hundredths of a second to the time records from 21 August 1972.

Records in short course (25 m) pools began to be officially approved as "short course world records" from 3 March 1991. Prior to this "record" times were not officially recognised, but were regarded a "world best time" (WBT). From 31 October 1994 records in 50 m backstroke, breaststroke and butterfly records were added to the official record listings.

FINA currently recognises world records in the following events for both men and women:

- Freestyle: 50 m, 100 m, 200 m, 400 m, 800 m, 1500 m
- Backstroke: 50 m, 100 m, 200 m
- Breaststroke: 50 m, 100 m, 200 m
- Butterfly: 50 m, 100 m, 200 m
- Individual medley: 100 m (short course only), 200 m, 400 m
- Relays: 4×100 m freestyle, 4×200 m freestyle, 4×100 m medley

Sports Nutrition

In swimming it is recommended that you eat healthy. Many competitive swimmers eat carbs and protein before their race. Swimming is an example of an endurance sport that requires a large amount of carbohydrates in order to maintain stamina throughout a swimming event. Carbohydrates are recommended for highly demanding sports due to the complete sources of energy that they provide. Carbohydrates promote muscle stamina and strength because the breakdown product of carbohydrate-glucose is a primary source of energy for muscles during exercise. Commonly the nutrient and energy needs of swimmers can be compromised by their intense schedules. Time should be allowed for a light meal before swimming, and time for a well-balanced generous meal should be allotted after the workout. Additionally, healthy snacking can at times be more efficient in fuelling the body than a main meal. Healthy snacking ideas include: low fat yogurt, fresh or dried fruit, crackers, oatmeal and raisins, granola, and cereal. Like all aerobic sports, swimmers need to be sure they remain hydrated and drink an adequate amount of water during training and competitions.

SQUASH

Squash is a racquet sport played by two players (or four players for doubles) in a four-walled court with a small, hollow rubber ball. Squash is recognised by the IOC and remains in contention for incorporation in a future Olympic programme.

The game was formerly called squash racquets, a reference to the "squashable" soft ball used in the game [compared with the harder ball used in its parent game Racquets (or rackets)].

History

Squash developed from at least five other sports involving racquets, gloves, and balls having roots in the early 1500s in France. It is stated that "Squash, with its element of hitting balls against walls, was for entertainment. For example, boys and girls slapped balls in narrow alleys and streets."

Religious institutions in France, such as monasteries, developed a similar game. Monks used gloves that were webbed to hit balls against a fishing net strung across the middle of the courtyards of the monasteries. This developed the early "racquets" used in tennis and squash. Then in late fifteenth century, tennis was developed and spread to other European nations. The next major development of squash took place in England where the game of "racquets" was developed in Fleet Prison, a debtor's prison. Similar to tennis, it involved racquets and balls, but instead of hitting over a net as in tennis, players hit a non-squeezable ball against walls. A variation of rackets that also lead to the formation of squash was called fives, similar to handball. Fives was essentially the game of racquets; without racquets (the ball was hit with the hand), played against a wall or walls.

These games gained popularity and were further developed in schools, notably Harrow School in England. The first courts built at this school were rather dangerous because they were near water pipes, buttresses, chimneys, and ledges. The school soon built four outside courts. Natural rubber was material of choice for the ball. Students modified their racquets to have a smaller reach to play in these cramped conditions.

In the 1900s the game increased in popularity with various schools, clubs and even private citizens building squash courts, but with no set dimensions. In April 1907 the Tennis, Rackets & Fives Association set up a sub-committee to set standards for squash. Then the sport soon formed, combining the three sports together called "Squash". It was not until 1923 that the Royal Automobile Club hosted a meeting to further discuss the rules and regulations and another five years elapsed before the Squash Rackets Association was formed to set standards for squash in Great Britain.

The sport spread to America and Canada, and eventually around the globe. Players such as F.D. Amr Bey of Egypt dominated the courts in the 1930s and during the 1980s and 1990s Jahangir Khan of Pakistan won the British Open a record of ten times and Jansher Khan of Pakistan won the World Open a record of eight times.

Court

The 'softball' or 'international' court size was codified in London, England in the late 1920s, at 32 ft (9.75 m) long and 21 feet (6.4 m) wide. The front wall was provided with an "out line" 15 feet (4.57 m) above the floor, connected by a raking "out" line meeting the "out" line on the back wall at 7 feet (2.13 m) above the floor. The front wall also has a "service line" (originally called the "cut line") 6 feet (1.83 m) above the floor with a 19 inch high (48 cm) "tin" acting as a 'net' (originally sheeted with metal in order to make a distinctive sound when hit by the ball). The floor is marked with a transverse "half-court" line and further divided into two rear "quarter courts" and two "service boxes".

The traditional "American" court for the U.S. game, (now referred to as "hardball squash") is a similar size, but narrower at

18 feet 6 inches (5.64 m). The floor and wall markings differ slightly from the "International" court and the tin is lower, at 15 inches (38 cm) high. However, hardball squash was replaced by softball in America as the standard version of squash and has since almost completely died out.

A "Converted Court" is the result of converting racquetball courts to squash. Racquetball courts are 20 feet (6.1 m) wide and 40 feet (12.2 m) in length, so it is relatively easy to install a back wall, producing a squash court of 20 feet (6.1 m) wide by 32 feet (9.75 m) long.

Playing Equipment

Standard rackets are governed by the rules of the game. Traditionally they were made of laminated timber (typically Ash), with a small strung area using natural gut strings. After a rule change in the mid-1980s, they are now almost always made of composite materials or metals (graphite, kevlar, titanium, boron) with synthetic strings. Modern rackets have maximum dimensions of 686 mm (27.0 in.) long and 215 mm (8.5 in.) wide, with a maximum strung area of 500 square centimetres (approx. 90 sq. in.), the permitted maximum mass is 255 grams (approx. 9 oz.), but most have a mass between 110 and 200 grams (4-7 oz.).

Squash balls are 39.5 mm and 40.5 mm in diameter, and have a mass of 23 to 25 grams. They are made with two pieces of rubber compound, glued together to form a hollow sphere and buffed to a matte finish. Different balls are provided for varying temperature and atmospheric conditions and standards of play: more experienced players use slow balls that are smaller and have less bounce than those used by less experienced players (slower balls tend to 'die' in court corners, rather than 'standing up' to allow easier shots). Depending on its specific rubber composition, a squash ball has the property that it bounces more at higher temperatures. Small coloured dots on the ball indicate its dynamic level (bounciness), and thus the standard of play for which it is suited. The recognised speed colours indicating the degree of dynamism are:

Colour	Speed	Bounce
Double Yellow	Extra Super Slow	Very Low
Yellow	Super Slow	Low
Green or White	Slow	Average
Red	Medium	High
Blue	Fast	Very High

Balls are manufactured to these standards by Prince, Dunlop, Pointfore, Wilson, Black Knight and others. The "double-yellow dot" ball, introduced in 2000, is currently the competition standard, replacing the earlier "yellow-dot" ball. There is also an "orange dot" ball, which is even less bouncy than the "double-yellow dot" ball, intended for use in areas of high altitude such as Mexico City, Calgary, Denver, and Johannesburg. The lower atmospheric pressure at these high altitude regions means that the ball bounces slightly higher, resulting in the need for such a ball.

Other balls available are:

- Dunlop "Max Blue" (aimed at beginners), which is 12 per cent larger and has 40 per cent longer "hang time" than a "double-yellow dot ball" and has "instant bounce".
- Dunlop "Max Progress" (red) (for players wishing to improve their technique), which is 6 per cent larger with a 20 per cent longer hang-time than a "double-yellow dot ball" and has instant bounce.

For the purpose of saving money, a faster (bouncier) ball should be bought. This is because the ball will lose its bouncing abilities over time and if you start off with something like a double-yellow ball, it will be barely playable with age. For competitive players this is not recommended.

Given the game's vigorousness, players wear comfortable sports clothing and robust indoor (non-marking) sports shoes. In competition, men usually wear shorts and a t-shirt or a polo shirt. Women normally wear a skirt and a t-shirt or a tank top, or a sports dress. Towelling wrist and head bands may also be required in humid climates. Polycarbonate lens goggles are recommended, as players might be struck with a fast-swinging racket or the ball, that typically reaches speeds exceeding 200 km/h (125 mph). In the 2004 Canary Wharf Squash Classic, John White was recorded driving balls at speeds over 270 km/h (170 mph). Many squash venues mandate the use of eye protection and some association rules require that all juniors and doubles players must wear eye protection.

Basic Rules and Gameplay

The Court

The squash court is a playing surface surrounded by four walls. The court surface contains a front line separating the front and back of the court and a half court line, separating the left and right hand sides of the back portion of the court, creating three 'boxes' - the front half, the back left quarter and the back right quarter. Both the back two boxes contain smaller service boxes. All of the floor markings on a squash court are only relevant during serves.

There are four walls to a squash court. The front wall, on which three parallel lines are marked, has the largest playing surface, whilst the back wall, which typically contains the entrance to the court, has the smallest. The out line runs along the top of the front wall, descending along the side walls to the back wall. There are no other markings on the side or back walls. Shots struck above the out line, on any wall, are out. The bottom line of the front wall marks the top of the 'tin', a half metre-high metal area which if struck means that the ball is out. The middle line of the front wall is the service line and is only relevant during serves.

Service

The players flip a racket to decide who commences serving at the start of the match. This player starts the first rally by electing to serve from either the left or right service box. For a legal serve, part of one of the server's feet must be in contact with the floor within the service box while not touching any part of the service box lines (the rest of that foot can reside over the line so long as it is not touching the ground) while striking the ball; after being struck by the racket, the ball must strike the front wall above the service line and below the out line and land in the opposite quarter court. The receiving player can choose to volley a serve after it has hit the front wall. If a server wins a point, the two players switch sides for the following point.

Play

After the serve, the players take turns hitting the ball against the front wall, above the tin and below the out line. The ball may strike the side or back walls at any time, as long as it hits below the out line. It must not hit the floor after hitting the racket and before hitting the front wall. A ball landing on either the out line or the line above the tin is considered to be out. After the ball hits the front wall, it is allowed to bounce once on the floor (and any number of times against the side or back walls) before a player must return it. Players may move anywhere around the court but accidental or deliberate obstruction of the other player's movements is forbidden. Players typically return to the centre of the court after making a shot.

English Scoring System

The scoring system is based on a "serving" system, in which one must gain the serve to obtain a point. Having the serve is sometimes considered to be on "offence". The opponent (who does not have the serve) is considered to be on the defencive and must score to win the serve and then score again to gain a point.

Points are awarded if, during the course of play:

- The receiver fails to strike the ball before it has bounced twice
- The receiver hits the ball out (either on or above the out line, or on the tin)
- The receiver fails to hit the front wall with the ball before the ball has bounced
- Stroke: where the receiver obstructs the server during the point (see "Interference and Obstruction")

Where the server does any of these things, or fails to hit the serve in, then the players change roles and the receiver will serve the next point, but no points are awarded.

Games are usually played to 9 points (alternatively, the receiver may opt to call "set two" and play to 10 when the score first reaches

8-8). Competition matches are usually played to "best-of-five" (i.e., the player to win the most out of 5 games). As the title suggests, this scoring system is preferred in Britain, but also among countries with traditional British ties, e.g. Australia, Pakistan, South Africa, India.

American Scoring System

Alternatively, in the point-a-rally scoring system (PARS), points are scored by the person who wins each rally, whether or not he or she served. Traditionally, PARS scoring was up to 15 points (or the receiver calls 15 or 17 when the game reaches 14-14). However, in 2004, the PARS scoring was reduced to 11 for the professional game (if the game reaches 10-10, a player must win by two clear points). PARS is now used on the men's Professional Tour, and the tin height has been lowered by two inches for the men's professional tournaments (these changes have been made in a hope to shorten the length of the rallies and therefore the match). The women's Professional Tour uses the original tin height, but started using the PARS to 11 scoring system as of July 2008. In the International game, club, doubles and recreational matches are usually played using the traditional British scoring system, but the European Squash Federation (ESF), World Squash Federation (WSF) and several national federations are now using PARS to 11 on a trial or permanent basis. Scoring systems and rules can be adapted subtly to accommodate shorter game time or multiple players.

Referee

The referee is usually a certified position issued by the club or assigned squash league. The referee has dominant power over the squash players. Any conflict or interference is dealt with by the referee. The referee may also issue to take away points or games due to improper etiquette regarding conduct or rules. Refer to "Interference and Obstruction" for more detail.

Types of Shots Played

There are many types of shots played that lead to interesting games and strategy.

1. *Straight drive or 'rail'*: The ball is hit parallel and close to a side wall to travel deep to the back of the court (the 'basic' squash shot). Often referred to as a 'good length' shot.
2. *Boast (or angle)*: The ball is played off a side wall at an angle, or the back wall, before hitting the front wall.
3. *Volley*: The ball is hit 'on the full' (before it touches the floor), usually directly to the front wall
4. *Drop Shot*: The ball is hit gently against the front wall, to fall softly to the floor in the front corner.
5. *Lob*: The ball is hit softly and high on the front wall and with a high arc, so that it falls in a back corner of the court.
6. *Cross Court*: The ball is hit to the front wall from the right side to the left (or *vice versa*).
7. *Kill*: The ball is hit hard and low on the front wall so that it travels no farther than half court.
8. *Trickle Boast*: A 'short' boast where the ball is hit to the side wall at the front of the court (often disguised as a drive or drop shot).
9. *Squeeze Boast*: A more difficult shot which is hit from the front of the court when the ball is very close to the side wall. Has the same effect as the trickle boast but is more deceptive because of its difficulty.
10. *Skid Boast*: The ball is hit high to the side wall near the front wall so that it travels cross court and falls in the opposite back corner.
11. *Nick Shot*: the ball is 'volleyed' or hit off a bounce, cross court and with power to strike the front wall then the junction of the side wall and floor (the 'nick'). When hit well, the ball will have little or no bounce or roll along the floor (this is a more advanced shot that is a variation of the kill shot).

Strategy and Tactics

A common strategy is to hit the ball straight up the side walls to the back corners referred to as a "rail," straight drive, wall, or "length", then move to the centre of the court near the "T" to be well placed to retrieve the opponent's return. Attacking with soft or "short" shots to the front corners (referred to as "drop shots") causes the opponent to cover more of the court and may result in an outright winner. "Angle" shots are used for deception and again to cause the opponent to cover more of the court.

A key strategy in squash is known as "dominating the T" (the intersection of the red lines near the centre of the court where the player is in the best position to retrieve the opponent's next shot). Skilled players will return a shot, and then move back toward the "T" before playing the next shot. From this position, the player can quickly access any part of the court to retrieve the opponent's next shot with a minimum of movement.

Rallies between experienced players may involve 30 or more shots and therefore a very high premium is placed on fitness, both aerobic and anaerobic. As players become more skilled and, in particular, better able to retrieve shots, points often become a war of attrition. At higher levels of the game, the fitter player has a major advantage.

Ability to change the direction of ball at the last instant is also important to off-balance the opponent. Expert players can anticipate the opponent's shot a few tenths of a second before the average player, giving them a chance to react sooner.

Interference and Obstruction

Interference and obstruction are an inevitable aspect of this sport, since two players are confined within a shared space. Generally, the rules entitle players to a clear view of the ball after it has struck the front wall, reasonable access to the ball, a reasonable swing and an unobstructed shot to any part of the front wall. When interference occurs, a player may appeal for a "let" and the referee (or the players themselves if there is no official) then interprets the extent of the interference. The referee may elect to allow a let and the players then replay the point, or award a "stroke" (either a point or the right to serve) to the appealing player, depending on the degree of interference, whether the interfering player made an adequate effort to avoid interfering, and whether the player interfered with was likely to have hit a winning shot had the interference not occurred. An exception to all of this occurs when the interfering player is directly in the path of the other player's swing, effectively preventing the swing, in which case a stroke is always awarded.

When it is deemed that there has been little or no interference, the rules provide that no let is to be allowed, in the interests of continuity of play and the discouraging of spurious appeals for lets. Because of the subjectivity in interpreting the nature and magnitude of interference, the awarding (or withholding) of lets and strokes is often controversial.

When a player's shot hits their opponent prior to hitting the front wall, interference has occurred. If the ball was travelling towards the side wall when it hit the opponent, it is usually a let. However, it is a stroke to the player who hit the ball if the ball was travelling straight to the front wall when the ball hit the opponent. Generally after a player has been hit by the ball, both players stand still, if the struck player is standing directly infront of the player who hit the ball he loses the stroke, if he is not straight infront a let is played. If it is deemed that the player who is striking the ball is deliberately trying to hit his opponent he will lose the stroke. An exception to all of this occurs when the player hitting the ball has "turned", i.e., let the ball pass him on one side, but then hit it on the other side as it came off the back wall. In these cases, the stroke goes to the player who was hit by the ball.

Cultural, Social, and Health Aspects

There are several variations of squash played across the world. In the U.S. hardball singles and doubles are played with a much harder ball and different size courts (as noted above). Hardball singles has lost much of its popularity in North America (in favour of the International version), but the hardball doubles game is still active. There is also a doubles version of squash played with the standard ball, sometimes on a wider court, and a more tennis-like variation known as squash tennis.

The relatively small court and low-bouncing ball makes scoring points harder than in its American cousin, racquetball, as the ball may be played to all four corners of the court. Since every ball must strike the front wall above the tin (unlike racquetball), the ball cannot be easily "killed". As a result, rallies tend to be longer than in racquetball.

Squash provides an excellent cardiovascular workout. In one hour of squash, a player may expend approximately 600 to 1000 calories (3,000 to 4,000 kJ), which is significantly more than most other sports and over 70 per cent more than either general tennis or racquetball. The sport also provides a good upper and lower body workout by utilising both the legs to run around the court and the arms and torso to swing the racquet. In 2003, Forbes rated squash as the number one healthiest sport to play. However, some studies have implicated squash as a cause of possible fatal cardiac arrhythmia and argued that squash is an inappropriate form of exercise for older men with heart disease.

Squash is getting very popular among the casual enthusiasts. Other than the positive health effect, it also allows males and females to play against each other without much advantage for either sex.

Squash around the World

According to the World Squash Federation, as of June 2009, there were 49,908 squash courts in the world, with 188 countries and territories having at least one court. England had the greatest number at 8,500. The other countries with more than 1,000 courts, in descending order by number were Germany, Egypt, the United States of America, Australia, South Africa, Canada, Malaysia, France, the Netherlands, and Spain.

As of June 2009, there were players from nineteen countries in the top fifty of the men's world rankings, with Egypt and England leading with eleven each. The women's world rankings featured players from sixteen countries, led by England with eleven.

The men's professional squash tour and rankings are run by the Professional Squash Association (PSA). The equivalent body for women is the Women's International Squash Players Association (WISPA).

Players and Records

The (British) Squash Rackets Association conducted its first British Open championship for men in December 1930, using a "challenge" system. Charles Read was designated champion in 1930, but was beaten in home and away matches by Don Butcher, who was then recorded as the champion for 1931. The championship continues to this day, but has been conducted with a "knockout" format since 1947.

Since its inception, the men's British Open has been dominated by relatively few players: F.D. Amr Bey (Egypt) in the 1930s; Mahmoud Karim (Egypt) 1940s; brothers Hashim Khan and Azam Khan (Pakistan) 1950s and 1960s; Jonah Barrington (Great Britain and Ireland) and Geoff Hunt (Australia) 1960s and 1970s; Jahangir Khan (Pakistan) 1980s; and Jansher Khan (Pakistan) 1990s.

The women's championship started in 1921, and has similarly been dominated by relatively few players: Joyce Cave and Nancy Cave (England) in the 1920s; Margot Lumb (England) 1930s; Janet Morgan (England) 1950s; Heather McKay (Australia) 1960s and 1970s; Vicki Cardwell (Australia) and Susan Devoy (New Zealand) 1980s; Michelle Martin (Australia) 1990s; and Sarah Fitz-Gerald (Australia) 1990s and 2000s.

Heather McKay, with her lengthy and absolute dominance of the game (she remained undefeated for 18 years during the 1960s and 1970s), is undoubtedly the greatest woman player of all time.

Because of its traditions, the British Open has been considered by many to be more prestigious than the World Open, which began in the mid-1970s. However, some have shown concern about the ability of the former to sustain its prominence, citing its failure in 2005 to attract top players, probably due in part to the disparity in prize money. In 2005 the combined men's and women's prize money for the British Open came to $71,000, compared with the 2005 World Open's prize money, estimated to be about $270,000.

Former world number one Peter Nicol stated that he believed squash had a "very realistic chance" of being added to the list of Olympic sports for the 2016 Olympic Games, but it ultimately lost out to golf and rugby sevens.

The current number 1 rank is held by Karim Darwish of Egypt in the men's competition and Nicol David of Malaysia in the women's competition. Currently there is no international standard method (other than for professional players) for evaluating skill levels for players.

Wider Acceptance

Squash players and associations have lobbied for many years for the sport to be accepted into the Olympic Games, with no success to date. Squash narrowly missed being instated for the 2012 London Games. It was again up for consideration for the 2016 Summer Games along with baseball, softball, rugby sevens, karate, golf, and roller sports, but squash again missed out as the IOC assembly decided to add golf and rugby sevens to the Olympic programme.

Squash is played throughout the world, and is similar to tennis in skills and fitness requirements, but the principal limitation has always been the difficulty in observing the sport as a spectator, either in person or on television. The ball travels so quickly that television audiences are hard-pressed to follow the action, even though some tournaments have attempted to remedy the problem by using a specially coated ball for increased visibility. To maximise the viewing audience at tournaments, promoters often use an all-glass court that is designed to permit spectators to be seated around all four walls but is specially tinted so as not to distract the players. Because of these viewer restrictions, professional squash players earn vastly less than their counterparts in the tennis world.

Popular Culture

The 1980 novel *Boast* by Miles Donald revolves around the game of squash.

In David Lean's Lawrence of Arabia a staff officer tells Lawrence about the new squash court at GHQ in Cairo when Lawrence asks what has been happening at base while he has been in the desert leading the Arab revolt.

In the TV sitcom "Frasier", squash was a game Frasier and his brother Niles would play.

In the movie Wall Street, Gordon Gekko (Michael Douglas) and Bud Fox (Charlie Sheen) play a game of squash.

In the television series "Friday Night Lights", Coach Eric Taylor and "Smash" Williams play a game of squash, which Smash describes as the "whitest sport ever."

In the novel *Digital Fortress* by Dan Brown David Becker's hobby is playing squash.

In the film Shallow Grave [2] the main characters play each other at squash.

In the 2005 novel Saturday by Ian McEwan, Henry Perowne plays a regular weekly squash game.

In the 1981 movie Outland, Marshal William T. O'Niel (played by Sean Connery) plays squash alone and against his female ally, Doctor Lazarus (Frances Sternhagen).

In the John Irving novel "A Widow for One Year" the character Ruth Cole plays squash and defends herself against an assault on the squash court.

In 2009, the first and only squash 3D video game, Touch Squash was launched on the iPhone App Store for iPhone and iPod touch.

The only other appearance of squash in a video game is a mini game from Super Monkey Ball: Banana Blitz, released as a launch title on the Nintendo Wii in December 2006.

HOCKEY

Hockey is any of a family of sports in which two teams play against each other by trying to maneuver a ball, or a hard, round, rubber or heavy plastic disc called a puck, into the opponent's net or goal, using a hockey stick.

Field Hockey

Field hockey is played on gravel, natural grass, sand-based or water-based artificial turf, with a small, hard ball. The game is popular among both males and females in many parts of the world, particularly in Europe, Asia, Australia, and South Africa. In most countries, the game is played between single-sex sides, although they can be mixed-sex.

The governing body is the 116-member International Hockey Federation (FIH). Men's Field Hockey has been played at each summer Olympic Games since 1908 (except 1912 and 1924), while Women's Field Hockey has been played each summer Olympic Games since 1980.

Modern field hockey sticks are J-shaped and constructed of a composite of wood, glass fibre or carbon fibre (sometimes both) and have a curved hook at the playing end, a flat surface on the playing side and curved surface on the rear side. While current field hockey appeared in the mid-18th century in England, primarily in schools, it was not until the first half of the 19th century that it became firmly established. The first club was created in 1849 at Blackheath in south-east London. Field hockey is the national sport of India and Pakistan.

Ice Hockey

Ice hockey is played on a large flat area of ice, using a three inch (76.2 mm) diameter vulcanised rubber disc called a puck. This puck is often frozen before high-level games to decrease the amount of bouncing and friction on the ice. The game is contested between two teams of skaters. The game is played all over North America, Europe and in many other countries around the world to varying extent. It is the most popular sport in Canada, Finland, Latvia, the Czech Republic, and in Slovakia.

The governing body is the 66-member International Ice Hockey Federation, (IIHF). Men's ice hockey has been played at the Winter Olympics since 1924, and was in the 1920 Summer Olympics. Women's ice hockey was added to the Winter Olympics in 1998. North America's National Hockey League (NHL) is the strongest professional ice hockey league, drawing top ice hockey players from around the globe. The NHL rules are slightly different from those used in Olympic ice hockey: the periods are 20 minutes long, counting downwards. There are three periods.

Ice hockey sticks are long L-shaped sticks made of wood, graphite, or composites with a blade at the bottom that can lie flat on the playing surface when the stick is held upright and can curve either way, legally, as to help a left- or right-handed player gain an advantage.

There are early representations and reports of ice hockey-type games being played on ice in the Netherlands, and reports from Canada from the beginning of the nineteenth century, but the modern game was initially organised by students at McGill University, Montreal in 1875 who, by two years later, codified the first set of ice hockey rules and organised the first teams.

Ice hockey is played at a number of levels, by all ages.

Roller Hockey (inline)

Inline hockey is a variation of roller hockey very similar to ice hockey, from which it is derived. Inline hockey is played by two teams, consisting of four skaters and one goalie, on a dry rink divided into two halves by a centre line, with one net at each end of the rink. The game is played in three 15-minute periods with a variation of the ice hockey off-side rule. Icings are also called, but are usually referred to as illegal clearing. For rink dimensions and an overview of the rules of the game, see IIHF Inline Rules (official rules). Some leagues and competitions do not follow the IIHF regulations, in particular USA Inline and Canada Inline.

Roller Hockey (quad)

Roller hockey (quad) is the overarching name for a roller sport that has existed since long before inline skates were invented. Roller hockey has been played in sixty countries worldwide and so has many names worldwide. The sport is also known as quad hockey, hóquei em patins, international style ball hockey, rink hockey and hardball hockey. Roller Hockey was a demonstration roller sport at the 1992 Barcelona Summer Olympics.

Street Hockey

Another form of popular hockey is Street hockey, sometimes known as road hockey. This is usually played with the same rules as ice hockey, or roller hockey, except it is on the street. Most of the time, a ball is used instead of a puck, because a puck generates too much friction when handled on an asphalt or cement surface and does not slide. Street hockey is played year round.

Other Forms of Hockey

Other games derived from hockey or its predecessors include the following:

- Air hockey is played indoors with a puck on an air-cushion table.
- Beach hockey, a variation of street hockey, is a common sight on Southern California beaches.
- Ball hockey is played in a gym using sticks and a ball, often a tennis ball with the fuzz removed.
- Unicycle hockey is similar to roller or inline hockey, however, each player must be mounted on their unicycle (with both feet on the pedals) to play at the ball.
- Deck hockey is traditionally played by the Royal Navy on the ships' decks, using short wooden 'L' -shaped sticks.

- Bandy is played with a ball on a football-sized ice arena, typically outdoors.
- Box hockey is a school yard game played by two people. The object of the game is to move a hockey puck from the centre of the box out through a hole placed at the end of the box (known as the goal). Each player kneels and faces one another on either side of the box, and each attempts to move the puck to the hole on their left.
- Broomball is played on an ice hockey rink, but with a ball instead of a puck and a "broom" (actually a stick with a small plastic implement on the end) in place of the ice hockey stick. Instead of using skates, special shoes are used that have very soft rubbery soles to maximise grip while running around.
- Floorball is a form of hockey played in a gymnasium or in sport halls. A whiffle ball is used instead of a plastic ball, and the sticks are made from composite materials. The sticks are only one metre long.
- Foot hockey or sock hockey is played using a bald tennis ball or rolled up pair of socks and using only the feet. It is popular at elementary schools in the winter.
- Gym hockey is a form of ice hockey played in a gymnasium. It uses sticks with foam ends and a foam ball or a plastic puck.
- Hurling and Camogie are Irish games bearing some resemblance to—and notable differences from—hockey.
- Indoor field hockey is an indoor variation of field hockey.
- Mini hockey, in the United States, is a form of hockey (also known as "mini-sticks") which is played in basements of houses. Players get down on their knees, using a miniature plastic stick, usually about 15 inches (38 cm) long to maneuver a small ball or a soft, fabric covered mini puck into a miniature goals. In England 'mini hockey' refers to a seven-a-side version of field hockey, played on an area equivalent to half a normal pitch for younger players.
- Nok hockey is a table-top version of hockey played with no defence and a small block in front of the goal.
- PowerHockey is a form of hockey for persons requiring the use of an electric (power) wheelchair in daily life.

PowerHockey is a competitive sports opportunity for the physically disabled.

- Ringette is an ice hockey variant that was designed for female players; it uses a straight stick and a rubber ring in place of a puck. Note: Ringette distances itself from hockey as it has its own set of rules and is closely related to a mix of lacrosse and basketball.
- Rinkball is a Scandinavian team sport, played in an ice hockey rink with a ball.
- Rossall hockey is a variation played at Rossall School on the sea shore in the winter months. Its rules are a mix of field hockey, Rugby and the Eton Wall Game.
- Shinny is an informal version of ice hockey.
- Shinty is a Scottish game now played primarily in the Highlands.
- Skater hockey is a variant of inline hockey, played with a ball.
- Sledge hockey is a form of ice hockey played by the disabled. The players sit on sleds, and push themselves up and down the ice with picks on the butt end of their shortened hockey sticks. The game is played with many of the same rules as regular ice hockey.
- Spongee is a cross between ice hockey and broomball and is most popular in Manitoba, Canada. A stick and puck are used as in hockey (the puck is a softer version called a "sponge puck"), and the same soft-soled shoes used in broomball are worn. The rules are basically the same as ice hockey, but one variation has an extra player on the ice called a "rover."
- Table hockey is played indoors with a table-top game.
- Underwater hockey is played on the bottom of a swimming pool.

FENCING

Fencing is a family of sports and activities that feature armed combat involving cutting, stabbing, or bludgeoning weapons that are directly manipulated by hand, rather than shot, thrown or positioned. Examples include swords, knives, pikes, bayonets, batons, clubs, and similar weapons. In contemporary common usage, fencing tends to refer specifically to European schools of swordsmanship and to the modern Olympic sport that has evolved out of them.

Fencing is one of the four sports which has been featured at every modern Olympic Games. Currently, three types of weapon are used in Olympic fencing:

- *Foil*—a light thrusting weapon; the valid target is restricted to the torso, the chest, shoulders, and back; double touches are not allowed (see priority rules below). This weapon follows the rule of "right of way".
- *Épée*—a heavy thrusting weapon; the valid target area covers the entire body; double touches are allowed. There is no "right of way".
- *Sabre*—a light cutting and thrusting weapon; the valid target area is the saddle line, which is from one side of your hip to the other and up, this also includes the head. The target area does not include the hands. This weapon follows "right of way."

The word *fence* was originally a shortening of the Middle English *defens*, which came from an Italian word, *defensio*, in origin a Latin word. The first known use of *defens* in reference to English swordsmanship is in William Shakespeare's *Merry Wives of Windsor*: "Alas sir, I cannot fence."

History

Origins

The origins of fencing date back to Egypt around 1200 BC. Carvings found depict bouts being fought using protected tips on swords, masks, and judges.

Renaissance

Fencing teachers and schools can be found in European historical records dating back at least to the 12th century. In later times some of these teachers were paid by rich nobles to produce books about their fighting systems, called treatises.

The earliest known surviving treatise on fencing, stored at the Royal Armouries Museum in Leeds, England, dates from around 1300 AD and is from Germany. It is known as I.33 and written in medieval Latin and Middle High German and deals with an advanced system of using the sword and buckler (small shield) together. From 1400 AD onwards there are an increasing number of fencing treatises surviving from across Europe, with the majority from the 15th century coming from Germany and Italy. In this period these arts were largely seen as reserved for the knighthood and the nobility—hence most of these treatises deal with the knightly weapons, such as the rondel dagger, longsword, spear, pollaxe and armoured fighting mounted and on foot. Some treatises do cover the weapons more usually used by the common classes however, such as großes Messer and sword and buckler. Wrestling, both with and without weapons, and armoured and unarmoured, is also featured heavily in the early fencing treatises.

By the 16th century, with the widespread adoption of the printing press and the increase in the urban population, together with other social changes, the number of fencing treatises being produced increased dramatically. Fencing schools had been forbidden in some European cities (particularly in England and France) during the medieval period, though court records show that such schools were kept illegally. After around 1500 it seems to have become more socially and legally acceptable to carry swords openly in most parts of Europe, and the increasing fortunes of the middle classes meant that more men were aspiring to carry swords, learn fencing and be seen as gentlemen. By the middle of the 16th century many European cities contained great numbers of fencing schools, often clustered together, such as in London in "Hanging Sword Lane". Italian fencing masters were particularly popular in the 16th century and they went abroad and set up schools in many foreign cities. The Italian styles of fencing at this time, bringing concepts of science to the art, were seen as revolutionary and new, and they appealed to the new Renaissance mindset.

In 16th century Germany compendia of older *Fechtbücher* techniques were produced, some of them printed, notably by Paulus Hector Mair (in the 1540s) and by Joachim Meyer (in the 1570s), based on the teachings of the 14th century Liechtenauer tradition. In the 16th century German fencing developed sportive tendencies. Eventually the newer Italian attitude to fencing grew in popularity in Germany as well as elsewhere.

Today there are many groups around the world recreating the old fencing systems, using the surviving treatises. Historical European Martial Arts (HEMA) are growing fast, bringing in people from many backgrounds, including those who have taken part in modern sport fencing and Asian martial arts.

Early Modern Period

Strictly, the European dueling sword is a basket and cage hilted weapon specifically used in duels from the late 17th to the 19th century. It developed through several forms of the rapier to the smallsword—reflecting the changes from a cutting style of swordplay to a thrusting style ('foining'). This was a result of increasing specialisation in their use on the dueling field, and the social stigma attached to carrying and using swords too obviously adapted to the actual "work" of warfare. The smallsword, and the last version of the rapier, were made possible only by metallurgical advances in the seventeenth century as high toughness steels became more readily available.

In England, it was not uncommon for fencing masters to take on other fencing masters in a fight, often to the death, often with intervals for medical staff to dress wounds. Such spectacles were generally held in beargardens, particularly in the Southwark neighbourhood near London.

The foil was invented in France as a training technique in the middle of the 18th century; it provided practice of fast and elegant thrust fencing with a smaller and safer weapon than an actual dueling sword. Fencers blunted its point by wrapping a foil around the blade or fastening a knob on the point ("blossom", French *fleuret*). In addition to practice, some fencers took away the protection and used the sharp foil for duels. German students took up that practice and developed the *Pariser* ("Parisian") thrusting small sword for the *Stoßmensur* ("thrusting mensur"). After the dress sword was abolished, the *Pariser* became the only weapon for thrust fencing in German colleges and universities.

Since thrust fencing with a sharply pointed blade of any kind is quite dangerous, many students died from (especially) pierced lungs (*Lungenfuchser*). However, a counter movement had already started in Göttingen in the 1750s, with the invention of the *Göttinger Hieber*, a predecessor of the modern *Korbschläger*, a new weapon for cut fencing. In the following years, the *Glockenschläger* was invented in Eastern Germany universities, also for cut fencing.

1800 to 1918

Thrust fencing (using the *Pariser*), and cut fencing (using *Korbschläger* or *Glockenschläger*), existed in parallel in Germany during the first decades of the 19th century, according to local preferences. Thrust fencing was especially popular in Jena, Erlangen, Würzburg and Ingolstadt/Landshut, two towns where the predecessors of Munich University were located. The last thrust *Mensur* is recorded to have taken place in Würzburg in 1860.

Until the first half of the 19th century all types of academic fencing can be seen as duels, since all fencing with sharp weapons was about honour. No combat with sharp blades took place without a formal insult. For duels involving non-students, e.g. military officers, the *academic sabre* became usual, apparently being derived from the military sabre. It was then a heavy weapon with a curved blade and a hilt similar to the *Korbschläger*.

The term "Classical Fencing" is a relatively new invention, retroactively applied to select periods and methods. As it is understood today, classical fencing derives most directly from the 19th and early-20th century national fencing schools, especially in Italy and France, although other pre-World War II styles such as Russian and Hungarian are also considered classical. Masters and legendary fencing figures such as Giuseppe Radaelli, Louis Rondelle, Masaniello Parise, the Greco brothers, Aldo Nadi and his rival Lucien Gaudin are today considered typical practitioners of this period.

Fencing was one of the disciplines at the very first Olympics Games in the summer of 1896. Épée and Sabre events have been held at every Summer Olympics; foil events have been held at every Summer Olympics except 1908.

Scoring was done by means of four judges who determined whether a touch had been made. Two side judges stood behind and to the side of each fencer, and watched for hits made by that fencer on the opponent's target. A director followed the fencing from a point several feet away from the centre of the action. At the end of each action, after calling "Halt!", the director would describe the action, and then poll the judges in turn. If the judges differed, or abstained, the director could overrule them.

This method had serious limitations, though it was universally used. As described in an article in the London newspaper, *The Daily Courier*, on June 25, 1896: "Every one who has watched a bout with the foils knows that the task of judging the hits is with a pair of amateurs difficult enough, and with a well-matched pair of maîtres d'escrime well-nigh impossible." There also were problems with bias: well-known fencers were often given the benefit of mistakes (so-called "reputation touches"), and in some cases there was outright cheating. Aldo Nadi complained about this in his autobiography *The Living Sword* in regard to his famous match with Lucien Gaudin.

The *Daily Courier* article is an early description of a new invention, the electrical scoring machine, that would revolutionise fencing.

1918 to Present

Dueling went into sharp decline after World War I. After World War II, dueling went out of use in Europe except for very rare exceptions. Training for duels, once fashionable for males of aristocratic backgrounds (although fencing masters such as Hope suggest that many people had only taken one or two lessons, and thus considering themselves trained), all but disappeared, along with the classes themselves. Fencing continued as a sport, with tournaments and championships. However, the need to actually prepare for a duel with "sharps" vanished, changing both training and technique.

Starting with épée in the 1930s, side judges were replaced by an electrical scoring apparatus, with an audible tone and a red or green light indicating when a touch landed. Foil was electrified in the 1950s, sabre in the 1980s. The scoring box reduced the bias in judging, and permitted more accurate scoring of faster actions, lighter touches, and more touches to the back and flank than were possible with human judges.

Forms of Fencing

Contemporary fencing is divided in three broad categories:

- Competitive fencing
- Fencing as a Western martial art
- Other forms of fencing.

Competitive Fencing

There are numerous inter-related forms of competitive fencing in practice, all of which approach the activity as a sport, with varying degrees of connectedness to its historic past.

Olympic fencing (or simply "fencing") refers to the fencing seen in most competitions, including the Olympic Games and the World Cup. Competitions are conducted according to rules laid down by the Fédération Internationale d'Escrime (FIE), the international governing body. These rules evolved from a set of conventions developed in Europe between mid 17th and early 20th century with the specific purpose of regulating competitive activity. The three weapons used in Olympic fencing are foil, épée, and sabre. In competition, the validity of touches is determined by the electronic scoring apparatus and a set of rules called right of way, so as to minimise human error and bias in refereeing. In the United States, athletes compete at a local and national level. At a local level, athletes register for tournaments in their division via a website called "Askfred.net." At a national level, athletes compete in tournaments called "North American Cups", or NAC's for short. At these tournaments, competitors fence each other depending on what age group or division they are in. Some of the age groups are Y12 (Youth 12, or 12 or younger), Y14, Junior (18 or younger), and Cadet (16 or younger). In fencing, your rating represents how good you are in general. Fencers are rated E through A, U if they do not have a rating, or are unrated. E being the lowest, and A being the highest. In certain competitions, fencers may be of any age, but must meet the rating criteria in order to fence. Division I fencing requires fencers to have a rating C through A. Division II requires fencers to have a rating of C or lower. And Division III requires fencers to have a rating D or lower. In tournaments, fencers first fence 5 or 6 other fencers in what are called "pools."

Depending on how the fencer does within that pool, the fencer is then put into a table chart with the other fencers of the tournament. In a NAC setting, if that fencer was one of the fencers in the bottom 20 per cent, then that fencer must go home immediately. If not, that fencer must fence the opponent they are paired with, and if they win, they advance in the table chart, if they lose, they must go home. This is why this table chart phase is called "Direct Elimination", or DE for short.

Wheelchair fencing, also known as jousting, an original Paralympic sport, was developed in post-World War II England. Minor modifications to the FIE rules allow disabled fencers to fence all three weapons. The most apparent change is that each fencer sits in a wheelchair fastened to a frame. Footwork is replaced by torso or arm movement, depending on the fencer's disability. The proximity of the two fencers tends to increase the pace of bouts, which require considerable skill. The weapons are identical to those used in Olympic fencing.

Other variants include *one-hit épée* (one of the five events which constitute modern pentathlon) and the various types of competitive fencing, whose rules are similar but not identical to the FIE rules. One example of this is the American Fencing League (distinct from the United States Fencing Association): the format of competitions is different, there is no electronic scoring, and the priority rules are interpreted in a different way. In a number of countries, the accepted practice at school and university level deviates slightly from the FIE format.

Fencing as a Western Martial Art

Some practitioners of fencing approach it as a Western martial art, with the goal being to train for a theoretical duel. The element of sport is absent (or nearly so) from these forms of fencing, but they all share a common origin with each other and with competitive fencing.

Classical fencing is differentiated from competitive fencing as being theoretically closer to swordplay as a martial art. Those who call themselves classical fencers may advocate the use of what they see as more authentic practices, including little or no emphasis on sport competition. There is strong interest within the classical fencing community in reviving the European fencing practices of the 19th and early 20th century, when fencers were expected to be able to fight a duel using their training. Weapons used are the standard (non-electric) foil, standard épée (often equipped with pointe d'arret), and the blunted dueling sabre. AFL fencing is often referred to as classical fencing, but this is a misnomer.

Historical fencing is a type of historical martial arts reconstruction based on surviving texts and traditions. Predictably, historical fencers study an extremely wide array of weapons from different regions and periods. They may work with bucklers, daggers, polearms, navajas, bludgeoning weapons, etc. One main preoccupation of historical fencers is with weapons of realistic weight, which demand a different way of manipulating them from what is the norm in modern fencing. For example, light weapons can be manipulated through the use of the fingers (more flexibility), but more realistically-weighted weapons must be controlled more through the wrist and elbow. This difference is great and can lead to drastic changes even in the carriage of the body and footwork in combat. There is considerable overlap between classical and historical fencing, especially with regard to 19th-century fencing practices.

Other Forms of Fencing

Finally, there are several other forms of fencing which have little in common besides history with either of the other two classifications.

Academic fencing, or *mensur*, is a German student tradition that has become mostly extinct but is still sometimes practiced in Germany, Switzerland and Austria as well as in Flanders, Poland and Latvia. The combat, which uses a cutting weapon known as the *schläger*, uses sharpened blades and takes place between members of student corporations - "Studentenverbindungen" - in accordance with a strictly delineated set of conventions. It uses special protective gear that leaves most of the head and face, excluding the eyes, unprotected. (The special goggles are called Paukbrille.) The ultimate goal is to develop personal character, therefore there is no winner or loser and flinching is not allowed. Acquiring a proper cut on the face with the sharp blade, called a Schmiss (German for "smile"), was considered a visible sign of manly courage and status as *"Akademiker"*, or member of the professional upper class. However, tales of cuts being intentionally manipulated by sewing in horsehairs or rubbing wounds with vinegar or salt have been discredited as popular myths since the 1880s.

Stage fencing seeks to achieve maximum theatrical impact in representing a wide range of styles, including both modern and historical forms of fencing. Theatrical fight scenes are choreographed by a Fight Director, and fencing actions are amended so that an audience with no understanding of the minutiae of fencing techniques can follow the narrative of the action, both physical and dramatic.

Recreational roleplaying often incorporates fencing in the context of historical or fantasy themes in the Society for Creative Anachronism or live-action roleplaying games. Technique and scoring systems vary widely from one group to the next, as do the weapons. Depending on local conventions, participants may use modern sport fencing weapons, period weapons, or weapons invented specifically for the purpose, such as boffers.

The Japanese sport of Kendo has no historic links to western fencing but is an example of parallel evolution, where a sport has developed for sword combat training.

Modern Weapons

Three weapons survive in modern competitive fencing: foil, épée, and sabre. The spadroon and the heavy cavalry-style sabre, both of which saw widespread competitive use in the 19th century, fell into disfavour in the early 20th century with the rising popularity of the lighter and faster weapon used today. The singlestick was featured in the 1904 Olympic Games, but it was already declining in popularity at that time. Bayonet fencing experienced a somewhat slower decline, with competitions organised by some armed forces as late as the 1940s and 1950s.

While the weapons fencers use differs in shape and purpose, their basic construction remains similar across the disciplines. Every weapon has a *blade* and a *hilt*. The tip of the blade is generally referred to as the *point*. The hilt consists of a *guard* and a *grip*. The guard (also known as the *coquille*, the *bell*, or the *bellguard*) is a metal shell designed to protect the fingers. The grip is the weapon's actual handle. There are a number of commonly used variants. In foil and épée the more traditional French grip is approximately straight and usually terminates with a *pommel* (a heavy nut intended to act as a counterweight for the blade and to hold the handle on the weapon). Some modern designs of French grip do not use a heavy pommel nut, in an effort to construct the lightest épée possible.

The French grip has been entirely replaced in higher level foil fencing, and partially replaced in épée fencing, by a variety of ergonomic designs, called as a group pistol grips or orthopaedic grips. All of the weapons used for modern competition have electrical wiring which allows them to register a touch on the opponent.

Foil

The foil is a light and flexible weapon, originally developed in the mid-17th century as a training weapon for the small sword, a light one-handed sword designed almost exclusively for thrusting.

In modern competitive fencing, 'electric' weapons are used. These have a push-button on the point of the blade, which allows hits to be registered by the electronic scoring apparatus. In order to register, the button must be depressed with a force of at least 4.90 newtons (500 grams-force) for at least 15 milliseconds. Foil fencers wear conductive (lamé) jackets covering their target area, which allow the scoring apparatus to differentiate between on- and off-target hits.

The target area is restricted to the torso, including the front and back. When fencing with electrical equipment, there is an area around each armpit that is not covered by the lamé, and is thus effectively not legal target as well.

A modification in FIE rules from 1 January 2009 onwards means that the valid target area includes that part of the bib below a straight line drawn between the shoulders; prior to this, the bib of the mask was not a valid target. The wisdom of this rule is currently widely disputed; the prevailing attitude in the US is that the rule will lead to a great increase in equipment failures and costs, while European opinion is that this will help prevent fencers from covering target.

This rule has not been implemented uniformly in all National fencing organisations. European fencing organizations have generally decided on September 1 2009 as the date for all competitions to use the new rule.

As of September 1, 2009, the USFA has decided not to implement the bib as target for foil. After reviewing international competitions, it was observed that very few hits were actually scored under the new rules. Given the expense of having to replace equipment, as well as the safety concerns of allowing hits in the region of the throat, the USFA rejected the change. All domestic competitions in the US will not require the bib target; however, international events such as Junior or Senior World Cup Events will require the bib target. There are currently no plans to adopt the rule in the future.

The target must be hit with the tip of the foil; a touch with any other part of the foil it has no effect whatsoever and fencing continues uninterrupted. A touch on an off-target area stops the bout but does not score a point. Foil fencing also features rules of *right of way* or *priority*, which determines which fencer's hit will prevail when both fencers have hit. The basic principle of priority is that the hit of the fencer who begins an offensive action first will prevail over his/her opponent's hit, unless the action of the former fails. A fencer's action fails when it falls short of his/her opponent, when it misses, or when it is parried. When one fencer's action fails, the other's current or next offensive action gains priority, unless they delay too long (longer than one period of "fencing time", the time taken to perform one action at the current tempo of the exchange), in which case the previously defending fencer loses priority. If priority cannot be determined when both fencers have hit each other, no point is awarded. The original idea behind the rules of foil fencing was to encourage fencers to defend and attack vital areas, and to fight in a methodical way with initiative passing back and forth between the combatants, thus minimising the risk of a double death.

When an exchange ends in a hit, the referee will call "halt", and fencing will cease. The referee will then analyse the exchange and phrase it in official terminology. The first offensive action is called the attack. All defencive actions successfully deflecting an opponent's blade are called parries. An offensive action of a parrying fencer directly following the parry is called a riposte. An offensive action of a fencer, who attacks without first withdrawing the arm directly after being parried, is called a remise. An offensive action of a fencer from the on-guard position, after being parried and then returning to the on-guard position, is called a reprise. An offensive action of a fencer after his/her opponent has lost the right to riposte via inaction is called a redouble. An offensive action begun by a fencer who is being attacked by his/her opponent is called a counter-attack.

Épée

Épée, as the sporting weapon known today, was invented in the second half of the 19th century by a group of French students, who felt that the conventions of foil were too restrictive, and the weapon itself too light; they wanted an experience closer to that of an actual duel. At the point of its conception, the épée was, essentially, an exact copy of a small sword but without the needle-sharp point. Instead, the blade terminated in a point d'arrêt, a three-pronged tip which would snag on the clothing without penetrating the flesh.

Like the foil, the épée is a thrusting weapon: to score a valid hit, the fencer must fix the point of his weapon on his opponent's target. However, the target area covers the entire body, and there are no rules regarding who can hit when (unlike in foil and sabre, where there are *priority rules*). In the event of both fencers making a touch within 40 milliseconds of each other, both are awarded a point (a *double hit*), except when the score is equal and the point would mean the win for both, such as in modern pentathlon's one-hit épée, where neither fencer receives a point. Otherwise, the first to hit always receives the point, regardless of what happened earlier in the phrase. Also épées are the heaviest of the weapons. However, with today's techniques, we see some épée blades as light as 150g. An épée is composed of a blade, a point, a bell guard, and a handle or grip (french or pistol grip).

The 'electric' épée, used in modern competitive fencing, terminates in a push-button, similar to the one on the 'electric' foil. In order for the scoring apparatus to register a hit, it must arrive with a force of at least 7.35 newtons (750 grams-force) (a higher threshold than the foil's 4.9 newtons), and the push-button must remain fully depressed for 1 millisecond. All hits register as valid, unless they land on a grounded metal surface, such as a part of the opponent's weapon, in which case they do not register at all. At large events, grounded conductive pistes are often used in order to prevent the registration of hits against the floor. At smaller events and in club fencing, it is generally the responsibility of the referee to watch out for floor hits. These often happen by accident, when an épéeist tries to hit the opponent's foot and misses. This results in a pause in the action but no points. However, deliberate hits against the floor are treated as "dishonest fencing," and penalised accordingly.

Épée has less restrictive rules for footwork and physical contact than the other two weapons. In Épée, a corps-à-corps (collision between fencers) is not penalised unless initialised with intent to harm or if it is excessively violent. There are no restrictions on crossing of the feet or use of the flèche attack in épée; if the fencers pass each other, the attacking fencer may score until he passes his opponent. The defending fencer has the right to one continuous riposte, and may still score after the attacker has passed.

The counterattack is very important in épée; direct, unprepared attacks are vulnerable to counterattacks to the hand or arm, or to the body if the attacker is shorter than his opponent. High level épée is often a game of provocation, with each player trying to lure the other into an attack. Distance in épée is even more important than in the conventional weapons.

Sabre

Sabre is the 'cutting' weapon: points may be scored with edges and surfaces of the blade, as well as the point. Although the current design with a light and flexible blade (marginally stiffer than a foil blade which bends easily up and down while a sabre blade bends easier side to side) appeared around the turn of the 19th and 20th century, similar sporting weapons with more substantial blades had been used throughout the Victorian era.

There is some debate as to whether the modern fencing sabre is descended from the cavalry sabres of Turkic origin, which became popular in Central and Western Europe around the time of Napoleonic Wars, or one of Europe's indigenous edged duelling weapons, such as the cutting rapier. In practice, it is likely to be a hybrid of the two. Most of the conventions and vocabulary of modern sabre fencing were developed by late 19th and early 20th century masters from Italy and Hungary, perhaps most notable among them being Italo Santelli (1866–1945).

The sabre target covers everything above the waist, except the hands (wrists are included) and the back of the head. Today, any contact between any part of the blade and any part of the target counts as a valid touch. This was not always the case, and earlier conventions stipulated that a valid touch must be made with the point or either the front or back cutting edge, and that a point attack must not merely graze the target and slip along (pass) the opponent's body. These requirements had to be abandoned, because of technical difficulties, shortly after electronic scoring was introduced into sabre fencing in late 1980s.

Like foil, sabre is subject to *right of way* rules, but there are differences in the definition of a correctly executed attack and parry. These differences, together with a much greater scoring surface (the whole of the blade, rather than the point alone), make sabre parries more difficult to execute effectively. As a result, sabre tactics rely much more heavily on footwork with blade contact kept to a minimum. Also, play is not halted by an off-target (hands/below the waist) hit in sabre. To prevent both fencers from immediately charging each other at the beginning of fencing action, crossing of the feet is not allowed, which also prohibits use of the flèche. This results in a penalty against the offending fencer (a warning, followed by awarding a penalty touch if the offense is repeated). A maneuver called a 'Flunge' is sometimes used as a replacement for the outlawed flèche: the fencer leaps at the opponent, being sure to keep his rear foot behind his front as long as possible. Safely landing following this move requires crossing the feet, thus the hit must be scored while airborne. Sabre matches are often decided very quickly compared to the other weapons.

Protective Clothing

The clothing which is worn in modern fencing is made of tough cotton or nylon. Kevlar was added to top level uniform pieces (jacket, breeches, underarm protector, lamé, and the bib of the mask) following the Smirnov incident at the 1982 World Championships in Rome. However, kevlar breaks down in chlorine and UV light, so the act of washing one's uniform and/or hanging it up in the sun to dry actually damaged the kevlar's ability to do the job.

In recent years other ballistic fabrics such as Dyneema have been developed that perform the puncture resistance function and which do not have kevlar's weakness. In fact, the FIE rules state that the entirety of the uniform (meaning FIE level clothing, as the rules are written for FIE tournaments) must be made of fabric that resists a force of 800 newtons (1600 N in the mask bib).

The complete fencing kit includes the following items of clothing:

- Form-fitting jacket covering groin and with strap (*croissard*) which goes between the legs (note that in sabre fencing, jackets that are cut along the waist and exclude the groin padding are also sometimes used), a small gorget of folded fabric is also sewn in around the collar to prevent a blade from slipping upwards towards the neck.
- Under-arm protector (plastron) which goes underneath the jacket and provides double protection on the sword arm side and upper arm. It is required to not have a seam in the armpit, which would line up with the jacket seam and provide a weak spot.
- One glove for the sword arm with a gauntlet that prevents blades from going up the sleeve and causing injury, as well as protecting the hand and providing a good grip.
- Breeches or knickers which are a pair of short trousers. The legs are supposed to hold just below the knee.
- Knee-length or Thigh high socks which should cover knee and thighs.
- Shoes with flat soles and reinforcement on the inside of the back foot and heel of front foot, to prevent wear from lunging.
- Mask including a bib which protects the neck. The mask can usually support 350 Newtons, however FIE regulation masks must withstand much more, 1600 Newtons. Some modern masks have a see-through visor in the front of the mask. These can be used at high level competitions (World Championships etc.).
- Plastic chest protector, mandatory for female fencers. While male versions of the chest protector are also available, they were, until recently, primarily worn by instructors, who are hit far more often during training than their students. Since the change of the depression timing (see above), these are increasingly popular in foil, as the hard surface increases the likelihood of point bounce and thus a failure for a hit to register. Plastrons are still mandatory, though the chest protector must be worn next to the skin.
- Fencing Masters will often wear a heavier protective jacket, usually reinforced by plastic foam to cushion the numerous hits an instructor has to endure. Sometimes in

practice, masters wear a protective sleeve or a leg leather for protection of their fencing arm or leg.

- Electric Fencing: In electric foil and sabre there is a layer of electrically conductive material (called a lamé) worn over the fencing jacket, and entirely covers the valid target area. In foil the lamé is sleeveless, and in sabre the lamé has sleeves and ends in a straight line across the waist. In all weapons, a body cord is also necessary to register scoring: it attaches to the weapon and is worn inside the sleeve of the normal jacket, down the fencer's back and is then attached to the scoring box. In sabre and foil, the body cord is connected to the lamé in order to create a circuit to the scoring box, where another part of the body cord attaches, can record where one has been hit.

Traditionally, the fencers' uniform is white in colour (black being the traditional colour for instructors). This may be to some extent due to the occasional pre-electric practice of covering the point of the weapon in dye, soot, or coloured chalk in order to make it easier for the referee to determine the placing of the touches. Recently the FIE rules have been relaxed to allow coloured uniforms (black still being reserved for the coaches). The guidelines delineating the permitted size and positioning of sponsorship logos are however still extremely strict.

Practice and Techniques

Competition Formats

Fencing tournaments are varied in their format, and there are both individual and team competitions. A tournament may comprise all three weapons, both individual and team, or it may be very specific, such as an Épée Challenge, with individual épée only. And, as in many sports, men and women compete separately in high-level tournaments. Mixed-gender tournaments are commonplace at lower-level events, especially those held by individual fencing clubs. There are two types of event, individual and team. An individual event consists of two parts: the pools, and the direct eliminations.

In the pools, fencers are divided into groups, and every fencer in a pool will have the chance to fence every other fencer once.

There are typically seven fencers in a pool. If the number of fencers competing is not a multiple of seven, then there will usually be several pools of six or eight. After the pools are finished, the fencers are given a ranking, or "seed," compared to all other fencers in the tournament, based primarily on the per cent of bouts they won, then based secondarily on the difference between the touches they scored and the touches they received. Once the seeds have been determined, the direct elimination round starts. Fencers are sorted in a table of some power of 2 (16, 32, 64, etc.) based on how many people are competing. Due to the fact that it is highly unlikely for the number of fencers to be exactly a power of two, the fencers with the best results in the pools are given byes or the bottom seeded fencers are eliminated. The winner carries on in the tournament, and loser is eliminated. Typically no one has to fence for third place (the exception is if the tournament is a qualifying tournament with limited slots for continuation). Instead, two bronze medals are given to the losers of the semi-final round.

Team competition involves teams of three fencers. A fourth fencer can be allowed on the team as an alternate, but as soon as the fourth has been subbed in, they cannot substitute again. The modern team competition is similar to the pool round of the individual competition. The fencers from opposing teams will each fence each other once, making for a total of nine matches. Matches between teams are three minutes long, or to 5 points, and the points then carry onto the next bout, thus making it a forty-five touch bout fought by six fencers. Unlike individual tournaments, team tournaments almost always fence for bronze.

Universities and Schools

Fencing has a long history of association with universities and schools. At least one style of Fencing, Mensur in Germany is practiced only within universities. University students compete against each other at an international level at the World University Games. The United States also holds a national level university tournament including the NCAA championship tournament in the USA and the BUCS Fencing Championships in the UK.

The cost of equipment and the relatively small scale of the sport means fencing at the school level has traditionally been dominated by a small number of schools. National fencing organisations have set up programmes to encourage a greater number of students to get involved with fencing at a school level examples include the Regional Youth Circuit programme or the Leon Paul Youth Development series in the UK.

In the UK there are two national competitions in which schools compete against each other directly; the Public Schools Fencing Championship, a competition only open to Independent Schools, and the Scottish Secondary Schools Championships, open to all secondary schools in Scotland it contains both a teams and individual event and is one of the most anticipated competition in Scottish youth fencing. However schools also organise matches directly against one another and school age pupils can compete individually against one another in the British Youth Championships.

4

Statistics Related to Commonwealth Games with Special Focus on 2004 Youth Games

COMMONWEALTH GAMES STATISTICS (1911—2006)

Year	*Venue*	*Competing Countries*	*Sports*	*Members*
1911 (Festival of Empire)	LONDON (England)	AUS; CAN; GBR; SAF (4)	Athletics; Boxing; Swimming; Wrestling (4)	Not known
1930 16-23 Aug	HAMILTON (Canada)	AUS; BER; BG; CAN; GBR; IRE; NFW; NZL; SAF; SCO; WAL (11)	Athletics; Boxing; Lawn Bowls; Rowing; Swimming; Wrestling (6)	approx 400 competitors 50 officials
1934 4-11 Aug	LONDON (England)	AUS; BER; BG; CAN; ENG; HKG; IND; JAM; NFW; NZL; NIR; RHD; SAF; SCO; TRI; WAL (16)	Athletics; Boxing; Cycling; Lawn Bowls; Rowing; Swimming; Wrestling (7)	approx 500 competitors 100 officials
1938 5-12 Feb	SYDNEY (Australia)	AUS; BER; BG; CAN, CEY; ENG; FIJ; IND; NZL; NIR; RHD; SAF; SCO; TRI; WAL (15)	Athletics; Boxing; Cycling; Lawn Bowls; Rowing; Swimming; Wrestling (7)	376M, 88W 43 officials (507)
1950 4-11 Feb	AUCKLAND (New Zealand)	AUS; CAN; CEY; ENG; FIJ; MAL; NGR; NZL; RHD; SAF; SCO; WAL (12)	Athletics; Boxing; Cycling; Fencing; Lawn Bowls; Rowing; Swimming; Water Polo; Weightlifting; Wrestling (10)	495M, 95W 73 officials (663)

(*Contd.*)

Year	*Venue*	*Competing Countries*	*Sports*	*Members*
1954 30 July - 7 Aug	VANCOU-VER (Canada)	AUS; BAH; BAR; BER; BG; CAN; ENG; FIJ; GC; HKG; IND; JAM; KEN; NGR; NIR; NRD; NZL; PAK; SAF; SCO; SRD; TRI; UGA; WAL (24)	Athletics; Boxing; Cycling; Fencing; Lawn Bowls; Rowing; Swimming; Weightlifting; Wrestling (9)	568M, 94W 127 officials (789)
1958 18-26 July	CARDIFF (Wales)	AUS; BAH; BAR; BG; CAN; CEY; DMA; ENG; FIJ; GHA; GIB; HKG; IND; IOM; JAM; JER; SEN; MAL; MLT; MRI; NB; NGR; NIR; NZL; PAK; RHD; SAF; SAR; SCO; SIN; SRI; SVI; TRI; UGA; WAL (35)	Athletics; Boxing; Cycling; Fencing; Lawn Bowls; Rowing; Swimming; Weightlifting; Wrestling (9)	967M, 163W 228 officials (1358)
1962 22 Nov - 1 Dec	PERTH (Australia)	ADN; AUS; BAH; BAR; BG; BH; CAN; CEY; COM; ENG; FIJ; GHA; BIG; HKG; IOM; JAM; JER; KEN; LCA; MAL; MLT; NB; NIR; NZL; PAK; PNG; RHD; SAR; SCO; SIN; TANG; TRI; UGA; WAL (35)	Athletics; Boxing; Cycling; Fencing; Lawn Bowls; Rowing; Swimming; Weightlifting; Wrestling (9)	727M, 136W 178 officials (1041)
1966 4-13 Aug	KINGSTON (Jamaica)	ANT; AUS; BAH; BER; BH; CAN; CEY; ENG, FIJ; GHA; GIB; GUY; IND; IOM; JAM; JER; KEN; MAL; MRI; NGR; NIR; NZL; PAK; PNG; SAF; SCO; SIN; SLE, SVI; TAN; TRI; WAL (32)	Athletics; Badminton; Boxing; Cycling; Fencing; Shooting; Swimming; Weightlifting; Wrestling (9)	854M, 196W 266 officials (1316)

(Contd.)

Year	*Venue*	*Competing Countries*	*Sports*	*Members*
1970 16-25 July	EDINBURGH (Scotland)	ANT; AUS; BAH; BAR; BER; CAN; CEY; DMI; ENG; FIJ; GAM; GHA; GIB; GRN; GUE; GUY; HKG; IND; IOM; JAM; JER; KEN; LCA; MAL; MAW; MLT; MRI; NGR; NIR; NZL; PAK; PNG; SCO; SIN; SLE; SVI; SWZ; TAN; TRI; UGA; WAL; ZAM (42)	Athletics; Badminton; Boxing; Cycling; Fencing; Lawn Bowls; Swimming; Weightlifting; Wrestling (9)	1095M, 288W 362 officials (1745)
1974 24 Jan - 2 Feb	CHRIST-CHURCH (New Zealand)	AUS; BAR; BER; BOT; CAN; COK; ENG; FIJ; GAM; GHA; GIB; GRN; CUE; HKG; IND; IOM; JAM; JER; KEN; LES; MAL; MAW; MRI; NGR; NIR; NZL; PNG; SCO; SIN; SRI; SVI; SWZ; TAN; TON; TRI; UGA; WAL; WSA; ZAM (39)	Athletics; Badminton; Boxing; Cycling; Lawn Bowls; Shooting; Swimming; Weightlifting; Wrestling (9)	977M, 299W 372 officials (1648)
1978 3-12 Aug	EDMONTON (Canada)	ANT; AUS; BAH; BAN; BAR; BER; BIZ; CAN; CAY; COK; CYP; ENG; FIJ; GAM; GHA; GIB; GRN; GUE; GUY; HKG; IND; IOM; JAM; JER; KEN; LCA; LES; MAL; MAW; MRI; NIR; NZL; PNG; SCO; SIN; SKN; SLE; SRI; SVI; SWZ; TCI; TAN; TRI; WAL; WSA; ZAM (46)	Athletics; Badminton; Boxing; Cycling; Gymnastics; Lawn Bowls; Shooting; Swimming; Weight-lifting; Wrestling (10)	1183M, 336W 481 officials (2000)

(*Contd.*)

Year	Venue	Competing Countries	Sports	Members
1982 30 Sept - 9 Oct	BRISBANE (Australia)	AUS; BAH; BAR; BER; BOT; CAN; CAY; CYP; ENG; FAI; FIJ; GAM; GHA; GIB; GUE; GUY; HKG; IND; IOM; JAM; JER; KEN; MAL; MAW; MLT; MRI; NGR; NIR; NZL; PNG; SCO; SIN; SOL; SHE; SRI; SWZ; TAN; TON; TRI; UGA; VAN; WAL; WSA; ZAM; ZIM (45)		
1986 24 July - 2 Aug	EDINBURGH (Scotland)	AUS; BOT; CAN; CAY; COK; ENG; FAI; FIJ; GIB; GUE; HKG; IOM; JER; LES; MAW; MDV; MLT; NFI; NIR; NZL; SCO; SIN; SWZ; VAN; WAL; WSA (26)	Athletics; Badminton; Boxing; Cycling; Lawn Bowls; Rowing; Shooting; Swimming; Weightlifting; Wrestling (10)	1662 competitors 461 officials (2123)
1990 24 Jan - 3 Feb	AUCKLAND (New Zealand)	AUS; BAH; BAN; BAR; BER; BOT; BRU; CAN; CAY; COK; CYP; ENG; FAI; GAM; GHA; GIB; GUE; GUY; HKG; IND; IOM; BVI; JAM; JER; KEN; LES; MAL; MAW; MDV; MLT; MRI; NFI; NGR; NIR; NRU; NZL; PAK; PNG; SCO; SEY; SIN; SKN; SLE; SOL; SRI; SWZ; TAN; TON; TRI; UGA; VAN; WAL; WSA; ZAM; ZIM (55)	Athletics; Badminton; Boxing; Cycling; Gymnastics; Judo; Lawn Bowls; Shooting; Swimming; Weightlifting (10)	2073 competitors 700 officials (2773)

(*Contd.*)

Year	Venue	Competing Countries	Sports	Members
1994 18-28 Aug	VICTORIA (Canada)	ANT; AUS; BAH; BAN; BAR; BER; BIZ; BOT; BRU; BVI; CAN; CAY; COK; CYP; DMA; ENG; FAI; GAM; GHA; GIB; GUE; GUY; HKG; IND; IOM; JAM; JER; KEN; LCA; LES; MAS; MAW; MDV; MLT; MRI; MTS; NZL; NAM; NGR; NFI; NIR; PAK; PNG; NRU; RSA; SCO; SEY; SLE; SIN; SOL; SRI; SKN; SVG; SWZ; TAN; TON; TRI; UGA; VAN; WAL; WSA; ZAM; ZIM (63)	Athletics; Badminton; Boxing; Cycling; Gymnastics; Lawn Bowls; Shooting; Swimming; Weightlifting; Wrestling (10)	2557 competitors 914 officials (3471)
1998 11-21 Sept	KUALA LUMPUR (Malaysia)	ANG; ANT; AUS; BAH; BAN; BAR; BER; BIZ; BOT; BRU; BVI; CMR; CAN; CAY; COK; CYP; DMA; ENG; FAI; FIJ; GAM; GHA; GIB; GRN; GUE; GUY; IND; IOM; JAM; JER; KEN; KIR; LCA; LES; MAS; MAW; MDV; MLT; MOZ; MRI; MTS; NAM; NFI; NIR; NRU; NZL; PAK; PNG; RSA; SAM; SCO; SEY; SLE; SHE; SIN; SOL; SRI; SKN; SVG;	Athletics; Badminton; Boxing; Cricket; Cycling; Gymnastics; Hockey (men & women); Lawn Bowls; Netball; Rugby; Shooting; Squash; Swimming; Tenpin Bowling; Weightlifting (16)	3638 competitors 1398 officials (5036)

(Contd.)

Year	Venue	Competing Countries	Sports	Members
		SWZ; TAN; TCI; TON; TRI; TUV; UGA; VAN; WAL; ZAM; ZIM (70)		
2002 25 July - 4 Aug	MANCHESTER (England)	ANG; ANT; AUS; BAH; BAN; BAR; BER; BIZ; BOT; BRU; BVI; CMR; CAN; CAY; COK; CYP; DMA; ENG; FAI; FIJ; GAM; GHA; GIB; GRN; GUE; GUY; IND; IOM; JAM; JER; KEN; KIR; LCA; LES; MAS, MAW; MDV; MLT; MOZ; MRI; MTS; NAM; NFI; NGR; NIR; NIU; NRU; NZL; PAK; PNG; RSA; SAM; SCO; SEY; SLE; SHE; SIN; SOL; SRI; SKN; SVG; SWZ; TAN; TCI; TON; TRI; TUV; UGA; VAN; WAL; ZAM; ZIM (72)	Athletics; Badminton; Boxing; Cycling; Gymnastics; Hockey (men & women); Judo; Lawn Bowls; Netball; Rugby; Shooting; Squash; Swimming; Table Tennis; Triathlon; Weightlifting; Wrestling (17)	3690 competitors 1784 officials (5474)
2006 15-26 March	MELBOURNE (Australia)	ANG; ANT; AUS; BAH; BAN; BAR; BER; BIZ; BOT; BRU; BVI; CMR, CAN, CAY; COK; CYP; DMA, ENG; FAI; FIJ; GAM; GHA; GIB; GRN; GUE; GUY; IND; IOM; JAM; JER; KEN; KIR; LCA; LES; MAS; MAW; MDV; MLT;	Athletics; Badminton; Basketball (men & women); Boxing; Cycling; Gymnastics; Hockey (men & women); Lawn Bowls; Netball; Rugby; Shooting; Squash; Swimming; Table Tennis; Triathlon; Weightlifting (16)	4071 competitors 2270 officials (6341)

(*Contd.*)

Year	Venue	Competing Countries	Sports	Members
		MOZ; MRI; MTS; NAM; NFI; NGR; NIR; NIU; NRU; NZL; PAK; PNG; RSA; SAM; SCO; SEY; SLE; SHE; SIN; SOL; SRI; SKN; SVG; SWZ; TAN; TCI; TON; TRI; TUV; UGA; VAN; WAL; ZAM (71)		

2004 COMMONWEALTH YOUTH GAMES

The 2004 Commonwealth Youth Games were held in Bendigo, Australia. They were the second Commonwealth Youth Games, which are held every four years.

Sports

Sports in this games:

- Athletics,
- Badminton,
- Bowls,
- Boxing,
- Cycling,
- Gymnastics,
- Rugby 7's,
- Swimming,
- Tenpin Bowling,
- Weightlifting.

Medal Count

This is the full table of the medal count of the Commonwealth Youth Games 2004. These rankings sort by the number of gold medals earned by a country. The number of silvers is taken into consideration next and then the number of bronze. If, after the above, countries are still tied, equal ranking is given and they are listed alphabetically. This follows the system used by the IOC, IAAF and BBC.

Rank	*Nation*	*Gold*	*Silver*	*Bronze*	*Total*
1	Australia (host)	58	41	30	129
2	England	31	29	26	86
3	South Africa	20	18	18	56
4	Scotland	12	17	23	52
5	New Zealand	6	0	0	6
6	Malaysia	6	9	3	18
7	Singapore	3	2	5	10
8	India	2	4	4	10
9	Nauru	2	1	0	3
10	Jersey	1	1	2	4
11	Sri Lanka	1	0	0	1
12	Wales	0	2	1	3
13	Northern Ireland	0	1	3	4
14	Samoa	0	1	2	3
15	Solomon Islands	0	1	1	2
16=	Cook Islands	0	0	2	2
16=	Fiji	0	0	2	2
18	Ghana	0	0	1	1

Jana Pittman - Face of the Games

100m World Champion hurdler Jana Pittman has been announced as The Face of the 2004 Commonwealth Youth Games.

The role of The Face of Games will be to promote the Games to state, national and even international markets, including media interviews, an advertising campaign, speaking engagements and attendance at the Games.

Jana's Profile

Date of Birth	9 November 1982
Born	Sydney
Residence	Melbourne
Height	1.81m
Weight	67kg

Jana's Athletic Profile

2004 Athens Olympic Games	
400m Hurdles	5th place (53.92 sec)
Personal Bests	
100m	11.77 sec
200m	23.52 sec
400m	50.43 sec
100m Hurdles	13.92 sec
400m Hurdles	53.22 sec
International Honours	
2003 World Championships	400m Hurdles - Gold
2002 World Cup	400m Hurdles - Bronze
2002 Commonwealth Games	400m Hurdles - Gold
2002 Commonwealth Games	4 x 400m Relay - Gold
2000 World Junior Champs	400m Hurdles - Gold
2000 World Junior Champs	400m – Gold
1999 World Junior Champs	400m Hurdles - Gold
World Records	
400m Hurdles	55.20 sec World Junior Record 2000
400m Hurdles	55.20 sec Australian U18 and U20 Record
4x400m Relay	3.25.63 sec Commonwealth Games Record 2002
400m	51.80 sec Australian U18 Record
300m	36.34 sec Australian Best

The Official Games Mascot

After much anticipation the official mascot for the 2004 Commonwealth Youth Games has been launched. Please welcome Ausca the Sugar Glider!

Over 140 entries were received for the mascot competition with each entry showing wonderful creative flair. Congratulations to class's 4B and 4/5W from Eaglehawk North Primary School for winning the mascot competition.

The students gave the following reason in their entry form: Ausca the Sugar Glider is a 'You can do it' animal, he is native to Bendigo and if he can glide 90 metres then a human can glide their way through achievements.

The Hon Jacinta Allan MP was given the role of unveiling Ausca to 300 thrilled young children in Bendigo. Ms Allan said that Ausca will now be out visiting local schools and community events encouraging many people to visit the Games from 30 November to 4 December.

About the Games Bendigo, Australia

The Commonwealth Games Federation discussed the idea of a Millennium Commonwealth Youth Games in 1997. In 1998 the concept was agreed on for the purpose of providing a Commonwealth multi-sport event for young people born in the calendar year 1986 or later.

The inaugural Commonwealth Youth Games were held in Edinburgh, Scotland from 10-14 August 2000. 14 countries contested 483 medals over 3 days of competition in 8 sports. A total of 733 athletes and team officials, 280 Technical Officials and around 500 volunteers participated in the event.

Eight sports were contested. These included: Athletics, Fencing, Gymnastics, Hockey, Lawn Tennis, Squash, Swimming and Weightlifting. The success of these Games in Scotland gained the support of the Commonwealth Games Federation who has pledged continued support for a Commonwealth Youth Games to be held every 4 years.

The second Commonwealth Youth Games were awarded to Australia in 2002. Following a formal submission process, Bendigo was awarded the honour of hosting these Games in Australia.

The Host City about Bendigo

Bendigo is a thriving regional city with a population of 95,000 people.

Bendigo is located in the geographic heart of the southern Australian State of Victoria, 150km north west of the state capital, Melbourne.

The Bendigo region developed from the heady gold rush days in the 1850's that brought thousands of people caught up with gold fever. Gold mining activity continued for over 100 years injected huge wealth into Bendigo. More than 20 million ounces of gold was won, much of which was invested in Bendigo, creating an impressive city of tree-lined streets and fine examples of Victorian architecture.

Welcome to Bendigo

Impressive Victorian buildings line the wide streets of Bendigo, as a reminder of the rich history built from one of the world's most exciting gold rushes. Today there are new treasures to be discovered in this thriving city. Bendigo is a place where art, culture, food, wine and heritage attractions are in the abundance, as was the gold of the late 1850's.

Attractions and Tours

A true Bendigo highlight is the range of quality experiences and things to do. Our major attractions are diverse and exciting. There is the authentic deep-shaft mine experience at Central Deborah, where you travel underground in a miners' cage. The famous Vintage Talking Tram Tour that weaves through the streets of Bendigo, telling wonderful stories of days gone by.

The original 1860's Chinese Joss House and the Golden Dragon Museum display the Chinese heritage of the area and house the world's oldest Imperial Dragon, Loong. Bendigo Art Gallery has a strong reputation with a significant collection. An award-winning architecturally designed café was added to the building in recent times.

The Bendigo Pottery is famous, with its display and sales complex set around vast old beehive kilns. Dozens of smaller studios and galleries in Bendigo profile artists of the region. For the curious at heart, there is a great experience for you at Confectionary Capers. A guided tour of Bendigo's magnificent Town Hall is a must.

For the active there is Australia's highest Vertical Slide at Discovery Science & Technology Centre and a host of physical challenges at Life Adventure Park. For an even more active visit try a walking trail or cycling trail through Bendigo's fabulous city centre or beyond. A bush-walk through the tranquil Whipstick Forest, fossicking for gold near historic Maldon or cycling around beautiful wineries on route to Castlemaine could be for you.

5

Case Study: 2006 Commonwealth Games Event, Ceremony and Festival

2006 COMMONWEALTH GAMES

The 2006 Commonwealth Games were held in Melbourne, Victoria, Australia between 15 March and 26 March 2006. It was the largest sporting event to be staged in Melbourne, eclipsing the 1956 Summer Olympics in terms of the number of teams competing, athletes competing, and events being held.

The site for the opening and closing ceremonies was the Melbourne Cricket Ground which was also used during Melbourne's 1956 Olympic Games.

The mascot for the games was Karak, a Red-tailed Black Cockatoo (a threatened species).

For the first time ever, the Melbourne 2006 Commonwealth Games appointed a Goodwill Partner, Plan International Australia.

Sports

The 2006 Commonwealth Games included 16 sports, with 12 individual sports and 4 team sports. In total there are 247 events at the Games.

Four of these sports are further broken down into separate disciplines, making a total of 24 disciplines:

- *Aquatics*: diving, swimming, synchronised swimming.
- *Cycling*: track, road, mountain bike.

- *Gymnastics*: artistic, rhythmic.
- *Shooting*: clay target, pistol, small bore and air rifle, full bore rifle.

The athletics, swimming, table tennis and weightlifting sports include fully integrated events for elite athletes with a disability (EAD). These events are included in the official medal tally.

Participating Nations

There were 71 countries, territories and bodies competing at the 2006 Commonwealth Games. The only difference between the countries competing at these games from the 2002 games is the absence of Zimbabwe, which has now withdrawn from the Commonwealth of Nations. In alphabetical order, the countries were:

- Anguilla
- Antigua and Barbuda
- Australia
- Bahamas
- Bangladesh
- Barbados
- Belize
- Bermuda
- Botswana
- British Virgin Islands
- Brunei Darussalam
- Cameroon
- Canada
- Cayman Islands
- Cook Islands
- Cyprus
- Dominica
- England
- Falkland Islands
- Fiji
- The Gambia
- Ghana
- Gibraltar
- Grenada
- Guernsey
- Guyana
- India
- Isle of Man
- Jamaica
- Jersey
- Kenya
- Kiribati
- Lesotho
- Malawi
- Malaysia
- Maldives
- Malta
- Mauritius
- Montserrat
- Mozambique
- Namibia
- Nauru
- New Zealand
- Nigeria
- Niue
- Norfolk Island
- Northern Ireland
- Pakistan
- Papua New Guinea
- Saint Helena
- Saint Kitts and Nevis
- Saint Lucia
- Saint Vincent and the Grenadines
- Samoa
- Scotland
- Seychelles
- Sierra Leone
- Singapore
- Solomon Islands
- South Africa
- Sri Lanka
- Swaziland
- Tanzania
- Tonga
- Trinidad and Tobago
- Turks and Caicos
- Tuvalu
- Uganda
- Vanuatu
- Wales
- Zambia

Medals Table

Rank	Nation	Gold	Silver	Bronze	Total
1	Australia	84	69	68	221
2	England	36	40	34	110
3	Canada	26	29	31	86
4	India	22	17	11	50
5	South Africa	12	13	13	38
6	Scotland	11	7	11	29
7	Jamaica	10	4	8	22
8	Malaysia	7	12	10	29
9	New Zealand	6	12	13	31
10	Kenya	6	5	7	18
11	Singapore	5	6	7	18
12	Nigeria	4	6	7	17
13	Wales	3	5	11	19
14	Cyprus	3	1	2	6
15	Ghana	2	0	1	3
16	Uganda	2	0	1	3
17	Pakistan	1	3	1	5
18	Papua New Guinea	1	1	0	2
19	Isle of Man	1	0	1	2
20	Namibia	1	0	1	2
21	Tanzania	1	0	1	2
22	Sri Lanka	1	0	0	1
23	Mauritius	0	3	0	3
24	Bahamas	0	2	0	2
25	Northern Ireland	0	2	0	2
26	Cameroon	0	1	2	3
27	Botswana	0	1	1	2
28	Malta	0	1	1	2
29	Nauru	0	1	1	2
30	Bangladesh	0	1	0	1

(Contd.)

Rank	Nation	Gold	Silver	Bronze	Total
31	Grenada	0	1	0	1
32	Lesotho	0	1	0	1
33	Trinidad and Tobago	0	0	3	3
34	Seychelles	0	0	2	2
35	Barbados	0	0	1	1
36	Fiji	0	0	1	1
37	Mozambique	0	0	1	1
38	Samoa	0	0	1	1
39	Swaziland	0	0	1	1
		245	**244**	**254**	**743**

Highlights

Opening Ceremony — 15 March

Both the Melbourne Cricket Ground and the Yarra River were centrepieces for the ceremony, which included many fireworks, and other spectacle. The Games were opened by Queen Elizabeth II, in her capacity as Head of the Commonwealth. The Queen is also Head of State of a number of Commonwealth countries, including Australia.

Day 1 — 16 March

Cycling

England managed a clean sweep of the 4,000 m individual pursuit gold medal on the cycle track. Paul Manning beat fellow team mate Rob Hayles in the final. Steve Cummings won the bronze medal race. Australian Ben Kersten manages to beat the World and Olympic champions in the 1 km time trial.

Swimming

Scotland's Caitlin McClatchey beat Australia's Libby Lenton in the Women's 200 m freestyle final, setting a new Games record of 1:57.25. England's Melanie Marshall came in third. David Carry of Scotland has won the 400 m freestyle final, winning the second swimming gold for his country. Canadian Andrew Hurd picked

Calandar

March	15th	16th	17th	18th	19th	20th	21st	22nd	23rd	24th	25th	26th
Ceremonies	?											?
Athletics					?	?	?	?	?	?	?	
Badminton		?	?	?	?	?????	?????	?????	?????	?????	?????	?????
Basketball		??	??	??	??	??	??	??	??	?		
Boxing		??	??	??	??	??	??	?	??	??	??	
Cycling		?		?	?		?	?		?	?	?
Diving		?				?	?					?
Gymnastics		?	?	??		?????	?????			??	?	????
Hockey		?	?	?	?	?						
Lawn Bowls		?	?	?	?	??	??		?	?		
Netball			?			?						
Rugby 7s		?	?									
Shooting		?				?						
Squash		?	?					?	?		?	
Swimming		?	?	?	?	?	?					
Synchronised Swimming			?	?			?	?				
Table tennis			?	?			?	?				
Triathlon			?	?			?	?				
Weightlifting			?	?			?	?				
March	15th	16th	17th	18th	19th	20th	21st	22nd	23rd	24th	25th	26th

up the silver in 3:49.08 and David Davies from Wales came third. Moss Burmester from New Zealand won gold in the 200 m butterfly in a new New Zealand and Commonwealth record time of 1:56.64.

Weightlifting

The Games' first gold medal was awarded in the Women's Weightlifting (48 kg class) to Kunjarani Devi Nameirakpam from India. Marilou Dozois-Prevost from Canada won the silver, and Erika Yamasaki of Australia picked up the bronze.

Day 2 - 17 March

Cycling

Australians Katherine Bates and Rochelle Gilmore get gold and silver respectively in the Women's 25 km Points Race, repeating their Manchester Games results. Their teammate Alexis Rhodes took ninth place after being seriously injured in Germany in an accident that took the life of Amy Gillett, in whose honour all three dedicated their ride.

Rugby Sevens

New Zealand won the gold medal at the Telstra Dome with a convincing 29-21 win over England. Fiji win the bronze medal with a 24-17 win over Australia in a game marred by a serious injury to Australian player Scott Fava.

Swimming

Australia gets all three medals in both the women's 50 m butterfly and women's 50 m breaststroke.

Day 3 - 18 March

Swimming

Australia swept gold, silver, and bronze in both the women's 50 m breaststroke and the 50 m butterfly. Leisel Jones and Danni Miatke, respectively, won the golds.

Triathlon

Day 3 saw the Australians and New Zealanders completely dominate the triathlon event. After missing out on qualification for the 2004 Athens Olympics, Emma Snowsill took the gold medal with a time of 1:58:02.59. New Zealand secured silver (Samantha Warriner), bronze (Andrea Hewitt) and fourth place for the Women's event. Continuing Australia's dominance in the triathlon, Brad Kahlefeldt won gold in the men's triathlon event with a time of 1:49:16. Australian Peter Robertson was just beaten by New Zealander, Bevan Docherty for silver, while Robertson took the bronze.

Cycling

Australian cyclist Ryan Bayley won the men's sprint, his second gold medal for these Games.

Weightlifting

Australian weightlifter Ben Turner won the men's 69 kg Division, the first Australian gold medal for weightlifting at the games.

Day 4 - 19 March

Athletics

Australian Kerryn McCann successfully defends her 2002 Commonwealth Games gold medal title by winning the women's marathon event with a time of 2:30:50.

Athletics

Tanzania retained the men's marathon title, Samson Ramadhani taking the gold. Kenya's Fred Mogaka took silver, and England's Dan Robinson took the bronze.

Cycling

The Isle of Man won their first Commonwealth gold in twenty years, when Mark Cavendish won the men's Scratch Race final. Cavendish held off Australia's Ashley Hutchinson on the final bend to triumph, with Scotland's James McCallum claiming bronze.

Swimming

World champion Jessicah Schipper of Australia swam a Games record in beating team-mate Libby Lenton for the women's 100 m butterfly gold.

Day 5 - 20 March

Athletics

Australian Craig Mottram and crowd favourite, is edged out by Augustine Choge in the men's 5000 m by 2 seconds. Choge won in a Games-record time of 12 min 56.41 s. At one stage during the race Mottram ran with 3 Kenyan racers in front of him and 3 Tanzanian racers behind him.

Athletics

Asafa Powell, world record holder, wins the men's 100 m sprint in a time of 10.03 seconds, ahead of Nigeria's Soji Fasuba and the Trinidadian Marc Burns. His Jamaican compatriot, Sheri-Ann Brooks won the women's 100 m in a personal best time of 11.19 s, ahead of South Africa's Geraldine Pillay and Delphine Antangana, of Cameroon.

Squash

The Grinham sisters (Australia) battled for the Gold medal. Natalie triumphed over Rachel 2-9 9-6 9-1 9-6. Peter Nicol won his third Commonwealth Games gold medal. He previously won the singles title in 1998, and the doubles in 2002. He recaptured the singles title in four games, defeating Australia's David Palmer 9-5 10-8 4-9 9-2.

Swimming

Scotland won two more gold medals in the pool, with Caitlin McClatchey and Gregor Tait each winning their second titles in the 400 m freestyle and 200 m individual medley respectively. Australia's Leisel Jones set the first world record of the swimming competition, breaking her own record in the 100 m breaststroke with a time of 1:05.09.

Day 6 - 21 March

Swimming

The Australian women's swimming team again asserted their dominance in the pool, breaking the 4 × 100 m medley relay world record in a time of 3:56.30, over a second faster than that set by the Australian women's swimming team in the 2004 Athens Olympics. The Australian women completed one of the most successful campaigns in games' history, finishing with 16 gold medals, just 3 short of the entire meet's offerings. The Australian men's swimming team finishes on a successful note, winning the 4 × 100 m medley relay. This was one of their least successful games meets with 3 gold medals.

Athletics

The Kenyan women finish with Lucy Wangui (31:29.66) and Evelyne Nganga (31:30.86) gold and silver respectively in the 10,000 m run. Wangui overtook Nganga in the final straight, after Nganga attempted to break away. Mara Yamauchi of England was third.

Athletics

Dean Macey of England overcame injury to win his first major title in the men's Decathlon. Maurice Smith of Jamaica took silver and Australian Jason Dudley earned bronze.

Day 7 - 22 March

Athletics

New Zealander Valerie Vili won gold in the women's shot put, setting a new Commonwealth Games record of 19.66 metres.

Day 8 - 23 March

Athletics

Australian Jana Pittman delighted the home crowd by retaining her 400 m hurdles title with Britons Natasha Danvers-Smith (England) and Lee McConnell (Scotland) picking up silver and bronze.

Jamaica won gold and silver in the women's 200 m with Sherone Simpson finishing ahead of Veronica Campbell and South African Geraldine Pillay in third.

Cycling

England's Liam Killeen led an England one-two in the men's mountain bike cross country race. The 23-year-old eased home in two hours 13.11 minutes, ahead of team-mate Oli Beckingsale.

Canada's Marie-Héléne Prémont took gold in the Women's mountain bike cross country race at 1:55:04, despite having to dodge a kangaroo on the course. New Zealand's Rosara Joseph finished second and Canada's Kiara Biasro finished third.

Shooting

India's Rajyavardhan Singh Rathore won gold medal in Men's Double Trap.

Day 9 - 24 March

Athletics

Australian Nathan Deakes won the men's 50 km walk in a time of 3:42:53, beating the previous record set by him at the 2002 Manchester Commonwealth Games by over 10 minutes. New Zealander Tony Sargisson took a silver medal in 3:58:05 while Australia's Christopher Erickson took the bronze in 3:58:22.

Basketball

The Australian men's team beat New Zealand 81-76 to win the first gold medal in this sport at the Commonwealth Games. The English men's team beat Nigeria 80-57 to take the bronze.

Day 10 - 25 March

Aquatics

Canadian Blythe Hartley won the Women's 3 m Springboard final with 690.05 points. Australians Chantelle Newbery and Kathryn Blackshaw took silver and bronze repectively.

Australian Matthew Helm won the Men's 10 m Platform with 1085.60 points. Silver went to England's Peter Waterfield with 1030.50 points and bronze went to Canadian Alexandre Despatie with 1016.95 points.

Athletics

England's Nicholas Nieland won the Men's Javelin with a season best throw of 80.10 m. Australians William Hamlyn Harris and Oliver Dziubak both threw 79.89 m with William Hamlyn Harris securing silver on a countback throw of 79.48 on his final throw. Oliver Dziubak took bronze on his countback throw of 78.43.

Nick Willis, gold medallist in the 1500 metres in a time of 3:38.49 mins, became the first athlete from New Zealand to win a track medal for twenty-four years.

Boxing

England dominated the boxing finals day, with Don Broadhurst, Frankie Gavin, Jamie Cox, James Russan, David Price, and Stephen Smith winning gold medals and Darran Langley winning silver.

Scotland's Kenny Anderson won the Light Heavyweight gold after defeating his opponent, Adura Olalehin, 23-19 after fighting back from 7-13 down after two rounds. During the fight, Olalehin had four points, the same as the margin of victory, awarded against himself for repeatedly holding Anderson.

Day 11 — Closing Ceremony - 26 March

Gymnastics

Canadian Alexandra Orlando completed the rhythmic gymnastics competition having won six gold medals - a gold in every rhythmic gymnastics event - to become the fourth competitor to win six gold medals at a single Commonwealth Games.

Cycling

Australians Natalie Bates and Matthew Hayman win the women's and men's road races respectively.

Hockey

In the men's final, the host nation beat Pakistan 3-0, after leading 1-0 before the break. In the bronze medal play-off, England lost to Malaysia 2-0.

Netball

New Zealand defeats Australia 60-55 in the gold medal match, to become the first country other than Australia to win Commonwealth Games gold in the sport.

Closing Ceremony

Both the Melbourne Cricket Ground and the Yarra River were again centrepieces for the ceremony. Samresh Jung of India was given the David Dixon Award at the closing ceremony. He was the "Best Athlete of the 18th Commonwealth Games". The games were closed by HRH Prince Edward.

Venues

The following venues were used at the 2006 Commonwealth Games. The sport(s) which were played at that venue is listed after it.

Melbourne Venues

- Docklands Precinct: Walks
- Melbourne Cricket Ground: Opening and Closing Ceremonies, and Athletics
- Melbourne Convention and Exhibition Centre: Badminton, Boxing and Weightlifting
- Melbourne Gun Club: Clay Target Shooting
- Melbourne International Shooting Club: Small Bore and Pistol Shooting
- Melbourne Sports and Aquatic Centre: Aquatics, Squash and Table tennis
- Multi Purpose Venue (Melbourne Park): Basketball Finals, Track Cycling and Netball Finals
- Rod Laver Arena (Melbourne Park): Gymnastics
- Royal Botanic Gardens Circuit: Cycling Road Race events
- State Lawn Bowls Centre: Lawn Bowls
- State Netball and Hockey Centre: Netball preliminaries and Hockey
- St. Kilda Foreshore and Beach Road: Triathlon and Cycling Time Trial
- Telstra Dome: Rugby 7s

Regional and Suburban Venues

Ballarat
Ballarat Minerdome: Basketball

Bendigo
Bendigo Stadium: Basketball
Wellsford Rifle Range: Full Bore Shooting
Geelong
Geelong Arena: Basketball
Lysterfield Park
State Mountain Bike Course: Mountain Bike Cycling
Traralgon
Traralgon Sports Stadium: Basketball

Impact on Host Nation

Early concerns arose about the large cost of staging the Games, with projected costs likely to be over 1 billion Australian dollars and a high likelihood the Victorian taxpayer would have to cover the expense. The cost was described in some local media as excessive. National Party leader Peter Ryan said that the Labour government should win "gold (medal) for burning money." However, not all of this money was wasted. Prior to the Games, accountants at KPMG were estimating that the gross income generated by this event could be as high as 1.5 billion dollars.

Melbourne's premier sporting ground, the Melbourne Cricket Ground (MCG), was redeveloped in preparation for the Games. An athlete's village in the inner suburb of Parkville housed approximately 7,000 athletes and support staff during the Games, and has been transformed into commercial housing with a distinctly eco-friendly image. The creation of this village attracted controversy, with critics claiming it was created by alienating public parkland, while proponents maintained that it represented the renewal of an otherwise derelict inner-city area.

The change from Daylight Saving Time to Standard Time in Australian states that follow it was delayed from 26 March to 2 April for 2006 to avoid affecting the games. In addition, state and private schools amended their usual term times so as to allow the first term end-of-term holidays to coincide with the Games.

Melbourne's public transport system—train, tram and bus—ran to altered timetables with some amended or substituted services for the duration of the Games. For the most part, timetabled services were unchanged but suffered due to higher loads.

Broadcasting

- The host broadcaster was Trans World International, while the domestic rights-holding broadcaster was the Nine Network in Australia. They showed rolling coverage, except for a break for the evening news and overnight.
- In Australia Fox Sports broadcast the Games on eight dedicated digital Pay-TV channels. These were available on the Foxtel, Austar and Optus Vision networks.
- The BBC covered the Commonwealth Games in the UK on BBC One and BBC Two. BBCi included a choice of two extra video streams on Freeview and four streams on Digital Satellite and Cable. Users with Broadband in the UK could also view all 5 video streams on bbc.co.uk, and the BBC Sport website.
- CBC, CBC Newsworld, and CBC Country Canada aired a daily one-hour highlights show of the Commonwealth Games in Canada. Compared to past games, the CBC's coverage was minimally staffed, with commentary from other broadcasting partners. At first, they did not even consider bidding for the broadcasting rights due to scheduling conflicts with events Canadians are more interested in, such as the Tim Hortons Brier, World Figure Skating Championships, and the 2006 Winter Paralympics (which itself had been reduced to five-to-ten minute daily coverage). None of Canada's metropolitan newspapers sent any journalists to report on the Games, instead relying on news agencies.
- TVNZ covered the games for the residents of New Zealand.
- In Malaysia, TV1 broadcast live coverage of the Games for three hours starting at 10 a.m. Malaysian time and for two hours starting at 3 p.m., with highlights at 12:30 a.m. Astro also included 3 dedicated channels to broadcast the Games live and delayed broadcast 24 hours to it Sports package subscribers.
- Singapore's MediaCorp TV had supposedly not broadcast the games due to the high cost of telecast rights, satellite charges and the lack of sponsors. However, on 17 March, the MediaCorp found other sponsors which is the Ministry of Community Development, Youth and Sports and the

Singapore Sports Council. Broadcast started from 18 March till the end of the games.

- In the United States, selected coverage was carried by Fox College Sports.

Missing Athletes

On 20 March 2006 it was reported that two athletes had gone missing from the Commonwealth Games village: Tanzanian boxer Omari Idd Kimweri and Bangladeshi runner Mohammad Tawhidul Islam.

On 22 March 2006 it was reported that seven athletes from Sierra Leone (three women and four men) had also disappeared. A further seven Sierra Leonean athletes also went missing during the course of the Games, bringing the total runaway count to fourteen (two-thirds of the team). Victoria Police believed that they had fled to Sydney where the Sierra Leonean community is much larger than Melbourne's.

Two hours before the Closing Ceremony on 26 March, officials from the Cameroon team reported to police that nine of their members had also vanished.

These incidents were not without precedent: 27 athletes similarly disappeared from the 2002 Commonwealth Games in Manchester, England (21 from Sierra Leone, 5 from Bangladesh and one from Pakistan), and over 80 athletes and officials overstayed their visas after the 2000 Summer Olympics in Sydney.

On request of Sierra Leone officials, the Commonwealth Games Federation cancelled those athletes' Games accreditation, allowing the Australian Department of Immigration and Multicultural Affairs (DIMA) to cancel their visas at midnight on 27 March, and begin investigating their disappearance.

At 7.20 a.m. on that day, New South Wales Police located six of the Sierra Leonean athletes in a house at Freshwater near Manly Beach in Sydney. All six indicated they wished to seek political asylum in Australia, and were granted bridging visas by DIMA while their refugee applications were arranged. The athletes claimed to have been subjected to violence and torture in their home country; seventeen-year-old Isha Conteh stated she could be forced into female genital cutting if she returned. On Tuesday

28 March, six further Sierra Leoneans turned themselves in to immigration authorities in Sydney and were also granted bridging visas.

Two of the missing Cameroon athletes were found in Perth, Western Australia.

OPENING CEREMONY

The Opening Ceremony of the 2006 Commonwealth Games was held on March 15, 2006 at Melbourne Cricket Ground in Melbourne, Victoria, Australia. The ceremony was directed by Andrew Walsh.

Description

The ceremony began with the temporary stage on the playing ground of the Melbourne Cricket Ground lighting up with previous host cities. The flags of Australia (current host), England (previous host) and India (next host) were raised. Surf boats which represented each of the past 18 host cities were on the Yarra River as were flags of the participating countries. A W-class Melbourne tram with wings attached was lowered into the stadium. A performance followed based on a poem by Michael Leunig, involving a boy with a duck which was an artificial one at first, and koalas, (people dressed in koala 'suits'). At the end of the display, the boy came into the Stadium with a real white duck. The opening ceremony had many themes, including Melbourne's Wurundjeri Indigenous heritage and Melbourne's fickle weather. The role of the boy was performed by 12-year old (almost 13) Sean Whitford, who had been selected from thousands of candidates. Australian rock band The Church played *Under The Milky Way* to accompany a performance by the Australian Ballet, with aerial work performed by students of the National Institute of Circus Arts (NICA).

Contrary to tradition, the nations did not enter the stadium in alphabetical order, but by regions of the Commonwealth. European nations entered the stadium first, followed by those from Africa, Asia, the Americas, the Caribbean and finally, Oceania. English athletes and officials entered the stadium first (as the host of the 2002 Commonwealth Games in Manchester) while the host nation,

Australia entered last. The athletes entered with The Cat Empire playing a specially written musical 'set', tailoring music to specific regions.

The final leg of the Queen's Baton Relay included the baton being handed to the 16 captains of the Australian Football League across the floating flags and fish along the Yarra River. After each of the captains had carried the baton, the last of the captains handed the baton to Ron Barassi, who walked on a semi-submerged pontoon, giving the effect that he was walking on water (some commentators joked that the stunt "proved what most of us suspected"). Barassi then handed the baton to Herb Elliott.

The Commonwealth Games Federation flag was then brought into the stadium by eight Young Australian of the Year recipients. The athlete's oath was taken by Adam Pine.

Harry White, a 13 year old boy, who was youth ambassador, presented a message to the Queen. After a rather controversial furore before the start of the Games regarding the decision by the Organising Committee not to include *God Save the Queen*, in the Opening Ceremony, a *Happy Birthday* medley was sung by Dame Kiri Te Kanawa in tribute of the Queen's 80th birthday (37 days hence), ending with eight bars from *God Save the Queen*. Michael Fennel, the president of the Commonwealth Games Federation then spoke.

The final bearers of the Queen's Baton were all former elite world-class athletes who had successfully competed at both the Olympic Games and Commonwealth Games. They were:

- Cathy Freeman (who lit the Olympic Flame at the 2000 Sydney Olympics), who brought the Queen's Baton into the stadium, and then handed the baton to
- Ron Clarke (who lit the Olympic Flame at the 1956 Melbourne Olympics), who then handed the baton to
- Marjorie Jackson-Nelson, then-Governor of South Australia, who then handed the baton to
- John Landy, then-Governor of Victoria, who presented the Queen's Baton to the Queen.

The Queen then read the message of greeting which she had placed in the baton (366 days earlier on Commonwealth Day, March 14, 2005), declaring the games open.

Australian singer Delta Goodrem sang *Together We Are One*, the theme song for the 2006 games while many fireworks were ignited, within the stadium, on the backs on roller-bladers circling the singer, and fireworks were also ignited on the banks of the Yarra, as well as the floating pontoons, and Melbourne's larger skyscrapers.

EVENTS

Sport	*Discipline*	*Event*	*Class*	*Scheduled Time of Final*	
				Local	*GMT*
Aquatics	Diving	1 m Spring-board	Men	Wed 22 19:07	Wed 22 08:07
			Women	Fri 24 19:07	Fri 24 08:07
		3 m Spring-board	Men	Thu 23 19.07	Thu 23 08:07
			Women	Sat 25 19:07	Sat 25 08:07
		10 m Platform	Men	Sat 25 20:30	Sat 25 09:30
			Women	Thu 23 20:44	Thu 23 09:44
		3 m Syn-chronised Springboard	Men	Fri 24 20:30	Fri 24 09:30
			Women	Wed 22 11:21	Wed 22 00:21
		10 m Syn-chronised Platform	Men	Fri 24 11:19	Fri 24 00:19
			Women	Wed 22 20:38	Wed 22 09:38
	Swimming	Freestyle 50 m	Men	TBC	TBC
			Men EAD	Sat 18 19:46	Sat 18 08:46
			Women	TBC	TBC
			Women EAD	Fri 17 19:50	Fri 17 08:50
		Freestyle 100 m	Men	TBC	TBC
			Men EAD	Mon 20 20:42	Mon 20 09:42
			Women	TBC	TBC
			Women EAD	Sun 19 20:09	Sun 19 09:09
		Freestyle 200 m	Men	TBC	TBC
			Women	TBC	TBC
		Freestyle 400 m	Men	TBC	TBC
			Women	TBC	TBC
		Freestyle 800 m	Women	TBC	TBC
		Freestyle 1500 m	Men	TBC	TBC

(Contd.)

Sport	Discipline	Event	Class	Scheduled Time of Final	
				Local	GMT
		Freestyle 4 x 100 m Relay	Men	TBC	TBC
			Women	TBC	TBC
		Freestyle 4 x 200 m Relay	Men	TBC	TBC
			Women	TBC	TBC
		Breaststroke 50 m	Men	TBC	TBC
			Women	TBC	TBC
		Breaststroke 100 m	Men	TBC	TBC
			Women	TBC	TBC
		Breaststroke 200 m	Men	TBC	TBC
			Women	TBC	TBC
		Butterfly 50 m	Men	TBC	TBC
			Women	TBC	TBC
		Butterfly 100 m	Men	TBC	TBC
			Women	TBC	TBC
		Butterfly 200 m	Men	TBC	TBC
			Women	TBC	TBC
		Backstroke 50 m	Men	TBC	TBC
			Women	TBC	TBC
		Backstroke 100 m	Men	TBC	TBC
			Women	TBC	TBC
		Backstroke 200 m	Men	TBC	TBC
			Women	TBC	TBC
		Individual Medley 200 m	Men	TBC	TBC
			Women	TBC	TBC
		Individual Medley 400 m	Men	TBC	TBC
			Women	TBC	TBC
		Medley 4 x 100 m Relay	Men	TBC	TBC
			Women	TBC	TBC
	Synchro-nised Swimming	Technical Routine - Solo	Women	Sat 18 14:10	Sat 18 03:10
		Technical Routine - Duet	Women	Sat 18 15:20	Sat 18 04:20
		Free Routine - Solo	Women	Sun 19 14:11	Sun 19 03:11

(*Contd.*)

Sport	Discipline	Event	Class	Scheduled Time of Final	
				Local	GMT
		Free Routine - Duet	Women	Sun 19 15:29	Sun 19 04:29
Athletics		100 m	Men	Mon 20 21:30	Mon 20 10:30
			Men EAD T12	Mon 20 20:05	Mon 20 09:05
			Women	Mon 20 21:20	Mon 20 10:20
			Women EAD T37	Mon 20 18:40	Mon 20 07:40
		200 m	Men	Thu 23 21:50	Thu 23 10:50
			Men EAD T46	Thu 23 19:32	Thu 23 08:32
			Women	Thu 23 21:40	Thu 23 10:40
		400 m	Men	Wed 22 21:20	Wed 22 10:20
			Women	Tue 21 21:40	Tue 21 10:40
		800 m	Men	Thu 23 20:50	Thu 23 09:50
			Women	Fri 24 20:42	Fri 24 09:42
			Women EAD T54	Fri 24 18:35	Fri 24 07:35
		1,500 m	Men	Sat 25 19:30	Sat 25 08:30
			Women	Tue 21 19:30	Tue 21 08:30
		5,000 m	Men	Mon 20 21:45	Mon 20 10:45
			Women	Fri 24 21:35	Fri 24 10:35
		10,000 m	Men	Sat 25 20:00	Sat 25 09:00
			Women	Tue 21 20:05	Tue 21 09:05
		3,000 m Steeplechase	Men	Fri 24 20:23	Fri 24 09:23
			Women	Wed 22 19:55	Wed 22 08:55
		100 m Hurdles	Women	Fri 24 19:10	Fri 24 08:10
		110 m Hurdles	Men	Tue 21 18:50	Tue 21 07:50
		400 m Hurdles	Men	Thu 23 19:50	Thu 23 08:50
			Women	Thu 23 21:15	Thu 23 10:15
		Decathlon	Men	Mon 20 10:05	Sun 19 23:05
		Heptathlon	Women	Tue 21 10:20	Mon 20 23:20
		4 x 100 m Relay	Men	Sat 25 19:00	Sat 25 08:00
			Women	Sat 25 18:40	Sat 25 07:40
		4 x 400 m Relay	Men	Sat 25 21:40	Sat 25 10:40
			Women	Sat 25 21:15	Sat 25 10:15

(Contd.)

Sport	Discipline	Event	Class	Scheduled Time of Final	
				Local	GMT
		Pole Vault	Men	Fri 24 20:18	Fri 24 09:18
			Women	Sat 25 19:00	Sat 25 08:00
		High Jump	Men	Wed 22 19:15	Wed 22 08:15
			Women	Thu 23 20:10	Thu 23 09:10
		Long Jump	Men	Wed 22 19:48	Wed 22 08:48
			Women	Fri 24 19:20	Fri 24 08:20
		Triple Jump	Men	Sat 25 18:50	Sat 25 07:50
			Women	Tue 21 18:40	Tue 21 07:40
		Shot Put	Men	Mon 20 19:42	Mon 20 08:42
			Women	Wed 22 20:15	Wed 22 09:15
		Seated Shot Put	Women EAD	Mon 20 10:00	Sun 19 23:00
		Hammer	Men	Fri 24 18:30	Fri 24 07:30
			Women	Mon 20 18:35	Mon 20 07:35
		Discus	Men	Thu 23 20:45	Thu 23 09:45
			Women	Tue 21 20:10	Tue 21 09:10
		Seated Discus	Men EAD	Wed 22 10:00	Tue 21 23:00
		Javelin	Men	Sat 25 18:30	Sat 25 07:30
			Women	Sun 19 12:30	Sun 19 01:30
		20 km Walk	Men	Mon 20 12:00	Mon 20 01:00
			Women	Mon 20 09:00	Sun 19 22:00
		50 km Walk	Men	Fri 24 08:00	Thu 23 21:00
		Marathon	Men	Sun 19 10:15	Sat 18 23:15
			Women	Sun 19 09:30	Sat 18 22:30
Bad-minton		Singles	Men	Sun 26 10:00	Sat 25 23:00
			Women	Sun 26 10:50	Sat 25 23:50
		Doubles	Men	Sun 26 11:50	Sun 26 00:50
			Women	Sun 26 12:50	Sun 26 01:50
			Mixed	Sun 26 13:50	Sun 26 02:50
		Team	Mixed	Sun 26 10:00	Sat 25 23:00
Basket ball			Men	Fri 24 20:15	Fri 24 09:15
			Women	Thu 23 20:15	Thu 23 09:15
Boxing		Light Fly-weight 48 kg	Men	Sat 25 19:00	Sat 25 08:00
		Flyweight 51 kg	Men	Sat 25 15:00	Sat 25 04:00
		Bantam-weight 54 kg	Men	Sat 25 19:25	Sat 25 08:25

(*Contd.*)

Sport	Discipline	Event	Class	Scheduled Time of Final	
				Local	GMT
		Feather-weight 57 kg	Men	Sat 25 15:15	Sat 25 04:15
		Lightweight 60 kg	Men	Sat 25 19:40	Sat 25 08:40
		Light Welterweight 64 kg	Men	Sat 25 15:40	Sat 25 04:40
		Welterweight 69 kg	Men	Sat 25 20:05	Sat 25 09:05
		Middleweight 75 kg	Men	Sat 25 16:00	Sat 25 05:00
		Light Heavyweight 81 kg	Men	Sat 25 20:30	Sat 25 09:30
		Heavyweight 91 kg	Men	Sat 25 16:25	Sat 25 05:25
		Super Heavyweight 91 kg+	Men	Sat 25 20:55	Sat 25 09:55
Cycling	Track	Sprint	Men	TBC	TBC
		Sprint	Women	TBC	TBC
		Team Sprint	Men	TBC	TBC
		500 m Time Trial	Women	TBC	TBC
		1,000 m Time Trial	Men	TBC	TBC
		3,000 m Individual Pursuit	Women	TBC	TBC
		4,000 m Individual Pursuit	Men	TBC	TBC
		4,000 m Team Pursuit	Men	TBC	TBC
		20 km Scratch Race	Men	TBC	TBC
		25 km Points Race	Women	TBC	TBC
		40 km Points Race	Men	TBC	TBC
		Keirin	Men	TBC	TBC
	Road	25 - 30 km Time Trial	Women	Fri 21 10:30	Thu 20 23:30

(Contd.)

Sport	Discipline	Event	Class	Scheduled Time of Final	
				Local	GMT
		30 - 40 km Time Trial	Men	Fri 21 13:00	Fri 21 02:00
		100 - 120 km Road Race	Women	Wed 26 09:00	Tue 25 22:00
		160 - 180 km Road Race	Men	Wed 26 13:00	Wed 26 02:00
	Mountain Bike	Cross Country	Men	Thu 23 14:00	Thu 23 03:00
			Women	Thu 23 10:30	Wed 22 23:30
Gym-nastics	Artistic	Artistic Individual All-Around	Men	Sat 18 13:30	Sat 18 02:30
			Women	Sat 18 19:00	Sat 18 08:00
		Artistic Individual Apparatus - Vault	Men	Tue 21 19:03	Tue 21 08:03
			Women	Mon 20 19:39	Mon 20 08:39
		Artistic Individual Apparatus - Uneven Bars	Women	Mon 20 20:51	Mon 20 09:51
		Artistic Individual Apparatus - Balance Beam	Women	Tue 21 19:39	Tue 21 08:39
		Artistic Individual Apparatus – Floor	Men	Mon 20 19:03	Mon 20 08:03
			Women	Tue 21 20:58	Tue 21 09:58
		Artistic Individual Apparatus-Parallel Bars	Men	Tue 21 20:20	Tue 21 09:20
		Artistic Individual Apparatus – Horizontal Bar	Men	Tue 21 21:39	Tue 21 10:39
		Artistic Individual Apparatus - Still Rings	Men	Mon 20 21:27	Mon 20 10:27
		Artistic Individual Apparatus - Pommel Horse	Men	Mon 20 20:15	Mon 20 09:15

(Contd.)

Sport	*Discipline*	*Event*	*Class*	*Scheduled Time of Final*	
				Local	*GMT*
		Artistic Team	Men	Mon 20 19:03	Mon 20 08:03
			Women	Mon 20 19:39	Mon 20 08:39
	Rhythmic	Rhythmic Individual All-Around	Women	Sat 25 12:30	Sat 25 01:30
		Rhythmic Individual Apparatus - Rope	Women	Sun 26 12:30	Sun 26 01:30
		Rhythmic Individual Apparatus - Ball	Women	Sun 26 13:18	Sun 26 02:18
		Rhythmic Individual Apparatus - Clubs	Women	Sun 26 14:00	Sun 26 03:00
		Rhythmic Individual Apparatus - Ribbon	Women	Sun 26 14:42	Sun 26 03:42
		Rhythmic Team	Women	Fri 24 18:00	Fri 24 07:00
Field Hockey			Men	Sun 26 13:00	Sun 26 02:00
			Women	Sat 25 13:00	Sat 25 02:00
Lawn Bowls		Singles	Men	Fri 24 19:00	Fri 24 08:00
			Women	Fri 24 17:00	Fri 24 06:00
		Pairs	Men	Wed 22 19:00	Wed 22 08:00
			Women	Wed 22 17:00	Wed 22 06:00
		Triples	Men	Mon 20 18:45	Mon 20 07:45
			Women	Mon 20 15:30	Mon 20 04:30
Netball			Women	Sun 26 16:00	Sun 26 05:00
Rugby Sevens			Men	Fri 17 21:52	Fri 17 10:52
Shooting	Clay Target	Trap	Men	Wed 22 10:00	Tue 21 23:00
			Women	Tue 21 10:00	Mon 20 23:00
		Trap Pairs	Men	Fri 17 10:00	Thu 16 23:00
			Women	Fri 17 10:00	Thu 16 23:00
		Skeet	Men	Sat 25 10:00	Fri 24 23:00
			Women	Fri 24 10:00	Thu 23 23:00
		Skeet Pairs	Men	Mon 20 10:00	Sun 19 23.00
			Women	Mon 20 10.00	Sun 19 23:00

(*Contd.*)

Sport	Discipline	Event	Class	Scheduled Time of Final	
				Local	GMT
		Double Trap	Men	Thu 23 10:00	Wed 22 23:00
			Women	Thu 23 10:00	Wed 22 23:00
		Double Trap Pairs	Men	Sun 19 10:00	Sat 18 23:00
			Women	Sun 19 10:00	Sat 18 23:00
	Pistol	10 m Air Pistol	Men	Wed 22 09:00	Tue 21 22:00
			Women	Thu 23 09:00	Wed 22 22:00
		10 m Air Pistol Pairs	Men	Sat 18 09:00	Fri 17 22:00
			Women	Sun 19 09:00	Sat 18 22:00
		25 m Rapid Fire Pistol	Men	Thu 23 09:00	Wed 22 22:00
		25 m Rapid Fire Pistol Pairs	Men	Sun 19 09:00	Sat 18 22:00
		25 m Pistol	Women	Tue 21 09:00	Mon 20 22:00
		25 m Pistol Pairs	Women	Fri 17 10:00	Thu 16 23:00
		25 m Centre Fire Pistol	Men	Fri 24 09:00	Thu 23 22:00
		25 m Centre Fire Pistol Pairs	Men	Mon 20 09:00	Sun 19 22:00
		25 m Standard Pistol	Men	Sat 25 09:00	Fri 24 22:00
		25 m Standard Pistol Pairs	Men	Sat 18 13:30	Sat 18 02:30
		50 m Pistol	Men	Tue 21 09:00	Mon 20 22:00
		50 m Pistol Pairs	Men	Fri 17 09:00	Thu 16 22:00
	Small Bore and Air Rifle	10 m Air Rifle	Men	Tue 21 09:00	Mon 20 22:00
			Women	Mon 20 09:00	Sun 19 22:00
		10 m Air Rifle Pairs	Men	Fri 17 09:00	Thu 16 22:00
			Women	Fri 17 11:30	Fri 17 00:30
		50 m Rifle 3 Position	Men	Fri 24 09:00	Thu 23 22:00
			Women	Thu 23 09:00	Wed 22 22:00
		50 m Rifle 3 Position Pairs	Men	Mon 20 09:00	Sun 19 22:00
			Women	Sun 19 09:00	Sat 18 22:00
		50 m Rifle Prone	Men	Thu 23 15:30	Thu 23 04:30
			Women	Wed 22 13:00	Wed 22 02:00

(Contd.)

Sport	*Discipline*	*Event*	*Class*	*Scheduled Time of Final*	
				Local	*GMT*
		50 m Rifle Prone Pairs	Men	Sat 18 11:00	Sat 18 00:00
			Women	Sat 18 13:00	Sat 18 02:00
	Full Bore Rifle	Singles	Open	Thu 23 10:00	Wed 22 23:00
		Pairs	Open	Sun 19 10:00	Sat 18 23:00
Squash		Singles	Men	TBC	TBC
			Women	TBC	TBC
		Doubles	Men	TBC	TBC
			Women	Sun 26 11:55	Sun 26 00:55
			Mixed	Sun 26 13:50	Sun 26 02:50
Table Tennis		Singles	Men	Sun 26 14:15	Sun 26 03:15
			Women	Sun 26 12:10	Sun 26 01:10
			Women EAD	Sun 26 10:30	Sat 25 23:30
		Doubles	Men	Sat 25 20:30	Sat 25 09:30
			Women	Sat 25 18:50	Sat 25 07:50
			Mixed	Fri 24 20:15	Fri 24 09:15
		Team	Men	Mon 20 18:15	Mon 20 07:15
			Women	Mon 20 16:00	Mon 20 05:00
Triathlon			Men	Sat 18 13:00	Sat 18 02:00
			Women	Sat 18 09:00	Fri 17 22:00
Weightlifting		48 kg category	Women	Thu 16 14:00	Thu 16 03:00
		53 kg category	Women	Fri 17 18:30	Fri 17 07:30
		56 kg category	Men	Thu 16 18:30	Thu 16 07:30
		58 kg category	Women	Sat 18 14:00	Sat 18 03:00
		62 kg category	Men	Fri 17 10:00	Thu 16 23:00
		63 kg category	Women	Sun 19 18:30	Sun 19 07:30
		69 kg category	Men	Sat 18 18:30	Sat 18 07:30
			Women	Mon 20 14:00	Mon 20 03:00
		75 kg category	Women	Tue 21 18:30	Tue 21 07:30
		75 kg+ category	Women	Wed 22 14:00	Wed 22 03:00
		77 kg category	Men	Sun 19 14:00	Sun 19 03:00

(Contd)

Sport	Discipline	Event	Class	Scheduled Time of Final	
				Local	GMT
		85 kg category	Men	Mon 20 18:30	Mon 20 07:30
		94 kg category	Men	Tue 21 14:00	Tue 21 03:00
		105 kg category	Men	Wed 22 18:30	Wed 22 07:30
		105 kg+ category	Men	Thu 23 18:30	Thu 23 07:30
		Open Powerlifting	Men EAD	Fri 24 14:00	Fri 24 03:00

OPERATION ACOLYTE

Operation Acolyte was the name given to the Australian Defence Force's (ADF) contribution to providing security, ceremonial and general support to the 2006 Commonwealth Games held in Melbourne, Australia.

The ADF contributed approximately 2600 personnel to Operation Acolyte from across the three defence services (Army, Navy, Air Force), and was commanded by Brigadier Andrew Smith.

FESTIVAL MELBOURNE

Festival Melbourne2006 is a cultural event which ran concurrently with the 2006 Commonwealth Games in Melbourne.

Wednesday 15 March — Sunday 26 March

Welcome to Festival Melbourne2006 - twelve days of non-stop music, dance, circus, street theatre and visual arts from all the corners of the Commonwealth that will add an extra sparkle to your whole Games experience. Best of all, everything is free during the Games!

Over 2,500 world-class performing artists from across Australia and the Commonwealth will descend on Melbourne for the duration of the Games as part of the largest free cultural festival ever held in Australia. So when you come to cheer on the world's elite athletes you can also catch a concert, see a circus, stroll amongst street performers, be dazzled by visual spectacles, celebrate Victoria's Indigenous culture, enjoy an array of exhibitions and even join in yourself with public classes of dance from around the Commonwealth in Federation Square.

The city will be buzzing day and night at Federation Square, the Alexandra Gardens, the Sidney Myer Music Bowl, around the Arts Centre, at Docklands and right across the CBD. The excitement will also reach out across the state, with regional festivals in Ballarat, Geelong, Moe and Bendigo. And all the great experiences of Festival Melbourne2006 are free!

Festival Melbourne2006 is an integral part of the Melbourne 2006 Commonwealth Games and is proudly funded and supported by the Victorian and Australian Governments.

Melbourne—We did it!

His Royal Highness Prince Edward has formally closed the Commonwealth Games, after a typically Melbourne Closing Ceremony.

Aussie rockers Grinspoon started the Ceremony with a bang, the first of a line-up of Australian music greats gracing the MCG celebrations.

Grinspoon performed centre-stage, surrounded by brightly costumed ballerinas wearing the colours of Australian Rules Football teams. Singer/songwriter Paul Kelly followed, performing his hit 'Leaps and Bounds' to an appreciative Melbourne crowd, before Ben Lee and BodyRockers took to the stage.

Sarah Blasko performed the Crowded House hit 'Don't Dream It's Over' in a tribute to the thousands of Games Volunteers, as snowflakes fell across the stadium to represent Melbourne's infamously unpredictable 'four seasons in one day' weather—thankfully absent for the duration of the Games.

This was the first time that volunteers have been invited to actively participate in a Closing Ceremony to receive their vote of thanks face-to-face.

Then followed a curtain-call for the Flag-bearers of all the competing nations, finishing with the raising of the Australian flag as a giant upside-down globe floated above the stadium, showing Australia to be on top of the world.

Melbourne 2006 Chairman Ron Walker addressed the crowd, saying the Closing Ceremony was a celebration of "the greatest coalition of Commonwealth nations ever seen."

"We have all been united by the moment," Mr. Walker said. "Melbourne – we did it!"

The Commonwealth Games Federation (CGF) flag was then lowered by a party representing Australia's three emergency services, and handed to Suresh Kalmadi, Chairman of the Organising Committee for the 2010 Delhi Games, before 800 Indian performers marked the hand over of the Games with a Bollywood spectacular.

Among the performers were 12 Bollywood superstars, including actress and former Miss Universe Aishwarya Rai, who played the lead in the recent film 'Bride and Prejudice'.

Commonwealth Games Federation (CGF) President, Mike Fennell, also named Indian Shooting athlete Samaresh Jung as the winner of the inaugural David Dixon Award.

Jung won an incredible seven medals at the Games, five gold, one silver and one bronze and set three new Games records along the way.

The CGF established the David Dixon Award, in memory of the man who served as its Honorary Secretary for 17 years, to honour the outstanding athlete at each Commonwealth Games.

His Royal Highness Prince Edward then formally closed the Commonwealth Games, before Moonee Pond's most famous housewife, Dame Edna Everage, addressed the MCG via satellite and introduced a stadium full of 1000 'Edna lookalikes'.

Musical legend John Farnham started the finale of the unforgettable evening, performing as athletes spilled out onto the field to party under the stars.

His closing song, 'You're The Voice', triggered an explosive city-wide pyrotechnics display - the final fireworks of Melbourne 2006.

Ceremonies Artistic Director and Executive Producer Andrew Walsh said, "If the Opening Ceremony was about theatre, the Closing is distinctly Melbourne."

The host of the 2010 Games, Delhi, staged a stunning showcase of Indian culture at the Closing Ceremony, showcasing its plans for the 19th Commonwealth Games.

Delhi 2010 will be a fantastic opportunity to bring the Commonwealth Games to a new generation of fans. India has a population of over 1 billion, of which half are under the age of 25.

India's fantastic contribution to the evening started with the sounds of shankhs and chimes filling the MCG, as giant video screens displayed images of India—a nation of diverse cultures, magnificent landscapes and a rich heritage.

Dancer Isha Sharwani treated the packed stadium to a yoga-inspired dance, as dancers with petals formed a rose which opened to reveal India's Miss World, Aishwarya Rai.

Bollywood superstar Rai began her career as a model and was crowned Miss World in 1994, before starting a hugely successful film career.

Bollywood - the informal name given to the hugely popular Mumbai-based film industry - is a significant part of the popular culture of not only India but also the Middle East, parts of Africa and south-east Asia. The output of the Indian film industry is the largest in the world in terms of number of films produced and audience tickets sold.

The Indian extravaganza continued with golden rays unfurling all around the stage to represent the sun in all its glory, as monuments of India and Delhi were projected onto the main stage.

A high-energy Bhangra performance followed - a lively form of north Indian folk music and dance - featuring Saif Ali Khan, Rani Mukherjee and hundreds of brightly costumed dancers.

As a grand finale, the theme song for Delhi 2010 was performed by some of India's finest singers including Sonu Nigam, Shiamak Davar, Sunidhi Chauhan and Shreya Ghoshal, before the MCG erupted in a dramatic pyrotechnics display, featuring the three colours of the Indian flag - saffron, white and green.

Nameste! See you in Delhi 2010! Swagatam!

Commonwealth Games Live Sites

Commonwealth Games Live Sites will be operating at outdoor venues around the city providing central locations for people to meet and enjoy the spirit of the Games by watching the sporting competition on giant screens.

Join in the fun at Live Sites at the following locations in your neighbourhood.

All Live Site start and finish times are approximate and subject to change. Sporting coverage will vary daily and will be subject to the television broadcast schedule. Sites operating for the Opening Ceremony will be open from approximately 6:30pm with actual ceremony coverage starting at 7:30pm.

Live Site Location Operating Hours

Alexandra Gardens
Opening Ceremony: 15 March 6:30pm - 11:00pm
Marathon: 19 March 9:00am - 2:00pm
Cycling Road Race & Closing Ceremony: 26 March 9:00am - 11:00pm

Melbourne Museum Plaza, Carlton Gardens

Opening Ceremony: 15 March 6:30pm - 11:00pm
Games time: 16-26 March 9:00am - 10:00pm

Queensbridge Square, Southbank Promenade

Opening Ceremony: 15 March 6:30pm - 11:00pm
Games time: 16-26 March 9:00am - 11:00pm

Federation Square

Opening Ceremony: 15 March 6:30pm - 11:00pm
Games time: 16-26 March 9:00am – midnight

Sidney Myer Music Bowl

Cycling Road Race & Closing Ceremony: 26 March 9:00am - 11:00pm

Waterfront City, Docklands

Queen's Baton Relay & Opening Ceremony: 15 March from 3:00pm - 11:00pm
Games time: 16-26 March 9:00am - 11:00pm

South Beach Reserve, St. Kilda

Triathlon, Marathon and Cycling Time Trial events: 17-21 March 9:00am - 11:00pm

About Festival Melbourne2006

Chairman's Message

What an enormous honour it is for our city to be hosting the Commonwealth Games; to see the best athletes of the Commonwealth coming together to compete at such a high level, and for us to celebrate their shared drive for excellence through sport. And what better way to enhance this wonderful Games sporting experience than to provide the opportunity for the best performing and visual artists from these countries to also come together to showcase their artistic skills and cultural diversity, and allow us to marvel at their energy and talent?

Welcome to Festival Melbourne2006, twelve days of non-stop music, dance, circus, street theatre and visual arts from all the corners of the Commonwealth. From large-scale performance works and exhibitions through to intimate events, workshops and cultural exchanges, Festival Melbourne2006 will entertain, challenge and add another joyful dimension to your whole Games experience. When you come to cheer on the worlds elite athletes, you can also catch a concert, see a circus, stroll amongst street performers, be dazzled by visual spectacles, and enjoy an array of exhibitions. You can join in, with public classes of dance from around the Commonwealth in Federation Square, lunchtime forums with the artists, and Artplays activity workshops for children. And you can celebrate Victoria's own Indigenous culture with a showcase of the best of Victorias Indigenous businesses, artists and performers. Throughout the Games, Melbourne will be buzzing - day and night! The excitement will reach out across the State centred around regional festivals in Ballarat, Bendigo, Geelong and Moe. Best of all, all the great experiences of the Festival are free!

Festival Melbourne2006 is also providing opportunities for artists and local communities to benefit from an exciting programme of cultural exchanges that has been put in place to celebrate the cultural diversity of the Commonwealth. For example, three leading youth circuses one from South Africa and two from Australia - have been living and working together to create a new, collaborative work, 3wAyXchange, to be performed under the Big Top in the Alexandra Gardens. And an extensive Youth Masterclass Programme brings some of the world's master percussionists together with Australia's leading tertiary percussion students to exchange ideas and skills. Their efforts will culminate in a public performance at the Sidney Myer Music Bowl in the All Star World Percussion Spectacular. Meanwhile artists from South Africa, Malta, Mauritius, Maldives, Sri Lanka, India, Samoa and New Zealand have been working in conversation with local artists and communities, using their traditional skills to produce work to be exhibited in Common Goods: Cultures Meet Through Craft at Melbourne Museum. The cultural legacy of these exchanges will live on long after the last star in Festival Melbourne2006 has performed.

It is my very great pleasure to invite you to come and help us to celebrate what we have in common and to appreciate what makes us different by sharing in Festival Melbourne2006.

6

India at the Commonwealth Games: An Analysis

SPORTS HISTORY OF INDIA

Sports have been the one podium to anchor the spirits of Indians. Sports not only promoted the country internationally, but also served as a pedestal to express and answer national rivalries. Who else can experience the joy and the pride which Indians feel for their achievements on the Oval Pitch! The ecstasy of triumph can only be felt with our very own dada flinging his shirt at Lord's. To say that 'sports have added vigour to the Indian aroma on the world stage' should not be considered as an exaggeration. This youthful sportsman spirit has not reserved itself to the young guns of India; it has a spell over the entire nation irrespective of age, sex, religion and even the understanding of a game.

An Indo-Pak cricket match is not only a matter of concern for sport-literates—it elicits a sizzle which unites the whole family, the whole community, the whole city, the whole generation, the whole nation. Elderly grandfathers might not know what do the players on the field need to do to make India win but they know that India needs to win.

The enthusiasm of a child waits for the glitter in the eye of his father watching the game when a run is scored. Envisaging this zeal, India's sports minister Uma Bharti could not resist herself on the occasion of Indian victory in the Champions Challenge hockey tournament held in Kuala Lumpur and announced it to the world by quoting, "This is the beginning of a distinguished and exciting chapter in Indian sports history." Everybody knew that the chapter was opened in the previous year by Viswanathan Anand and

Pullela Gopichand in their stirring deeds for chess and badminton respectively.

Such vivid descriptions of a nation with such diversified sports behaviours would leave a curiosity in any sane mind about the country's own accomplishments. Therefore, I would like to bring to the fore the triumphs achieved by our spearheads of various sports. Hockey is officially the national sport of India in which she holds an impressive record boasting of 8 Olympic Golds. While bidding a good-bye, the year 2001 witnessed India joining the world's 'elite top six club' in hockey. The feat was achieved by emerging as champions in Champions Challenge Trophy. At one point the team was almost down and out; however, once again the team did a phoenix and the paradigm resulted in the South African defeat.

While talking of individual performances, Leander Paes made sure that the presence of Indian tennis is felt by the world. In the year 1990, he became third Indian to lift Wimbledon Junior Championship. He managed to earn India a bronze in tennis singles of 1996 Olympics. The task is now overtaken by the young lady. Ever since she emerged on the global arena, Sania Mirza never looked back. Indian tennis was brought to the fore with Sania's continuous success. Her consistent performance made her first ever Indian to thrust into the top 50 of WTA rankings. Year 2005 gifted her the Hyderabad Open Trophy in the month February to make her first Indian woman to win WTA Tourney.

INDIA AT THE 2006 COMMONWEALTH GAMES

India was represented at the 2006 Commonwealth Games in Melbourne by a 270-member strong contingent comprising 183 sportspersons and 77 officials. 2004 Summer Olympics silver medalist Rajyavardhan Singh Rathore was the flag bearer for India.

Samresh Jung was chosen as the winner of the inaugural David Dixon Award, which honours the outstanding athlete at each Commonwealth Games. Jung won seven medals at the 2006 Games, five gold, one silver and one bronze and set three new Games records along the way. As in the previous 2002 Commonwealth Games, India came fourth overall in the medals table, behind Australia, England and Canada. India is also the host nation for the 2010 Commonwealth Games, which will be held in Delhi, India's Capital.

Medals

Gold

Shooting:

- Samaresh Jung, Men's 50m Pistol
- Gagan Narang, Men's 10m Air Rifle
- Tejaswini Sawant, Women's 10m Air Rifle
- Samaresh Jung and Jaspal Rana, Men's 25m Centre Fire Pistol (Pairs)
- Samaresh Jung and Vivek Singh, Men's 10m Air Pistol (Pairs)
- Samaresh Jung and Ronak Pandit, Men's 25m Standard Pistol (Pairs)
- Tejaswini Sawant and Avneet Sidhu, Women's 10m Air Rifle (Pairs)
- Abhinav Bindra and Gagan Narang, Men's 10m Air Rifle (Pairs)
- Abhinav Bindra and Gagan Narang, Men's 50m Rifle 3 Positions (Pairs)
- Saroja Jhuthu and Sushma Rana, Women's 25m Pistol (Pairs)
- Vijay Kumar and Pemba Tamang, Men's 25m Rapid Fire Pistol (Pairs)
- Anuja Jung, Women's 50m Rifle 3 Positions
- Samresh Jung, Men's 10m Air Pistol
- Vijay Kumar, Men's 25m Rapid Fire Pistol
- Rajyavardhan Singh Rathore, Men's Double Trap
- Gagan Narang, Men's 50m Rifle 3 Positions

Weightlifting:

- Yumnam Chanu, Women's 58kg
- Kunjarani Devi, Women's 48kg
- Geeta Rani, Women's +75 kg

Table Tennis:

- Sharath Achanta, Men's Singles
- Men's Team Event

Boxing:

- Akhil Kumar, Bantamweight 54kg

Silver

Shooting:

- Avneet Kaur Sidhu, Women's 10m Air Rifle
- Samresh Jung and Vivek Singh, Men's 50m Pistol (Pairs)
- Rajyavardhan Singh Rathore and Vikram Bhatnagar, Men's Double Trap (Pairs)
- Anjali Bhagwat and Anuja Jung, Women's 50m Rifle 3 Positions (Pairs)
- Pemba Tamang, Men's 25m Rapid Fire Pistol
- Vivek Singh, Men's 10m Air Pistol
- Abhinav Bindra, Men's 50m Rifle 3 Positions

Weightlifting:

- Mohammed Asdullah, Men's 77kg
- Vicky Batta, Women's 56kg
- Arun Murugesan, Men's 62kg
- Laishram Monika Devi, Women's 69kg
- Simple Kaur BHUMRAH, Women's +75kg

Athletics:

- Seema Antil, Women's Discus Throw
- Women's 4 × 600m Relay

Boxing:

- Vijender Kumar, Welterweight 69kg
- Harpreet Singh, Heavyweight 91kg

Hockey:

- India women's national field hockey team

Bronze

Badminton:

- Chetan Anand, Men's Singles
- Mixed Team Event

Table Tennis:

- Women's Team Event

Shooting:

- Abhinav Bindra, Men's 10m Air Rifle
- Sanjeev Rajput, Men's 50m Rifle Prone
- Manavjit Singh Sandhu, Men's Trap
- Samresh Jung, Men's 25m Centre Fire Pistol

Weightlifting:

- Sudhir Kumar Chitradurga, Men's 69kg

Athletics:

- Ranjith Kumar Jayaseelan, Men's Seated Discus Throw EAD

Boxing:

- Jitender Kumar, Flyweight 51kg
- Varghese Johnson, Super Heavyweight +91kg

India's Teams at the 2006 Commonwealth Games

Field Hockey

Men's Team

- Bharat Kumar Chetri
- Deepak Thakur
- Kanwalpreet Singh
- Sandeep Singh
- Tejbir Singh
- Ignace Tirkey
- Prabodh Tirkey
- Didar Singh
- Baljit Singh
- Rajpal Singh
- Sardara Singh
- Viren Rasquinha
- Arjun Halappa
- William Xalxo
- Vikram Pillay
- Tushar Khandekar

Head Coach: Rajinder Singh

Women's Team

- Helen Mary
- Kanti Baa
- Nilima Kujur
- Rajwinder Kaur
- Sumrai Tete
- Masira Surin
- Subhadra Pradhan
- Asunta Lakra
- Jyoti Sunita Kullu
- Mamta Kharab
- Jasjeet Kaur Handa
- Surinder Kaur
- Saba Anjum Karim
- Sanggai Chanu
- Sarita Lakra
- Rajni Bala

Head Coach: Maharaj Krishan Kaushik

COMMONWEALTH BUSINESS CLUB INDIA

The Commonwealth Business Club India will strive to draw high-power business delegations from offshore to India during the Games and enable them to leverage the unfolding opportunity for transacting business and enjoy the Games.

The OC CWG Delhi 2010 joined hands with the Federation of Indian Chambers of Commerce and Industry (FICCI) on 22 September 2010 to effectively use the Delhi 2010 platform to facilitate deeper economic and trade relationships amongst the Commonwealth fraternity.

This coming together of a national sports body and a national business chamber with a huge global presence and outreach is expected to galvanise the sporting and the business communities into spearheading and spreading the culture of sports and endeavour to raise sports sponsorships and also market India as a preferred business partner and destination.

Towards this end, the OC CWG Delhi 2010 and FICCI have signed a Memorandum of Understanding (MoU) to enable the OC

CWG Delhi 2010-led Commonwealth Business Club India (CBCI), achieve these objectives.

Going forward, OC CWG Delhi 2010 and FICCI will work towards spreading the culture of sport. They will share information on events, publications and activities of interest to the organisations and their stakeholders, work towards raising awareness among sports bodies and academic institutions and ensure safe working and sporting environment.

IMPACT OF COMMONWEALTH GAMES 2010 ON INDIA

So, the question that is in our minds is that, how exactly it affects us and what is all this fuss about? Why is government spending so much money in all the commonwealth games event, and estimated Rs. 37.50 billion ($805.81 million)? The answer is, that apart from being just a matter of reputation for the country, it is a matter of opportunity and business. Experts say that 2010 will be a year of business for tourism and sports and many other related industries. That will give India return for all its investments in a very efficient way. India has been holding many different games events in past:

- 1951 - 1st Asian Games, New Delhi, India
- 1982 - 9th Asian Games, New Delhi, India

That was the time when India was recognised well and appraised for its efforts. As far as Indian performance in sports is concerned, we are all very much aware that the conditioning that our children have in schools and homes is anti-sports. There are different sayings in India to discourage a child from getting into sports. Whatever one has accomplished in India, be it a Sachin Tendulkar or a Sania Mirza, it was all in a very raw form and without any professional practice, conditioning and guidance. It is a matter of great debate. This even reflects truly that what we know is only about the Flyovers, metros, roads, hotels and business plans than we talk about the sports and the sports personalities. We hardly know about them. But, on the contrary, the performance in the year 2006 in the Commonwealth Games in Melbourne has been splendid. India ranked fourth in the tally. Let us see how it exactly turns out to be for India in 2010 but this is clear from the media, businesses and politicians that the main focus is on infrastructure. To rebuild everything as if everything is truly international experience. Eventually, we all know what is going to happen, the rise in prices for property, stuffs of general use (there was no mother dairy till the 1982 Asiad happened, they removed all the cows from houses and this concept was floated).

Government of India has long back initiated the process for Bed and Breakfast facility for economic stay. Also, the Ashoka Hotel is official hotel for the Commonwealth Games 2010 official guests.

For Best Shopping Experience

For Inexpensive Items

- Janpath
- Sarojini Nagar
- Dilli Haat
- Karol Bagh.

For Brand Shopping

- Visit Gurgaon Shopping Malls
- Ansals Plaza.

The Places in and around New Delhi that you must see

Places to see within New Delhi & National Capital Region

- Akshardham Temple
- Qutub Minaar
- Laal Quila or Red Fort
- Jantar Mantar
- Humayun's Tomb
- India Gate
- Purana Quila
- Lotus Temple
- Jaama Masjid.

Places to see around New Delhi

- Jaipur
- Agra
- Udaipur
- Gurgaon.

7

2010 Commonwealth Games in Delhi: A Brief Overview

2010 COMMONWEALTH GAMES: AN INTRODUCTION

The 2010 Commonwealth Games are the nineteenth edition of the Commonwealth Games, and the ninth to be held under that name. The Games are scheduled to be held in New Delhi, India between 3 October and 14 October 2010. The games will be the largest multi-sport event conducted to date in Delhi and India generally, which has previously hosted the Asian Games in 1951 and 1982. The opening ceremony is scheduled to take place at the Jawaharlal Nehru Stadium, Delhi. It will also be the first time the Commonwealth Games will be held in India and the second time the event has been held in Asia (after 1998).

In addition to the Commonwealth Games, the city of Pune, India hosted the 3rd Commonwealth Youth Games between October 12 and 18, 2008. The Youth Games offered nine sports: athletics, badminton, boxing, shooting, swimming, table tennis, tennis, weightlifting and wrestling.

Games Preparation

In January 2005, the Commonwealth Games Federation vice-president Raja Randhir Singh expressed concern that Delhi was behind schedule in forming an organising committee. On 18 January 2008, however, the Commonwealth Games Federation expressed its approval of Delhi's progress.

On 15 October 2009, Jarnail Singh, a former Secretary of the Government of India was appointed as the Chief Executive Officer of the Organising Committee.

India's Sports Minister will head the apex committee for conducting the games while the Indian Olympic Association president Suresh Kalmadi will head the organising committee. The Games will be held from the 3rd to 14 October 2010.

The total budget estimated for hosting the 19th Commonwealth is US$ 1.6 billion and this amount excludes non sports related infrastructure development in the city like airports, roads and other structures. This makes the 2010 Commonwealth Games as the most expensive Commonwealth Games ever (compared to Manchester 2002 - approx. US$420 million, and Melbourne 2006 - approx. US$ 1.1 billion).

Infrastructure

Delhi already has many international features of a modern and well-planned city. However, to get ready for the huge influx of tourists visiting Delhi during the Games, the Government of India has taken many steps to improve the city. This includes city beautification, transportation development, upgrading of many old structures etc.

Transport

Delhi proposed a four-lane, 2.2 km underground stretch from Lodhi Road to trans-Yamuna, linking the Games Village to the Jawaharlal Nehru Stadium and reducing travelling time for athletes travelling between the Village and the Stadium by six minutes.

In response to concerns over the large number of trains that pass by the Delhi metropolitan region daily, construction of road under-bridges and over-bridges along railway lines has been started.

To expand road infrastructure, flyovers, cloverleaf flyovers, and bridges have been planned to provide connectivity to the Games Village, to sports venues, to hospitals, and for intra-city connectivity. Road-widening projects have been under process, with an emphasis being placed on expanding national highways. To improve traffic flow on existing road, plans are underway to make both the inner and outer Ring roads signal free.

To support its commitment to mass transport, nine corridors have been identified and are being constructed as High Capacity Bus Systems (for example, one from Ambedkar Nagar to Red Fort). Six of these corridors are expected to be operational in 2010.

Additionally, the Delhi Metro will be expanded to accommodate more people and boost the use of public transport during the 2010 games. By then it will have the second longest network in the world and later the longest, which will be more than 420 km. To achieve this exponential increase in the network's length, the Delhi Metro has deployed 14 tunnel boring machines (TBMs). The Delhi Metro reports that no country in Asia has ever put to work so many TBMs at the same time.

To further support air travel, the Indira Gandhi International Airport is being modernised, expanded, and upgraded. By the 2010 games, a new terminal (Terminal 3) will have been constructed at a cost of nearly US$ 1.94 billion, with the capability to cater to more than 37 million passengers a year by 2010 and the planned expansion programme will increase its capacity to handle 100 million passengers by 2030. Terminal 3 will be a two tier building, with the bottom floor being the arrivals area, and the top being a departures area. This terminal will have over 130 check in counters, 55 aerobridges, 30 parking bays, 72 immigration counters, 15 X-ray screening areas, duty free shops, and much more. The airport will also have a new runway to cater more than 75 plus flights an hour; the runway will be more than 4400 metres long and one of Asia's longest. The entire airport will be connected to the city via a 6 lane highway (National Highway 8) and the Delhi Metro.

Energy Consumption

To prepare for the energy-usage spike during the Games and to end chronic power cuts in Delhi, the government is undertaking a large power-production initiative to increase power production to 7,000 MW (from the current 4,500 MW). To achieve this goal, the government plans to streamline the power distribution process, direct additional energy to Delhi, and construct new power plants. In fact, the government has promised that by 2010, Delhi will have a surplus of power.

Security

In preparation for the Games and to promote security at major tourist destinations, Indian states will be deploying a force of "tourist police" far before the Games begin. These tourism police are regular state police forces, but will be trained to handle tourist-related aspects. A number of states have already implemented this programme; other states are expected to emulate this model within the end of the year.

Tourism

India is expected to use the Games to provide a major boost to tourism in India. According to official estimates, two million foreign tourists and 3.5 million domestic tourists are likely to arrive in Delhi in 2010 as a result of the Games. To prepare for this influx, the government is providing tax incentives for hotel rooms to be constructed in India, with a focus on tourist regions of Agra and Jaipur.

Additionally, the government has extended a five-year tax rebate to the tourism industry to create jobs and increase development.

Delays

In September 2009, Commonwealth Games federation Chief Mike Fennell reported that the games were at risk of falling behind schedule and that it was "reasonable to conclude that the current situation poses a serious risk to the Commonwealth Games in 2010". A report by the Indian Government released several months prior found that construction work on 13 out of the 19 sports venues was behind schedule. The Chief of the Indian Olympic Association Randhir Singh has also expressed his concerns regarding the current state of affairs. Singh has called for the revamp of the games' organising committees commenting that India now has to "retrieve the games". Other Indian officials have also expressed dismay at the ongoing delays but they have stated that they are confident that India will succesfully host the games and do so on time.

Other Preparation

In addition to physical preparation, India and Delhi will be offering a myriad of amenities to all athletes. These include traditional Commonwealth Games services, such as free accommodation for all athletes, a modern, comfortable Games Village, cutting-edge health facilities, security, a pollution-free environment, entertainment for non-competition times, transportation, and other unique amenities as well. Delhi will also be offering all athletes a free trip to the famed Taj Mahal and will provide a reserved lane for participants on selected highways.

The Delhi High Court is also set to implement a series of "mobile courts" to be dispatched throughout Delhi to relocate migrant beggars from Delhi streets. The mobile courts would consider each beggar on a case-by-case basis to determine whether the beggar should be sent back to his/her state of residence, or be permitted to remain in government-shelters.

In preparation for a rush of English-speaking tourists for the Games, the Delhi Government is implementing a programme to teach English to low-income individuals who will have a high-frequency of contact with tourists. This subset includes city cab drivers, waiters, gatemen, and service staff. Over the past two years, the city has successfully taught 2,000 drivers English, and is continuing the programme to reach as many as possible before the Games. The city plans to teach 1,000 people English per month, and hopes to reach everyone necessary by March 2009. In addition to Delhi, the Indian Government plans to expand the programme to teach people in local tourist destinations, including Agra and Mathura in Uttar Pradesh, Bhopal and Gwalior in Madhya Pradesh, Gaya in Bihar and Puri in Orissa.

Participating Nations

There are currently 71 nations planning to field teams at the 2010 Commonwealth Games. In alphabetical order, these nations are:

- Anguilla
- Antigua and Barbuda
- Australia
- Bahamas
- Bangladesh
- Barbados
- Belize
- Bermuda
- Botswana
- British Virgin Islands
- Brunei
- Cameroon
- Canada
- Cayman Islands
- Cook Islands
- Cyprus
- Dominica
- England
- Falkland Islands
- Gambia
- Ghana
- Gibraltar
- Grenada
- Guernsey
- Guyana
- India
- Isle of man
- Jamaica
- Jersey
- Kenya
- Kiribati
- Lesotho
- Malawi
- Malaysia
- Maldives
- Malta

- Mauritius
- Montserrat
- Mozambique
- Namibia
- Nauru
- New Zealand
- Nigeria
- Niue
- Norfolk Island
- Northern Ireland
- Pakistan
- Papua New Guinea
- Saint Helena
- Saint Kitts and Nevis
- Saint Lucia
- Saint Vincent and the Grenadines
- Samoa
- Scotland
- Seychelles
- Sierra Leone
- Singapore
- Solomon Islands
- South Africa
- Sri Lanka
- Swaziland
- Tanzania
- Tokelau
- Tonga
- Trinidad anc Tobago
- Turks and Caicos Islands
- Tuvalu
- Uganda
- Vanuatu
- Wales
- Zambia

Sports

There are 17 disciplines planned for the 2010 Commonwealth Games.

- Aquatics
- Archery
- Athletics (track and field)
- Badminton
- Boxing
- Cycling
- Gymnastics
- Hockey
- Lawn Bowls
- Netball
- Rugby sevens
- Shooting
- Squash
- Table Tennis
- Tennis
- Weightlifting
- Wrestling

Kabaddi will also be a demonstration sport at the 2010 Games.

The triathlon appears likely to be excluded from these games as there is no suitable location for the swimming stage. The organisers have also proposed removing basketball, but want to include archery, tennis, and billiards and snooker for men. Cricket, although in strong demand, may not make a come-back as the Board of Control for Cricket in India were not keen on a Twenty20 tournament, but the organisers did not want a one day tournament.

Calendar

The official calendar for the 2010 Commonwealth Games is as follows:

? Opening ceremony ? Event competitions ? Closing ceremony

October	3	4	5	6	7	8	9	10	11	12	13	14	Venue
Ceremonies	?											?	Jawaharlal Nehru Stadium
Aquatics		?	?	?	?	?	?	?	?	?	?		SPM Swimming Pool Complex
Archery													I.G. Indoor Stadium Complex & India Gate / Red Fort
Athletics				?	?	?	?	?	?	?	?		Jawaharlal Nehru Stadium
Badminton		?	?	?	?	?	?	?	?	?	?		Siri Fort Sports Complex
Boxing		?	?	?	?	?	?	?	R	?			Talkatora Indoor Stadium
Cycling		?	?	?	?		?				?		I.G. Indoor Stadium Complex
Gymnastics		?	?	?	R	?	?		?	?	?		I.C. Indoor Stadium Complex
Hockey		?	?	?	?	?	?	?	?	?	?		Maj. Dhyan Chand National Stadium
Lawn Bowls		?	?	?	?	?	?	?	?	?			Jawaharlal Nehru Stadium
Netball		?	?	?	?	?	?	?	?	?	?		Tyagaraj Sports Complex
Rugby 7s			?	?									Delhi University
Shooting		T	?	?	?	?	?	?	?	?	?		Dr. Karni Singh Shooting Range
Squash		?	?	?	?	?	?	?	?	?	?		Siri Fort Sports Complex
Table Tennis		?	?	?	?	?	?	?	?	?	?		Yamuna Sports Complex
Tennis													RK Tennis Complex
Weightlifting			?	?	?	?	?	?	?	?			Jawaharlal Nehru Stadium
Wrestling			?	?	?	?							I.G. Indoor Stadium Complex
October	3	4	5	6	7	8	9	10	11	12	13	14	Venue

Venues

Existing and new stadia will be used to house the following sports: Archery, Aquatics, Athletics, Badminton, Boxing, Cycling, Elite Athletes with a Disability (EAD) Events, Gymnastics, Hockey, Lawn Bowls, Netball, Rugby 7s, Shooting, Squash, Table Tennis, Tennis, Weightlifting and Wrestling. Specific venues for 2010 games in Delhi are following:

- Jawaharlal Nehru Stadium - Opening and Closing ceremonies, Athletics, Lawn bowls, Weightlifting
- Dhyan Chand National Stadium - Hockey

- Indira Gandhi Arena - Archery, Cycling, Gymnastics, Wrestling
- Delhi University sports complex - Rugby 7s
- Tyagaraj Sports Complex - Netball
- Siri Fort Sports Complex - Badminton, Squash
- Dr. Karni Singh Shooting Range - Shooting
- Talkatora Stadium - Boxing
- SPM Swimming Pool Complex - Aquatics
- RK Khanna Tennis Complex - Tennis
- Yamuna Sports Complex - Table tennis

Jawaharlal Nehru Stadium

The opening and closing ceremonies, athletics, lawn bowls, and weightlifting will take place at the massive Jawaharlal Nehru Stadium, Delhi, which will have a capacity of 75,000 spectators for the Games. The stadium will be renovated and improved in time for the Games.

Indira Gandhi Arena

The events of archery, cycling, gymnastics, and wrestling will take place at the Indira Gandhi Arena, the largest indoor sports arena in India and the second largest in Asia, which seats 25,000 people. Located at the Indraprastha Estate in the eastern region of New Delhi, the arena will be connected to other venues via dedicated bus lanes and mass transportation. The arena will be renovated for the Games.

XIX COMMONWEALTH GAMES AT DELHI: A BRIEF OVERVIEW

The XIX Commonwealth Games 2010 Delhi, to be held in October 2010, will be the largest and the most spectacular sports event that the country – and Delhi – will witness. The Games will showcase the economic, social and technical prowess of modern day India and provide lasting legacies of national infrastructure and economic benefits.

If you would like to be a part of this exciting historic event, you could be involved in various ways. As a businessperson you could become a member of Business Club India or partner with the OC CWG Delhi 2010 to mount the most successful Games ever; as an entrepreneur, you could be part of the Bed and Breakfast scheme and play host to the visitors to our city during the Games; as a sports lover you could join the Volunteers Programmes; or as a citizen of India, you could "Come out and Play."

COMMONWEALTH GAMES MOVEMENT

The three core values of the Commonwealth Games movement are Humanity, Equality and Destiny, which were adopted by the Games movement in 2001. These values inspire and unite millions of people and symbolise the broad mandate for holding the Games within the Commonwealth.

A sporting contest that brought together members of the British Empire was first proposed by Reverend Ashley Cooper when he suggested a Pan-Britannic, Pan-Anglican Contest and Festival every four years to foster goodwill and understanding within the Empire. In 1928, a key Canadian athlete, Bobby Robinson, was given the responsibility of organising the first British Empire Games, which culminated in the first-ever Commonwealth Games being held in Hamilton, Ontario, Canada, in 1930. These first Games saw the participation of 400 athletes from 11 countries.

Since then 18 Commonwealth Games have been held every four years, except during World War II (1942 and 1946). Initially the Games were known as the British Empire and Commonwealth Games, then as British Commonwealth Games and simply as the Commonwealth Games since 1978. But more than that, they have always been known as the 'Friendly Games'. India hopes to take this legacy forward.

There are currently 53 members of the Commonwealth of Nations, and 71 teams participate in the Games. The four constituent countries of the United Kingdom—England, Scotland, Wales and Northern Ireland—send separate teams to the Commonwealth Games, and individual teams are also sent from the British Crown dependencies—Guernsey, Jersey and the Isle of Man—and many of the British overseas territories. The Australian external territory of Norfolk Island also sends its own team, as do the Cook Islands and Niue, two non-sovereign states in free association with New Zealand. The Commonwealth dependency of Tokelau is expected to take part in the Games in Delhi.

The Games have evolved and changed over the years. Only single competition games were featured until team sports were introduced in 1998 and continue to be featured since then; a fully inclusive sports programme for Elite Athletes with a Disability (EAD) was first introduced in 2002 and has become an integral part of the Games; since 2004 Commonwealth Youth Games have been organised regularly for athletes of 18 years of age.

QUEEN'S BATON 2010 DELHI

The Queen's Baton 2010 Delhi was unveiled at a spectacular cultural show held at India Gate in New Delhi on 8 March 2009.

The Queen's Baton 2010 Delhi is a combination of handcrafted excellence and precision engineering, it is a true symbol of India: its ancient roots and present vibrant, modern identity. It is also representative of India's diversity—the baton's colour scheme showcases 'soils' from every corner of the country, a rich palette ranging from white sands to yellow clay, deep reds to dark browns and an array of other hues.

The shape and design of the baton has been created using a triangular section of aluminium which is twisted in the form of a helix and coated with soil in a graduating pattern. Interweaving of the intricate hand layered soil pattern creates a very distinctive design, form and texture never before seen in the styling of a Queen's Baton.

Culminating at the pinnacle of the Queen's Baton 2010 Delhi is a precious jewellery box containing the Queen's 'message to the athletes'. The Queen's message has been symbolically engraved onto a miniature 18 carat gold leaf, representative of the ancient Indian 'pathras'. The gold leaf inscription reflects the essence and the richness of culture in ancient India. Modern laser technology known as micro calligraphy has been used for the first time to reproduce the Queen's message in this style.

The Queen's Baton 2010 Delhi stands at 664 millimetres high is 34 millimetres wide at the base, and 86 millimetres wide at the top and weighs a mere 1,900 grams. The baton's ergonomic contours allow for convenient holding and good balance.

The Queen's Baton 2010 Delhi technology features include:

- The ability to capture images and sound as it travels throughout all nations of the Commonwealth;

- The latest global positioning system (GPS) technology through which the exact location of the baton can be tracked on the XIX Commonwealth Games 2010 Delhi website;
- Embedded light emitting diodes (LEDs) which will change into the colours of a country's flag whilst in that country; and
- Text messaging capability so that anyone anywhere can send their messages of congratulations and encouragement to the Batonbearers throughout the Queen's Baton Relay 2010 Delhi.

The Queen's Baton 2010 Delhi is created using processes and technologies existing in India by Foley Design in partnership with Titan Industries and a technology consortium led by Bharat Electronics Limited.

The baton's journey symbolises the unity and shared ideals of the Commonwealth of Nations, and enables communities beyond the Host City to share the Games celebrations. It also serves a functional purpose in carrying Her Majesty Queen Elizabeth II's 'message to the athletes' from Buckingham Palace in London to the opening ceremony of the Games.

The Queen's Baton Relay 2010 Delhi will commence from Buckingham Palace, London, on the 29 October 2009. The baton will then travel through all other 70 Commonwealth nations – a historic journey that will cover a distance of more than 170,000 kilometres in 240 days. On its 100 day national tour, the baton will visit the capital of each of India's 28 states and seven union territories, plus many other cities along the way, covering more than 20,000 kilometres.

By the end of its journey, the baton will have traversed over 190,000 kilometres in 340 days, making the Queen's Baton Relay 2010 Delhi one of the longest relays in the history of the Commonwealth Games. The baton will also have passed through thousands of hands, and travelled by different modes of transport across land, air and sea.

The relay will conclude after the final Batonbearer enters the Jawaharlal Nehru Stadium during the Opening Ceremony of the XIX Commonwealth Games on 3 October 2010 where Her Majesty's message will be removed from the baton and read aloud, officially opening the Games.

TRADITION

The Queen's Baton Relay is one of the great traditions of the Commonwealth Games, having been the curtain-raiser to every games since Cardiff, Wales, in 1958. The relay symbolises the gathering of people from across the Commonwealth at the four-yearly festival of sport and culture.

The relay traditionally begins with a commencement ceremony at Buckingham Palace, London, which coincides with the city's Commonwealth Day festivities. There Her Majesty Queen Elizabeth II entrusts the baton containing Her 'message to the athletes' to the first honorary relay runner.

The relay concludes at the Opening Ceremony, as the final relay runner hands the baton back to Her Majesty, or Her representative, and the message is read aloud. At that moment the relay ends and the Games begin.

Over the years, the Queen's Baton Relay has evolved into a powerful symbol of the unity and diversity of the Commonwealth of Nations. With each Games, the tradition grows in scale and significance – including more nations, involving more participants and generating more excitement than ever before.

The Kuala Lumpur 1998 Queen's Baton Relay was the first to deliver the relay to other nations of the Commonwealth, besides England and the host country. The Manchester 2002 Queen's Jubilee Baton travelled more than 100,000 kilometres in 87 days, and visited 23 Commonwealth nations.

The Melbourne 2006 Queen's Baton travelled an epic journey of more than 180,000 kilometres in a year and a day, and visited all 71 nations of the Commonwealth – home to almost one-third of the world's population.

The Melbourne 2006 Queen's Baton Relay was the world's longest, most inclusive relay. No other Games relay has visited all member nations.

The Queen's Baton Relay 2010 Delhi will commence at Buckingham Palace on 29 October 2009 and end 340 days later at the Opening Ceremony of the XIX Commonwealth Games 2010 Delhi on 3 October 2010. During this period the baton will visit the home of one-third of the world's population and cover a distance in excess of 190,000 kilometres. This marathon event will involve travelling for 240 days through the other 70 nations of the Commonwealth, before spending 100 days visiting all the capital cities in India's 28 states and seven union territories.

QUEEN'S BATON RELAY FACTS

The Queen's Baton Relay is one of the great traditions of the Commonwealth Games. It symbolises the gathering of people from across the Commonwealth at a four yearly festival of sport and culture. Queen's Baton Relays have been the curtain-raiser to every games since Cardiff, Wales, in 1958.

The relay traditionally begins with a commencement ceremony at Buckingham Palace, London, which coincides with the city's Commonwealth Day festivities. There, Her Majesty Queen Elizabeth II entrusts the baton containing Her 'message to the athletes' to the first honorary Batonbearer.

The relay concludes at the opening ceremony of each games, when the final Batonbearer hands the baton back to Her Majesty, or Her representative, and the message is read aloud. At that moment the relay ends and the games begin.

Over the years, the Queen's Baton Relay has evolved into a powerful symbol of unity and diversity of the Commonwealth of Nations. With each games, the tradition of the relay grows in scale and significance—visiting more nations, involving more participants and generating more excitement than ever before.

The Kuala Lumpur 1998 Queen's Baton Relay was the first to deliver the relay to other nations of the Commonwealth, besides England and the host country.

The Manchester 2002 Queen's Jubilee Baton Relay visited 23 Commonwealth nations over an 87 day period and travelled more than 100,000 kilometres.

The Melbourne 2006 Queen's Baton Relay was the first Queen's Baton Relay to visit all 71 nations of the Commonwealth. This epic journey lasted one year and one day and covered a distance of more than 180,000 kilometres—taking the baton to the home of one-third of the world's population.

The Queen's Baton Relay 2010 Delhi will commence at Buckingham Palace on 29 October 2009, and will end 340 days later at the Opening Ceremony of the XIX Commonwealth Games 2010 Delhi on 3 October 2010. During this 11 month period the baton will cover a distance in excess of 190,000 kilometres. This marathon event involves travelling for 240 days through the other 70 nations of the Commonwealth, before spending another 100 days visiting all the capital cities in India's 28 states and seven union territories, and many other cities along the way. The Queen's Baton Relay 2010 Delhi will be one of the longest relays in history.

For each games, the host country designs a unique baton.

For Kuala Lumpur 1998, the baton design was inspired by a traditional Malay artefact, the 'Gobek', which is a unique cylindrical areca nut-pounder widely used and displayed in Malay homes.

For Manchester 2002, the baton had special significance as it marked the Golden Jubilee of Her Majesty Queen Elizabeth II and was designed to symbolise the uniqueness of the individual and the common rhythm of humanity.

For Melbourne 2006, the baton harnessed the very latest in digital and other communication technology which enabled people across the globe to join the baton on its epic journey to the opening ceremony of the Melbourne 2006 Commonwealth Games. The high tech baton tracking technology housed in Melbourne's baton allowed schoolchildren, adults, families and friends to pinpoint the baton's location via the Games website.

The Queen's Baton 2010 Delhi is a fusion of handcrafted elements interplayed with a precision engineered body, and ornamented with an intricate hand layered soil pattern. The shape and design of the baton is created using a triangular section of aluminium which has been twisted in the form of a helix and then coated with a diverse range of coloured soils collected from all corners of India.

The interweaving of coloured soils, including white sands, deep reds, warm yellows, dark browns and an array of other hues creates a very distinctive design, form and texture never before seen in the styling of a Queen's Baton. The very essence of India with its diversity and unrelenting endeavour towards a harmonious and progressive nation has shaped the inspiration of the baton. The Queen's Baton 2010 Delhi is a true Indian masterpiece.

QUEEN'S BATON RELAY 2010 DELHI

The Queen's Baton Relay is one of the great traditions of the Commonwealth Games. It symbolises the gathering of people from across the Commonwealth at a four yearly festival of sport and culture. Queen's Baton Relays have been the curtain-raiser to every games since Cardiff, Wales, in 1958.

The Queen's Baton 2010 Delhi contains Her Majesty's 'message to the athletes', and will be carried from Buckingham Palace, London, throughout all nations of the Commonwealth to the Opening Ceremony of the XIX Commonwealth Games 2010 Delhi.

Uniting the Commonwealth, the Queen's Baton Relay 2010 Delhi will be a rousing celebration that showcases India to the world.The relay begins when Her Majesty Queen Elizabeth II entrusts the baton containing Her message to the first of many thousands of Batonbearers.

The Queen's Baton 2010 Delhi will leave Buckingham Palace on 29 October 2009, and arrive at the Opening Ceremony of the XIX Commonwealth Games 2010 Delhi after visiting the other nations of the Commonwealth and travelling throughout India. The Queen's Baton Relay 2010 Delhi will take the baton to the home of one-third of the world's population, enabling many millions of people across the globe to join in the celebrations for the Games.

It will take the Queen's Baton 2010 Delhi 240 days to complete the epic journey to all 70 nations of the Commonwealth. During this time the baton will cover a distance of more than 170,000 kilometres.Whilst on its 100 day national tour, the baton will visit all the capital cities in India's 28 states and seven union territories and many other cities along the way, covering in excess of 20,000 kilometres.This will make the national sector of the Queen's Baton Relay 2010 Delhi twice as long as the Manchester and Melbourne relays, which each lasted for 50 days. By the end of its marathon journey, the Queen's Baton 2010 Delhi will have passed through many thousands of hands on many different modes of transport across land, air and sea.

On arrival at the opening ceremony, the Queen's Baton 2010 Delhi will have travelled in excess of 190,000 kilometres over a 340 day period; this will make the Queen's Baton Relay 2010 Delhi one of the longest relays in the history of the Commonwealth Games.

The relay will conclude in Jawaharlal Nehru Stadium at the Opening Ceremony of the XIX Commonwealth Games 2010 Delhi on 3 October 2010. During the ceremony, the final Batonbearer will hand the baton back to Her Majesty, or Her representative, where the Queen's message that was placed in the baton some 11 months ago, is then removed and read aloud, officially opening the Games.

INTERNATIONAL SECTOR

The Queen's Baton Relay is one of the great traditions of the Commonwealth Games. It symbolises the gathering of people from across the Commonwealth at a four yearly festival of sport and culture. Queen's Baton Relays have been the curtain-raiser to every games since Cardiff, Wales, in 1958.

Uniting the Commonwealth, the Queen's Baton Relay 2010 Delhi will be an exciting national celebration that will showcase India to the world. The relay begins when Her Majesty Queen Elizabeth II entrusts the baton containing Her message to the first of many thousands of Batonbearers.

A highlight for the XIX Commonwealth Games 2010 Delhi will be the Queen's Baton Relay 2010 Delhi. One of the longest relays in history, will commence when the Queen's Baton 2010 Delhi leaves Buckingham Palace on 29 October 2009. The baton will then traverse the length and breadth of the Commonwealth for 240 days, visiting all of the other 70 nations, before embarking upon a 100 day national tour of India. By the end of this epic journey, the baton will have travelled for 340 days and covered in excess of 190,000 kilometres, passing through the hands of many thousands of individuals, across land, air, sea, and on many different modes of transport—from bicycle and boat to hot air balloon, steam train and even on an elephant, conveying the Queen's message to its final destination Delhi, India.

During this marathon journey, the Queen's Baton 2010 Delhi will visit the smallest country per square kilometre in the Commonwealth, Malta, and the largest, Canada. The baton will also travel to some of the most remote places in the Commonwealth including St Helena—an island off the west coast of Africa, which is only accessible by boat, before venturing onto the Falkland Islands. Many famous landmarks, areas of great beauty and places of historical significance will be graced by the presence of the Queen's Baton 2010 Delhi. Heads of State, dignitaries and athletes will also be on hand, to herald the arrival of the Queen's Baton

2010 Delhi into many different cultures and communities, promoting diversity and calling on all competing athletes to participate in the XIX Commonwealth Games 2010 Delhi.

The relay will conclude in Jawaharlal Nehru Stadium at the Opening Ceremony of the XIX Commonwealth Games 2010 Delhi on 3 October 2010. During the ceremony, the final Batonbearer will hand the baton back to Her Majesty, or Her representative, where the Queen's message that was placed in the baton some 11 months ago, is then removed and read aloud, officially opening the Games.

ARRIVAL DATES FOR THE QUEEN'S BATON 2010 DELHI

Day No of Relay	*Days to Games*	*Country No.*	*Date*	*Location*	*Day No. of Relay*	*Days to Games*	*Country No.*	*Date*	*Location*
1	339	1	Thu 29 Oct 2009	Buckingh-am Palace, England	132	208	36	Tue 9 Mar 2010	St Lucia
1	339	1	Thu 29 Oct 2009	England	135	205	37	Fri 12 Mar 2010	Antigua and Barbuda
11	329	2	Sun 8 Nov 2009	Wales	138	202	38	Mon 15 Mar 2010	Dominica
15	325	3	Thu 12 Nov 2009	Northern Ireland	140	200	39	Wed 17 Mar 2010	Montserrat
18	322	4	Sun 15 Nov 2009	Isle of Man	142	198	40	Fri 19 Mar 2010	St Kitts and Nevis
21	319	5	Wed 18 Nov 2009	Jersey	145	195	41	Mon 22 Mar 2010	British Virgin Islands
25	315	6	Sun 22 Nov 2009	Guernsey	148	192	42	Thu 25 Mar 2010	Anguilla
28	312	7	Wed 25 Nov 2009	Gibraltar	150	190	43	Sat 27 Mar 2010	Jamaica
31	309	8	Sat 28 Nov 2009	Scotland	154	186	44	Wed 31 Mar 2010	Cayman Islands
35	305	9	Wed 2 Dec 2009	Cyprus	156	184	45	Fri 2 Apr 2010	The Bahamas

(*Contd.*)

Day No. of Relay	Days to Games	Country No.	Date	Location	Day No. of Relay	Days to Games	Country No.	Date	Location
38	302	10	Sat 5 Dec 2009	Malta	158	182	46	Sun 4 Apr 2010	Turks and Caicos
42	298	11	Wed 9 Dec 2009	Sierra Leone	161	179	47	Wed 7 Apr 2010	Belize
44	296	12	Fri 11 Dec 2009	The Gambia	165	175	48	Sun 11 Apr 2010	Bermuda
48	292	13	Tue 15 Dec 2009	Ghana	167	173	49	Tue 13 Apr 2010	Canada
51	289	14	Fri 18 Dec 2009	Nigeria	172	168	50	Sun 18 Apr 2010	Australia
54	286	15	Mon 2l Dec 2009	Cameroon	176	164	51	Thu 22 Apr 2010	Papua New Guinea
58	282	16	Fri 25 Dec 2009	Kenya	179	161	52	Sun 25 Apr 2010	Vanuatu
61	279	17	Mon 28 Dec 2009	Tanzania	181	159	53	Tue 27 Apr 2010	Solomon Islands
63	277	18	Wed 30 Dec 2009	Uganda	184	156	54	Fri 30 Apr 2010	Nauru
67	273	19	Sun 3 Jan 2010	Seychelles	188	152	55	Tue 4 May 2010	Kiribati
70	270	20	Wed 6 Jan 2010	Mauritius	190	150	56	Thu 6 May 2010	Fiji
73	267	21	Sat 9 Jan 2010	South Africa	193	147	57	Sun 9 May 2010	Samoa
77	263	22	Wed 13 Jan 2010	Lesotho	196	144	58	Wed 12 May 2010	Niue
79	261	23	Fri 15 Jan 2010	Swaziland	200	140	59	Sun 16 May 2010	New Zealand
82	258	24	Mon l8 Jan 2010	Mozambi-que	203	137	60	Wed 19 May 2010	Tonga
85	255	25	Thu 21 Jan 2010	Malawi	207	133	61	Sun 23 May 2010	Cook Islands
87	253	26	Sat 23 Jan 2010	Zambia	212	128	62	Fri 28 May 2010	Tuvalu

(*Contd.*)

Day No. of Relay	*Days to Games*	*Country No.*	*Date*	*Location*	*Day No. of Relay*	*Days to Games*	*Country No.*	*Date*	*Location*
89	251	27	Mon 25 Jan 2010	Botswana	217	123	63	Wed 2 Jun 2010	Norfolk Island
92	248	28	Thu 28 Jan 2010	Namibia	220	120	64	Sat 5 Jun 2010	Singapore
100	240	29	Fri 5 Feb 2010	St Helena	223	117	65	Tue 8 Jun 2010	Brunei Darussalam
110	230	30	Mon 15 Feb 2010	Falkland Islands	226	114	66	Fri II Jun 2010	Malaysia
117	223	31	Mon 22 Feb 2010	Trinidad and Tobago	229	III	67	Mon I4 Jun 2010	Maldives
120	220	32	Thu 25 Feb 2010	Guyana	232	108	68	Thu I7 Jun 2010	Sri Lanka
123	217	33	Sun 28 Feb 2010	Barbados	235	105	69	Sun 20 Jun 2010	Bangladesh
127	213	34	Thu 4 Mar 2010	Grenada	238	102	70	Wed 23 Jun 2010	Pakistan
129	211	35	Sat 6 Mar 2010	St Vincent and The Grenadines	**240**	**100**	**71**	**Fri 25 Jun 2010**	**INDIA**

Source: The information contained in the table above reflects the date the Queen's Baton 2010 Delhi is sheduled to arrive in each Nation/Territory and is correct at the time of printing. Please note, dates may change due to circumstances outside the control of the XIX Commonwealth Games 2010 Delhi. All arrival dates should be confirmed with the respective Commonwealth Games Association.

ALPHABETICAL LISTING OF QUEEN'S BATON 2010 DELHI DESTINATIONS

Day No. of Relay	Days to Games	Country No.	Date	Location	Day No. of Relay	Days to Games	Country No.	Date	Location
148	192	42	Thu 25 Mar 2010	Anguilla	70	270	20	Wed 6 Jan 2010	Mauritius
135	205	37	Fri 12 Mar 2010	Antigua and Barbuda	140	200	39	Wed 17 Mar 2010	Montserrat
172	168	50	Sun 18 Apr 2010	Australia	82	258	24	Mon 18 Jan 2010	Mozambi-que
235	105	69	Sun 20 Jun 2010	Bangladesh	92	248	28	Thu 28 Jan 2010	Namibia
123	217	33	Sun 28 Feb 2010	Barbados	184	156	54	Fri 30 Apr 2010	Nauru
161	179	47	Wed 7 Apr 2010	Belize	200	140	59	Sun 16 May 2010	New Zealand
165	175	48	Sun II Apr 2010	Bermuda	51	289	14	Fri 18 Dec 2009	Nigeria
89	251	27	Mon 25 Jan 2010	Botswana	196	144	58	Wed 12 May 2010	Niue
145	195	41	Mon 22 Mar 2010	British Virgin Islands	217	123	63	Wed 2 Jun 2010	Norfolk Island
223	117	65	Tue 8 Jun 2010	Brunei Darussalam	15	325	3	Thu 12 Nov 2009	Northern Ireland
1	**339**	**1**	**Thu 29 Oct 2009**	**Buckingham Palace, England**	238	102	70	Wed 23 Jun 2010	Pakistan
54	286	15	Mon 21 Dec 2009	Cameroon	176	164	51	Thu 22 Apr 2010	Papua New Guinea
167	173	49	Tue 13 Apr 2010	Canada	193	147	57	Sun 9 May 2010	Samoa
154	186	44	Wed 31 Mar 2010	Cayman Islands	31	309	8	Sat 28 Nov 2009	Scotland
207	133	61	Sun 23 May 2010	Cook Islands	67	273	19	Sun 3 Jan 2010	Seychelles

(Contd.)

Day No. of Relay	*Days to Games*	*Country No.*	*Date*	*Location*	*Day No. of Relay*	*Days to Games*	*Country No.*	*Date*	*Location*
35	305	9	Wed 2 Dec 2009	Cyprus	42	298	11	Wed 9 Dec 2009	Sierra Leone
138	202	38	Mon 15 Mar 2010	Dominica	220	120	64	Sat 5 Jun 2010	Singapore
1	339	1	Thu 29 Oct 2009	England	181	159	53	Tue 27 Apr 2010	Solomon Islands
110	230	30	Mon 15 Feb 2010	Falkland Islands	73	267	21	Sat 9 Jan 2010	South Africa
190	150	56	Thu 6 May 2010	Fiji	232	108	68	Thu 17 Jun 2010	Sri Lanka
48	292	13	Tue 15 Dec 2009	Ghana	100	240	29	Fri 5 Feb 2010	St Helena
28	312	7	Wed 25 Nov 2009	Gibraltar	142	198	40	Fri 19 Mar 2010	St Kitts and Nevis
127	213	34	Thu 4 Mar 2010	Grenada	132	208	36	Tue 9 Mar 2010	St Lucia
25	315	6	Sun 22 Nov 2009	Guernsey	129	211	35	Sat 6 Mar 2010	St Vincent and The Grenadines
120	220	32	Thu 25 Feb 2010	Guyana	79	261	23	Fri 15 Jan 2010	Swaziland
240	**100**	**71**	**Fri 25 Jun 2010**	**INDIA**	61	279	17	Mon 28 Dec 2009	Tanzania
18	322	4	Sun 15 Nov 2009	Isle of Man	156	184	45	Fri 2 Apr 2010	The Bahamas
150	190	43	Sat 27 Mar 2010	Jamaica	44	296	12	Fri 11 Dec 2009	The Gambia
21	319	5	Wed 18 Nov 2009	Jersey	203	137	60	Wed 19 May 2010	Tonga
58	282	16	Fri 25 Dec 2009	Kenya	117	223	31	Mon 22 Feb 2010	Trinidad and Tobago
188	152	55	Tue 4 May 2010	Kiribati	158	182	46	Sun 4 Apr 2010	Turks and Caicos

(*Contd.*)

Day No. of Relay	Days to Games	Country No.	Date	Location	Day No. of Relay	Days to Games	Country No.	Date	Location
77	263	22	Wed 13 Jan 2010	Lesotho	212	128	62	Fri 28 May 2010	Tuvalu
85	255	25	Thu 21 Jan 2010	Malawi	63	277	18	Wed 30 Dec 2009	Uganda
226	114	66	Fri 11 Jun 2010	Malaysia	179	161	52	Sun 25 Apr 2010	Vanuatu
229	111	67	Mon I4 Jun 2010	Maldives	11	329	21	Sun 8 Nov 2009	Wales
38	302	10	Sat 5 Dec 2009	Malta	87	253	26	Sat 23 Jan 2010	Zambia

Source: The information contained in the table above reflects the date the Queen's Baton 2010 Delhi is sheduled to arrive in each Nation/ Territory and is correct at the time of printing. Please note, dates may change due to circumstances outside the control of the XIX Commonwealth Games 2010 Delhi. All arrival dates should be confirmed with the respective Commonwealth Games Association.

The Commonwealth is primarily an organisation in which countries with diverse economic backgrounds have an opportunity for close and equal interaction. The primary activities of the Commonwealth are designed to create an atmosphere of economic co-operation between member nations, as well as the promotion of democracy, human rights, and good governance in those nations.

As you might have guessed by now, the various sports activities like Aquatics, Athletics, Badminton, Bowls, Boxing, Cycling, EAD Events, Gymnastics, Hockey, Netball, Rugby 7s, Shooting, Squash, Table Tennis and Weightlifting are all meant to bring the countries together to strengthen the relationships. This time (2006) it was Australia next time (2010) it will be India.

The important part to remember here is, just because you are a member country, this does not give you the right to organise the Commonwealth Games in your country. There are criterion that the member country has to meet before it can even "bid" for the Commonwealth Games to be held on its land.

You got a new term there, BID. Yes you heard that right, a member country actually has to place a bid and win the bid so that the games could be played on its land. India has won the bid last time over Canada. This is a moment of great pride that the events are going to be held in India, they not only won the bid but they are actually very close to meet all the deadlines that were given to prepare for the games and improve the infrastructure according to the international standards.

2010 NEW DELHI COMMONWEALTH GAMES

Welcome to Commonwealth Games 2010 (unofficial) website. It is just about time that you get informed about Commonwealth Games 2010 that is to be held in India. Information that will make you a part of the international event the whole world is waiting for. The event that involves the elite of the athletes and the best of the nations.

The 2010 Games also presents an opportunity for India to showcase itself as a sporting and cultural nation and economic power.

New Delhi is beaming with pride to host the Commonwealth Games 2010. India's distinct culture, where the traditional is successfully combined with the modern, will make the Delhi Games special. Right now what you see and really experience are the infrastructural changes that are taking place, to be honest, on daily basis. But now we even have news from across the country informing us about the preparation of athelets.

As in the words of Indian sports minister Suresh Kalmadi, "The colour, costumes, the traditions and heritage will be world class, the public will be welcoming and friendly and the flair of India is what will make the next Games really unique."

India will be only the third developing country to host the event after Jamaica in 1966 and Malaysia in 1998. This is only the second time the event will be held in Asia. The success of these games may also strengthen India's bid for 2016 Summer Olympics.

This will be the biggest multi-sport event conducted in India. In past New Delhi has proudly experienced playing host to the Asian Games in 1951 and 1982 (Asiad). Preparations are in full swing and New Delhi is comfortably meeting all the target dates. Every venue event is getting ready for the important year.

The proposed dates for the Games are 3—14 October 2010 inclusive of the Opening and Closing Ceremonies.

The Delhi Games Village is to be constructed as a low rise medium development on a 40 acre site in the heart of the capital with a possible capacity for 8,500 athletes and officials. Existing and new stadium will be used to house the following sports:

The culture, infrastructure and sport all will be successfully combined to create yet another memorable experience for Commonwealth Games.

The 2010 Games will be staged in the heart of Delhi itself with existing venues and facilities being given a major facelift that includes construction of new venues like New Delhi games village.

8

Legacy of Delhi City for Hosting Commonwealth Games Participants and Tourists

AN OVERVIEW OF COMMONWEALTH 2010

Delhi, the political and tourist hub of India is passionate about sport and games. The Commonwealth Games will be the most imperative sport event ever staged in India. Since it is going to be the most costly event ever organised by India so far, the Organising Committee of Commonwealth is doing its best to offer smooth effective transport and security for this meaningful and significant event.

Energy Consumption

To increase power production to 7,000 MW (from the current 4,500 MW), the government is undertaking a huge power-manufacture scheme. Thus, government plans to streamline the power distribution process to reach its goal. Direct additional energy to Delhi and construction of new power plants has been introduced in Delhi for advancement of the Game. In fact, as per the government assurance of Commonwealth 2010, Delhi will have a surplus of power very shortly.

Security

A tight security is being provided for your safety and protection by the Government of India during this occasion. The state will be deploying a force of "tourist police" lot before the Games begin.

This tourism police will be alert to handle tourist-related aspects. All the Indian states are going to follow this process. A number of states have already implemented this programme; other states are expected to emulate it within a short while.

Delhi and the 2010 Commonwealth Games

World Class Sport to bring Economic and Tourist Boom to Indian Capital

The 2010 Commonwealth Games were launched in traditional fashion on the 3rd of March 2009. The Queen's relay baton was unveiled at India Gate among great public celebrations, marking the start of its long journey between participating nations. On the 3rd of October 2010, it will return to Delhi where the enclosed royal message will be read and the games will begin. The Delhi baton is made of aluminium with multicoloured layers of soil from every corner of the land.

In the meantime, India's capital is in the throes of an unprecedented economic boom bringing its infrastructure up to date.

Economic Boom in Indian Capital, Games and Tourism

The 2010 Commonwealth Games should be a major boost for Delhi. Labour is cheap and plentiful, foreign investors have moved in and despite a few hiccups, work appears to be moving at a frantic pace.

Most apparent are improvements to the transport system with flyovers, underpasses, multi-lane roads and high capacity bus corridors. Efforts to combat pollution continue with more taxis and buses running on natural gas. Meanwhile Delhi boasts new trains and buildings in the Cantonment Station, the Metro is fast expanding to become the world's second longest and the modernised Indira Gandhi Airport will have a new runway and terminal.

Add increased energy and water supplies, thousands of extra hotel rooms and a green village to house over 8000 athletes and officials and Delhi seems all set for world class sport and a major boost in tourism. Over five million visitors from India and abroad are expected in the capital as a result of the games.

Delhi and the 2010 Commonwealth Games

India will be hosting the Commonwealth Games for the first time and is only the second Asian country to do so, after Malaysia. Delhi won the vote by a sizeable majority against Hamilton in Canada where the first games were held in 1930.

There are currently 72 nations planning to attend the 19th Commonwealth Games in Delhi and 17 disciplines from Aquatics and Wrestling to Hockey, Gymnastics and Athletics. Triathlon, basketball and cricket are still in the balance but a demonstration of Kabaddi, a Tamil Nadu team sport, is likely to be included.

India hopes to beat its 2002 record of 138 medals, including 30 gold. Indian gold medals in 2006 went to boxing, shooting, table tennis and women's weightlifting.

World Class Sport in India, Commonwealth Games Venues and Information

The 2010 Commonwealth Games will be held in a number of venues across Delhi, including the Indira Gandhi Indoor Stadium Complex, the Siri Fort Sports Complex and the Jawaharlal Nehru Stadium where the opening and closing ceremonies will take place, on October 3rd and 14th respectively.

Tickets are available on a number of websites but it is advisable to book through a reputable tour operator or agent. Visit the games official site www.cwgdelhi2010.com for the latest news and for general information on India, see www.incredibleindia.org.

The copyright of the article Delhi and the 2010 Commonwealth Games in India Travel is owned by Solange Hando. Permission to republish Delhi and the 2010 Commonwealth Games in print or online must be granted by the author in writing.

LEGACY OF DELHI

Hosting a sporting event at a scale such as the Commonwealth Games is a matter of international prestige for the country, and is bound to boost brand India. The country is heralded as the next world economic superpower and the Games will be another opportunity to project the nation on the world stage. Delhi too, as the host city, will get the chance to exhibit a new image for itself – that of a world class city with international standards. Improved infrastructure and appearance of the host city, and global media exposure will serve to transform the image of the city.

Another legacy of the Games will be the social, economic and physical regeneration of Delhi. The Games will help to boost urban renewal, create jobs, increase investment and transform the landscape of the city. Delhi will get a major facelift due to the Games: its monuments and heritage buildings will be restored and areas such as East Delhi and the Yamuna riverfront will be developed. Not only will the Games leave behind improved infrastructure and facilities for the citizens of Delhi, but will also promote investment in the city. The hospitality sector is an area that will see a huge growth spurt, with the help of the XIX Commonwealth Games 2010 Delhi.

Another sector that will see huge improvements will be transportation: flyovers, bypasses, broader roads, a larger metro system, an integrated Rail Bus Transport system and a High Capacity Bus system. These will all serve to ease traffic congestion and transit for Delhi's citizens. The modernisation of the Indira Gandhi International Airport will treble capacity and go a long way towards improving connectivity within India and with the rest of the world. Apart from this, two new power plants to enhance electricity supply, improved water distribution and solid waste management systems will add considerably to the Delhi citizen's comfort levels post Games.

And, of course, the Games will leave behind dramatically improved, world-class sports facilities that generations of Indian sportspersons can use in the future. The establishment of an Olympic-size pool as well as a gym in the Delhi University will boost sports among the youth of Delhi.

More than all this, the legacy of the XIX Commonwealth Games 2010 Delhi will be to boost the sports culture as a part of the daily life of every Indian, particularly the youth.

CITY MAKE-OVER

The historic city of Delhi will look its best for visitors during the XIX Commonwealth Games 2010 Delhi. One of the legacies of the event will be that it will leave behind a city much more beautiful and charming than it currently is. The colonial city-centre and Delhi's main shopping area, Connaught Place, has been given a new façade and is already experiencing a resurgence. Rajpath, the main avenue in Lutyens' Delhi, is being rejuvenated. The city's monuments, an integral part of the rich heritage of Delhi's past, are being cleaned and revitalised.

New international standard signages and bus shelters will add to Delhi's modern look as will new public conveniences such as call booths, shopping areas, etc.

CITY INFRASTRUCTURE

GNCTD has allocated a sum of Rs 11.89 billion to enhance, expand and upgrade city infrastructure.

Indira Gandhi International Airport

Delhi's airport is being modernised, upgraded and expanded to handle the passenger traffic envisaged during the XIX Commonwealth Games 2010 Delhi. Passenger and baggage handling facilities have been upgraded and a new 4.43 km runway, the longest operational runway in Asia, became operational in 2008. It is fitted with the highly-sophisticated Instruments Landing System (ILS) on both sides, and is built to the highest Code F standards. Expansion plans include the construction of a new state-of-the-art terminal (T3) with a capacity to handle 35 million passengers per year.

It will have 75 aero-bridges, of which nine will be compatible to handle operations of mammoth A-380 aircraft. It will have 20 parking bays for passengers.The terminal, connected with all types of transport systems, will have an advanced five-level in-line baggage-handling device with explosive-detection technology for high-class efficiency and security. There will be 160 check-in counters for fast clearance and more number of immigration counters. The departure complex will be situated on the upper deck of the two tier building and arrival on the lower deck. The roof of the building will have stylised incisions to allow daylight, but it will be angled to protect the interior from direct sun-rays. The airport's connectivity with the city will be enhanced through a six-lane highway (National Highway 8). The Metro Rail will also have a dedicated corridor from the airport to the Games Village for easy transfer of athletes and officials.

Transportation and Road Network

Delhi will have a dedicated Metro line from the airport to the city centre – Connaught Place – by 2010. The Games Village as well as the main competition venues such as the Jawaharlal Nehru Stadium and the Indira Gandhi Stadium will be connected through the Metro. The inter-city connectivity as well as passenger capacity will be enhanced. All Metro stations are planned to be Wi-Fi enabled by 2010.

A four-lane, 2.2 km underground stretch from Ring Road to Lodhi will link the Games Village to the Jawaharlal Nehru Stadium, reducing travelling time for athletes. Twelve new flyovers and several bridges and under-bridges have been planned to improve road connectivity with the Games Villages, the sports venues, and within the city. Road widening also is in progress. The new eight-lane expressway from Gurgaon to Delhi is functional. A total of 1,100 new low-floor, high-capacity air-conditioned buses will ply on Delhi roads by 2010 to ease commuting.

Civic Services

Delhi plans to be power surplus by the time the Games are held. To ensure additional power to Delhi, the government is undertaking a large power-production initiative to increase production to over 5,880 mega watts (MW) from the current 4,500 MW. The power distribution system will be streamlined, more power directed to Delhi and new power plants constructed.

Delhi Jal Board is planning to augment water supply substantially by 2010. Two new initiatives have been undertaken to boost water supply from the current 670 million gallons per day (MGD) to 941 MGD. Plans are also underway to streamline Delhi's solid waste management system.

Twenty new hospitals will be functional by 2010 to enhance Delhi's healthcare and medical infrastructure. Special trauma ambulances will be on call during the Games to provide immediate relief in cases of emergencies.

Nine new automated car parks are being built in the vicinity of the Games venues with a capacity for 7,500 vehicles.

Hospitality

Delhi has a vibrant hospitality industry with almost all major world-class hotels and restaurants located here. However, the current capacity will be insufficient to handle the huge influx of visitors expected into Delhi for the XIX Commonwealth Games

2010 Delhi. An additional 25,000 rooms are being built to meet the requirements of the Games; this will be supplemented by the Bed and Breakfast Scheme launched by the Delhi Government.

In addition, the State-owned India Tourism Development Corp. Ltd. (ITDC) and private hotels have embarked on make-over and upgradation plans to welcome visitors to Delhi and make their stay an enjoyable experience.

XIX COMMONWEALTH GAMES 2010 DELHI

These are scheduled from 3 October to 14 October, 2010. This is the best time to travel to Delhi, which has average daytime temperatures of 22°C (71.5°F) in October. You can visit many of Delhi's numerous heritage sites and monuments, sample world class cuisine and entertainment at the city's numerous hotels and restaurants, shop till you drop at the various malls and shopping outlets the city provides, and experience all that this vibrant, exciting city has to offer.

Delhi is located a few hours away from the world's greatest monument to love, the majestic Taj Mahal in Agra. Also close by is the colourful state of Rajasthan with its forts and palaces, tales of valour, and unbeatable exotic experiences. The sheer scale and diversity of India offers a range of destinations and experiences found nowhere else in the world: the mystical and breathtaking Himalayas in the north; vast beaches with an exciting range of water sports and other activities; peaceful lagoons and inland waterways; yoga and meditation to lift your spirits; wildlife parks to commune with nature; and ancient heritage sites to remind you of India's ancient past. Incredible India has it all—waiting to be experienced!

The Accommodation Functional Area (FA), Organising Committee Commonwealth Games 2010 Delhi (OC CWG Delhi 2010) in conjunction with the Games Travel Office (GTO) has secured a comprehensive range of hotel accommodation in and around Delhi exclusively for visitors who will travel to Delhi for the Games. It is important to note that all accommodation options listed in this document are subject to availability at the time of request and will be allocated in order of receipt of bookings.

Kindly go through the Accommodation manual to view the hotel options before submitting the accommodation booking form.

BED AND BREAKFAST

Hosting the Games is a matter of pride for the city of Delhi, and an opportunity to showcase traditional Indian hospitality. If you have rooms to spare and the desire to play host to our visitors during the Games, you can become a proactive participant in making Delhi—and India—proud.

The Delhi Government has initiated a Bed & Breakfast Scheme, which allows you, as a citizen of Delhi, to lodge tourist coming from abroad and other parts of the country as paying guests within a regulated framework. You will, of course, gain from the fee charged to the guests. If you have suitable space and facilities to host guests, and are looking for an additional source of income, you can make use of this opportunity.

HOTEL FACT SHEET

The Ashok Hotel

Classification/Category	5 Star Deluxe (as classified by Government of India, Department of Tourism)
Total no. of rooms	550
Address	50-B, Chanakaya Puri, New Delhi 110 021
Contact details	Tel: 011-26110101 Fax: 011-26873216 E-Mail : ashoknd@ndb.vsnl.net.in
Access	15 kms from International Airport, 12 kms from Domestic Airport, 10 kms from City Centre (Connaught Place)
Special room facilities	Wi-Fi in all the guest rooms, 24 hrs room service, Hot & Cold running water, Telephone, Tea/Coffee maker, Electronic safe, Cable T.V.
Other facilities	Business centre, Separate executive floor with club lounge, Non-smoking guest rooms, rooms for physically challenged, Banquet & Conference facilities, Shopping arcade, International State-of-Art Health SPA, Swimming pool, Putting Green, Billiards room
Services	Doctor on call, Theatre evenings, Laundry, Money changer, Banking, Safe deposit, Valet, Travel desk service, Dry cleaning

Food & Beverages	Indian (Awadhi, South Indian, Northwest Frontier), Continental, Chinese, Korean, Lebanese, Bar
Credit Card	Major Credit Cards accepted

Hotel Janpath

Classification/Category	4 Star (as classified by Government of India, Department of Tourism)
Total no. of rooms	209
Address	Janpath Road, New Delhi 110 001
Contact details	Tel: 011-23340070 Fax: 011-23347083 E-Mail : janpath@ndf.vsnl.net.in
Access	20 kms from International Airport, 15 kms from Domestic Airport, 2 kms. from Railway Station & 1 km from City Centre (Connaught Place)
Special room facilities	Hot & Cold running water, Telephone, T.V., Refrigerator
Other facilities	Centrally Air-conditioned, Non-smoking rooms, Business Centre, Shopping Arcade, 24-hour Money Changer, Beauty Parlour and Hair Dresser, Unique Health Check-up and Lab Test Services
Services	Doctor on call, Theatre evenings, Laundry, Money changer, Banking, Safe deposit, Valet, Travel desk service, Dry cleaning
Food & Beverages	Indian, Continental and Chinese delicacies with live ghazals in the glow of candle light. South Indian vegetarian food paradise. The hotel has a well stocked Bar
Credit Card	Major Credit Cards accepted

Ramada Plaza Hotel

Classification/Category	4 Star (as classified by Government of India, Department of Tourism)
Total no. of rooms	419
Address	19, Ashok Road, New Delhi 110 001
Contact details	Tel. 011-43555555 Fax: 011-43555566 E-Mail : ramadaplazadelhi@gmail.com

Access	16 kms from International Airport, 3 kms from New Delhi Railway Station, & 2 kms from City Centre (Connaught Place)
Special room facilities	Tea/Coffee maker, In Room safe, Wi-Fi, Club Floors, Express check-in
Other facilities	Business centre, Club Floors with Lounge, Conference & meeting facilities
Services	Express laundry, Doctor on call, Money changer facility, 24 hrs room service
Food & Beverages	Indian, Oriental, Multi-cuisine & 02 Bars
Credit Card	Major Credit Cards accepted

ITC Maurya Hotel

Classification/Category	5 Star Deluxe (as classified by Government of India, Department of Tourism)
Total no. of rooms	469
Address	Diplomatic Enclave, S.P. Marg, New Delhi 110 021
Contact details	Tel: 011 - 26112233, Fax: 011-26113333 E-Mail : itcmaurya@itcwelcomgroup.in
Access	14 kms from International Airport, 7 kms from Domestic Airport, 10 kms from New Delhi Railway Station & 7 kms from City Centre (Connaught Place)
Special room facilities	Direct dial telephone, Mini bar, Ironing equipments, Voice mail, Coffee making services. In house music system, fruit basket, Television with satellite channels, Direct dial telephone, 24 hour room service
Other facilities	Wi-Fi broad band internet access, 24 hour Business centre, Shopping arcade, gourmet shop, florist, 24 hour room service, 24 hour currency exchange, doctor on call, travel desk, banquet/conference facilities, health club, beauty parlor, barber shop, outdoor swimming pool, exclusive arrangement with classic golf resort
Services	Spa, Gym, Baby Sitting
Food & Beverages	Indian, Continental, Oriental, Grills, Contemporary Chinese & 02 Bars
Credit Card	Major Credit Cards accepted

The Oberoi Hotel

Classification/Category	5 Star Deluxe (as classified by Government of India, Department of Tourism)
Total no. of rooms	283
Address	Dr. Zakir Hussain Road, New Delhi 110 003
Contact details	Tel: 011-24363030 Fax: 011-24360484 E-Mail : reservations.tond@oberoihotels.com
Access	18 kms from the International Airport (30 minutes), 15 kms from Domestic Airport, 10 kms from the Central Railway Station (15 minutes) 7 kms from City Centre (Connaught Place)
Special room facilities	Bed, 32.5 square metres (348 square feet), Pool, Monument, Golf club view, DVD player, Bathroom scale and telephone, Wireless internet access (Surcharge), Tea/Coffee maker, Complimentary newspapers
Other facilities	Spa, Swimming Pool, Gymnasium
Services	Doctor on call, 24 hrs Laundry, money changer, baby sitting, valet, car rental, travel desk service, safe deposit in all rooms
Food & Beverages	Italian, Szechwan, Cantonese, World cuisine & Bar
Credit Card	Major Credit Cards accepted

Hyatt Regency Hotel

Classification/Category	5 Star Deluxe (as classified by Government of India, Department of Tourism)
Total no. of rooms	524
Address	Bhikaji Cama Place, Ring Road, New Delhi 110 066
Contact details	Tel: 011-26791234 Fax: 011-26791024 E-Mail : hrdelhi@hyatt.com
Access	13 kms from International Airport, 9 kms from Domestic Airport, 10 kms from Railway Station & 12 kms from City Centre (Connaught Place)
Special room facilities	24 hrs Shopping Arcade, Flower ship, Mini Bar, Data port, Non-smoking rooms
Other facilities	Business Centre, Separate Executive Floor, Executive Lounge, 24 hrs Cafe, Banquet &

	Conference Facilities, Health Club, Swimming Pool, Tennis
Services	Doctor on Call, Laundry, Money Changer, Banking, Safe Deposit, Baby Sitting, Valet, Travel Desk Service, Car Rental, On-site parking
Food & Beverages	Indian, Continental, Italian, Oriental, Middle Eastern, Chinese & Bar
Credit Card	Major Credit Cards accepted

Taj Palace Hotel

Classification/Category	5 Star Deluxe (as classified by Government of India, Department of Tourism)
Total no. of rooms	419
Address	2, Sardar Patel Marg, Diplomatic Enclave, New Delhi 110 021
Contact details	Tel: 011-26110202 Fax: 011-26110808 E-Mail : palace.delhi@tajhotels.com
Access	14 kms from International Airport, 7 kms from Domestic Airport, 15 kms. from New Delhi Railway Station & 7 kms from City Centre (Connaught Place)
Special room facilities	Room Service, Hot & Cold running water, Telephone, T.V., Safe Deposit, Channel Music, Tea/Coffee maker, Wi-Fi
Other facilities	Business Centre, Separate Executive Floor, Executive Lounge, Banquet & Conference Facilities, Wireless Internet, Beauty Parlour, Shopping Arcade, Health Club, Swimming Pool, Tennis, Golf, Fitness Centre
Services	Doctor on Call, Laundry, Money Changer, Banking, Safe Deposit, Baby Sitting, Valet, Travel Desk Service, Fax
Food & Beverages	Indian, Continental & 2 Bars
Credit Card	Major Credit Cards accepted

Le Meridien Hotel

Classification/Category	5 Star Deluxe (as classified by Government of India, Department of Tourism)

Total no. of rooms	358
Address	Windsor Place, Janpath, New Delhi 110 001
Contact details	Tel: 011-23710101 Fax: 011-23714545 E-Mail : info@lemeridien-newdelhi.com
Access	15 kms from International Airport, 12 kms from Domestic Airport, 2 kms from New Delhi Railway Station & 3 kms from City Centre (Connaught Place)
Special room facilities	Each guest room and suite has a large flat screen TV, DVD, VCD, and CD Player, WI-Fi + High-Speed Internet Access, Separate Sofa seating, individually controlled air conditioning, International direct-dial telephone lines, a hair dryer and an in-room safe
Other facilities	Equipped Gymnasium, the Amatra Spa, and swimming pool with crystal clear water jogging track, bank, shopping arcade, beauty saloon & barber shop, live band at Le Belvedere
Services	Doctor on Call, Laundry, Money Changer, Banking, Safe Deposit, Baby Sitting, Valet, Travel Desk Service
Food & Beverages	Indian, Chinese, Continental & 2 Bars
Credit Card	Major Credit Cards accepted

Hotel Radisson

Classification/Category	5 Star Deluxe (as classified by Government of India, Department of Tourism)
Total no. of rooms	256
Address	National Highway 8, New Delhi 110 037
Contact details	Tel: 011-26779191 Fax: 011-26119090 E-Mail : reservationc@radissondel.com
Access	3 kms from International Airport, 5 kms from Domestic Airport, 18 kms from New Delhi Railway Station; & 18 kms from City Centre (Connaught Place)
Special room facilities	Complimentary Wi-Fi internet facility, Tea/Coffee maker, Room safe, Ironing board
Other facilities	The Spa-an ultra modern three level spa spread

	over 20,000 sq feet dedicated to your rejuvenation, relax & replenishment
Services	Doctor on call, Laundry, Money Changer, Banking, Safe Deposit, Baby Sitting, Valet, Travel Desk Service
Food & Beverages	Indian, Italian, Continental, Mediterranean, Spanish & Bar
Credit Card	Major Credit Cards accepted

The Claridges Hotel

Classification/Category	5 Star (as classified by Government of India, Department of Tourism)
Total no. of rooms	137
Address	12, Aurangzeb Road, New Delhi 110 011
Contact details	Tel: 011-41335133 Fax: 011-23010625 E-Mail : info@claridges.com
Access	17 kms from International Airport, 8 kms from Domestic Airport; 4 kms from New Delhi Railway Station & 3 kms from City Centre (Connaught Place)
Special room facilities	Tea/Coffee maker, Electronic Safe, Mini Bar, Interactive TV
Other facilities	Doctor on Call, Beauty Parlour & Men's Salon, Fitness Centre, Shopping Arcade, Swimming Pool, Business Centre, Board Room, Catering & Meeting Facilities, Laundry, Travel Desk
Services	Baby Sitting facility on request, Currency Changer
Food & Beverages	Indian, Chinese, Continental, Mediterranean & Bar
Credit Card	Major Credit Cards accepted

The Park Hotel

Classification/Category	5 Star Deluxe (as classified by Government of India, Department of Tourism)
Total no. of rooms	220
Address	15, Parliament Street, New Delhi 110 001
Contact details	Tel: 011-23743000 Fax: 011-23744000 E-Mail : gm.del@theparkhotels.com

Access	15 kms from International Airport, 12 kms from Domestic Airport; 2 kms from New Delhi Railway Station & 100 metres from City Centre (Connaught Place)
Special room facilities	Voice mail, international direct dial, email, internet facilities, safe deposit lockers and in-room safes, minibar, multi-channel colour television with satellite TV, in-room temperature control, hairdryers, in-house laundry, fresh flowers, seasonal fruits, newspaper of choice
Other facilities	Doctor on call, disabled access and no smoking rooms and confectionery shop
Services	24 hrs currency exchange, 24 hrs car hire, and travel services, baby sitting, free car parking and valet services
Food & Beverages	Coffee Shop, Indian & Bar
Credit Card	Major Credit Cards accepted

Hotel Radisson Marina

Classification/Category	4 Star (as classified by Government of India, Department of Tourism)
Total no. of rooms	94
Address	G-59, Connaught Circus, New Delhi 110 001
Contact details	Tel: 011-23324658 Fax: 011-23328609 E-Mail : reservations@rdmardel.com
Access	15 kms from International Airport, 12 kms from Domestic Airport; 1 km from New Delhi Railway Station & located in the City Centre (Connaught Place)
Special room facilities	Attached bathrooms, running Hot & Cold water, refrigerator, colour TV with satellite channels, direct dial telephone, mini bar and 24 hour room service
Other facilities	Travel Desk, Barber shop, Front Desk, Free Newspaper, Parking, Bar, Banquet, Safe Deposit Box, Conference Facilities, Business Centre
Services	Doctor on Call, Laundry, Currency Exchange, Safety Deposit Box, Secretarial Services, Wake up service

Food & Beverages	Indian, Continental & Chinese Cuisine & 01 Bar
Credit Card	Major Credit Cards accepted

Eros Intercontinental Hotel

Classification/Category	5 Star Deluxe (as classified by Government of India, Department of Tourism)
Total no. of rooms	218
Address	S-2, American Plaza, International Trade Tower, Nehru Place, New Delhi 110 019
Contact details	Tel: 011-41223344 Fax: 011-26239029 E-Mail : del-nehruplace@interconti.com
Access	18 kms from International Airport, 14 kms from Domestic Airport; 10 kms from New Delhi Railway Station & 12 kms from City Centre (Connaught Place)
Special room facilities	Direct high speed internet access, Wireless & wired broad band connectivity
Other facilities	Non-smoking rooms, A room for the physically challenged available on request, Club Intercontinental Lounge on the 12th floor terrace.
Services	24 hrs currency exchange, 24 hrs car hire, and travel services, baby sitting, free car parking and valet services
Food & Beverages	Indian, Chinese, Continental & 02 Bar
Credit Card	Major Credit Cards accepted

Hotel Vikram

Classification/Category	4 Star (as classified by Government of India, Department of Tourism)
Total no. of rooms	72
Address	Lajpat Nagar, New Delhi 110 024
Contact details	Tel: 011-46515151 Fax: 011-46515152 E-Mail : hotelvikramdelhi@hotelvikram.com
Access	19 kms from International Airport, 14 kms from Domestic Airport; 10 kms from New Delhi Railway Station & 9 kms from City Centre (Connaught Place)

Special room facilities	Room service, Hot & cold running water, Telephone, T.V., Safe deposit
Other facilities	Banquet facilities, Conference facilities, Swimming pool
Services	Doctor on call, Laundry, Money changer, Safe deposit, Travel desk, Fax, Cyber cafe
Food & Beverages	Indian, Chinese, Continental & 01 Bar
Credit Card	Major Credit Cards accepted

The Connaught Hotel

Classification/Category	4 Star (as classified by Government of India, Department of Tourism)
Total no. of rooms	79
Address	37, Shaheed Bhagat Singh Marg, New Delhi 110 001
Contact details	Tel: 011-23364225 Fax: 011-23340757 E-Mail : theconnaughtnewdelhi@yahoo.com
Access	15 kms from International Airport, 12 kms from Domestic Airport; 2 kms from New Delhi Railway Station & Located in the City Centre (Connaught Place)
Special room facilities	Room Service, Hot & Cold running water, Telephone, Multichannel T.V., Wi-Fi, Tea/Coffee maker
Other facilities	Banquet & Conference Facilities, Shopping Arcade, Business Centre
Services	Doctor on Call, Laundry, Money Changer, Safe Deposit, Baby Sitting, Valet, Travel Desk Service
Food & Beverages	Indian, Chinese, Continental & 01 Bar
Credit Card	Major Credit Cards accepted

Parkland Hotel, Kailash Colony

Classification/Category	3 Star (as classified by Government of India, Department of Tourism)
Total no. of rooms	29
Address	A-56, Kailash Colony, New Delhi 110048
Contact details	Tel: 011-42266655 Fax: 011-46688800 E-Mail : reservations@hotelparkland.in

Access	20 kms from International Airport, 16 kms from Domestic Airport; 12 kms from New Delhi Railway Station & 11 kms from City Centre (Connaught Place)
Special room facilities	Central Air-conditioning, Minibar, Hot & Cold running water, Telephone, Multichannel T.V., Tea/ Coffee maker
Other facilities	Conference Facilities, Business Centre
Services	Doctor on Call, Laundry, Money Changer, Safe Deposit, Valet, Travel Desk Service
Food & Beverages	Thai & Chinese cuisine
Credit Card	Major Credit Cards accepted

Parkland Hotel, Safdarjung Enclave

Classification/Category	3 Star (as classified by Government of India, Department of Tourism)
Total no. of rooms	42
Address	A-2/5, Safdarjung Enclave, New Delhi 110029
Contact details	Tel: 011-42266655 Fax: 011-46688800 E-Mail : reservations@hotelparkland.in
Access	18 kms from International Airport, 14 kms from Domestic Airport; 12 kms from New Delhi Railway Station & 11 kms from City Centre (Connaught Place)
Special room facilities	Central Air-conditioning, Minibar, Hot & Cold running water, Telephone, Multichannel T.V., Tea/ Coffee maker
Other facilities	Conference Facilities, Business Centre
Services	Doctor on Call, Laundry, Money Changer, Safe Deposit, Valet, Travel Desk Service
Food & Beverages	European cuisine & Bar
Credit Card	Major Credit Cards accepted

Parkland Hotel, Kalkaji Colony

Classification/Category	3 Star (as classified by Government of India, Department of Tourism)
Total no. of rooms	48
Address	CC-30,31, Nehru Enclave, Opposite Nehru Place, New Delhi 110 019

Contact details	Tel: 011-42266655 Fax: 011-46688800 E-Mail : reservations@hotelparkland.in
Access	21 kms from International Airport, 17 kms from Domestic Airport; 17 kms from New Delhi Railway Station & 16 kms from City Centre (Connaught Place)
Special room facilities	Central Air-conditioning, Minibar, Hot & Cold running water, Telephone, Multichannel T.V., Tea/ Coffee maker
Other facilities	Conference Facilities, Business Centre
Services	Doctor on Call, Laundry, Money Changer, Safe Deposit, Valet, Travel Desk Service
Food & Beverages	Multi Cuisine
Credit Card	Major Credit Cards accepted

Hilton Garden Inn Hotel

Classification/Category	4 Star (as classified by Government of India, Department of Tourism)
Total no. of rooms	116
Address	A4 DLF Place Saket District Centre, New Delhi 110 017
Contact details	Tel: 011-39191919 Fax: 011-39191920
Access	16 kms from International Airport, 12 kms from Domestic Airport; 12 kms from New Delhi Railway Station & is located 11 kms from the City Centre (Connaught Place)
Special room facilities	Garden Sleep® System bed, which enables guests to adjust the firmness or softness of the bed; Herman Miller Mirra ergonomic chairs, spacious, clutter free work desk, complimentary wired and wireless Wi-Fi with remote printing, two phones, 32 inch flat panel LCD TV, ample plugs, electronic safe, hot water tea kettle, iron and ironing board
Other facilities	Business Centre, Baby sitting service, Fitness Centre, pool, Foreign exchange, valet, Laundry, Room Service, Safety Deposit Box
Services	Doctor on Call, Travel Desk Service

Food & Beverages	Coffee shop, Pavilion Pantry which will offer a selection of healthy snacks, microwaveable meals, beverages and sundries & a bar
Credit Card	Major Credit Cards accepted

Hotel Hilton, Janakpuri

Classification/Category	4 Star (as classified by Government of India, Department of Tourism)
Total no. of rooms	228
Address	Janakpuri District Centre Complex, New Delhi 110 058
Contact details	Tel: 011-41234123 Fax: 011-41234124
Access	18 kms from International Airport, 14 kms from Domestic Airport, 16 kms from New Delhi Railway Station & 15 kms located in the City Centre (Connaught Place)
Special room facilities	In-room facilities offer attached bathroom, plasma TV, Iron & Ironing board, Mini bar, Coffee/ Tea maker and an Electronic safe
Other facilities	Business Centre, Baby sitting service, Fitness Centre, pool, Foreign exchange, valet, Laundry, Room Service, Safety Deposit Box
Services	Doctor on Call, Travel Desk Service
Food & Beverages	Indian, Chinese, Mediterranean, Italian & 01 Bar
Credit Card	Major Credit Cards accepted

The Hans Hotel

Classification/Category	4 Star (as classified by Government of India, Department of Tourism)
Total no. of rooms	67
Address	Hansalaya Building,15, Barakhamba Road, New Delhi 110 001
Contact details	Tel: 011-23316861 Fax: 011-23314830 E-Mail : info@hanshotels.com
Access	23 kms from International Airport, 16 kms from Domestic Airport, 2 kms from New Delhi Railway Station & Located in the City Centre (Connaught Place)

Special room facilities	24 hrs Room Service, Hot & Cold running water, Telephone, T.V., Channel Music
Other facilities	Business Centre, Separate Executive Floor, Banquet & Conference Facilities, Secretarial Services
Services	Doctor on Call, Laundry, Money Changer, Fax, Safe Deposit, Baby sitting, Travel Desk Service
Food & Beverages	Indian, Continental, Mediterranean, Italian & 01 Bar
Credit Card	Major Credit Cards accepted

Crowne Plaza Hotel

Classification/Category	5 Star Deluxe (as classified by Government of India, Department of Tourism)
Total no. of rooms	240
Address	New Friends Colony, New Delhi 110025
Contact details	Tel: 011-26835070 Fax: 011-26837758 E-Mail : crowneplaza@crowneplazadelhi.com
Access	22 kms from International Airport, 15 kms from Domestic Airport; 12 kms from New Delhi Railway Station & 11 kms From City Centre (Connaught Place)
Special room facilities	Tea/Coffee maker, Mini Bar in all rooms, Butler in club Rooms
Other facilities	Health Club, Ayurvedic Massage
Services	WIFII Enabled Hotel
Food & Beverages	Indian, Continental, Chinese & 01 Bar
Credit Card	Major Credit Cards accepted Svelte, Personal
Svelte, Personal Suites	Suites
Classification/Category	4 Star (as classified by Government of India, Department of Tourism)
Total no. of rooms	83
Address	A-3, District Centre, Select City walk, Saket, New Delhi 110017
Contact details	Tel: 011-40512000 Fax: 011-40512001 E-Mail : info@svelte.in
Access	15 kms from International Airport, 12 kms from Domestic Airport; 12 kms from New Delhi Railway

	Station & 11 kms From City Centre (Connaught Place)
Special room facilities	Designer kitchenette equipped with refrigerator, microwave oven, hot plate, cookware and service ware, Specially designed pillow menu, Electronically controlled lighting and temperature controls, LCD television in the living and bedroom Functional workstation and study desk with internet connectivity and data port
Other facilities	Hi-speed internet and broadband access, 24-hour room service, International direct dialing, voice messaging and fax line capability, Housekeeping, In room dining, Health Centre
Services	Doctor on Call, Security Services
Food & Beverages	Indian, Continental, Chinese
Credit Card	Major Credit Cards accepted

The Claridges, Surajkund

Classification/Category	5 Star Deluxe (as classified by Government of India, Department of Tourism)
Total no. of rooms	285
Address	Shooting Range Road, Faridabad, Haryana – 121001
Contact details	Tel: 129-4190000 Fax: 129-4190001 E-Mail : tcsk@claridges.com
Access	25 kms from International Airport, 20 kms from Domestic Airport; 20 kms from New Delhi Railway Station & 19 kms From City Centre (Connaught Place)
Special room facilities	Centrally air conditioned,24 hour room service, Tea/Coffee maker, Bedside master control for lights, Separate work desk, Bath tub & glass shower cubicle, Premium bathroom amenities, Mini bar, In room interactive LCD television, Dual line telephone with voice mail, In room electronic safe, Four fixture bathroom
Other facilities	Fitness Centre, Swimming pool

Services	WIFI Enabled Hotel
Food & Beverages	Indian, Mediterranean & 01 Bar
Credit Card	Major Credit Cards accepted

ACCOMMODATION MANUAL

The XIX Commonwealth Games 2010 Delhi is scheduled from 3 October to 14 October, 2010. This is the best time to travel to Delhi, which has average daytime temperatures of 22°C (71.5°F) in October. You can visit many of Delhi's numerous heritage sites and monuments, sample world class cuisine and entertainment at the city's numerous hotels and restaurants, shop till you drop at the various malls and shopping outlets the city provides, and experience all that this vibrant, exciting city has to offer.

Delhi is located a few hours away from the world's greatest monument to love, the majestic Taj Mahal in Agra. Also close by is the colourful state of Rajasthan with its forts and palaces, tales of valour, and unbeatable exotic experiences.The sheer scale and diversity of India offers a range of destinations and experiences found nowhere else in the world: the mystical and breathtaking Himalayas in the north; vast beaches with an exciting range of water sports and other activities; peaceful lagoons and inland waterways; yoga and meditation to lift your spirits; wildlife parks to commune with nature; and ancient heritage sites to remind you of India's ancient past. Incredible India has it all—waiting to be experienced!

The Accommodation Functional Area, Commonwealth Games Delhi 2010 in conjunction with the Games Travel Office has secured a comprehensive range of hotel accommodation in and around Delhi exclusively for visitors to Delhi for the Games. It is important to note that all accommodation option listed within this document are subject to availability at the time of request and will be allocated in order of receipt of bookings.

Games Family Hotels

Flagship Hotel—The Ashok

The Ashok is an Indian Tourism Development Corporation Ltd. (ITDC) hotel, and has been nominated as the Flagship Hotel for the XIX Commonwealth Games 2010 Delhi. No hotel symbolises the traditional grandeur and hospitality of the historic capital of India more than The Ashok. Set in a prime location in New Delhi's Diplomatic Enclave, The Ashok is the foremost of Delhi's five-star hotels, a distinctive landmark and pride of Indian hospitality. It has also played host to many international events, and has hosted 103 Heads of State in the past.

The hotel offers a choice of 550 rooms and suites, ranging from executive to theme suites and an emperor—The Ashok Presidential Suite. It is well equipped, offering facilities such as broadband Internet access in all rooms. There are special rooms for the physically challenged, a most magnificent convention venue of the capital, international and national specialty cuisine restaurants, and an in-house discotheque, a world class state-of-the-art health spa and Fitness Centre, 24 hour money changer and safe deposits in each room.

This hotel will host members of the Commonwealth Games Federation members (CGF), Commonwealth Games Associations (CGAs), International Sports Federations, and the International Olympic Committees members (IOCs). The Ashok will also have offices of the President of the CGF, One Stop Shop and Games Family Accreditation Centre. It will host all major conferences, events, dinners, etc., that will be held during Games time. The hotel will act as a nerve centre during Games time from where all major decisions and policies will be taken and monitored.

Facilities on Additional Payment

Airline counters, business centre, baby sitter, bank, billiards room, beauty salon and barber shop, business centre, chemist, theatre evenings, confectionery, courier service, credit cards (Diners, American Express, Master Card, Visa), dentist by appointment, doctor on call, florist, golf, health club, laundry and dry cleaning same-day service and 24 hour room service.

Room Allocation

Constituent with our bid commitment each CGA has been allocated 2 rooms (double/single occupancy) at the Games Family Hotel free of charge for the period of 29th Sept 2010—15th Oct 2010. Additional rooms have been protected for CGA's and at this stage each CGA can secure up to 2 additional rooms at a cost of USD 225 (double occupancy) or USD 200 (single occupancy) plus taxes.

CGA's will have the opportunity to book these rooms up till 31 March, 2010 after which the rooms will be made openly available to other games constituents.

Adjacent to The Ashok Hotel is the Samrat Hotel that offers 4 Star accommodation and easy access for accredited personnel to the Games Family Hotel. Rates for this hotel are USD 185 (double occupancy) or USD 175 (single occupancy).

Media Hotels

Tariff in USD

S. No.	*Hotel Name*	*Room Category*	*Single*	*Double*	*Location*	*Distance from Main Media Centre*
1.	Janpath	Standard Room	140	150	*Connaught Place*	*3 km*
		Suite	*200*	*210*		
2.	Ramada Plaza	*Deluxe Room*	*170*	*175*	*Connaught Place*	*3 km*

Other Hotels

A range of hotel accommodation is offered by the GTO as featured in this brochure. A selection of properties and applicable room rates has been detailed below. For a complete list of available properties, including descriptions and facilities available at the hotels on additional charges, please refer to www.cwgdelhi 2010.org/accommodation

			Tariff in USD		*Location*	*Approx Distance*	
S. No.	*Hotel Name*	*Room Category*	*Single*	*Double*		*Domestic Airport*	*International Airport*
1.	ITC Maurya	Executive Club Room	275	300	South Delhi	7 Km	14 Km
		The Towers	350	375			
2.	The Oberoi	Deluxe Room	275	290	South Delhi	15 Km	18 Km
		Luxury Room	370	380			

(*Contd.*)

			Tariff in USD		Location	Approx Distance	
S. No.	Hotel Name	Room Category	Single	Double		Domestic Airport	International Airport
		King Room & win Room	275	300		9 Km	13 Km
3.	Hyatt	View King Room & View Twin Room	350	375	South Delhi		
		Regency Club Room King & Win	375	400			
4.	The Taj Palace	Deluxe Room	250	275	South Delhi	7 Km	14 Km
		Luxury Room	275	300			
5.	Le Meridien	Executive Room	250	275	CP/Central	12 Km	15 Km
		Royal Club Room	350	375			
		Executive Suite	425	450			
6.	Radisson	Superior Room	250	250	South Delhi	5 Km	3 Km
		Club Room	270	275			
7.	Claridges Delhi	Deluxe Room	250	275	South Delhi	8 Km	17 Km
		Club Room	280	325			
8.	The Park	Luxury Room	250	270	CP/Central	12 Km	15 Km
		Luxury Premium Room	275	300			
9.	Radisson Marina	Superior Room	200	250	CP/Central	12 Km	15 Km

(Contd.)

			Tariff in USD		Location	Approx Distance	
S. No.	Hotel Name	Room Category	Single	Double		Domestic Airport	International Airport
10.	Eros Intercontinental	Superior Room	250	270	South Delhi	14 Km	18 Km
11.	Hotel Vikram	Executive Club	170	170	South Delhi	14 Km	19 Km
12.	The Connaught	Standard Room	170	175	CP/Central	12 Km	15 Km
13.	Parkland	Deluxe Room	170	175	South Delhi	14 Km	18 Km
14.	Hilton Garden INN	Hilton Evolution Room	250	275	South Delhi	12 Km	16 Km
		Garden View Guest Room	275	300			
15.	Hilton	Standard Room	250	275	West Delhi	14 Km	18 Km
16.	The HANS	Executive Room	170	175	CP/Central Delhi	16 Km	23 Km
17.	Crowne Plaza	Superior Room	250	275	South Delhi	15 Km	22 Km
		Deluxe	275	300			
18.	Svelte	Executive Suite	175	200	South Delhi	12 Km	15 Km
		Royal Suite	250	275			
19.	Claridges Surajkund	Standard Room	250	270	Surajkund	20 Km	25 Km
		Premium Room	275	300			
20.	Country Inn & Suites	Superior Room	175	200	Sahibabad	30 Km	35 Km

- All quoted rates are in US Dollar, per room per Night including a Buffet Breakfast/Fixed Menu Breakfast.
- The rates quoted above are discounted rates secured by OC CWG D 2010 which we are passing on at cost to CGA's. Government taxes are levied on a Hotel published tariff which differs from the above. These are Nett October 1st

each year. Currently this is 10 per cent. As this figure will not be known until Games Time these taxes will have to be paid directly to the Hotel at the time of checking out.

- All extras to be paid directly to the hotel, at the time of checkout.
- Country Inn and suites serves Vegetarian food only.

Process of Booking in Media and other Hotels

The Booking Request Forms will be available on the website www.cwgdelhi2010.org/accommodation from 15 October 2009.

Process of Booking during General Assembly

Booking Request Forms will be launched for delivery during the General Assembly through 'One Stop Shop on 7 October 2009.

On receipt of your booking request, the GTO will forward you a written confirmation outlining your deposit payment requirement. Spot bookings can be done on payment of 30 per cent advance by credit card.

Please review the accommodation options mentioned above and e-mail the GTO at acco.gto@cwgdelhi2010.org for your booking request as soon as possible to ensure that your preferences can be met.

Process of Booking from 15 October 2009

Booking Request Forms are available online at www.cwg delhi2010.org/accommodation.

Terms of Payment

- A deposit payment of 30 per cent of the total billing should be made by 30 January 2010 to secure your reservation.
- Second installment of another 30 per cent of the total billing to be paid by 30 March 2010.
- Balance 40 per cent to be paid by 30 May 2010.

All accommodation during the Games period is subject to a four-night minimum stay.

Room Rate

All prices are per room per night in US Dollars. Room rates do not include Government taxes. Hotel prices are based on up to two persons sharing a room. All prices are based on use of existing bedding; additional charges will apply for use of a roll-away extra bed.

Full Payment

Full payment for all travel services on/before 30 May, 2010 is mandatory. Booking requests received after 31 May, 2010 shall be entertained on the basis of one-time full payment only.

Cancellations

Deposit payments of 30 per cent will be forfeited for each room cancelled. Following full payment (i.e., by 30 June, 2010), a cancellation fee equal to one hundred per cent (100%) will apply after 1 September, 2010.

Methods of Payment

All room rates are valid for payments made by bank transfer via SWIFT mode and credit cards (Visa/Master/Amex), bank or card charges on the total payment will be as applicable.

Accommodation Information

Distances from Games Family Hotel and Games Village have been provided by individual properties as a guide only.

Check-in and check-out at Hotels at 12 noon

General Terms

The OC CWG Delhi 2010 (including its GTO) does not accept any liability of whatever nature for the act, omissions or default, whether negligent or otherwise, of third party suppliers such as airlines, coach operators, shipping companies, hoteliers or other persons providing services in connection with your accommodation package over which we have no direct control. We do not accept liability in contract or in tort for any injury, damage, loss, delay, additional expenses or inconvenience caused, directly or indirectly, by *force majeure* or other events which are beyond our control, or which are not preventable by reasonable diligence on our part including, but not limited to war, civil disturbance, fire, floods, unusually severe weather conditions, acts of God, acts of government or any other authorities, accidents to or failure of equipment or machinery or industrial action. In the event of cancellation or change on account of the above, the GTO will offer alternative arrangements if any are available or, if alternatives are not available or are reasonably acceptable to you, it will refund that part of any money paid which relates to the accommodation package or service that has been cancelled or changed. In particular, the GTO will not be liable (subject to any statutory provisions having contrary effect) for any loss or damage sustained because of delays or inconvenience that might be experienced during your stay of accommodation.

Ms. Moti Irani. DDG Accommodation

(M): +91 9650714040, +91 9923760007
Email:moti.irani@cwgdelhi2010.org/moti.cwgd2010@gmail.com

Accommodation

Organising Committee Commonwealth Games 2010 Delhi
New Delhi City Centre, Tower II,
Opposite Jantar Mantar, Jai Singh Road,
New Delhi 110001, India.
Phone: +91 11 24500400, +91 11 24500539
Email: acco.gto@cwgdelhi2010.org/Online Bookings: www .cwgdelhi2010.org/accommodation
Games Travel Office
Mr. Sunil Kundu
(M): +91 9810798617
Email: sunil@lpti.in

9

Other Programmes, Mascot, Logos and Organising Committee for XIXth Commonwealth Games

VOLUNTEER PROGRAMME

It is a chance of a lifetime after 20 years: the chance to make a difference, the chance to see the world at your own doorstep, the chance to join the team of XIX Commonwealth Games 2010 Delhi volunteers. As Delhi prepares to roll out the red carpet to the world, every contribution will matter.

Volunteers are often known as the 'Face' of the Games and the 'Building Blocks' of the Organising Committee Commonwealth Games 2010 Delhi, for, without their selfless, 'we can do it' attitude, it would be difficult to conduct a successful event of this magnitude. Stability and strength come from the blocks when they are placed symmetrically—side by side, one on top of the other . . . . with each and every person contributing to the success of the Games.

By becoming a volunteer, you could be part of a team of 20,000 who will welcome the world to India. We are looking for a team that shares our values of sportsmanship, integrity, excellence, solidarity, diversity, competence, transparency, discipline and fairness.

The Volunteer Programme will be formally launched in mid-2009. If you are interested in being a part of the 20,000-strong volunteer team, watch this space for more details and updates.

SHERA—THE MASCOT

Shera, mascot of the XIX Commonwealth Games 2010 Delhi, is the most visible face of the XIX Commonwealth Games 2010 Delhi. His name comes from the Hindi word Sher – meaning tiger. Shera truly represents the modern Indian. He is an achiever with a positive attitude, a global citizen but justifiably proud of his nation's ancient heritage, a fierce competitor but with integrity and honesty. Shera is also a 'large-hearted gentleman' who loves making friends and enthusing people to 'come out and play'.

In Indian mythology, the tiger is associated with Goddess Durga, the embodiment of Shakti (or female power) and the vanquisher of evil. She rides her powerful vehicle—the tiger—into combat, especially in her epic and victorious battle against Mahishasur, a dreaded demon.

Shera embodies values that the nation is proud of: majesty, power, charisma, intelligence and grace. His athletic prowess, courage and speed on the field are legendary. He is also a reminder of the fragile environment he lives in and our responsibility towards the protection of his ecosystem.

Games Look

The logo of the XIX Commonwealth Games 2010 Delhi is inspired by the Chakra, the national symbol of freedom, unity and power. Spiralling upwards, it depicts the growth of India into a proud, vibrant nation. Her billion people coming together to fulfil their true destinies. India's journey from tradition to modernity, her economic transformation into a super power... reaching out to the world and leading the way, even as she enthusiastically embraces all the 71 CGA nations and territories of the Commonwealth to become one and host the best ever Commonwealth Games in Delhi.

Come Out and Play: The logo tagline is in an invitation to every person across all divides – Indian and Commonwealth—to let go of themselves and participate in the Games to the best of their abilities, in the true spirit of the Games. It is an exhortation to them to set new records, to outperform, and to raise the bar by scaling new peaks of achievement. It is also a call to the people of India, especially Delhi, to come out in support of the Games and play the perfect hosts at the XIX Commonwealth Games 2010 Delhi.

Colour Palette: The colour palette for the Delhi 2010 look programme combines two of the distinctive colours of the Delhi 2010 Emblem with the official colours of the Commonwealth Games.

Green: The colour that signifies life, energy and high spirits also represents the fact that Delhi 2010 will be the firstever Green Games. With a spring in your step, face every challenge and overcome hurdles with radiance and gusto.

Purple: Combining the stable and calming aspects of blue with the mystical qualities of pink, this colour satisfies the need for reassurance, while adding a hint of mystery and excitement.

Red, Yellow & Blue: Commonwealth Games colours, representing the 'Trinity of Values' that symbolise the games; unifying Humanity (Red) giving all athletes a chance to realise their Destiny (Yellow) and promoting Equality (Blue).

Pink: This colour has also been introduced to the palette adding an element of surprise and luxury to the Games look programme. It plays to the crowd and truly reflects India in all its resplendent glory.

COMMONWEALTH GAMES 2010 OFFICIAL LOGOS

Get ready to see them every now and then, everywhere. These are the logos that are going to make you proud for next 4-5 years in some or the other way. Remember Appu, well he was the one who was with us at the time of Asiad. Most of us have forgotten about him but he is still there. The same way the lion that you see in the Commonwealth Games 2010 logo is going to be present and is going to speak to you always.

KEY STAKEHOLDERS

The Host City Contract identifies and binds the five key stakeholders who are responsible for the successful delivery of the XIX Commonwealth Games 2010 Delhi. It is incumbent upon these stakeholders to undertake all measures, including adequate financial provisions, to deliver the Games in the most befitting manner within the framework of the Constitution, Protocol and Guidelines of the Commonwealth Games Federation (CGF). The key delivery partners are:

- Commonwealth Games Federation (CGF);
- Indian Olympics Association (IOA);
- Organising Committee (OC);
- Government of the National Capital Territory of Delhi (GNCTD);
- Government of India (GoI).

The requirement to fulfil multiple functional roles as well as several support areas in the organisation and management of an event of the stature of the XIX Commonwealth Games 2010 Delhi also includes several ministries, departments and agencies of GoI and several local and municipal bodies of the GNCTD within the purview of delivery partners.

CGF

The CGF, headquartered in London, is the organisation that is responsible for the direction and control of the Commonwealth Games. The CGF is the supreme authority in all matters concerning the Commonwealth Games. In effect, the CGF "owns" the Commonwealth Games in the same way as the International Olympic Committee "owns" the Olympic Games. The governance of the CGF is through the General Assembly and the Executive Board of the Federation. Ultimate authority lies with the General Assembly of member countries and territories, which meets once a year. The Executive Board consists of the Officers of the CGF and a Regional Vice-President from each of the CGF' six regions.

The Commonwealth Games is awarded to a Commonwealth Games Association's (CGA's) candidate city by the CGF at its General Assembly. This city is chosen seven years in advance of the eventual hosting. The CGF entrusts the CGA of the Host Country with the organisation of the Games.

Through the mechanisms of its Constitution, regulations, rules of conduct, Host City Contract, manuals and knowledge management programmes, the CGF facilitates the preparation for and conduct of the Games while fulfilling its mission of maintaining the integrity of the Commonwealth Games. It also provides an interface between International Federations and CGAs and ensures their complete cooperation during the Games.

ORGANISING COMMITTEE COMMONWEALTH GAMES 2010 DELHI

The IOC has delegated the responsibility for fulfilling the obligations of the Host City Contract—under Protocol 2 of the Contract, in accordance with Article 27 C of the Constitution and with the approval of the Commonwealth Games Federation (CGF)—to the Organising Committee Commonwealth Games 2010 Delhi. The OC CWG Delhi 2010 is thus empowered to plan, manage and deliver XIX Commonwealth Games 2010 Delhi. It was formed on 10 February 2005, as a registered society under the Societies Registration Act 1860 of India. It is a non-profit autonomous body that works in collaboration with its partners to build a committed team and adopt best practices for the successful delivery of the Games.

The Organising Committee Commonwealth Games 2010 Delhi (OC CWG Delhi 2010) came into being on 10 February 2005, as a registered society under the Societies Registration Act 1860. It was resolved by the Commonwealth Games Federation (CGF) in the General Assembly held in Jamaica on 13 November 2003 to entrust the organising and hosting of the XIX Commonwealth Games to the Indian Olympic Association (IOA). As per Clause 2(C) of the Host City Contract, signed by the Government of India (GoI), the Government of National Capital Territory of Delhi (GNCTD), IOA, and CGF, IOC has delegated the organisation of the Games to the OC CWG Delhi 2010.

The OC CWG Delhi 2010 has set itself the goal of conducting the best Commonwealth Games to date, including the provision of impeccable standards of service to athletes, officials and the general public, in close collaboration with its partners. It hopes to set new benchmarks for other Host nations with regards to urban sustainable development by showcasing excellent infrastructure and facilities which could be used by the society and the general public for generations to come.

KEY OBJECTIVES

- Prepare for, organise and conduct the XIX Commonwealth Games 2010 Delhi in the National Capital Region (NCR) of Delhi;

- Prepare for, organise and conduct other events (including sports and cultural activities and festivals) as part of the XIX Commonwealth Games 2010 Delhi including the Commonwealth Youth Games;
- Promote all such activities that may be useful, necessary or helpful and which contribute towards the conduct of the XIX Commonwealth Games 2010 Delhi;
- Conduct XIX Commonwealth Games 2010 Delhi in a manner that would encourage sports development and physical recreation and promote the shared values of integrity, fair play, competence, team work, commitment to excellence, respect for gender equality and tolerance including the fight against the use of drugs and unhealthy or performance enhancing substances;
- Advise all offices, institutions, government and other bodies of associations that may be associated with the holding of the XIX Commonwealth Games 2010 Delhi;
- Decide on all matters connected with the preparations and holding of the XIX Commonwealth Games 2010 Delhi and bringing it to a successful completion; and
- Do all such lawful things that are incidental or conducive to the attainment of the above objectives or of any of them.

Vision, Mission and Values

Vision

The vision of the Organising Committee Commonwealth Games 2010 Delhi is to inculcate sports consciousness and culture in every Indian.

Mission

- Deliver the 'Best Commonwealth Games Ever'
- Build state-of-the-art sporting and city infrastructure for the facilitation of the Games
- Create a suitable environment and opportunities for the involvement of the citizens in the Games
- Showcase the culture and heritage of India
- Project Delhi as a global destination
- Project India as an economic power
- Leave behind a lasting legacy.

Values

In fulfilling its mission, the OC CWG Delhi 2010 will exhibit and abide by the following values in its day-to-day operations:

- Sportsmanship
- Integrity
- Excellence
- Solidarity
- Diversity
- Competence
- Transparency
- Discipline.

Secretariat

This team is responsible for planning, coordination and execution of all Functional Area plans in order to deliver the Games.

The Team

Chairman Secretariat and Executive Office			
Name	*Designation*	*Contacts*	*Email*
Mr. Suresh Kalmadi	Chairman	24500401	suresh.kalmadi@cwgdelhi2010.org
Mr. Randhir Singh	Vice Chairman	24500402	randhir.singh@cwgdelhi2010.org
Dr. Lalit K. Bhanot	Secretary General	24500403	lalit.bhanot@cwgdelhi2010.org
Mr. A.K. Mattoo	Treasurer	24500405	ak.mattoo@cwgdelhi2010.org
Mr. V.K. Verma	Director General	24500406	vk.verma@cwgdelhi2010.org
Mr. T.S. Darbari	JDG (Revenue, Marketing & Chairman Secretariat)	24500411	ts.darbari@cwgdelhi2010.org
Ms. Shovana Narayan	JDG (Ceremonies)	24500409	shovana.narayan@cwgdelhi2010.org
Mr. Anil Kumar Saxena	JDG (Venue Development & Operations)	24500410	ak.saxena@cwgdelhi2010.org

(Contd.)

Chairman Secretariat and Executive Office			
Name	*Designation*	*Contacts*	*Email*
Mr. R.K. Sacheti	JDG (Coordination)	24500511	rk.sacheti@cwgdelhi2010.org
Mr. M. Jeychandren	JDG (Finance & Accounts)	24500503	m.jeychandren@cwgdelhi2010 .org
Mr. A.S.V. Prasad	JDG (Sport)	24500521	asv.prasad@cwgdelhi2010.org
Mr. B.B. Kaura	JDG (Revenue)	24500568	bb.kaura@cwgdelhi2010.org
Mr. Vijay Kumar Gautam	Chief Operating Officer	24500407	vijay.gautam@cwgdelhi2010.org
Mr. N.P. Singh	ADG (Workforce and Administration)	24500408	n.p.singh@cwgdelhi2010.org
Lt. Gen. (Retd.) Raj Kadyan	ADG (Ceremonies)	24500523	raj.kadyan@cwgdelhi2010.org
Lt. Gen. (Retd.) Ashok Vasudeva	ADG (Chairman's Office)	24500465	ashok.vasudeva@cwgdelhi2010. org
Mr. Sujit Panigrahi	ADG (Technology)	24500420	sujit.panigrahi@cwgdelhi2010. org
Lt. Gen. (Retd.) Ashok Kapur	ADG (Games Village)	24500517	ashok.kapur@cwgdelhi2010.org
Group Captain K.U.K. Reddy	ADG (Finance)	24500475	kuk.reddy@cwgdelhi2010.org
Ms. Sangeeta Wellinkar	ADG (Chairman's Office and Image & Look)	24500412	sangeeta.w@cwgdelhi2010.org
Mr. Uday Sahay	ADG (Communi-cations)	24500447	uday.sahay@cwgdelhi2010.org
Mr. V.K. Saksena	ADG (Revenue)	24500530	vk.saksena@cwgdelhi2010.org

Functional Area and its Head			
Functional Area	*FA Head*	*Contacts*	*Email*
Accommo-dation	Ms. Moti Irani	24500459	moti.irani@cwgdelhi2010.org
Accredition	Mr. R.K. Sacheti	24500511	rk.sacheti@cwgdelhi2010.org
Broadcasting	Mr. Goverdhan Sharma	24500512	govardhan.sharma@cwgdelhi2010.org
Catering	Mr. V.K. Gautam	24500407	vijay.gautam@cwgdelhi2010.org
Ceremonies	Mrs. Shovana Narayan	24500409	shovana.narayan@cwgdelhi2010.org
CGA Relations	Mr. V.K. Gautam	24500407	vijay.gautam@cwgdelhi2010.org
Co-ordination & Govt. Relation	Mr. R.K. Sacheti	24500511	rk.sacheti@cwgdelhi2010.org
Cleaning and Waste Management	Mr. V.K. Gautam	24500407	vijay.gautam@cwgdelhi2010.org
Communica-tions	Mr. Uday Sahay	24500447	uday.sahay@cwgdelhi2010.org
Finance & Accounts	Mr. Jeychandren	24500503	m.jeychanderen@cwgdelhi2010.org
Games Village Develop-ment and Operation	Lt. Gen. Ashok Kapur (Retd.)	24500465	ashok.kapur@cwgdelhi2010.org
Image and Look	Ms. Sangeeta Wellinkar	24500544	sangeeta.w@cwgdelhi2010.org
Legacy	Mr. R.K. Sacheti	24500511	rk.sacheti@cwgdelhi2010.org
Legal	Mr. Ram Mohan	24500540	ram.mohan@cwgdelhi2010.org
Logistics	Mr. R K Singh	24500472	rakesh.singh@cwgdelhi2010.org

(*Contd.*)

Functional Area and its Head			
Functional Area	*FA Head*	*Contacts*	*Email*
Medical & Doping Control	Mr. Ak. Mendiratta (Medical)	24500553	ak.mendiratta@cwgdelhi2010.org
	Mr. Munish Chander (Doping)	24500501	munish.chander@cwgdelhi2010.org
Merchandising & Licensing	Mr. V.K. Saksena	24500530	vk.saksena@cwgdelhi2010.org
Office Adminis-tration	Mr. N.P. Singh	24500408	np.singh@cwgdelhi2010.org
Procure-ment	Mr. Surjit Lal	24500443	surjit.lal@cwgdelhi2010.org
Protocol	Mr. Nachiketa Kapur	24500532	nachiketa.kapur@cwgdelhi2010.org
Queen's Baton Relay	Lt. Gen. Raj Kadyan (Retd.)	24500523	raj.kadyan@cwgdelhi2010.org
Revenue	Mr. V.K. Saksena	24500530	vk.saksena@cwgdelhi2010.org
Risk Mana-gement	Mr. V.K. Gautam	24500407	vijay.gautam@cwgdelhi2010.org
Security	Col. R.K. Yadav	24500566	rk.yadav@cwgdelhi2010.org
Spectator Services	Mr. V.K. Gautam	24500407	vijay.gautam@cwgdelhi2010.org
Sponsor-ship	Mr. V.K. Saksena	24500530	vk.saksena@cwgdelhi2010.org
Sports	Mr. ASV Prasad	24500521	asv.prasad@cwgdelhi2010.org
Sustaina-bility & Environment	Mr. N.P. Singh	24500408	np.singh@cwgdelhi2010.org
Technology	Mr. Sujit Panigrahi	24500420	sujit.panigrahi@cwgdelhi2010.org
Ticketing	Mr. V.K. Saksena	24500530	vk.saksena@cwgdelhi2010.org

(Contd.)

Functional Area and its Head			
Functional Area	*FA Head*	*Contacts*	*Email*
Transportation	Mr. A.K. Chaturvedi	24500551	ak.chaturvedi@cwgdelhi2010.org
TV Rights	Mr. B.B. Kaura	24500568	bb.kaura@cwgdelhi2010.org
Venue Development & Operations	Mr. A.K. Saxena	24500410	ak.saxena@cwgdelhi2010.org
Workforce	Mr. N.P. Singh	24500408	np.singh@cwgdelhi2010.org

BUSINESS PARTNERS

The Organising Committee Commonwealth Games 2010 Delhi is looking for business partners in the following areas to achieve its goals of holding a successful Commonwealth Games.

Sponsors

Through participation in the Games as a sponsor, corporate businesses can access an outstanding marketing opportunity with the largest and most significant sporting and community event ever to be staged in the country. Your association with this event will provide not only a brand leadership position but an opportunity to win the hearts and minds of the community at large.

The Games can be used to support the achievement of a range of corporate, sales and marketing objectives. The sponsorship team for Delhi 2010 would be pleased to discuss with you a tailor made proposal to meet your individual corporate needs. For more information, contact sponsorship@cwgdelhi2010.org

Broadcasting Rights

The Organising Committee Commonwealth Games 2010 Delhi is appointing Prasar Bharti as the Host Broadcaster for XIX Commonwealth Games 2010 Delhi. The world class International Broadcasting Centre (IBC) will cater to the needs of the Rights Holder Broadcasters.

International Broadcasting Rights

With the help of our International Broadcast Rights sales and strategy consultant, we have already contracted for Broadcasting Rights with major television channels for some international territories with high sports viewership ratings. Interested international channels could contact revenue@cwgdelhi2010.org for details on the sale of the International Broadcasting Rights of D2010.

Domestic Rights

TV Rights: The exclusive rights in India to televise on free to air television will be granted to Prasar Bharti.

New Media Rights: These rights would include existing New Media and new technologies including Internet, Mobile, Digital Video Broadcasting – Handheld (DVB-H), etc. Interested organisations could contact revenue@cwgdelhi2010.org for details on the sale of New Media Rights of D2010.

10

Sports, Competition and Non-Competition Venues for XIXth CWG: A Detailed Account

INTRODUCTION

XIX Commonwealth Games 2010 Delhi will feature 17 sports: Aquatics (Swimming, Synchronised Swimming and Diving), Archery, Athletics (Track and Field, Road Walk and Marathon), Badminton, Boxing, Cycling (Track, Road Mass Start and Road Time Trials), Gymnastics (Artistic and Rhythmic), Hockey, Lawn Bowls, Netball, Rugby 7s, Shooting (Pistol, Small Bore, Full Bore and Clay Target), Squash, Table Tennis, Tennis, Weightlifting and Wrestling. The competition schedule of the Games was presented to, and approved by, the CGF General Assembly meeting in Colombo, 5 - 9 November.

The 17 sports to feature in the XIX Commonwealth Games 2010 Delhi will be held at six venue clusters and five stand alone venues in Delhi. Ceremonies, Athletics, Lawn Bowls and Weightlifting will be held at Cluster I: Jawaharlal Nehru Sports Complex; Cycling, Gymnastics and Wrestling at Cluster II: Indira Gandhi Sports Complex; Archery (Qualification Rounds) and Table Tennis at Cluster III: Yamuna Sports Complex; Badminton and Squash at Cluster IV: Siri Fort Sports Complex; Hockey and Archery Finals (India Gate) at Cluster V: MDC National Stadium Complex; and Swimming and Boxing at Cluster VI: Talkatora Garden Complex.

Twenty-six new training venues are being constructed for the Delhi 2010 for different sports. Work has been initiated on all the training venues and is progressing satisfactorily. Apart from this, 16 training venues are being upgraded and will be ready on schedule.

COMMONWEALTH GAMES 2010 SCHEDULE

Welcome to Commonwealth Games 2010 unofficial website. What you will provide here will generalize information about Commonwealth Games 2010 that is to be held in India. Information that will help you prepare yourself with all the required information about the event when it happens.

Sports Programme (October 3-14, 2010)													
Event		S	M	T	W	T	F	S	S	M	T	W	T
	Date	3	4	5	6	7	8	9	10	11	12	13	14
	Day	1	2	3	4	5	6	7	8	9	10	11	12
Opening Ceremony	J.N. Stadium (JNS)	?											
Closing Ceremony	J.N. Stadium (JNS)												?
1. Aquatics	Delhi University		?	?	?	?	?	?	?	?	?	?	
2. Athletics	J.N. Stadium (JNS)					?	?	?	?	?	?	?	
3. Badminton	Siri Fort Sports Complex		?	?	?	?	?	?	?	?	?	?	
4. Boxing	Talkatora Indoor Stadium		?	?	?	?	?	?	?	R	?		
5. Cycling	I.G. Indoor Stadium Complex		?	?	?	?		?				?	
6. Gymnastics	I.G. Indoor Stadium Complex		?	?	?	R	?	?		?	?	?	
7. Hockey	Maj. Dhyan Chand National Stadium		?	?	?	?	?	?	?	?	?	?	
8. Lawn Bowls	J.N. Stadium (JNS)		?	?	?	?	?	?	?	?	?		
9. Netball	Tyagaraj Sports Complex		?	?	?	?	?	?	?	?	?	?	
10. Rugby 7s	Delhi University			?	?								

(Contd.)

Sports Programme (October 3-14, 2010)													
Event		S	M	T	W	T	F	S	S	M	T	W	T
	Date	3	4	5	6	7	8	9	10	11	12	13	14
	Day	1	2	3	4	5	6	7	8	9	10	11	12
11. Shooting	Dr. Karni Singh Shooting Range		T	?	?	?	?	?	?	?	?	?	
12. Squash	Siri Fort Sports Complex		?	?	?	?	?	?	?	?	?	?	
13. Table Tennis	Yamuna Sports Complex		?	?	?	?	?	?	?	?	?	?	
14. Weightlifting	J.N. Stadium (JNS)			?	?	?	?	?	?	?	?		
15. Wrestling	I.G. Indoor Stadium Complex			?	?	?	?						

COMPETITION SCHEDULE

Event		*Venue*	*Event Dates*
Opening Ceremony		JN Stadium	3 October 2010
Closing Ceremony		JN Stadium	14 October 2010
Aquatics	Diving	Dr. SPM Swimming Complex	10-13 October 2010
	Swimming	Dr. SPM Swimming Complex	4-9 October 2010
	Synchronised	Dr. SPM Swimming Complex	6-7 October 2010
Archery		Yamuna Sports Complex/India Gate	4-10 October 2010
Athletics	Track & Field	JN Stadium	6-12 October 2010
	Marathon	JN Stadium/Marathon Course	14 October 2010
	Walk	India Gate	9 October 2010
Badminton		Siri Fort Sports Complex	4-14 October 2010
Boxing		Talkatora Indoor Stadium	5-11, 13 October 2010
Cycling	Track	IG Sports Complex	4-7 October 2010
	Road Mass Start	India Gate	10 October 2010
	Road Time Trials	Noida Highway Express Road	13 October 2010
Gymnastics	Artistic	IG Sports Complex	4-8 October 2010
	Rhythmic	IG Sports Complex	12-14 October 2010

(*Contd.*)

Event		Venue	Event Dates
Hockey		Maj. Dhyan Chand National Stadium	4-14 October 2010
Lawn Bowls		JN Sports Complex	4-13 October 2010
Netball		Thyagaraj Sports Complex	4-12, 14 October 2010
Rugby 7s		Delhi University	11-12 October 2010
Shooting	Clay Target	Dr. Karni Singh Shooting Range	8, 10-13 October 2010
	Full Bore	CRPF Campus, Kadarpur	7, 9, 11 October 2010
	Pistol and Small Bore	Dr. Karni Singh Shooting Range	5-13 October 2010
Squash		Siri Fort Sports Complex	4-13 October 2010
Table Tennis		Yamuna Sports Complex	4-14 October 2010
Tennis		RK Khanna Tennis Stadium	4-10 October 2010
Weightlifting		JN Sports Complex	4-12 October 2010
Wrestling		IG Sports Complex	5-10 October 2010

PARA-SPORTS

1. Swimming

Venue: Dr. S.P.M. Aquatics Complex, Talkatora Gardens *Competition Dates*: 5-9 October 2010

Men	Women
Freestyle (50 m – S9)	Freestyle (50 m – S9)
Freestyle (100 m – S8)	Freestyle (100 m – S9)
Freestyle (100 m – S10)	Butterfly (100 m –S9)

Entry: A CGA can enter maximum of 9 men and 9 women for three Para-sports swimming events.

2. Athletics

Venue: Jawaharlal Nehru Stadium (JNS)
Competition Dates: 6-12 October 2010

Men	*Women*
100 m – T46	100 m – T37
1500 m – T54 (Wheel Chair)	1500 m – T54 (Wheel Chair)
Shot Put – F32/34/52	Shot Put – F32-34/52/53

3. Table Tennis

Venue: Yamuna Sports Complex
Competition Dates: 10-14 October 2010
Women Wheelchair – (TT1-5)
Team Size: Maximum 3 Women

4. Powerlifting

Venue: J.N. Sports Complex
Competition Dates: 12 October 2010
Bench Press (Men &Women)
Entry: Maximum 3 lifters per CGA

SPORTS PERSONNELS

The following Technical Delegates, Competition Managers and Sports Managers have joined the Organising Committee Commonwealth Games 2010 Delhi:

Technical Delegates

Sr.	*Sport*	*Name*	*Country*
1.	Aquatics	Mr. Sam Ramsamy	South Africa
2.	Archery	Mr Dion Buhagiar	Malta
3.	Athletics	Mr. Bill Bailey	Australia
4.	Badminton	Mr. Henry Boon Kong Ee	Singapore
5.	Cycling	Mr. Ray Godkin	Australia
6.	Gymnastics		
	a) Artistics (M)	Mr Andrew Tombs	UK
	a) Artistics (F) (M)	Ms. Kym Dowdell	Australia
	Rhythmic	Ms. Tamara Bompa	Canada
7.	Hockey	Mr. Dennis Meredith	Australia
8.	Lawn Bowls	Mr. Kerry Clark	New Zealand
9.	Netball	Ms. Lindy Murphy	Australia

(Contd.)

Sr.	Sport	Name	Country
10.	Rugby 7s	Ms. Beth Coalter	Ireland
11.	Shooting	Mr. David R.V. Parish	UK
12.	Squash	Mr. Andrew Shelly	UK
13.	Table Tennis	Mr. Alan Ransome	UK
14.	Tennis	Mr. Paul Smith	UK
15.	Weightlifting	Dr. Tamas Ajan	Hungary
16.	Boxing	Mr. Raymond Silvas	USA
17.	Wrestling	Mr. Chang Kew Kim	Korea

Competition Managers

Sr.	Sport	Competition Manager	Sports Manager
1.	Aquatics	Mr. Kamlesh Nanavati	
2.	Archery	Mr. Rathin Datta	Ms. Zhang Xiuhu, China
3.	Athletics	Mr. C.K. Valson	
4.	Badminton	Mr. S. Muralidharan	
5.	Boxing	Mr. Jay Kowli	
6.	Cycling	Mr. William Patrick Clinch	
7.	Gymnastics	Dr. G.S. Bawa	
8.	Hockey	To be appointed	
9.	Lawn Bowls	Mr. Bill Fowlie, New Zealand	
10.	Netball	Ms. Carmel M. Wright, Australia	
11.	Rugby 7s	Mr. Kevin G. Culliver, Australia	
12.	Shooting	Mr. Avtar Singh Sethi	Mr. Graeme Hudson, New Zealand
13.	Squash	Mr. Manan Mushruwala	
14.	Table Tennis	Mr. Dhanraj Choudary	
15.	Tennis	Ms. Manpreet Kandhari	
16.	Weightlifting	Mr. K. Subramanya	
17.	Wrestling	Mr. Raj Singh	

COMPETITION VENUES

Construction of the following new venues is underway in full swing and progressing satisfactorily: Badminton and Squash (Siri Fort Sports Complex); Netball (Thyagaraj Sports Complex); Rugby 7s (Delhi University); Table Tennis (Yamuna Sports Complex); Weightlifting and Wrestling (Indira Gandhi Sports Complex); Shooting (Dr. Karni Singh Shooting Range); Archery Preliminaries (Yamuna Sports Complex); and Lawn Bowls (Jawaharlal Nehru Sports Complex).

Renovation of the following existing venues will be completed on schedule: Athletics (Jawaharlal Nehru Stadium); Boxing (Talkatora Indoor Stadium); Gymnastics (Indira Gandhi Stadium); Hockey (Major Dhyan Chand National Stadium); Swimming (Dr. S.P. Mukherjee Aquatics Complex); and Tennis (R.K. Khanna Tennis Stadium).

These are the following venues:

1. Jawaharlal Nehru Sports Complex
2. Thyagaraj Sports Complex
3. Indira Gandhi Sports Complex
4. Dr. S.P. Mukherjee Swimming Stadium
5. Talkatora Indoor Stadium
6. Major Dhyan Chand National Stadium
7. Siri Fort Sports Complex
8. Dr. Karni Singh Shooting Range
9. R.K. Khanna Tennis Complex
10. Yamuna Sports Complex.

NON-COMPETITION VENUES

OC CWG Delhi 2010 Headquarters

The OC CWG Delhi 2010 is located in the iconic New Delhi Municipal Council (NDMC) building, opposite Jantar Mantar, Connaught Place, New Delhi. The office is spread over nine floors with a capacity to accommodate a workforce of over 1,200. Its effective structural design, modern facilities, accessibility from all parts of Delhi, multi-level parking space and 24-hour power backup make it a state-of-the-art workspace. The design concept of the interiors of this uniquely shaped building showcases India of the 21st century, an amalgamation of tradition and technological advancement. The interiors complement contemporary design elements with usage of indigenous, eco-friendly and traditional materials.

Main Media Centre

XIX Commonwealth Games 2010 Delhi's state-of-the-art Main Media Centre (MMC), which will comprise the International Broadcasting Centre (IBC) and the Main Press Centre (MPC), will be set up in close proximity to the Games Village and the main venues at Pragati Maidan. While the IBC will be managed by the host broadcaster Prasar Bharti, the MCP will be managed by the Press Information Bureau (PIB), both state owned agencies. GoI plans to stop analogue broadcast in New Delhi before the D2010. Prasar Bharti will start high definition TV service on an experimental basis soon. New Delhi will become the first city in India to have digital broadcast through conditional access system by the time Games are held.

Games Family Hotel—Hotel Ashok

Hotel Ashok, in New Delhi, has been officially recognised as the Games Family Hotel. On 4 June 2009, a Memorandum of Understanding (MoU) was signed between OC CWG Delhi 2010 and India Tourism Development Corporation (ITDC) in this regard. Hotel Ashok offers 500 rooms and as the flagship family hotel, it will serve as host to members of CGAs, the CGF, International Sports Federations, Technical Delegates and the IOA. The hotel's rooms and suites as well public areas hotel such as the lounge, lobby and restaurants are being renovated and given a major facelift. The hotel will host the facilitation offices of the OC CWG Delhi 2010 and the CGF. All events, meetings and conferences, etc., will be held at the Games Family Hotel.

Training Venues

Sport	*No. of Venues*	*Venue Names*
ARCHERY	1	Yamuna Sports Complex
AQUATICS	4	Major Dhyan Chand National Stadium
		Shivaji Stadium
		Yamuna Sports Complex
LAWN BOWLS	2	Yamuna Sports Complex (2 greens)
		Delhi Public School, R.K. Puram (2 greens)
NETBALL	2	Delhi University (2 courts)
		Thyagaraj Sports Complex (2 courts)
RUGBY 7s	8	Delhi University (7)
		1. St. Stephan's College
		2. Hindu College
		3. Khalsa College
		4. Ramjas College
		5. Kirorimal College
		6. Sri Ram College of Commerce
		7. Daulatram College
		Jamia Milia Islamia University (1)
SHOOTING	2	Dr. Karni Singh Shooting Range
		CRPF Campus, Kadarpur (Full Bore)
SQUASH	1	Siri Fort Sports Complex (3)
TABLE TENNIS	2	Yamuna Sports Complex
		Jamia Milia Islamia
WEIGHTLIFTING	1	Games Village (12 platforms)
WRESTLING	3	Sri Ram College of Commerce (Women) (4 mats)
		Games Village (4 mats)
		Ludlow Castle (4 mats)
TENNIS	2	R.K. Khanna Sports Complex (6 courts)
		Siri Fort Sports Complex (9 courts)

11

Commonwealth Games, Tourism and India: Factors, Impacts and Institutions

COMMONWEALTH TOURISM 2010

This is the second time India is going to organise such a delightful multi-sport event - the Commonwealth 2010. India is anticipated to make this event into a major boost to tourism. As per official estimates, two million foreign tourists and 3.5 million domestic tourists are likely to arrive in Delhi in 2010. As a result of the Games, there will be a huge influx of tourists from all the nooks and corners of the globe. For the better benefit and comfort of foreign guests, a huge number of hotels and resorts are pulling up their services. The government is providing tax incentives for hotel rooms to prepare for this influx. With a focus on highly in demand tourist regions as Agra and Jaipur, several developments are to be implemented within a very short while.

In addition, the government has extended a five-year tax refund to the sightseeing and tourism industry to generate jobs and increase development. The Tourism ministry of Delhi is working intimately with the ministries of railways and civil aviation for setting up budget hotels. These budget hotels can accommodate 1,30,000 rooms and convention centres in all over the state. To improve connectivity and accommodation of 2010 Commonwealth Games, Tourism department is working at their level best.

During this event, the ministry also plans to organise four shopping events in three states of the country to attract more tourists. They are also keen to popularise the hallmarked jewellery in India with the help of this event. The Indian Ministry is going to host at least four shopping events before CWG 2010.

The Commonwealth Games Organising Committee expects almost one lakh tourists, including officials for the Games to be hosted in Delhi. Speaking to a national daily recently, Suresh Kalmadi, Chairman, Organising Committee for the Commonwealth Games 2010 said that all steps will be taken to ensure complete branding of Delhi. Kalmadi added that preparations for the Games were going in the right direction and infrastructure work linked with the Games, including the stadiums, will be complete well before the Games next year.

Commenting on the accommodation facilities in the capital city and the NCR region, Kalmadi said the problem of shortage of good three-star accommodation, will be partly solved with the Delhi Development Authority (DDA) offering around 3,300 rooms. As reported by TravelBiz Monitor earlier, these rooms will be furnished and managed by India Tourism Development Corporation (ITDC) for guests during the Games. Kalmadi also informed that a Games Travel Office will be opened at The Ashoka Hotel and all information regarding travel and accommodation will be made available through the Commonwealth Games website starting October 2009. He said that security of athletes and venues was being given maximum attention and a security buffer will be erected on routes where athletes and officials will move.

IMPACT OF COMMONWEALTH GAMES ON TOURISM

A big boost for brand India comes in form of Delhi, the National Capital Territory (NCT) of India, having won the bid to host the 2010 Commonwealth Games in 2003. This Indian capital of Delhi, stretching for 1483 km, skims border areas of States of Haryana, Rajasthan and Uttar Pradesh and the impact of CWG (Commonwealth Games) Delhi 2010 on tourism is bound to effect these surrounding areas, apart from the host region, that's for sure.

Going by that surmise, the true impact of the Commonwealth Games on tourism, scheduled for October 2010, can be judged better if one is to look at the various possibilities for marketing, advertising, educating and introducing a new India for the sportspersons, their entourage and other global visitors to the country. Knowing this definite time frame for the CWG taking place, the tourism and other related ministries get a chance to develop some public-private demonstration projects as a show-case for domestic, regional and international cities. What makes the CWG so important in sporting events and a coup for Indian economy and hospitality sector and its sister branch, tourism segment, is that the Olympic and Commonwealth Games are the second largest sports events held in modern times. Other cities that have hosted the CWG have recorded major spurt in tourism since their chance at this excellent reason for global travellers to come together in a spirit of competition, learning and life experiences while also giving the countries a chance to present a newer, vibrant youth-appeal to their land. The examples for this kind of cultural showcasing and effective gift-wrapping of sectors of interest like tourism—be it adventure, spa or spirituality - can be seen from the earlier hosts of world sporting events: Beijing, China and Barcelona, Spain benefited from hosting the Olympics while Manchester, UK and Melbourne, Australia received greater tourist inflow during and after playing host to CWG 2002 and 2006, respectively.

Factors raising Effective Impact of Commonwealth Games on Tourism

State-of-art technology deployments will help in ensuring world-class management of Delhi city during the event and also leave a sure, culturally strong imprint as valuable legacy of classy Indian hospitality on visitors to the CWG Delhi, 2010 while major economic boost from the CWG will raise tourism opportunities for our country, if basic amenities and modern tourist needs are kept in mind while formulating and promoting specialised tourism sectors.

The CWG Delhi 2010 can well prove to be a catalyst for major investment in the country's sporting, social and environmental fabric since it will effect the tourism sector directly as well as indirectly.

Eco-tourism and total wellness packages including ancient exercise and relaxation, toning, breathing and strengthening routines are likely choices that guarantee global tourist interest and are bound to be crowd-pullers during CWG. While earlier host nations of CWG directed their tourism budget towards raising standards of basic and luxury amenities, including novelty factor for tourists and sportspersons, other areas of redevelopment covered bridge and road links to and from the host city to neighbouring regions and specialty tourism spots. These can be developed as mini-villages offering bountiful shopping, eating, local customs, drama and theatre, music, dance and associated learning and living experiences that are essentially Indian, therefore attractive to outsiders. Planting of trees, arranging meetings with trained-up volunteers assisting local community/ youth/social service and cultural awareness groups and events and such like are likely to generate almost 13,600 full time equivalent jobs created from the Games. Naturally then, the expected economic return will be higher than before thanks to the impact of the Commonwealth Games on Tourism and the higher number of international tourists.

2010 COMMONWEALTH GAMES AND INDIA TOURISM INDUSTRY

Delhi—the capital city of India, is the new born host of eminent Commonwealth Games that are supposed to be held in 2010 starting from 3th October to 14th October. In the past, Delhi has also hosted Asian Games in 1951 and 1982. It is believed that Commonwealth Games are likely to boost India Tourism Industry, as the foreign tourists who will be coming to India next year will be greatly dependent upon the travel agents for the tour itineraries, hotel bookings, flight reservations and visa.

According to the estimates over 2.5 million foreign tourists and 4.5 million domestic tourists are likely to arrive in Delhi on the eve of the Commonwealth Games. So it is no doubt that the event will be great hit for the India Tourism Industry. Along with that Indian hospitality, aviation and hotel industry will also be equally beneficial with the event.

Commonwealth Games will provide dual enjoyment to the tourists—first of all, it is a opportunity for tourists to be a part of the different sports activities and on the other they can enjoy great tourism in the country. The Government of India in collaboration with the Ministry of Tourism has come up the new development plans to change the look and feel of the city, for the better.

Hotel owners and apartment builders in the city are working really hard to provide the most delightful experience of India tour during the eve of the Commonwealth Games. Further new projects have come up to discover new heritage, religious, adventurous tourists sites in the northern states of India bordering Delhi including the Punjab, Uttarakhand, Uttar Pradesh, Haryana and Rajasthan.

New Delhi is already a well planned modern city with the great infrastructure. But to host such a great event is really a big challenge. The Government of India wants to leave no stone unturned to make a big hit. To make the transportation more easily, government is extending its metro train stations, recently it has launched large of AC buses in the city, stadiums are being renovated, new flyovers have come up and last but not the least airports of all the major Indian cities Delhi, Nagpur, Mumbai, Bangalore, Goa, Cochin, etc. are being modernised especially for the Commonwealth Games.

So, it is no doubt that Commonwealth Games are going to benefit the Indian Tourism Industry in a big way. It is also going to boost the various job opportunities in the country. With that the private sectors like the hotels, travel agencies, tour operators, airlines, airports are going to hire more employees in order to handle large flux of tourists from all over the world.

The Commonwealth Games 2010 are expected to lift the Indian Tourism Industry in a big way, which is definitely more important now after the horrifying terror attacks on the country last year. According to the estimates the percentage of foreign tourists arrival in the country will increase by 15-20 per cent, as compared to the last year growth of merely six per cent which was hurt by the Mumbai attacks.

The Government of India in collaboration with the Ministry of Tourism and Archaeological Survey of India (ASI) has plans to launch special programme 'Discover India in CWG 2010' and for same must they are supposed to organise road shows in Australia, South Africa, US, Singapore, Canada, Mauritius etc. as tourists, arrival in India is expected to be more from these countries.

Since the Commonwealth Games are scheduled to be held in the India's capital city – Delhi, the government has come up the new development plans to change the look and feel of the city, for the better. Further the new projects have come up to discover new heritage, religious, adventurous tourists' sites in the northern states of India bordering Delhi including the Punjab, Uttarakhand, Uttar Pradesh, Haryana and Rajasthan.

All the athletes would be offered free accommodation, security, a pollution free environment, free transportation and entertainment options for the non-competition times. They will be offered a free trip to the famed Taj Mahal – the 'Seventh Wonder of the World' clubbed with the other heritage sites such as the Fort, Fatehpur Sikri, Sikandra Itmad-ul-Daulah's Tomb, Chini Ka Rauza, Ram Bagh, Soami Bagh/Dayal Bagh and many more.

Apart from that other major tourists' spots in India including the Shimla, Jhansi, Kerala Backwaters, Goa Beaches, Andaman and Nicobar Islands, Rajasthan Forts and Palaces, Dehradun, Haridwar, Ranikhet, Himlayas, Punjab etc. are likely to attract large number of foreign tourists in the year 2010.

Medical and Ayurvedic sectors will also be equally beneficiary during the Commonwealth Games in view of India's popularity in ancient tradition of Yoga and Ayurveda and the availability of low cost medical treatments in India.

Tour agencies in India are opened with the new hot travel deals for 2010 Commonwealth Games for the foreign tourists. They have come up with the exclusive packages at the most attractive prices that are truly rewarding from the economic point of view. Tourists have been making online reservation in advance for the upcoming Commonwealth Games.

ASSOCHAM'S VIEWPOINT

Commonwealth Games are likely to push India's Foreign Exchange Earnings (FEE) through Tourism alone in Calendar 2010 to an estimated levels of over US$ 16915 million as these are expected to grow at cumulative rate of 20 per cent in next two years, according to The Associated Chambers of Commerce and Industry of India (ASSOCHAM). Through tourism only in Calendar 2008, FEE's were measured at US$ 11747 million.

The optimism as to why tourism would register a cumulative growth of 20 per cent in next two years is based on the fact that by then global meltdown would have subsided to make India a lead tourist destination, especially due to the fact the focus its policy makers are attaching on hospitality sector.

In October 2008, tourism alone fetched India US$ 900 million with tourist arrivals of over 4.50 lakhs especially from countries like UK, Japan, South Africa, Australia, Singapore, Mauritius, Middle East and Far East etc.

Releasing the analysis 'Impact of CWG 2010 on India's Tourism Sector', the ASSOCHAM Secretary General, D.S. Rawat said that in the last couple of years, FEE's earnings on an average have been growing at robust average of over 10 per cent and there is no reason that their average rate of growth would accelerate during Commonwealth Games for which India is creating lot of facilities by renovating its majority of tourist sites.

Also, advertising strengths and intellectual superiority and skills of India's ayurvedic, medical and clinical tourism including religious tourism which are expected to draw a large crowd during the forthcoming Games for multi-purposes.

The ASSOCHAM estimates that if India's tourist arrivals in October 2008 was 4.53 lakhs, during 2010 Commonwealth Games which would conclude in October, the foreign tourist arrival is likely to double, said Rawat. It may be mentioned here that in calendar 2008, total tourist arrivals in India were 5.37 million and since India will emerge a lead tourist destination in South East Asian region in next two years, the total tourist arrivals in calendar 2010 is likely to be around 10 million.

The ASSOCHAM has suggested that Ministry of Tourism in partnership with Archaeological Survey of India (ASI) and State Governments should introduce a Special Programme 'Explore India in CWG 2010' and must organise road shows in UK, South Africa, Australia, Singapore, Canada, South Africa, Mauritius etc., because from these countries, large tourist arrivals are expected towards India.

Since the Games will be held in the capital, the Chamber has also recommended the government to identify new heritage, religious, adventurous and attractive tourists' spots in northern regional states of Uttar Pradesh, Uttarakhand, Punjab and Haryana, Rajasthan etc. to lure the foreign and domestic tourists.

India's hospitality industry, tour operators and travel agents who are currently reeling under global slowdown will "feel good" during the CWG 2010 as foreign tourists will be mainly dependent on them for their hotel accommodation, travel itinerary, visa, etc.

To grab future opportunities, India's travel and tour operators should come out with exclusive packages, designed for foreign tourists. These packages should comprise hotel accommodation, short trips to nearby destinations, yoga and ayurvedic therapies, food and taxi etc.

Ayurvedic and Medical Tourism sectors will also be beneficiary during CWG 2010 in view of India's strength in ancient tradition of ayurveda and the availability of low-cost medical tourism facilities in India.

The Chamber estimates reveal that each foreigner visiting India during the period is likely to spend Rs.10,000 to Rs. 30,000 in availing ayurvedic expertise in various ayurvedic and herbal centres.

The key private hospitals in Delhi and NCR should also unveil the 'Special Medical Tourism and Healthcare Packages' during 2010 to tap the large inflow of foreign tourists. The private hospitals in Delhi and NCR like Sir Ganga Ram, Fortis, Moolchand, Apollo, Metro, Dharmshila, Max etc. can start these kinds of packages and services. Better connectivity from the games villages and hotels in Delhi will also pave the way for these hospitals to contribute the medical tourism sector.

India's famous tourist places in these states like Taj Mahal, Fatehpur Sikri, Lucknow, Jhansi in UP, Shimla, Kufri, Manali, Panchkula in Himachal Pradesh, Jaipur, Jabalpur, Udaipur, Bhilwara, Kota in Rajasthan, Nainital, Musoorie, Aulli, Dehradun, Haridwar, Ranikhet, Almora in Uttarakhand, Amritsar in Punjab can attract huge forex earnings and large number of foreign tourists will also explore these tourists' sites.

DELHI AND THE 2010 COMMONWEALTH GAMES

World Class Sport to Bring Economic and Tourist Boom to Indian Capital

The 2010 Commonwealth Games were launched in traditional fashion on the 3rd of March 2009. The Queen's relay baton was unveiled at India Gate among great public celebrations, marking the start of its long journey between participating nations. On the 3rd of October 2010, it will return to Delhi where the enclosed royal message will be read and the games will begin. The Delhi baton is made of aluminium with multicoloured layers of soil from every corner of the land.

In the meantime, India's capital is in the throes of an unprecedented economic boom bringing its infrastructure up to date.

Economic Boom in Indian Capital, Games and Tourism

The 2010 Commonwealth Games should be a major boost for Delhi. Labour is cheap and plentiful, foreign investors have moved in and despite a few hiccups, work appears to be moving at a frantic pace.

Most apparent are improvements to the transport system with flyovers, underpasses, multi-lane roads and high capacity bus corridors. Efforts to combat pollution continue with more taxis and buses running on natural gas. Meanwhile Delhi boasts new trains and buildings in the Cantonment Station, the Metro is fast expanding to become the world's second longest and the modernised Indira Gandhi Airport will have a new runway and terminal.

Add increased energy and water supplies, thousands of extra hotel rooms and a green village to house over 8000 athletes and officials and Delhi seems all set for world class sport and a major boost in tourism. Over five million visitors from India and abroad are expected in the capital as a result of the games.

Delhi and the 2010 Commonwealth Games

India will be hosting the Commonwealth Games for the first time and is only the second Asian country to do so, after Malaysia. Delhi won the vote by a sizeable majority against Hamilton in Canada where the first games were held in 1930.

There are currently 72 nations planning to attend the 19th Commonwealth Games in Delhi and 17 disciplines from Aquatics and Wrestling to Hockey, Gymnastics and Athletics. Triathlon, basketball and cricket are still in the balance but a demonstration of Kabaddi, a Tamil Nadu team sport, is likely to be included.

India hopes to beat its 2002 record of 138 medals, including 30 gold. Indian gold medals in 2006 went to boxing, shooting, table tennis and women's weightlifting.

World Class Sport in India, Commonwealth Games Venues and Information

The 2010 Commonwealth Games will be held in a number of

venues across Delhi, including the Indira Gandhi Indoor Stadium Complex, the Siri Fort Sports Complex and the Jawaharlal Nehru Stadium where the opening and closing ceremonies will take place on October 3rd and 14th respectively.

Tickets are available on a number of websites but it is advisable to book through a reputable tour operator or agent. Visit the games official site www.cwgdelhi2010.com for the latest news and for general information on India, see www.incredibleindia.org.

COMMONWEALTH GAMES 2010 IN DELHI AND TOURISM INDUSTRY

Gone are days when Indian Tourism Industry had received a set-back. A new era of Indian tourism is ushering and things are now falling into their right place. India is too happy to host the exciting Commonwealth Games in 2010. And equally enthusiastic is Delhi where these Games are scheduled. 85 teams of Commonwealth Nations would be seen contesting for 17 disciplines. The 12 day long event will have matches of swimming, wrestling, weightlifting, cycling, marathon, badminton, boxing, shooting, athletics, table tennis and tennis etc. which would be held from 3rd to 14th October 2010.

India and more importantly Delhi and neighbouring states have geared themselves up for the upcoming Commonwealth Games next year. The tourists will be much excited to witness the participants competing in the newly built Khelgaon near Yamuna River Bank which is very close to Swami Narayan Akshardham temple.

Delhi Government and Indian Government had ventured into upgradation of infrastructure of the country. The Aviation, Hospitality as well as Tour and travel industry will be highly benefited from the Games. Keeping this in mind, the transportation services are being improved, metro trains will be soon seen plying passengers, new hotels are mushrooming and the existing ones are being renovated.

In addition to this, the monumental heritage of Delhi and surrounding states as Rajasthan, Uttar Pradesh, Himachal Pradesh, Madhya Pradesh is specially taken care of. The old structures are being restored into their natural condition. Tour and Travel agents have started making reservations from the tourists. They are providing car rentals, transfers, accommodations, sightseeing tours, lodging and boarding etc.

The tourists coming to Delhi will have excellent chances of visiting the world famous Taj Mahal in Agra which is very close to Delhi. The beauty in marble is a must visit. Other popular tourist destinations like Mathura, Gaya, Bhopal, Puri, Goa, Kerala, Shimla will be also receiving a number of tourists.

Back with a new vigour is the Indian Tourism Industry and this time more so because of the deadly terrorist attacks on the country in the recent past. But times have now moved on and so has our hospitality industry. The country has taken the event hosting of Commonwealth Games 2010 with great enthusiasm. Scheduled from 3rd October to 14th October, this 12 days gala affair will be a matter of pride for everyone in India and from India. This gala event is also extravagant affair of US$17.5 billion that is approximately Rs. 87.5 thousand crores.

Preparations for Commonwealth Games 2010

To boost Indian tourism through Commonwealth Games, Delhi has already made preparations and improved the infrastructure of the city and neighbouring states as well. The beautification process of the city is on its peak and transportation system has been upgraded along with renovation of old historical monuments. Government of Delhi and Indian Government are taking every possible step to pep up tourism in and around Delhi.

The games village which is being built along the Yamuna River at a cost of USD 230.7 million, is a venture of Delhi Government to provide world class amenities to the participants, the tourists and the audience. The security of tourist and athletes is not at all an issue as Government has beefed up security measures.

Impact of Commonwealth Games on Indian Tourism Industry

The gala event will prove a boon for the tourism of India as there will be huge influx of tourists coming to India which will stir up Tour and Travel, Hotel, Airlines, Industries. ASSOCHAM

(Associated Chambers of Commerce and Industry of India) has estimated the influx of tourists may be higher than ten million. The event also has generated many job opportunities. The current growth of Indian Hospitality Industry is 12 per cent which will surely rise to at least 20 per cent and thereby the occupancy rate of it would be 70 per cent. Many new projects have come up and numerous others are in their developmental stage.

Not only Hospitality Industry, but Medical Tourism will also a high boom in 2010 because of the upcoming event. If the reports of RNCOS are to be seen, it states that India will be receiving many Medical Tourists because of the gala affair. The industry experts also believe that Commonwealth Games would make a considerable and influential impact on Indian Tourism Industry.

With India to host the Commonwealth Games next year, hoteliers in the country are rushing to make the most of the likely spurt in tourist traffic by providing new rooms, leading to a boom in development, global consultancy firm Deloitte has said.

"In 2010, India will host the Commonwealth Games for the first time, and hoteliers here will be hoping to emulate the success of Melbourne, which was the host in 2006," it said in a report, 'Hospitality Vision—Global Performance Review'.

"International and domestic hotel chains are rushing to maximise India's potential by providing new rooms, leading to a boom in development. Mumbai and Delhi are expected to see an influx of new rooms in 2009, with 305 added to New Delhi's inventory, while Mumbai will see 1,158 rooms enter the market," it added.

The report said the economic slowdown and Mumbai's terror attacks of last November notwithstanding, India will make a mark as a preferred tourist destination globally.

"There have also been bombings in several Indian cities (tourist hubs such as Jaipur, Bangalore and Ahmedabad), including the outrage in Mumbai, where terrorists targeted the tourism icon, the Taj Mahal Palace Hotel. These events may deter visitors in the short term, but tourists quickly come back and their presence helps the healing process," it said.

Although Asia-Pacific will not escape the general slowdown, robust economies in China and India make them better placed than other regions, Deloitte said.

"There are predictions that international visitor arrivals will more than double by the end of 2010. China and India will continue to make their mark, both regionally and globally."

Citing a survey by World Travel and Tourism Council (WTCC), the report said that between now and 2018, India will be a tourism hotspot followed by China, Libya and Vietnam.

"The world's fastest growing tourism destinations over the next decade will be India, China, Libya and Vietnam."

Cautioning that 2009 will be challenging for hoteliers and only the fittest will survive, Deloitte said, "Hotels will need to focus on value for money more than ever before."

Occupancy in hotels was down by 14 per cent throughout 2008, but average room rates rose 4.5 per cent to $257.

The report said while it may be tempting to slash room rates to bring in business, the move could be damaging as it takes average room rates much longer to recover than occupancy levels.

"Tempting though it is to slash room rates to bring in business, this is not a long-term solution, as it takes average room rates much longer to recover than occupancy levels," Deloitte said.

The glimmer of hope, however, could be the reduction in airfares through low global oil prices - $35 a barrel in February 2009 compared to $147 last July, it added.

Deloitte's India Head for Tourism, Hospitality and Leisure, P.R. Srinivas, told PTI that while the swine flu scare may have been the latest dampener to the global tourism scenario, traffic to India has not been drastically affected.

"Not really very much as there have been very few suspected cases of swine flu in India. The European and Trans-Atlantic traffic has been drastically affected," Srinivas said.

INDIA TOURISM ALL SET FOR THE COMMONWEALTH GAMES

"Get set and go"—like sports, this also seems to be the present motto for the Indian tourism industry. It is all set to cater to the

Commonwealth Games which will be held in New Delhi in October 2010. This prestigious event will really add a feather in the cap of India and the tourism and hospitality industry also hopes to gain from it.

The event will draw huge number of spectators, athletes, officials, sportspersons and media persons from various parts of the world and this is exactly what the Indian tourism industry is hoping to capitalise on. Lots of foreigners will make trips to various parts of the country, mainly North India and this will help the tourism sector to earn good revenue.

In order to cater to the tourists, the tourism, hospitality, hotel and aviation sectors in Delhi and the surrounding areas are putting considerable effort to improve their services. Some of the tours which are already experiencing good demand are Rajasthan Tours, Golden Triangle Tours, North India Tours and so on. Most of these tours are centred on Delhi and the itineraries consist of visit to Rajasthan, Agra and other attractions of North India.

In fact, the government is keen to promote tourism as one of the brands to foreign tourists in view of the forthcoming Commonwealth Games 2010. Initiatives are already in place to make the country a more tourist friendly, cleaner, greener and safer place. Emphasis has also been put to improve the transport and communication infrastructure. In view of the Commonwealth Games, private tour operators are also putting their step forward. Tour packages by preparing tours to Rajasthan, Amritsar, Ranthambore, Taj Mahal, Khajuraho Temples, Corbett National Parks, Shimla, Mussoorie, Nainital, Jammu and Kashmir and other places. These places are well preferred by the foreign tourists and more foreign tourist inflow is being expected to these places.

The tourism department of the government is not behind too. They are putting emphasis to promote the lesser known destinations to the foreign tourists. Places like the Northeastern India, Virgin Islands of Andaman and Nicobar, Ladakh and so on are being promoted as favourite tourist destinations for the foreigners.

Another good thing about October is that it is the festive season in India. Keeping this in mind, the tourism industry will also try to promote the festivals and events to the foreign tourists when they come in October next year. The government plans to endorse

Pushkar Fair, Durga Puja, Dussehra, Diwali and other festivals by introducing various festive tours and packages.

The Indian tourism is highly optimistic that the Commonwealth Games will help India become more popular to the tourists from abroad.

SHARE IN TOURIST ARRIVALS

The Commonwealth Games in 2010 will push up India's share in foreign tourist arrivals to about 1.5 per cent in 2010 from mere 0.52 per cent in 2006 out of 842 million tourist arrivals globally, according to Assocham.

The Games will generate additional employment opportunities for over five lakh workforce in sectors such as airlines and airports, hotels, tour operators, flyover, stadia developers, besides medical and eco-tourism.

With modernisation of Delhi and Mumbai international airports and revamping of 35 metro airports, airlines and airport industry will alone create over 2.5 lakh jobs, according to the Chamber.

INDIA TO BOOST TOURISM USING COMMONWEALTH GAMES

India is going to exploit the 2010 Commonwealth Games in New Delhi to boost tourism in a big way, Minister of State for Tourism Kanti Singh said here Tuesday. "We are looking at the 2010 Commonwealth Games to boost our tourism industry in a big way," Singh told reporters on the sidelines of the Arabian Travel Market (ATM) 2008 tourism exhibition.

"Leading up to the event, we are focusing on increasing the number of hotel rooms in the country significantly," she said after inaugurating the Indian pavilion at ATM 2008.

Observing that the government has extended a five-year tax rebate to the tourism sector, she said her ministry was laying great stress on promoting India as a monsoon and medical tourism destination.

"We all know medical treatment in India can be done at a fraction of the cost compared to other parts of the world. That is why we are promoting this sector besides starting a new campaign for monsoon tourism," Singh told IANS.

Joint Secretary in the tourism ministry E.K. Bharat Bhushan said monsoon tourism is a new offering from India Tourism.

"We are attracting people for monsoon tourism and Kerala is a major destination for this," he said.

Apart from this, religious tourism in India is also being promoted.

"The Cheraman Mosque in Kerala, which was built in 600 AD, is a good example. Similarly we will promote temples, churches and synagogues which have great historical value," Bhushan said.

Pointing out that the Gulf is a big market for the Indian tourism industry, he said 120,000 tourists from the region visited India in 2007.

"Of this, around 60,000 came from the United Arab Emirates (UAE) alone," he said.

A total of 31 participants from India, including the state tourism boards of Andhra Pradesh, Arunachal Pradesh, Jammu and Kashmir and Kerala, have put up stalls at the three-day ATM 2008, the Middle East's premier travel and tourism event, which got under way Tuesday.

This year's event has the largest exhibitor base of 2,208 participants from 70 countries—an eight per cent increase on the 2007 edition.

Reed Travel Exhibitions, organisers of the event, said floorspace bookings from international representatives in Asia, the Americas, Europe and Africa had grown by 10 per cent, with Middle East companies increasing their allocation by five per cent.

"The increased regional and international exhibitor participation is a clear indication of this market's expansion," Richard Mortimore, Managing Director of Reed Travel Exhibitions, said in a statement.

"The diversification of the products and services on display further underlines the industry's growing dynamism and competitiveness," he added.

APPEAL FOR LOOKING THROUGH THE EYES OF TOURISTS

"We should look through the eyes of tourists about what they expect from us," Tourism Minister Kumari Selja said here

Wednesday, calling upon experts and all stakeholders to help put India on the world tourism map.

"We need good hotels, infrastructure, connectivity for tourists. We have to specially think about tourism infrastructure in view of the 2010 Commonwealth Games. We should take it as an opportunity and a boon for us," said Selja while inaugurating a workshop on World Class Tourism Infrastructure.

"I call upon experts and stakeholders in the tourism sector to develop world class tourism infrastructure for putting India's tourism industry on the world tourism map," she added.

"We should look at comprehensive development of infrastructure which includes roads, water, sanitation, cleanliness, hygiene, proper lighting, landscape, signages and proper maintenance of tourism destinations and heritage sites," she said.

"We have to see the tourism industry from the point of view of tourists rather than our officialdom," she said.

She said her ministry, through rural tourism projects, is evolving a system to bring villages of the country on the main tourist map.

Selja said that world class tourism infrastructure facilities should not be limited to cities like Delhi but also should reach far-flung areas of the country.

The main objective of the one-day workshop was to develop world class tourism infrastructure in consultation with architects, engineering organisations, tourism managers and consultants.

The participants of the workshop included heads of the engineering departments of implementing agencies in the states and union territories, officers from the tourism ministry and experts from agencies like INTACH, CPWD, RITES, NBCC, HUDCO and ITDC.

Said Selja: "We are looking at all aspects of the Commonwealth Games such as security, sanitation, comfort and zero harassment to tourists. Games are a matter of pride for our country."

"I talked to Minister of Road Transport and Highways Kamal Nath about developing the golden triangle (Delhi-Agra-Jaipur) as hassle free so that tourists can have seamless travel. He has shown a very positive response to that," she told reporters later.

"I also talked to the minister about developing wayside amenities on highways," she added.

PLANNED ROADSHOWS TO ATTRACT TOURISTS

India will hold tourism roadshows in London and other capitals of Commonwealth countries in a bid to cash in on the Commonwealth Games here next year, Tourism Minister Kumari Selja said here Monday.

"The Commonwealth Games in India next year will be an important event, especially from the tourism point of view. Teams that will arrive here can take the opportunity to explore India thus giving a major boost to tourism," Selja said at the inaugural function of the two-day meet of the ministry's overseas tourism officials and the private sector.

Selja said that thanks to the ministry's efforts in promoting India as the ideal destination for tourists, there was a 0.2 per cent positive growth in the tourist arrival to India.

Because of the global meltdown, foreign tourist arrivals from January to June this year fell by 9.3 per cent as compared to last year.

Tourism ministry joint secretary Leena Nandan said special roadshows will be organised in London to attract people to explore India when they come here for the Commonwealth Games that will be attended by athletes from 71 countries.

"Our overseas office in London is actively promoting India and will organise special roadshows there in this regard, so that people travel across India when they come here for the Commonwealth Games," Nandan told IANS.

The tourism ministry also has a number of other initiatives to attract tourists to the country.

"We want to encourage tourist arrival from those countries from which we are already getting a good tourist arrival. Therefore, we have a series of roadshows in the Scandinavian countries—Finland, Sweden and Norway—at the end of this month to promote India. Next month we will go to Russia with a similar aim," Selja said.

To promote niche tourism products, like medical tourism, the ministry will have a series of roadshows in Dubai in October this year, adventure tourism roadshows in Australia and New Zealand. The UN Development Programme is helping the tourism ministry to promote rural tourism.

IMPACT OF COMMONWEALTH GAMES 'TOURISM BOOM'

A two-member parliamentary delegation expressed dissatisfaction at the near chaotic traffic, bad drainage system and poor maintenance of monuments in this Uttar Pradesh city and said it may miss the 2010 Delhi Commonwealth Games 'tourism boom'.

The committee of MPs Sitaram Yechury and P. Karunakaran Sunday also said a dry Yamuna presented a very "ugly and disturbing backdrop" to the beautiful Taj Mahal.

Yechury said in a meeting with State Government officials that the maintenance of "Baby Taj" Etmaduddaula across the river was not satisfactory, the marble stones at the Taj were losing their shine, and the issue of cross-city movement needed to be resolved.

The MPs were caught in traffic jams twice within the city.

Yechury said that in his report he would suggest filling Yamuna with water so that boating could be possible.

"River Yamuna should have enough water so that the tourists could be ferried across from the Taj to the Etmaduddaula," Yechury told reporters.

He told the district officials that the other lesser known monuments in the city should be highlighted and approach roads cleaned up. He also wanted adequate number of signages close to the monuments.

He said the games would give a fillip to the tourism industry not only in Delhi but also in the surrounding areas.

"The committee in its report will suggest ways to give a boost to tourism which can offset the process of recession and generate jobs," he added.

"Heaps of dirt and garbage, pollution in the river and perpetual traffic jams due to encroachments are the major problems that need to be urgently addressed," Surendra Sharma, President of the Braj Mandal Heritage Conservation Society said in a memorandum to the district authorities.

Ravi Singh, a green activist, said the Yamuna should have water round the year. "For this, a weir or a barrage downstream of the Taj Mahal should be constructed and additional water released from the Okhla barrage."

TRANSPORT INDUSTRY AS AN INTEGRAL PART OF TOURISM

Union Minister of Tourism and Culture Ambika Soni said that the onus of making India a successful tourist destination lies not only with the Ministry of Tourism but also on the entire tourism industry, which includes transport industry.

Soni was speaking at the Convention of the Indian Tourist Transporters Association (ITTA) at Ashoka Hotel, New Delhi today.

When we in the Ministry of Tourism talk about inclusive growth through tourism we are also thinking about those people who are involved in the transport sector as they are vital for sustaining India's tourism industry, said Soni.

She further said that these people are the real ambassadors of tourism and likely to make India a tourist hub.

Their positive and pleasant attitudes create welcoming environment for tourists, which in turn encourages repeat visitors to India, Soni added.

While talking of opportunities for the transport industry, Soni said, The 2010 New Delhi Commonwealth Games is a big opportunity for the transport industry.

She suggested that ITTA as a service provider should take up the challenge to provide quality services during the Commonwealth Games in 2010 and sighted the example of efficient service provided by the Melbourne Commonwealth Game and the Beijing Olympics. The Tourism Minister also emphasised on the safety and security of tourists for the success of tourism in the country. Please take care of your tourists as if they are your guests in the true spirit of Atithi Devo Bhava, said Soni while referring to incidents of harassment in the recent past.

India is projecting itself as a tourist destination through the phrase Incredible India to attract prospective tourists. (ANI)

A leading association of tourist transporters Wednesday sought active cooperation from the government in providing better transport facility for visitors to the city during the Commonwealth Games in 2010. "The government at the centre and in the state should extend all possible help to tourist transporters to ensure visitors coming to Delhi for the event do not face any hardship," said Indian Tourist Transporters Association (ITTA).

Delhi's Commonwealth Games 2010 are scheduled to start October 3, 2010.

"Looking at the magnitude of the event, there is a need for coordinated efforts from all the stakeholders to make the Commonwealth Games a stupendous success," ITTA President Sarabjit Singh told reporters here.

He said ITTA's city-based members have over 7,500 tourist vehicles, including around 300 luxury coaches.

"The organising committee for the Games should decide on the type of vehicles required and suited for the event and prospective users. Accordingly, we will work out our fleet building strategy," he said.

Singh also sought incentives like tax exemption for the tourist transporters to help them upgrade their fleet.

"The tourist transport operators should be allowed duty-free import of luxury vehicles, and should be given exemption from excise duty and value added tax on the purchase of vehicles within India," said Singh.

SPORTS AND ADVENTURE TOURISM IN INDIA

India the land yet unexplored can easily be the new millennium's adventure tourism destination. Its vast geographical diversity and the pristine nature of its facilities enable all tastes to be catered for, from the gentlest to the fast paced and for people of every level of competence—the beginner and the expert. From the daunting Himalayan peaks in the North to the azure coastal areas on the South, from the rain forests of the North East to the coral paradise in the South West, it is variety that is as bewildering as it is diverse.

What is so fascinating and so compelling almost to the point of addition in adventure sports? It must be the daunting thrill of dashing down the ski slopes or the landscape trekking or pedalling along sheer mountain slopes, white water rafting along the dangerous, roaring waters of great services, hang gliding over enormously deep mountain gorges and climbing serrated glaciers or, mountain summits is believable only through experience.

And, yet, these aspects form just a small part of the exhilaration and excitement of the fast developing area, which is increasingly being recognised as adventure tourism.

Wait that is not all. How can one forget the serenity of scuba diving along the coral reefs or floating high above terra firma on hot air balloons, yes, even the slow steady ambling along deserts on the gentle camels or horse riding, elephant riding safaris—all these would have been dismissed as fanciful had it not been true and existing on India.

And believe it—India is a perfect destination for adventure tourism because it is as enjoyable, exciting, thrilling and invigorating as one makes it. What helps is the destination which is custom made. In India, the mighty Himalayan and the never, never ending coastline and not to forget the two island territories are open invitations to the fun loving and the adventurous souls.

It is not only India's vast geographical diversity that provides a huge scope for the adventure tourist but also that it is relatively unforayed into and comparatively inexpensive too. Those who want to fancy the wild and see mother-nature in its original form, to see man and nature surviving in each other's arms is rediscovering one's own self.

The intrigue of age-old monasteries and temples, the Himalayan peaks and slopes, with its dense tropical forests providing diverse fauna and flora and the 3000km of long-long coastline promises the most exciting of sports and adventure imaginable. The best part is that these facilities exist all year through and in different places with affordable prices.

Summer has the spotlight on the mountains in the northern most states with its breath taking, views, winter has the country's coastline to explore and in between the shoulder period is covered with a variety of other sports. Season is not the restriction.

Neither is there a constrain of places to go to. Rock climbing is not restricted to Himalayan foothills, it can be done in the adventure park at Lado Sarai in Delhi too. Similarly kayaking and canoeing is not merely done in the Himalayan slopes or the sea beaches, but also the Bhulasawa lake on the northern tip of Delhi has a multisports leisure complex for the purpose. So it is with parasailing and paddling, boating and fishing, often such sports are available all over India.

List of Flying Clubs/Schools in India

Sl. No.	Name	State	Total No. of Aircraft	Name of C.F.I.	Telephone No.
1.	Delhi Flying Club, Delhi	Delhi	12	Capt. M.S. Beniwal	4618931
2.	Gujarat Flying Club, Baroda	Gujarat	9	Capt. B.K. Manha	442631
3.	Madras Flying Club, Chennai	Tamil Nadu	7	Capt. N. Jai Prakash	91-44-22561709
4.	Patiala Aviation Club, Patiala	Punjab	6	Capt. G.S. Brar	301823
5.	Haryana Institute of Civil Aviation, Karnal + 2 branches at Hissar & Pinjore	Haryana	6	Capt. Kamal Kishore	0814-252320/ 250731
6.	Andhra Pradesh Flying Club, Hyderabad	Andhra Pradesh	8	Capt. G.B. Reddy	7753759
7.	Madhya Pradesh Flying Club, Indore + 1 Branch – Bhopal	Madhya Pradesh	12	Capt. Manoj Chabria	413959
8.	Ludhiana Aviation Club, Ludhiana	Punjab	6	Capt. Rachpal Singh	844539
9.	Bihar Flying Training Institute, Patna	Bihar	5	Capt. N.K. Singh	
10.	Govt. Flying Training School, Bangalore	Karnataka	6	Capt. N. Jai Prakash	332251
11.	Hissar Aviation Club - Branch of Haryana Institute of Civil Aviation	Haryana	5	Capt. M.S. Baniwal	37556
12.	Bombay Flying Club, Mumbai	Maharashtra	8	Capt. A.J. Bodas	6185100
13.	Kerala Aviation Training Instt. Thiruvananthapuram	Kerala	4	Capt. Anil Prakash	
14.*	Nagpur Flying Club, Nagpur	Maharashtra	5	Nil	
15.*	Coimbatore Aviation Training Academy, Coimbatore	Tamil Nadu	6	Capt. P. Ganpathiappan	

(Contd.)

Sl. No.	*Name*	*State*	*Total No. of Aircraft*	*Name of C.F.I.*	*Telephone No.*
16.	Rajasthan State Flying School, Jaipur	Rajasthan	4	Capt. Mohinder Singh	
17.	Government Aviation Training Institute, Bhubaneshwar	Orissa	4	Capt. B.P.S. Budhiraja	
18.*	Government Flying Training Institute, Calcutta	West Bengal	4	Capt. Bhasker Pandey	
19.	Government Flying Training Centre, Lucknow	Uttar Pradesh	12	Capt. Anjit Singh	
20.*	Assam Flying Club, Guwahati	Assam	2	Nil	
21.	Northern India Flying Club, Jullandhar Cantt. (camp at Patiala)	Punjab	5	Capt. S.S. Kang	
22.	Amritsar Aviation Club, Amritsar	Punjab	6	Capt. Rachpal Singh	
23.	Jamshedpur Co-operative Flying Club, Jamshedpur	Bihar	3	Capt. Santosh Kumar	
24.*	Bansathali Vidyapith Gliding & Flying Club, Banasthali	Rajasthan	1	Nil	
25.	Pinjore Aviation Club, Pinjore (Distt. Ambala)	Haryana	4	Capt. G.S. Cheema	
26.*	Andaman & Nicobar Flying Training Institute, Port Blair	U.T. Andaman & Nicobar Islands	1	Nil	
27.	Ajanta Flying Club, Aurangabad	Maharashtra		Nil	
28.	Kanpur Branch of SCAUPFTC, Lucknow	U.P.		Capt. K.B. Singh	
29.	Faizabad Branch of SCAUPFTC, Lucknow	U.P.		Capt S.K. Bhatnagar	

(Contd.)

Sl. No.	Name	State	Total No. of Aircraft	Name of C.F.I.	Telephone No.
30.	Varanasi Branch of SCAUPFTC, Lucknow	U.P.		Capt. V.V. Singh	
31.	Bhopal Branch of MP Flying Club, Indore	Madhya Pradesh		Capt. A.K. Singh	
32.	Indira Gandhi Rashtriya Urban Akademi, Fursatganj, under Ministry of Civil Aviation not covered unser subsidy scheme	Uttar Pradesh		Air Cdr. P. Bharadwaj	0535-202808

Source *These Flying Clubs are not operational.

List of Private Training Institutes

Sl. No.	Name	State	Total No. of Aircraft	Name of C.F.I.	Telephone No.
1.	Orient Flight School, Pondicherry	(U.T.) Pondicherry	5	Capt. P.S. Guron Chennai Pondicherry	234041
2.*	Bangalore Aeronotics Technical Services Pvt. Ltd. (BATS), Bangalore	Karnataka	3	Nil	5571566/573900
3.	Tata Nagar Aviation, Jamshedpur	Bihar	6	Capt. T.N. Sridhar	0657-407594/ 407816
4.	Ahmedabad Aviation Academy Ahmedabad	Gujarat	9	Capt. Jasbir Singh	079-2863468
5.	Garg Aviation Ltd., Kanpur	Uttar Pradesh	3	Capt. Arun Man	0512-300248
6.	Flytech Aviation Ltd., Hyderabad	Andhra Pradesh	7	Capt. P.D. Rao	040-7800331, 7801109
7.	Rajputana Aviation Academy, Kota	Rajasthan	4	Capt. Keshari Sing Rathore	91-0141-384200 91-0744-427331

(*Contd.*)

Sl. No.	*Name*	*State*	*Total No. of Aircraft*	*Name of C.F.I.*	*Telephone No.*
8.*	Udan Research & Flying Institute Pvt. Ltd., Indore Renamed Frank Airways (P) Ltd.,	Madhya Pradesh	6		
9.	Academy of Carver Aviation Pvt. Ltd., Belgaum	Karnataka	3	Capt. K.K. Sharma Bombay Belgaum	3892643 420906
10.	Tetra Aviation Academy, Salem	Tamil Nadu	3	Capt. K.S. Sinha	
11.	Wings Aviation Pvt. Ltd., Hyderabad	Andhra Pradesh	3	Capt. R.K. Kaura	
12.	Teneja Aerospace and Aviation Ltd., Bangalore	Karnataka	5	Capt. M.K. Aggarwal	91(080)5550609 5550610 5550944

CASE STUDY: HIMACHAL TOURISM TO OFFER COMMONWEALTH GAMES PACKAGE

Shimla. Himachal Pradesh Tourism Development Corporation (HPTDC) hotels would endeavour to give boost to its business promotional activities to attract participants and foreigners to visit Himachal Pradesh proposed Commonwealth Games scheduled to be held in New Delhi during the year 2010 by offering them an attractive package. This was revealed by Prof. Prem Kumar Dhumal, Chief Minister, in the 121st Board of Directors Meeting of the Himachal Pradesh Tourism Development Corporation held here under his Chairmanship last evening.

He said that the ensuing Commonwealth Games would be one additional opportunity for the Corporation to gain additional business by offering special package to the players and sports lovers visiting New Delhi and attract them to visit Himachal Pradesh as also gain word of mouth publicity beyond national boundaries.

He said that hospitality was one of the fastest growing industry in the world and HPTDC needs to keep pace with the global trends by updating its professional capabilities and catering to the requirements of the customers.

He said that since the online booking of hotels was available and the Corporation needs to take benefit of the same to offer packages to the prospective tourists to visit Himachal Pradesh.

He said that the packages could also be offered for promotion of health tourism by incorporating 'Panch Karma' system and could be beneficial in attracting more health loving tourists to the pollution free environment of the State.

He said that State had varied local cuisines which needed to be prepared in the traditional style and offered to the visitors to acquaint them to the local dietary habits of the people and could generate income to the Corporation. He said that additionally different types of international cuisines also needed to be introduced to customers to make them permanent customers of the HPTDC.

Mrs. Asha Swaroop, Chief Secretary, advised that regular exchange of the food and beverage staff of HPTDC needed to be carried with best addresses in the hospitality industry so that the professional skill of the staff was upgraded to match the prevailing trend in the industry.

AN OVERVIEW OF TOURISM RELATED PREPARATIONS FOR XIX CWG IN INDIA

Racing against time to ensure 1,50,000 hotel rooms before 2010 Commonwealth Games to be held in Delhi, the tourism ministry has asked the finance ministry to incentivise the tourism industry, which is pounded by the rupee appreciation.

In the pre-Budget consultations with the finance ministry, the tourism ministry has put up a strong case for providing tax benefits and a relief package for the industry.

"Devaluation of the dollar against the Indian rupee is affecting travel trade industry a lot. The industry is after us and we have taken it up at different levels in the finance ministry," minister for tourism and culture Ambika Soni said.

India played host to five million tourists last year, and the industry would have been in the midst of good times, but for the impact of 12.3 per cent rise in the value of rupee in comparison to the US dollar.

The profitability has been severely hit because the conversion value of the foreign exchange earned by the hotels and other components of the industry has been reduced to the extent of 15 per cent in the last 16 months.

Soni said that the focus of incentives would be on providing budget accommodation not only in Delhi but also heritage sites throughout the country.

"We have asked the finance ministry to give tax holidays for budget accommodation at places which are most visited like world heritage sites. India has 27 of them," Soni said.

Soni said that her ministry was giving Rs. 50 crore as incentives for developing infrastructure in large revenue generating circuits and Rs. 25 crore for development in destinations like Agra, Varanasi, Sarnath, Hampi.

While an assessment done by the ministry puts the requirement hotel rooms at 1,50,000 in less than three years, Soni was not sure how the target would be met and expressed concern over the lack of adequate response from the State Governments and the Union urban development ministry.

"We are certainly racing against time... the ministry itself gives subsidy up to Rs. one crore for building budget hotels, but there is a very little we can do or which is in our hand to get land," she said.

High land prices is proving to be a big obstacle for enthusing investment in increasing the room capacity. "Some of the land auctions were so high that people did not even go for the bidding," she added. This is despite the fact that Finance Minister P. Chidambaram in the last budget had... .

12

Draft National Sports Tourism Strategy: A Case of Australia

SPORTS TOURISM: AN OVERVIEW OF AUSTRALIAN INITIATIVES

Estimates of the size of the sports tourism sector vary, mainly because there is no single, agreed definition of what constitutes "sports tourism". While definitions of tourism are well accepted and fairly consistent throughout the world, definitions of sports tourism range from narrow ones involving travel solely for participation in competitive sporting activity to broader definitions where the "sporting" activity might be more leisure or adventure activity incidental to the main purpose of travel. For the purposes of developing a National Sports Tourism Strategy, a relatively narrow definition has been adopted. It is:

- *Domestic sports tourism:* any sports-related trip of over 40 kms and involving a stay of at least one night away from home; and
- *International sports tourism:* any trip to Australia a prime purpose of which is to participate in a sporting activity, either as a spectator, participant or official.

The sport or sporting activity under this definition are organised activities—unstructured activities undertaken by individuals have been excluded, as government's ability to influence such activities is relatively limited. Under such a definition, it appears that sports tourism in Australia might represent about 5 per cent of the overall tourism market, equating to tourism expenditure of about $3 billion per annum.

Evaluating Tourism and Sport—A Comparison of World and Australian Markets

Tourism and travel have grown to become not only one of Australia's, but also one of the world's most significant industries. The World Tourism Organisation predicts that global international tourism, which in 1999 generated, directly and indirectly, 11 per cent of global GDP, will expand by 4.1 per cent per year over the next two decades. Australian international visitor arrivals are predicted to grow more quickly at around 7 per cent per year through to 2008. Based on these predictions, tourism is destined to continue playing a vital role in Australia's economic and social development. Accompanying the growth in tourism has been a significant expansion in the worldwide sport and recreation industry. These industries come together in the sports tourism sector, and with the emergence of "niche" markets as a major factor in tourism development, the potential for growth in the sector is considerable. Apart from economic factors, notably increases in disposable income, there is a range of other factors influencing the future growth. These include: continuing increases in the number of sporting events and accompanying media exposure; increased professionalism in sport and consequent demand for training camps; the growth of mass participation events such as Masters Games; and the growth in "manufactured" events—both made for television and made specifically to help promote tourism to a region.

Analysing Opportunities for Australia at various Levels

The hosting of the Sydney 2000 Olympics also provides Australia with a unique opportunity. Apart from showcasing Australia to the world, both as a tourism destination and as a country with the ability to successfully stage major sporting events, the Olympics will leave a legacy of expertise in a range of sports-tourism related fields as well as a legacy of world-class sporting venues. The challenge for sports tourism development is to take advantage of all the opportunities this presents.

Industry Coordination

Sports tourism opportunities, and especially the tourism benefits, are sometimes lost or not maximised because the linkages between the sports and tourism sectors are not well established. Sporting activities, especially events, have historically been organised by sporting organisations for purely sporting purposes. Maximising the tourism potential of the events has often not been a major consideration for the organiser, representing a potential failure of the market. Further, many sporting organisations rely on volunteers, and may not have well developed business or organisational skills or experience. Both of these factors can lead to lost tourism opportunities.

To overcome this, better linkages need to be established between the sporting and tourism groups at all levels—regional, state/territory and national. Regional "sports tourism clusters" provide a model for building these linkages at the local level. Similar groupings at state and national levels would also be beneficial. While the State and Territory events units are working to improve linkages, there may be a role for the Commonwealth to disseminate information and take on a coordination and facilitation role at the national level.

Education and Training

Education and training is critical to the success of both the sports and tourism sectors. For sports tourism, the issue of education and training is especially important in ensuring that sporting bodies in particular have the requisite business skills both to run successful events and to recognise and take advantage of the tourism opportunities which accompany the hosting of those events. While training in this area is certainly available, there may be an issue with ensuring such training is appropriate to the needs of the sector and is affordable and accessible.

Regulatory Issues

Government regulation can and does impact on the sports tourism sector—at the local, State/Territory and Commonwealth levels. This can range from the need to obtain permits for road closures etc. at the local level, to visa requirements for international athletes or international visitors generally, involved in a sporting activity. It is important to try to minimise any adverse impacts of such regulation.

A basic problem for many organisers is simply trying to deal with what can seem like a maze of different agencies with differing requirements. While some States/Territories have developed information kits to help address this issue, the Commonwealth could also play a major role in assisting organisers to navigate through this maze.

Infrastructure

Most if not all sporting activities and events rely on there being appropriate infrastructure in place. The most obvious form of infrastructure is the sporting facilities themselves, however other infrastructure is often more important if sports tourism opportunities are to be maximised.

Adequate accommodation and transport are often critical to the success of events where large numbers of people may need to be moved and accommodated. This can provide difficulties in regional areas, where accommodation may be in short supply and where transport links, both to and within a region, may be expensive and/or suffer from inadequate capacity.

A starting point in addressing these issues, and one which the Commonwealth and a number of States and Territories have already embarked on, would be to conduct facilities audits to identify just what sporting facilities and at what standard, are available. A further logical step down this track would be to conduct a broader "asset audit" of all relevant infrastructure, to assist organisers in assessing the ability of a region to support a particular sporting activity or event.

Research and Data Collection

Like many niche tourism sectors, the sports tourism sector suffers from a lack of reliable data on which to base strategic decision-making. Even data which might help measure the size of the sector is not readily available. Indeed, there is no agreed definition of just what constitutes "sports tourism", hence any discussion of research and data needs must start with the need to come to some consensus as to just what "sports tourism" comprises. Limited data is available from the major tourism surveys—the International

Visitor Survey and the National Visitor Survey. At best, however, the picture they draw is very partial but does indicate that sports tourism is significant in the overall tourism market.

A further issue is that most of the available research tends to focus on individual events and not on improving our overall understanding of the sports tourism market and how it operates at a national or regional level.

Evaluation of Events

There are numerous "models" employed to evaluate events which can lead to different outcomes and a consequent inability to compare results. A more consistent methodology, and in the case of smaller regional events, a simplified methodology would be of considerable benefit. The Cooperative Research Centre for Sustainable Tourism, through its events sub-programme and its recently established sports tourism "node", may be able to better coordinate activity in this area, and help provide a more "macro level" focus. Australia can learn from international experience in the sports tourism field. The United Kingdom, through the British Tourist Authority, has developed a sports tourism marketing strategy and has recently appointed a sports tourism coordinator in their Sydney office. Canada has been pursuing a programme of developing sports tourism "clusters" or networks in regional areas, to bring together relevant players, raise awareness and maximise tourism benefits. South Africa also has identified sports tourism as a growth sector.

Implementation

Successful implementation of a national strategy will require a concerted and coordinated effort from a range of organisations, including governments at all levels (Commonwealth, State/Territory and local), the tourism industry, the sports sector including national and state/territory sporting organisations and researchers.

At the State/Territory level, State departments and events corporations take on much of the responsibility for building these links. At the local level, there may be a greater need for development of networks or "clusters" focusing on sports tourism development. At the national level, there may also be a need for better coordination.

In sum, sports tourism in Australia has enormous potential. A number of factors, including strong inbound tourism growth, a sporting culture, good sporting and tourism infrastructure, and the catalytic effect of the Sydney 2000 Olympic Games, are combining to make this a key growth area. The challenge is to maximise that growth in a manner that can provide genuine economic and social benefits for Australia and Australians. This draft Strategy poses a number of questions, with the aim of identifying key measures which would need to be implemented to facilitate growth of the sports tourism industry.

DRAFT NATIONAL SPORTS TOURISM STRATEGY: A CASE STUDY OF AUSTRALIA

Overview

Tourism has in recent decades become firmly established as a major Australian industry, providing significant economic and employment benefits. It accounts for 8 per cent of employment, 5.8 per cent of Gross Domestic Product and nearly 15 per cent of export earnings. Forecast growth, especially for inbound tourism, is very strong.

Similarly, the sports sector has a major economic impact, contributing billions of dollars to the economy and employing tens of thousands of Australians. Furthermore, sport occupies a central place within Australian culture and identity, based on a long history of achievement across a wide range of sports.

It is not surprising then that travel for the purpose of participating in some manner of sporting activity is both significant and growing—in Australia and worldwide.

Key Elements of the Strategy

The aim of the Strategy is to facilitate a viable and internationally competitive sports tourism industry which can maximise its contribution to Australia's economic and social well-being, especially in regional Australia.

The draft Strategy identifies a number of issues that impact on the development of the sports tourism industry, and discusses developments in these areas and possible actions. The issues include: industry coordination; education and training; government regulation; sport and tourism infrastructure; evaluation of the economic benefits of sports tourism; research and data; and Strategy implementation.

Background

The development of the National Sports Tourism Strategy has its genesis in the *National Action Plan for Tourism*. The Plan, released in 1998, provides a policy framework for the future growth of the tourism industry in Australia. It identifies the development of a range of niche tourism products as one of the avenues which will promote strong future growth and diversification of the industry, and identifies sports tourism as one of the sectors showing enormous potential for further development.

In November 1999 the Federal Minister for Sport and Tourism, the Hon Jackie Kelly MP, announced the Government's intention to develop a National Sports Tourism Strategy in recognition of the need for a planned and consistent approach to building a larger sustainable base for the sports tourism sector.

The development of the Strategy to date has involved extensive consultation with a wide range of stakeholders; desk research; the production of a preliminary discussion paper; and the organisation of a series of focus group workshops around Australia.

Reasons for developing a National Sports Tourism Strategy

In the past decade tourism has been firmly established as a major industry in Australia, economically, socially and as a job provider for Australians. In 1996-97, tourism directly accounted for 5.8 per cent of expenditure on Gross Domestic Product (GDP). Growth in the tourism industry is forecast to continue well into the next decade, especially for international tourism, with the Tourism Forecasting Council predicting that international visitor arrivals will grow at an average annual rate of 7.3 per cent to 2008 when we will welcome 8.4 million visitors. In 1999, international tourism to Australia generated export earnings of $17 billion and accounted for 14.9 per cent of Australia's total export earnings. Expenditure derived from domestic tourism was $44.8 billion in 1998-99.

Sport has always been an integral part of Australian life and it is increasingly being recognised that sporting events and activities have the potential to be a major tourism drawcard. Australia has something of a natural advantage in this niche market given our strong international image as a sporting nation. This reputation is largely based on the achievements of our sports men and women and images from international events held here. It also forms part of the Australian "lifestyle", an experience which is consistently rated as a major motivating factor in bringing international visitors to Australia.

The popularity of sports events, which constitute a significant proportion of all events held in Australia, guarantees that they are a major component of tourism agencies' strategies for destination development. For the Australian Tourist Commission (ATC), the promotion of Australia as a destination for a holiday featuring sports activity is a logical development of Australia's strong sporting image and the ATC has incorporated a "sports" theme in its overseas marketing.

Sports tourism, or tourism which is associated with sporting activity, therefore has the potential to develop into a highly significant niche sector which provides Australia with economic and social benefits.

The hosting of the Olympic Games in Sydney in 2000 is undeniably a definitive moment for sports tourism in Australia and has the potential to bring significant ongoing benefits to the Australian tourism sector. While mega-events of this ilk are definitely not the "bread and butter" of sports tourism, the Olympics will provide many lessons in organising, running and capitalising on the tourism benefits of sporting events. We need to ensure that Australia obtains every possible advantage from hosting this one-off special event, in order to build a more sustainable base for the long-term future viability of the sports tourism sector in Australia.

The Key Elements of the Strategy

The aim of the strategy is to facilitate a viable and internationally competitive sports tourism industry and to ensure that the benefits of this niche market are maximised and spread widely throughout Australia. This objective has been identified because of the perception that the tourism benefits which sporting activities and events can provide are not currently being maximised. The strategy identifies *opportunities* for the development of the sports tourism sector as well as identifying and addressing *impediments* to the growth of the industry.

The key elements of the strategy are a range of possible actions which can help to:

- Improve the coordination and competitiveness of the sports tourism industry
- Identify and address education and training issues for the industry
- Minimise the impact of regulatory issues (e.g. visas, customs) on the industry
- Identify and address the infrastructure requirements of the industry
- Identify and address the research and data collection requirements of the industry
- Improve the means of evaluation of the economic benefits of sports tourism
- Coordinate the implementation of the strategy.

Revisiting Sports Tourism

Sports tourism is a niche market which can be broadly described as a tourism activity generated by participation in sporting activity. That activity can be a sporting event or competition, a tour of a sporting facility, or a training camp. Participation might involve being a competitor/participant, official, or spectator. The Australian definitions of international and domestic tourism are well understood and accepted and are used as the basis for the definitions of sports tourism adopted for the development of this Strategy. These are:

- *Domestic sports tourism*: any sports-related trip of over 40 kms and involving a stay of at least one night away from home; and

- *International sports tourism*: any trip to Australia a prime purpose of which is to participate in a sporting activity, either as a spectator, participant or official.

As to what constitutes a sporting activity in this context some decisions need to be made in relation to activities that could be seen more as recreational (e.g. fishing, golf, skiing, horse-racing) and also to adventure activities (e.g. sky surfing, para-sailing, rock-climbing, etc.). All of these activities require skill and also offer potential for competition, however they are also frequently pursued by individuals in an unstructured way and maybe entirely incidental to their main reason for travelling.

While this may not matter in some respects, structured, organised sports events, tours, camps and so on arguably offer more potential for industry and governments to target with a view to increasing the tourism potential, than do leisure and adventure activities–important though they are in their own right. It is therefore those activities which can be targeted for further development which are included within the ambit of this Strategy.

Tourism and Sport—The World Market

Tourism

Tourism and travel make up one of the world's largest industries. In 1999 the World Travel and Tourism Council (WTTC) also reports that across the global economy, travel and tourism generates, directly and indirectly:

- 11 per cent of GDP;
- 200 million jobs;
- 8 per cent of total employment, and
- 5.5 million new jobs per year until 2010

World Tourism Organisation (WTO) data for 1999 show that 663 million people spent at least one night in a foreign country, up 4.1 per cent over the previous year. Spending on international tourism reached US$453 billion—a growth rate of nearly 3 per cent over 1998. These results are in line with WTO's long-term growth forecast *Tourism: 2020 Vision* which predicts that the tourism sector will expand by an average of 4.1 per cent a year over the next two decades. Annual international arrivals are expected to surpass one billion by the year 2010 and reach 1.6 billion by the year 2020.

Reasons for this sustained growth include greater disposable income in tourism generating countries, and, especially in some of the emerging economies of Asia, more leisure time, earlier retirement, improvements in infrastructure and transport (particularly air transport), and changes in consumer spending preferences.

Sport

Sport and active recreation have become very large and successful industries worldwide. A 1994 European Commission Report on the European Community and Sport estimated that the sports industry is responsible for 2.5 per cent of world trade.

The factors influencing the growth of sport and recreation are similar to those influencing tourism growth—notably increased disposable income, greater availability of leisure time and changing consumer preferences. An increased awareness of the benefits for all ages of greater physical activity has also been important.

In addition, the role of the media in promoting sports has been critical. A number of factors have contributed to this greater international media attention on sport and recreation, especially in western economies:

- increased demand for sports programming from television broadcasters to meet consumer demand, the advent of dedicated sports channels (e.g. Fox Sports, ESPN, C7 Sports), and the availability of satellite technology allowing live coverage;
- increased prominence of professional sportspersons across a range of sports, e.g. golf, tennis, basketball, baseball, surfing, rugby and soccer;
- large amounts of money being spent by corporations directly and indirectly sponsoring events, teams and individuals for commercial advantage;
- sports associations becoming more like large-scale business enterprises;

- growth of merchandise associated with particular sports, sporting activities and sporting teams;
- significant advertising, promotion, and activity associated with high-profile international sporting events, e.g. the Olympic Games, Soccer World Cups, Grand Slam tennis, Formula One Grand Prix, and national sporting competitions;
- increasing opportunities for participation, especially in western economies, through changing leisure patterns, ageing of the population, increased disposable income, and increased awareness of the benefits of physical activity.

Sports Tourism

Having regard to the trends emerging in both the tourism and sports sectors, it is not surprising that significant growth is also occurring in travel for sports related purposes. In fact, this growth is also linked to another trend—that of travelling for specific "niche" purposes, of which sporting activity is one.

The British Tourist Authority and English Tourism Board claim as many as 20 per cent of tourists trips are for the prime purpose of sports participation, whilst up to 50 per cent of holidays include incidental sports participation. This level of activity is broadly consistent with Canadian data, with the 1998 Canadian Travel Survey finding that 37 per cent of domestic trips that year were for sports-related purposes. In the case of the United States, the Travel Industry Association of America found that in the past five years, 38 per cent of US adults attended an organised sports event, competition or tournament as either a spectator or participant, while on a trip of 50 miles or more. These figures are based on rather broad definitions of the "sport" in sports tourism.

Significantly, perhaps, the sports market, and hence the sports tourism market, is becoming increasingly internationalised. As previously mentioned, the availability of sports-only TV channels which display sports from numerous countries around the world, as well as increasing coverage of an ever-expanding range of sporting events through more mainstream media outlets, means there is an increasing awareness of the range of sporting activities being pursued around the world, including in countries such as Australia.

Tourism and Sport—The Australian Market

Tourism

Tourism has grown to be one of Australia's most significant industries. While a small player in terms of world arrivals, Australia is a major tourism destination in terms of tourism receipts, ranking 12th in the world for 1999.

In 1996-97, tourism accounted directly for 5.8 per cent of expenditure on Gross Domestic Product (GDP), and was directly responsible for the employment of over 670,000 persons and indirectly for a further 290,000. This accounts for 11.5 per cent of total Australian employment.

In 1998/99, expenditure derived from domestic tourism was $44.8 billion. In 1999, international tourism to Australia generated exports of $17 billion and accounted for 14.9 per cent of Australia's total export earnings.

Tourism is destined to continue playing a vital role in Australia's economic and social development. The Tourism Forecasting Council (TFC) predicts that international visitor arrivals will grow at an annual average rate of 7.3 per cent to 2008 and generate nearly $32 billion in export earnings in 2008. This means international visitor number in excess of 8.4 million in 2008—almost double the current level of tourist visitation to Australia. Much higher levels of growth are predicted from emerging Asian markets including China (21.1%), South Korea (23.7%) and Thailand (18.3%). On the domestic front growth is anticipated to be steady with an average annual growth rate of 1.6 per cent for the period 1998-99 to 2008-09.

Sport

Australia has long been regarded as a sporting nation. Significant interest by the Australian public in sports of one type or another across wide demographic boundaries ensures that the sport industry in Australia assumes a significant economic, social and even political profile.

Involvement in sport and sporting activity not only benefits both the health and general well-being of our nation, it also makes a sizeable contribution to the Australian economy. Precise figures are extremely difficult to find—a problem for sports tourism also, and one which is discussed later in this strategy. What is clear is that the sports sector generates many billions of dollars within the economy and provides employment for tens of thousands of people.

Despite its size and significance, many sectors of the industry are not highly commercialised, although some, such as the businesses supplying goods and services which support sporting activities, are very commercially focused. There is a large "not-for-profit" segment of the sports sector, exemplified by the number of volunteers working within it. In 1994/95 there were 112,877 volunteers working in the sports industries which was almost double the formal employment in sports industries at that time. The majority of these volunteers (89%) worked within the sports, or in the provision of services to sports sectors.

Structurally, the sports sector is very decentralised. An important part of the sector is the local sporting club—bodies dedicated to the development of single sports run by and for its members. These clubs often affiliate with regional and state associations which, in turn, unite to form National Sporting Organisations (NSOs). Volunteers administer sport at all levels—particularly the club level. At state and national levels professional administrators begin to play a role, although even here volunteers may still make a significant contribution.

Professional clubs also exist in parallel with this system in the major sports like the football codes, basketball, cricket and baseball. They belong to state or national leagues and are managed predominantly by full-time professional administrators and coaches.

Special purpose associations exist to promote particular interests such as sports medicine, coaching, school and university competition, physical education, legal issues and professional development for sports workers. These usually affiliate with an umbrella body which operates at the national level.

Government involvement in sport occurs at each of the three levels of government—local, state and national, through the various departments dealing with sport and recreation, the Australian Sports Commission, the Australian Institute of Sport, and the State Institutes of Sports and Academies. There are also a range of non-government organisations which administer, coordinate and promote particular interests at both state and national levels.

Within the government sector, there are a number of vehicles for seeking to discuss and coordinate issues relating to sport industry development. The Sport and Recreation Ministers Council (SRMC) is the peak body for discussion between the Commonwealth and State and Territory Governments for issues concerning sport and recreation needs across Australia. It is supported by the Standing Committee on Recreation and Sport (SCORS), whose members are senior officials in the sports departments of each State and Territory.

The Commonwealth Government has also given recognition to the many commercial businesses which service Australian participation in sport, through the development of a strategic plan to facilitate the growth of the commercial sports and leisure services sector.

Sports Tourism

Both the tourism industry and the sports industry in Australia come together in the sports tourism sector. Those involved include sport and tourism departments; major events corporations; sporting bodies; facilities managers; event organisers and promoters; tour operators and accommodation providers; transport operators; retailers; and the full range of organisations providing goods and services to both sporting and tourism operators.

However, not all of these groups necessarily perceive themselves as being part of a broader sports tourism industry, resulting in potential lost opportunities associated with the staging of Australia's many and various sporting events.

While it is difficult to establish the size of the industry, some efforts have been made to quantify its value to the Australian economy.

For example, during the focus group process forming part of the development of this draft strategy, a number of participants suggested that the sector accounts for about 5 per cent of the total tourism market, based on the relatively narrow definition proposed in the Strategy. If this is the case across both international and domestic tourism, sports tourism in Australia would account for annual expenditure of about $3 billion per annum.

This estimate is consistent with analysis undertaken by the Bureau of Tourism Research and published in the recent paper *Sports Tourism: An Australian Perspective*, which found that 6 per cent of day trips and 5 per cent of overnight trips taken by Australians in

Australia, were taken with sport as the primary motivation. This corresponds to expenditure of $1847 million by domestic sports tourists, of which $461 million was on day trips and the remaining $1386 million was spent on overnight trips.

Australian domestic sports tourists appear to generate a higher dollar yield than other domestic travellers, with 31 per cent staying in hotel, resort, motel or motor inn accommodation on their sports trip compared with 23 per cent for all domestic travellers. Consequently, their estimated average daily expenditure of $130 is higher than the $112 estimated for other domestic travellers.

OPPORTUNITIES FOR AUSTRALIA AT THE INTERNATIONAL, NATIONAL AND REGIONAL LEVELS

Australia has many competitive advantages in the sports tourism marketplace, including a climate conducive to outdoor activities, a diverse range of sporting activities, access to quality sports facilities, well developed tourism infrastructure and an internationally renowned image as a sporting nation and tourism destination.

Even the fact that our seasons are the reverse of those in the major tourism source markets of the Northern Hemisphere provides a range of opportunities in areas such as pre-season training camps. Similarly, our expertise in areas such as sports science and sports medicine, as well as leading edge facilities such as the Australian Institute of Sport, help to encourage international sporting teams and individuals to travel to Australia.

These assets form the basis for an internationally competitive tourism product. However they have to be managed in a way that delivers the maximum benefits for the country as a whole.

While there are numerous opportunities within the broader sports tourism fields, some sectors and some markets appear to have particular potential for Australia to exploit.

International Opportunities

The Olympics

The sport mega-event is the most widely recognised example of sports tourism. And, with mega-events such as the Olympic Games and the World Cup Football it is not surprising that they involve the largest volumes of spectators and the largest revenues of all special events and festivals.

The value of hosting an Olympic Games has been the subject of much research with wide ranging views on the benefits and costs of such an event. A significant increase in tourism is not a guaranteed certainty with many impacts dependent upon the organisation and marketing of the Olympic Games. Regardless, the staging of an Olympic Games is recognised as being a unique opportunity for the host city and country to engage in high-profile promotion their tourism products at a worldwide level.

Development of international standard sporting facilities, and the upgrading of facilities required for pre-Games training, is both an obvious and tangible legacy. High quality facilities combined with a successful hosting of the Olympics will give Australia a head start in bidding for major sporting events in the years immediately following the Games.

It is also in these years that the Tourism Forecasting Council predict Australia will receive a major tourism benefit from the Olympic Games with additional international visitor numbers of 342,000 in 2000, 335,000 in 2001 and 350,000 in 2002. If these numbers are realised, and they may well be, Australia will have received an immediate and major dividend from the hosting of the Games. Many of those additional visitors will no doubt participate in sporting activities while in Australia.

Just as importantly perhaps, the lessons that have been learned by governments, sporting bodies and business will play a major role in the further development of the sports tourism sector.

The Olympics will also expose Australia's sporting and tourism assets to vast new audiences and markets, providing significant opportunities in the sports tourism field.

Australia's traditional international "sports tourism" markets have been North America, Europe and New Zealand. Rugby tests in particular, but also rugby league, cricket and to a lesser extent netball, generate significant trans-Tasman traffic flows. More recently, however there appears to be considerable emerging growth potential from upper middle and high income Asian economies, including Japan, Korea and Taiwan. Other emerging markets (e.g. India, Latin America and South Africa) offer similar promise where the distribution of wealth is changing and there is an expanding middle class with an increasing level of disposable income.

National Opportunities

Masters Games

Masters Games provide sports tourism opportunities at the international, national and regional levels.

They may well prove to be the greatest potential growth area in sports tourism over the next decade. A relatively recent phenomenon, these games have already grown to occupy a central place among sports tourism activities and are keenly fought over and bid for by potential hosts, because of the sheer numbers of participants involved and their demographic profile – i.e. Masters—which generally equates to high levels of disposable income.

At the top of the Masters Games tree—which comprises local, inter-state, national and international events—is the World Masters Games. Recognised as the world's biggest multi-sport festival, the World Masters Games are considered the premier international event for Masters competitors, allowing them to compete regardless of ability, gender, race or religion. In terms of competition, they are twice as big as the Olympic Games.

Held every four years, the World Masters Games are participant focused, with competitors only being required to meet each sports age qualification.

In Australia, the first sanctioned Masters Games were held in 1986 in Alice Springs. The first Australian (i.e. national) Masters Games were held in Tasmania in 1987. Since then the Australian Masters Games have been held in Adelaide (1989), Brisbane (1991), Perth (1993), Melbourne (1995),Canberra (1997) and Adelaide (1999). The eighth Australian Masters Games will be held in Newcastle and the Hunter region in 2001.

The overall philosophy of the Australian Masters Games is to provide an incentive for mature age persons to begin, or continue active participation in sport. It aims to provide a focus for individual sports to develop their own mature age sport events and to maintain mature sports as a continuing aspect of their programmes and focus. There is a definite aim of the Games to promote community interest and participation in mature age sport and to thereby contribute to the health of its citizens and the nation.

The organisers of the 2001 Australian Masters Games in Newcastle have also identified the potential for the Games to have a significant impact on tourism, sport and culture in the Newcastle and Hunter region and to increase both tourism and brand awareness of the area at a domestic and business level.

"Manufactured" Events

Over the past twenty years or so the interest in sport, especially elite sporting events, has grown at a phenomenal rate. Sport is no longer just about playing the game, it is now perceived to have an obligation to provide public entertainment.

This growth has been in parallel with advances in technology and the evolution of the digital age. People now expect to be entertained by worldwide sporting events telecast live direct to their television sets—or perhaps on their home computer.

According to a survey conducted by the Australian Bureau of Statistics in November 1997, sporting programmes were the most commonly watched on television after news and current affairs, and were viewed regularly by over half of all Australians aged over 18 (55%).

A relatively recent concept is the "manufacture" of sporting events for television – events such as the "One Summer" sporting festival of beach related sporting events is a case in point of what is almost exclusively a television event. There can be a number of tourism-related benefits, including marketing benefits, from events such as these.

Another variation on the "manufactured" event theme is an event which is designed from the outset to promote tourism, rather than being designed as a purely sporting event with the tourism aspect an added extra. The main emphasis in events of this nature, of which there are still relatively few, is on the promotion of tourism to the region where the event is being held, rather than just on the event itself. An excellent example is the Jacobs Creek Tour Down Under in South Australia, which sees cyclists racing through regional South Australia, receiving national and international media coverage and by careful planning and route selection, promoting the region to potential tourists.

One of the major benefits of this type of event is that they can be designed using existing locations, and to suit the capabilities of the region. Examples include cycle races, triathlons, road races, "challenges" such as the Omeo challenge, etc. Critically, these events can be introduced to even out peaks and troughs in tourism activity, and can be tailored to fit into a regional tourism package of events, attractions and activities. They can also spread the accommodation load across a region if necessary. Given that the region which created the event then "owns" the event, they can be conducted on an annual basis which in the longer term reduces the costs associated with their staging.

Regional and Local Opportunities

Masters Games and "manufactured" events can have significant impact at the regional and local level, as well as nationally. Indeed, there are numerous market sectors within sports tourism which lend themselves to regional areas and the lower level of facilities and infrastructure which these areas generally possess.

A key issue for regional areas is to identify the range and level of resources and infrastructure which they do possess, and to use this information as the basis for identifying and pursuing suitable sports tourism opportunities.

Some examples of events which might well lend themselves to hosting by regional or local areas include:

- Schools and underage championships, which can vary in size from quite small to very large (e.g. Albury has been very active in pursuing this part of the market);
- National or indeed international events in "lesser" sports (e.g. Corowa has hosted a world parachuting championship recently while Manilla is a world-renowned paragliding centre);
- Regional championships in a variety of sports; and
- Sports which can be held at a number of locations throughout a region.

Marketing Opportunities

Sports tourism events at the international, national and regional levels have a double-barrelled effect – the direct effect of the attendance of the competitors and/or spectators and accompanying persons, and the indirect effect of the marketing of the destination which will lead to subsequent tourism flows. This indirect effect can be very large – most of the tourism benefits of the Olympics are expected to be of this nature. Even for non-mega events, for example events like the Gold Coast Indy Car Race, the Australian Formula 1 and 500cc Motor Cycle Grand Prix and even events such as the Australian Surf Life Saving Championships, this impact can be very significant.

There is a marketing effect through the word-of-mouth recommendation of attendees at the event, (such as with Masters competitions) but potentially a much greater effect if the event attracts widespread media interest—especially live television coverage.

The marketing spin-offs from sports tourism events can vary enormously depending on a range of factors, including whether the tourism aspects were considered as an integral part of the event and were "built-in" to the development process. For example, the Gold Coast Indy Car Race is deliberately designed to showcase Australia's premier beach destination – the Gold Coast – with parts of the track running right beside Surfers Paradise beach.

Given Australia's status as a relatively little known tourism destination in world terms, the marketing benefits from events, particularly from mega-events such as the Olympics, may be greater than for countries which are already well-known tourist destinations. This presents a genuine opportunity for better showcasing Australia's tourism assets through sporting events.

INDUSTRY COORDINATION

It is clear that major sports events can play a significant role in generating tourism activity on a national and international scale. Such events can have positive economic and social benefits, and have in recent years been increasingly recognised by both national and State Governments as a legitimate focus for tourism and general economic development strategies.

One manifestation of governments' support of events-based strategies is the provision of funding for events and infrastructure by Commonwealth, State and Territory sport departments, and the creation in most states of dedicated events corporations. As this investment in events increases, Governments are being increasingly required to justify their expenditure in these areas, with the attendant challenge being how to enhance sporting events as tourism products so as to maximise returns on investment.

Developing a Strategic Approach

The Commonwealth Government is currently developing a Strategic National Plan for the Sport and Leisure Services Industry. The plan will articulate a vision for the industry and ways for the industry to become world class in the provision of sport and leisure goods and services. Success in realising this vision will require advanced business networks and better relationships between business, governments, sporting organisations and consumers of leisure activities.

A similar challenge faces the sports tourism sector. The sports tourism focus group discussions identified the need for the sports tourism sector to identify itself as a discrete industry group and to establish the linkages necessary to capture commercial opportunities.

The current lack of an identity and cohesiveness was identified as one of the major impediments to the growth of the sports tourism sector. In addition, the lack of recognition by both government and the private sector of the economic potential of sports tourism has led to many opportunities being overlooked. Some of the key issues which need to be addressed to encourage and enable the growth of sports tourism include *establishing linkages* to enable the raising of awareness of the mutual benefits and advantages of establishing alliances; coordinating planning and the *sharing of resources and information;* and identifying opportunities and mechanisms for *maximising the tourism benefits* of sporting activities.

Establishing Linkages

The fact that most events are organised by sporting bodies as sporting events first and foremost with tourism almost an optional extra, represents a failure of the market. Sporting bodies arguably have little incentive to pursue the tourism benefits which can flow from sporting activities, especially sporting events, because they themselves cannot directly capture many of those benefits. The great majority of those benefits accrue to other parties—tour operators, accommodation providers, transport operators, retail outlets, restaurants and so on. And yet many of these people may not even perceive that they stand to benefit significantly from tourism activity associated with sporting events.

To some extent, States and Territories have moved to address this by establishing major events corporations, to bring together the sports and tourism players and to bid for events. This works very well for some events – most notably the larger, higher profile events on which the events corporations generally focus.

However, the needs of second-tier or regional events are not necessarily adequately met through this process. At a regional level, governments could play a role in facilitating the establishment of "cluster" groups comprising the full range of stakeholders in the sports tourism process. A useful model could be the cluster formed in Cairns following the focus group conducted there—"Sports Tropical North Queensland." Significantly, the Cairns group is being coordinated by the economic development corporation, reflecting the broad benefit which sports tourism events can provide throughout the regional economy.

Sharing of Resources and Information

At the regional level, clusters or networks can play a number of roles to help coordinate activities, assist in the sharing of physical resources and encourage information sharing. For smaller sporting bodies, the level of resources required (e.g. signage, barriers, marquees) may be a deterrent to running events, as can be the lack of knowledge for first time organisers. Simply sharing these resources can assist in the planning and running of successful events, with region-wide benefits for both sporting and tourism groups.

At a national level, the Commonwealth could play a role which would largely be one of the provision of information, including providing links and referrals to the enormous range of information already available, much of which has been produced by States and Territories, but which is currently not being accessed by event organisers or tourism groups.

Maximising the Tourism Benefits

There are a number of ways to maximise the returns from investment in events. These include:

- improving the yield from existing events;

- staging more events;
- targeting and supporting events that offer the biggest potential returns in terms of tourism;
- spreading the benefits of new and existing events to more regions, rather than just the major metropolitan centres; and
- better coordination of sporting events with other tourism related activities to maximise visitor stay and yield.

Success in each of these areas relies on the establishment of alliances between sport and tourism bodies at all levels—national, state/territory and regional—and greater emphasis on cooperative planning and coordination. This emerged as the top priority in almost every focus group discussion held around Australia.

Recent international experience such as that in the UK (see Appendix 4) has illustrated that simply bringing the sport and tourism sectors together is not sufficient to encourage the development of working alliances. It will therefore be important to demonstrate clearly to both the sport and tourism sectors the practical advantages of creating and encouraging alliances.

While sporting events continue to be organised purely as sporting events with tourism a secondary consideration, progress towards fully capturing the business opportunities associated with sports tourism will remain difficult. What is required is for events or activities to be seen as sports tourism opportunities and for organisers to give equal weight to the requirement to run a technically and administratively successful sporting event and the opportunity to maximise the visitation and yield by producing an appropriate tourism package.

Possible Commonwealth Facilitation Role

One of the key suggestions arising from the focus group discussions is for the Commonwealth Government to play a facilitation role for the development of sports tourism in Australia. In doing so, the Commonwealth Government could help address a perceived general lack of coordination between private sector, government, and sport and tourism bodies, and rectify the absence of an effective and appropriate mechanism for the dissemination of information throughout the sports tourism sector. This facilitation role could focus primarily on the provision and dissemination of information, referral to appropriate agencies, and the encouragement of better communication between key sports and tourism players.

Project Facilitation

The Commonwealth Government could also play a role in the facilitation of major projects—the so-called mega events—which impact on national interests as well as individual State/Territory interests. A possible model could be the approach adopted for the Olympics, where a coordination unit brought together the many Commonwealth agencies necessary to make the event a success. This role would be undertaken on an "as needs" basis, when events of this magnitude are being considered or planned.

Network Facilitation

More generally, as already mentioned, there is a need to help facilitate the establishment of sports tourism networks or clusters, especially at a regional level, to ensure opportunities are not lost and are indeed maximised. There are existing models in other industries.

By way of example, as part of the Furnishing Industry Action Agenda, which aims to improve the competitiveness of the furnishing industry, the Commonwealth Government has recently announced the establishment of a Furnishing Industry Unit within the Department of Industry, Science and Resources. This unit will act as a focal point within the Commonwealth for issues of concern to the sector, and will aim to improve networking and statistical data collection.

A similar mechanism could be established for sports tourism and might play a similar role, although broader, to that being undertaken by Soar International in Canada. Soar International is a sports information and event management company contracted by the Canadian Tourism Commission to facilitate the development of sports tourism networks in regional areas.

Possibilities of Development of Sports Tourisn in Australia

- Information dissemination

    - development of a website to bring together a range of information relating to international, national, state, regional and local events, funding, planning, management, research and economic evaluation, with links to other relevant websites
- Project facilitation
    - form a "one-stop-shop" for events organisers to access information and facilitate liaison with other government portfolios and agencies
- Establishing networks between sports and tourism organisations and agencies
    - develop a database of key stakeholders at national level, and develop a similar model for use by state and regional areas to bring together the relevant organisations and agencies
- Hosting workshops
    - to promote and establish sports tourism "clusters" such as the one formed in Cairns following the Focus Group workshop conducted as part of the development of this Strategy. (See Case Study: Cairns Cluster)
- Assessing research needs
    - work with CRC Tourism Events sub-programme and researchers to establish, maintain and disseminate a register of research undertaken, and identify research needs
- Assessing education and training needs
    - work with educational institutions, training bodies and the industry to identify education and training needs and provide information on appropriate courses available to stakeholders
- Providing advice on infrastructure development
    - provide advice to government on requirements for facilities and asset audits, disseminate results of audits
- Promoting best practice
    - disseminate information on best practice, assist in development of standards, particularly with regard to economic evaluation of events
- Establishing appropriate industry awards
    - consider possibility of developing industry "award

for excellence" for sports tourism in conjunction with a peak body such as Tourism Council Australia or Sport Industry Australia

- Promoting international competitiveness
  - disseminate information and resources which promote competitiveness and assist in capturing international markets (e.g. access to Government programmes such as the Export Markets Development Grants Scheme).

Is a strategy of encouraging the development of regional sports tourism "clusters" an appropriate way to assist sports tourism development in regional Australia?

—if so, whose responsibility is it to undertake this role?

EDUCATION AND TRAINING

There is widespread recognition that a high level of business expertise and management skill is critical if the sports tourism sector is to successfully meet the needs of the increasingly discerning sports tourism consumer.

The focus group discussions highlighted the demand for appropriate and accessible education and training, particularly in the area of management, where many not-for-profit sporting organisations rely on part-time staff or volunteers. Equally, tourism organisations would benefit from greater awareness of sports tourism opportunities and some education and training to enable them to maximise the tourism potential of sporting events and activities.

Sport and Recreation

Sport and recreation industry specific education and training is provided through a combination of graduate/post graduate university education, Vocational Education and Training (VET), on the job training (sometimes with a VET component), industry based training and accreditation and a range of short courses. The most common VET providers are the Technical And Further Education (TAFE) institutions, although some sectors, for example the fitness industry, mainly use private training providers. Other training providers include community based organisations, individual businesses and some secondary schools.

A national industry training advisory body, Sport and Recreation Training Australia, which is jointly funded by industry and government with employer and employee representation, provides advice on the range of industry training needs. A National Sport Industry Training package became available in 1999.

Some areas of the industry have introduced training and accreditation systems for instructors, primarily as a result of the threat of litigation in an area of high risk of injury to participants. Employment in these areas is generally dependent on possession of an industry qualification in addition to specific industry skills.

Tourism

As in the sport and recreation sector, the tourism industry has access to industry specific education and training from a combination of graduate/post graduate university education, Vocational Education and Training (VET), on the job training, industry based training and accreditation and a range of short courses.

A national industry training advisory body, Tourism Training Australia (TTA) develops and delivers integrated tourism packages for the tourism industry. Many forms of management and staff training are available, including in-house or on the job training, self-paced and distance learning packages, and formal courses offered by TAFE colleges, universities and private tourism training enterprises.

Among the priority areas identified by TTA for future skills development are management and business skills for medium and small enterprises, marketing skills and specific management and operational skills for the meetings, conferences, exhibitions and events sector.

The Sports Tourism Sector

Despite the education and training opportunities available in the sport and recreation and tourism industries, there remains a continuing need for improving workforce and management skills.

This is particularly so in areas characterised by volunteers or low wage employees or where there is a predominance of part time jobs and high staff turnover. In particular, organisations relying on government funding find it difficult to attract and retain skilled employees.

In terms of higher education, new courses focusing specifically on sports tourism are starting to emerge. For example, Southern Cross University recently introduced a degree course in Sports Tourism. However, more generally, as was suggested at the focus group discussions, a more comprehensive range of education and training opportunities is needed if the sports tourism sector is to fully realise its growth potential.

This could be achieved through the development of an industry training package that identifies the skill requirements for qualifications in various occupations, and the appropriate training courses to acquire these skills. Development of such a package would require input from industry associations, government sport and tourism bodies, industry training bodies and universities and TAFE institutions. A range of accreditation opportunities could be also developed to enhance professional development opportunities for employees, trainees, and volunteers.

Improved access and take-up of management courses would also assist businesses improve their performance. This is particularly so for many not-for-profit sporting organisations whose personnel may have a high degree of technical knowledge about their sport but are less skilled in business management. Volunteers can also pose particular challenges in the take up of management training due to time and resource constraints.

One means of improving management training could be to augment generic management courses with elements tailored to the sports tourism sector, for example, on strategic planning and development of an event calendar, how to create and maintain linkages between sport and tourism organisations, and ways to prepare an appropriate tourism package for a particular sporting market.

One suggestion made in the focus group discussions was for agencies responsible for funding sporting bodies to provide greater recognition for sporting organisations whose executive hold relevant qualifications or undertake appropriate courses or participate in the existing volunteer and management improvement programmes. Another suggestion was for State and Territory funding agencies or regional organisations to arrange mobile "in-service" training for regional areas.

Specific sports tourism development courses could also assist in the formation and development of sports tourism clusters, such as the one established in Cairns. There could be a role for regional development and tourism associations to develop and make available 'value adding' packages to regional tourism and sporting organisations that include, for example, checklists and guidelines for organising committees. Such packages could include tourism product marketing material for sporting organisers and information about the event participants for tourism agencies and businesses.

REGULATORY ISSUES

Governments at all levels can and do impose requirements which impact on sports tourism events and activities. These can be broad requirements such as the need for international competitors or spectators to sporting events to obtain a visa or electronic travel authority to enter Australia or they can be specific to a particular event, for example, the closure of roads for the holding of a fun run or triathlon.

Dealing with Commonwealth, State/Territory and local government departments and agencies can be a daunting prospect for event organisers. This can be especially so for organisers who may be tackling the task of organising their event for the first time or for volunteers in sporting organisations who have neither experience in dealing with regulatory requirements or the time available to deal with these.

During the focus group discussions, the issue of government regulatory requirements was frequently raised as a significant barrier to the successful organisation of sporting events and activities, and the maximisation of tourism opportunities from those activities. It was suggested on numerous occasions that governments could play a role by providing event organisers with a mechanism to help deal with complex regulatory requirements.

A number of State and Territory governments have already developed assistance packages that go some way towards providing just such a service. For example, the Canberra Tourism and Events Corporation (CTEC) has developed a publication entitled *Assistance for Special Events – Information Handbook for Event Organisers*, which contains a section on Government liaison with relevant contact details for organisations such as police, emergency services, roads and traffic bodies, venue hire, litter disposal and so on. The Handbook provides a how-to guide for organising an event, covering issues such as budgeting, sponsorship, media relations, general organisation tips, and evaluating the outcome of the event.

This kind of assistance is not available in all States and Territories. Even where advice is available through Events Corporations, this may not always be available at the local or regional level—i.e. contact details may not be available for all local government agencies with whom event organisers in regional areas might have to deal. Further, the CTEC publication does not deal with liaison with Commonwealth agencies such as Customs, Immigration and Quarantine for events where there may be international competitors involved.

There is therefore a clear information gap for event organisers in dealing effectively with government agencies—at the local, Commonwealth, and in some instances at least, State/Territory level. There may be a need for Commonwealth, State/Territory and local governments to cooperate more fully in the provision of information to help fill this gap.

Commonwealth Agencies

At the Commonwealth level, a number of agencies oversee regulatory requirements which impact on event organisers, in particular where there are international competitors, spectators or other participants involved.

Visas

Visitors to Australia are required to obtain a visa to enter the country. In the case of most visitors travelling as tourists, this takes the form of an Electronic Travel Authority (ETA) which is, in effect, an "invisible visa."

There are different categories of visas, including business visas and sport visas. The latter are often used by professional sports people who will be staying for some time in Australia pursuing their sporting interests. Depending on the nature and duration of the sporting activity being undertaken, people travelling to Australia who will be participating in some form of sports tourism activity may choose to travel under all of these different visa types.

Two recent innovations by the Department of Immigration and Multicultural Affairs (DIMA) which administers Australia's visa system, will assist organisers and international participants in sporting events in Australia. These are the *International Event Coordinator Network (IECN)*, and *Streamlined Short Term Business Entry*. The IECN is a network of immigration officers located within the DIMA Business Centre in each State and Territory capital city. The role of these officers is to alert event organisers of immigration requirements and to advise Australian posts overseas of details of forthcoming events. The network is potentially of great benefit to event organisers, including organisers of sporting events, who appear not to have utilised its services greatly to this point.

The Streamlined Short Term Business Entry arrangements have been put in place in the lead up to the Olympics, and have enabled sports people to enter Australia on business visas, including the ETA version of the business visa. This is a quicker and more streamlined option for many sports people and will help facilitate travel to Australia to participate in sporting activities. This arrangement may continue following the Olympics.

Customs

The Australian Customs Service maintains Australia's border integrity by ensuring that prohibited goods are not brought into Australia and that other goods brought in either permanently or temporarily, pay the appropriate rate of duty or tax. This may include sporting goods brought in by international visitors for use in competition.

As with immigration requirements, the Australian Customs Service can make special arrangements to cater for the needs of teams competing in international events, provided it receives sufficient notice of forthcoming events. For example, special dispensation may be obtained to enable temporary duty-free entry of goods for sporting events.

The special arrangements put in place for the Sydney 2000 Olympic Games will no doubt provide valuable lessons in facilitating the movement of goods and people for future major sporting events.

Quarantine

The Australian Quarantine Inspection Service (AQIS) seeks to protect Australia against the introduction of exotic plant and animal matter which could pose a disease risk for Australia's unique environment and its agricultural industries.

For this reason, AQIS inspects goods entering Australia, including sporting equipment, food supplements, and therapeutic substances.

Where horses are brought to Australia to compete in races or in equestrian events, a period of quarantine is required. Early contact with AQIS helps minimise any quarantine difficulties which might otherwise impact on a sporting event.

AQIS also anticipate that the knowledge and experience gained from the Olympics will help them to adopt best practice approaches to future major sporting events.

Infrastructure

The ability of cities or regions to host successful sports tourism activities and events depends on there being adequate infrastructure in place. This includes sporting facilities, accommodation, air, road and rail transport networks both to and within the region, and other tourism related facilities such as restaurants, retail outlets and entertainment venues.

While the focus of event organisers tends to be on the actual sporting infrastructure, the existence of adequate sporting facilities does not necessarily mean that an event can be held at that location. If accommodation and transport requirements cannot be met or are inadequate, even small regional events will be difficult to host. Accordingly, a strategic approach which considers the adequacy and availability of all relevant infrastructure needs to be adopted when planning sporting events and activities.

Sporting facilities are expensive to provide. For this reason, their funding has almost always been the domain of governments—local, State and Territory and Commonwealth. This can lead to distortions in the provision of facilities, with priorities sometimes influenced by factors other than the perceived benefits to a community. Arguably, this has led to an over-investment in sporting facilities in some areas, and consequent excess capacity.

This excess capacity represents a genuine opportunity for sports tourism development—significant benefits can be gained through better facilities utilisation, without the need for further costly investment.

The relationship between facilities and the hosting of events is complex. Investment in facilities can rarely be justified on the basis of being used only for major sporting events. Also, it cannot be assumed that the mere provision of high quality sporting facilities will guarantee a region or a state a flow of major sports tourism opportunities. It is ultimately then incumbent upon a region itself to attract facilities funding, possibly through the hosting of a "catalytic" event, and thereafter to "sell" those facilities effectively to event organisers to help ensure their sustainable use.

Cost-effectiveness is a key consideration in attracting facilities funding. It may be that the costs associated with the construction and maintenance of national or international standard facilities simply cannot be justified for community use alone or even taking into consideration increased use associated with the hosting of national or international events. The commercial viability of facilities can be further reduced when accompanying accommodation and transport infrastructure is inadequate for the hosting of major events.

More recently there has been a trend towards the construction of multi-purpose facilities which can be utilised for a variety of community and entertainment functions as well as the holding of a variety of sporting activities and events. This kind of facility can prove more cost effective than traditional facilities dedicated to a narrow focus on a particular sport or range of sports.

When considering facilities investment, it is also important—both for governments and private investors—to consider the regional facilities environment so as to avoid duplication and maximise the synergies with complementary facilities in nearby regions. The development of regional sporting "hubs" for particular sports can also help reduce the risk of constructing sports specific facilities which are economically unsustainable.

More generally, a strategy by governments and sporting organisations of "sharing" State or national events around regional Australia would help justify the financial investment in regional facilities as well as help ensure a more even distribution of the economic benefits associated with sporting events.

State/Regional Facilities and Asset Audits

Facilities investment and prioritisation of facilities funding would also be enhanced by improved information about the supply and demand for regional sporting infrastructure. This would also help address the difficulties faced by event promoters, organisers or prospective organisers who often lack awareness of just what facilities and of what standard, are available in various regions.

Currently, the Commonwealth is working with the State and Territory governments on undertaking a facilities audit of state, national and international standard facilities. To complement this work regions could benefit if similar audits were conducted at the regional level.

Frequently, events may be organised with little knowledge of, or regard to, other events planned for the same time. This can have serious ramifications for all events staged at that time, with multiple demands on infrastructure and services, which may well exceed the capacity of the region to manage. Data on the utilisation of sporting facilities is therefore important, particularly where there may be strong seasonal variations. In this way, sports tourism activities, along with other events-based tourism activity, can be targeted at low or shoulder season times, to help minimise peaks and troughs.

Accommodation Infrastructure

One of the key issues for maximising the tourism benefits of sporting activity and events is the availability of a range of accessible accommodation, covering the budget to the luxury markets. As part of each region's asset audit, an accommodation directory should be produced detailing the bed numbers in each sector of the market. By identifying the range of accommodation available, local sports tourism organisers can more effectively target particular events, knowing that suitable accommodation for the specific market is available. For example, under age championships may well have quite different accommodation needs from a masters competition.

As part of this accommodation audit, consideration could be given to utilising or upgrading existing facilities such as school dormitories, barracks etc., which may well provide adequate accommodation for the lower end of the market.

A vital part of encouraging the development of sports tourism in a region is identifying the benefits which can accrue to the whole community. In particular the businesses directly involved in the provision of services should be made aware of the importance of catering for the needs of their guests to ensure they have a good experience. In the case of accommodation providers, they need to address the particular needs of athletes including bed lengths and adequate and appropriate catering.

Transport Infrastructure

A key issue emerging from the focus group discussions is high cost of transportation in many areas of regional Australia—both to and within regions. An associated issue was lack of transport capacity—the inability to move large numbers of participants in and out of many regions in a short space of time.

Ongoing reforms and deregulation in the transport sector, especially domestic aviation, have the potential to deliver significant benefits to regional Australia, and to help encourage the development of sports tourism and other events based tourism in regional Australia.

RESEARCH AND DATA COLLECTION

Sports tourism is a relatively new area of study given its recent rise as a significant niche sector for the Australian tourism industry. A number of Australian researchers have begun to specialise in this field but the current information base available to the industry is still relatively small and a range of research needs to be conducted.

The effects of the Sydney Olympic Games will undoubtedly provide the focus for many research efforts in the coming year but this needs to be complemented by a more grassroot approach to research across a range of sports tourism activities.

A major inhibitor to more and better quality research is the current lack of data available. While some data is collected in relation to individual events, there is no widespread or systematic data series across all sports tourism activities at a state or national level.

The International Visitor Survey (IVS) and National Visitor Survey (NVS) produced by the Bureau of Tourism Research (BTR) currently include limited questions regarding activities undertaken by visitors while travelling throughout Australia. The NVS includes the categories of Sport—Participant or Spectator under Main Purpose of Visit in its survey form. In the IVS 'to participate in or watch an organised sporting event' is a response to a question regarding factors that influenced the decision to visit Australia.

This data provides at best a very partial picture of the level of sports tourism activity in Australia. To improve the available data, there may be some scope to expand the range of questions regarding sports related activities within these surveys or to initiate a stand-alone sports tourism baseline study.

The BTR have also undertaken initial research profiling Australian 'sports tourists'. (Tourism Research Report 3rd edition – *Sports Tourism: An Australian Perspective*) This research extends the definition of sports tourism further than that adopted for this Strategy to include day trips, i.e. a round trip of at least 50 kilometres, where the traveller stays away from home for at least 4 hours but does not spend a night away from home as part of that travel. The Survey results showed that 6 per cent of day trips and 5 per cent of overnight trips taken by Australians in Australia, were taken with sport as the primary motivation. (It could be anticipated that a significant further number of trips were undertaken with sport as a secondary motivation.) The paper found that that Australians who travelled to take part in sports, either as spectators, officials or participants (day and overnight) are likely to be male; aged between 15 and 24 years; from an upper income household (earning more than $78000 per year); and that they generate higher yield per night.

The slightly different definition employed in the BTR study suggests what should probably be the first step in data collection for the sports tourism sector—the establishment of a uniform set of standard definitions for sports tourism. The adoption of standard definitions provides the opportunity for various researchers to produce data which has comparability across the sports tourism sector. An extensive range of agreed definitions should be developed, allowing researchers to choose those required for specific data sets while retaining commonality. The definition adopted in this Strategy might provide the basis for discussion towards such agreement.

Data types which might provide the basis for a range of research in the sports tourism field include (for both domestic and international visitors):

- expenditure on trips involving sporting activities (including expenditure on total trip and on the "sports" component);
- more detailed questions on motivation for travel, especially for domestic travellers;
- satisfaction information;
- length of stay data (including length of stay for total trip and for the "sports" component);
- demographic information (age, gender, income, occupation);
- type of accommodation used while travelling for sports related purposes; and
- type of transport used while travelling for sports related purposes.

Areas of research which may be useful to the industry include:

- appraisal of potential and proposed sport events;
- estimation of market for new or proposed sport tours;
- identification of infrastructure needed for sports tourism;
- specification of new tourism uses for existing sports infrastructure;
- recommendations for modifications to existing sports infrastructure to enhance tourism value; and
- profiling of sports tourism segments (e.g. training camps, tours of facilities).

Other possible areas of research could be:

- measuring the economic impact of sport events at a regional, State/Territory and national level;
- measuring the economic impact of sporting infrastructure;
- measuring the social impact of sports tourism; and
- assessment of the environmental impacts of sport infrastructure and sports tourists.

Work by government bodies such as the Bureau of Tourism Research and the Australian Bureau of Statistics can often provide useful broader contexts for specific research and in the case of BTR often more targeted baseline data. Specific research needs can also be met through academic and industry collaboration. For example, the Cooperative Research Centre for Sustainable Tourism has an events sub-programme which potentially can address some of the research and data needs, especially if its activities are focused towards sports events and activities at the non-micro level. The CRC has also recently established a sports tourism "node", located at the University of Canberra, to provide a focus for its research into the sports tourism market.

There is considerable scope for cooperation between industry and research bodies in improving the information available to the sports tourism sector. There is also scope for industry to address its own information needs in terms of local environments and of its specific marketing and development requirements.

EVALUATION OF EVENTS

Ongoing public sector reform and rationalisation have placed public tourism authorities and sporting organisations under increasing pressure to operate cost effectively. Government agencies have to be more accountable for policies, programmes and funding decisions and this includes funding for sporting events.

Governments lend their support to events on the basis of decisions made regarding benefits and costs ranging from financial to social and cultural. Such events may have the capacity to create income and employment in the short term and generate increased visitation and related investment in the longer term.

Determining the value of sporting events has been a perennially difficult issue for governments to resolve. There are no standard criteria for evaluating the economic significance of staging events. There also appears to be an absence of rigorous and comprehensive criteria for evaluating publicly funded tourism events, with great disparity between States, regions and research companies in their approach, both to the assessment of economic impact and to less tangible cultural and social impacts.

These differing approaches have made it difficult for governments not only to justify expenditure on events, but also to compare the economic success of various events. It is imperative for the credibility of the industry that sound methodologies are used to measure the return on the investment, and that these methodologies are widely accepted.

Development of a commonly accepted framework for evaluation would allow event organisers to compare and predict outcomes for their events with similar sized events. The ability to establish these areas of comparability (as well as differences) is important in gaining an overall view of sports tourism events in Australia and making assessments about the size and characteristics of this industry. This would also facilitate national and international comparisons.

Given the limited budgets of organisations expected to undertake evaluations of events and the often complex methodology, a framework for evaluation is essential for smaller/regional organisations. Several of the State events bodies have developed basic evaluation models which are appropriate but more importantly are financially accessible to the smaller sporting and tourism organisations. It may be appropriate to develop a national standard model for events of this size and nature, possibly based on one of the existing models.

Mega-events such as the 2000 Sydney Olympics Games stand alone in terms of developing methodology to assess their impact—the impact is felt at regional, state and national levels. Much preparatory work has already been completed by researchers in this area leading up to the Games and this will continue post Games. Notable in this regard is the Federal Government publication *The Olympic Effect* which assesses the likely tourism impact of the Games. A particular challenge will be to ensure that some of the innovative modelling approaches and methodologies developed for, and implemented during, the Games, can filter down to evaluation for smaller events.

IMPLEMENTATION

The proposals contained in this strategy will require the concerted efforts of a range of organisations if they are to be successfully implemented and if the sports tourism sector is to achieve its full potential. Those organisations include governments at all levels (Commonwealth, State/Territory and local), the tourism industry, the sports sector including national and state/territory sporting organisations and researchers.

A key theme of the strategy is the need for better coordination between what is a very diverse range of stakeholders involved in the sports tourism sector. Lack of communication and coordination, especially between sporting groups and the tourism sector, has been identified as a major impediment to maximising the tourism potential of sporting activities and events.

At the state/territory level, events corporations take on much of the responsibility for building these links. At the local level, there is arguably a greater need for development of networks or "clusters" focusing on sports tourism development. At the national level, there may also be a role for an overarching coordination mechanism of this nature.

Such a national-level group, which could be similar to the Canadian Sports Tourism Coalition, could be comprised of representatives of key stakeholders across industry and government, and could play a significant role in:

- raising the level of awareness about the sports tourism sector within both industry and government;
- identifying and pursuing specific research needs and priorities;
- identifying and overseeing the role of any facilitation unit which might be established following the release of this strategy; and
- overseeing and reporting on progress in implementing the strategy.

DEVELOPMENT PROCESS STRATEGY

The development of a National Sports Tourism Strategy has its genesis in the *National Action Plan for Tourism*. The Plan, released in 1998, provides a policy framework for the future development of the tourism industry and identifies the development of a range of niche tourism products as one of the avenues which will promote strong future growth and diversification of the Australian tourism industry. Sports tourism is identified as once of the sectors showing enormous potential for further development.

Against this background, the Minister for Sport and Tourism announced in November 1999 that the Commonwealth would develop a National Sports Tourism Strategy to examine impediments and opportunities impacting on the development of the sector and to see what role the Commonwealth might play to facilitate its growth.

Given the historical role of the States and Territories in attracting, developing, promoting and hosting major events, including sporting events, consultations were undertaken at an early stage with State and Territory government agencies and a range of other key stakeholders. These included Sport Industry Australia, the Australian Tourist Commission, the Australian Sports Commission, industry associations and academic researchers prominent in sports tourism and/or events research, including the Co-operative Research Centre for Sustainable Tourism.

At the same time, desk research was being undertaken and an inclusion on Sports Tourism was developed for the Commonwealth's Discussion paper, *End Goal 2006—Moving the Sport and Recreation Industry to a Higher Growth Path*. The discussion paper, released in December 1999, was an initial step in the development of a Strategic National Plan for the Sport and Recreation Industry, in fulfilment of an election commitment made by the Government during the 1998 election campaign.

On the basis of the initial consultations and feedback from the *End Goal* Paper, a short discussion paper was developed, drawing together themes and issues associated with sports tourism development. This paper was utilised in a series of focus group discussions convened around Australia in May and June 2000. The group discussions were held in every capital city, as well as two key regional centres, Cairns and Tamworth.

Typically, the focus group discussions brought together industry and government sport, tourism and events representatives. They included representatives of major sporting organisations from each centre or region, managers of major sporting facilities, tour operators with an interest in sporting events or activities, economic development agencies, regional tourism bodies and event organisers.

A number of common themes and issues emerged in many or most groups, but specific issues were also identified impacting on particular regions or States/Territories.

This draft, *"Towards a National Sports Tourism Strategy"* has been prepared on the basis of these consultations and accompanying research. There will be further opportunity for interested parties to comment, following its release in October 2000. Feedback received at that stage will be taken into account in the finalisation of the Strategy.

SUMMARY OF FOCUS GROUP OUTCOMES

The focus groups were convened with two primary objectives. Firstly to identify issues of importance to sports tourism stakeholders; and secondly to elicit comment on the discussion paper prepared based on the initial consolations, feedback and research. A number of issues were identified, which were then allocated priority rankings by the groups participants. The outcomes of the ten focus groups have been collated and summarised.

Nine common issues have been identified through this process, and the following is a summary of these in priority order and the suggested strategies for addressing each of these.

Issue	*Suggested Strategies*
1. Strategic Approach	
Lack of strategic approach to sports tourism development.	1. Promote network of sport and tourism organisations to improve communication and coordination. 2. Develop industry profile – establish peak body. 3. Clarify roles of stakeholders. 4. Educate national sporting organisations and tourism organisations on commercial opportunities sports tourism provides. 5. Promote development of business and event management skills in sporting organisations. 6. Encourage coordination of event calendars. 7. Encourage development of events-based tourism strategies.
2. Coordination and Communication	
Need for better communication at national, State and regional level.	1. Establish national coordination/communication/facilitation unit to assist the development of sports tourism.

(*Contd.*)

Issue	*Suggested Strategies*
	2. Improve information dissemination through website with links to existing relevant databases. 3. Facilitate access to research findings and resources. 4. Improve lines of communication between stakeholders. 5. Maintain project facilitation mechanisms established for Olympics for future major events. 6. Encourage cross-agency linkages to give access to tourism product marketing resources and material.
3. Regional Development	
Promote the development of sports tourism in regional areas and address impediments to its growth.	1. Develop region specific databases for event managers of stakeholders, services, facilities, accommodation and infra-structure. 2. Encourage sharing of information and expertise – through development of "sports tourism clusters" in regional areas. 3. Target niche events appropriate to area and facilities. 4. Address access issues—transport, sponsorship, media. 5. Encourage coordination to avoid duplication of facilities. 6. Encourage integrated view of sport, tourism and business opportunities at regional level. 7. Encourage rotation of national events throughout all of Australia.
4. Research	
Need to develop sound research base.	1. Clearly define sports tourism. 2. Coordinated development of research agenda. 3. Conduct further research into economic and social impacts of events, include consideration of both direct and flow-on effects and disseminate findings to stakeholders.

(*Contd.*)

Issue	*Suggested Strategies*
	4. Conduct accurate market analysis for identification of existing and potential markets. 5. Encourage better understanding of the sports tourism market needs. 6. Undertake post event research—long-term tracking of benefits of events.
5. Facility development	
Need coordinated and sound economic approach to development and use of facilities.	1. Need to conduct thorough facilities audit, also develop "asset audit" of regional infrastructure to assist in effective planning. 2. Encourage capacity utilisation of existing facilities. 3. Examine cost effectiveness of developing different standards of facilities in regional areas, consider multi-use facilities.
6. Funding	
Address difficulties in accessing funding for conducting events.	1. Encourage State Governments to recognise difficulties faced by State and regional areas in accessing funding and sponsorship for events. 2. Identify funding sources—communicate to organisations what funding is available and how to access it. 3. Ensure funding is equitable as possible across States and Territories. 4. Assist regional areas to access financial and in-kind sponsorships, possibly as a group. 5. Encourage partnerships between government and private sector—recognise role of private sector in supporting second tier events.
7. Education and Training	
Identify and address education and training needs in sports tourism sector.	1. Develop profile of the industry to identify opportunities for education, employment and experience. 2. Promote implementation of event management training courses. 3. Develop appropriate sports tourism training modules.

(*Contd.*)

Issue	*Suggested Strategies*
	4. Improve business skills through effective training tailored to sector, including volunteers. 5. Encourage development and distribution of manuals and educational resources.
8. Standardised Economic Modelling	
Need standardised approach to evaluation of events.	1. Develop standardised approach to economic, cultural, social and environmental modelling. 2. Develop standardised evaluation model which is affordable and appropriate for regional areas. 3. Develop methods to deliver meaningful information to local businesses on impact of sports tourism. 4. Develop best practice guidelines for evaluation of major events.
9. Participation	
Need to recognise need to provide ongoing support for mass participation in sport.	1. Recognise that participation underpins sports tourism. 2. Address needs of all sectors of the population 3. Encourage and support volunteers.

DISCUSSION OF DEFINITIONS

The strong linkages between sport and tourism are well recognised, and the literature contains many studies devoted to the topic, however, as discussed earlier, to date there has been no consensus on a definition of sports tourism, and a wide range of definitions have been adopted by different parties.

Definitions used may be influenced by the availability of data, the intent of research being undertaken, current sport and tourism definitions in the country or region concerned, etc.

There is broad agreement about the tourism side of the definition with most countries generally accepting definitions similar to those observed in Australia for international and domestic tourists. (Although there could be some disagreement over whether day trips should be included in a definition of domestic sports tourism—see for example, the article *Sports Tourism: An Australian Perspective* in BTR Tourism Research Report 3rd issue.)

However, there are wide-ranging views on what constitutes sport. Should recreational and adventure activities be included, is sport only sport when it is "organised", are non-competitive events such as fun runs still considered sporting activities? Some other examples of sports tourism definitions are set out below:

Sport Tourist: A temporary visitor staying at least twenty-four hours in the site visited and the purpose of whose journey is to attend sport related events. Specific activity categories are sports events; sports attractions; sports tours; sports resorts; and sports cruises. (Douvis *et al*, p. 2)

Sport: The whole range of competitive and non-competitive active pursuits that involve skill, strategy, and/or chance in which human beings engage, at their own level, simply for enjoyment and training or to raise their performance to levels of publicly acclaimed excellence.

Tourism: The temporary movement of people beyond their own home and work locality involving experience unlike those of everyday life. The experiences might take place as part of a holiday or as an ancillary to business travel.

Sport Tourism: All forms of active and passive involvement in sporting activity, participated in casually or in an organised way for non-commercial or business/commercial reasons that necessitate travel away from home and work locality. (Standeven & DeKnop, p. 12)

Sports tourism is a combination of sports activities and travel. From a sport marketing and sport management perspective, it consists of two broad categories of products:

- sports participation travel (travel for the purpose of participating in a sports, recreation, leisure or fitness activity); and
- sports spectatorial travel (travel for the purpose of spectating sports, recreation, leisure or fitness activities or events). (Pitts 1997, p. 31)

INTERNATIONAL CASE STUDIES

Britain

In 1992 the creation of the Department of National Heritage (DNH) pulled together under one roof the leisure sectors of sport, tourism, and the arts. For the first time there appeared to be a formal connection between sport and tourism which might lead to some development of the sports tourism sector. Unfortunately this turned out not to be the case, and for all practical purposes, no significant relationship between sport and tourism was established at either the policy or operational level.

In fact, rather than further integrate sport and tourism, the subsequent policies of the DNH tended to reverse previous policies that allowed greater integration e.g. reduction of English Tourist Board core funding and a narrower focus for the Sports Council. (Bull and Weed 1997(1); Standeven and DeKnop)

However, the historical difficulties of linking sport and tourism in Britain may be a thing of the past. The Department of Culture, Media and Sport (formerly DNH) announced in February 1999 the Government's intention to develop innovative niche markets such as sports tourism. The announcement forms part of a 15 point plan for tourism to unlock the full potential of Britain's unique cultural and natural heritage. UK Sport has also created an economic impact "guidance document" to assist with the undertaking of impact studies to determine the value of sports events. (Dept. of Culture, Media and Sport; English Tourism Council)

Furthermore, the British Tourist Authority has recently developed a sports tourism marketing strategy which is backed up by three staff in England and a recently appointed staff member in their Sydney office. This innovative move to place a dedicated sports tourism officer in a key source market may place the UK at the forefront of international sport tourism development. While it is very early in the process, the appointment of a dedicated officer in this role may open up a range of opportunities for sports tourism in the UK.

There may be lessons for Australia and in particular, our marketing body, the Australian Tourist Commission, should the UK's approach prove to be successful.

Canada

In 1998, 37 per cent of Canada's 73.7 million domestic trips were for sports tourism purposes. In Canada, sport tourists are defined as individuals who travelled and in doing so participated in or attended a sport event during the reference period. Sport tourists account for between 2.5 and 5 million individuals from June to September, July and August being the most popular months for sport tourist activities (15% and 18%). (Statistics Canada—1998 Canadian Travel Survey) (Note that this does not mean that 37% of tourism activity was sports tourism – rather than 37% of travellers travelled at least once for sports purposes).

Since 1996 the Canadian Tourism Commission (CTC) has been involved in a programme designed to promote community and tourism industry interest in development of sports tourism as a viable contributor to the economic well-being of local communities. The Canadian Sports Tourism Initiative is a programme designed to increase the quality and quantity of sports events hosted in Canada and has a number of objectives:

- to create a viable sports tourism industry in Canada;
- to organise Canadian communities to pursue sports tourism by providing them with assistance in organising the appropriate local resources and infrastructures to be effective;
- to assist communities in developing sports tourism commissions, appropriately organised to recruit sports events;
- to create linkages with the Canadian national, provincial and local sports system and event hosts to assist in the development of the sports tourism industry;
- to create new revenue streams and resources for local event organisers, sports friendly businesses and sport in general;
- to provide effective communication channels to facilitate business to business relationship marketing opportunities between event rights holders and potential host cities; and
- to create an industry-led, Canadian Sports Tourism Coalition to provide a forum for education, market intelligence and sports tourism marketing for communities and sports involved in the sports tourism business.

Based on positive support demonstrated by communities across Canada, in 1997, a partnership between the CTC, client communities and sport/tourism industry was borne. Soar International, a Vancouver based sports information and event management company was contracted to manage the process.

Communities that have decided to be part of the Sports Tourism Initiative's community planning programme participated in a comprehensive planning process. To start the process, a Soar International facilitator presents a half day session to a broad constituency of local sports, tourism and community leaders, covering such topics as what is sports tourism, who are sports tourists, how are sports events organised, where are the opportunities to work together and how a sports tourism commission can be developed. Secondly, using a local project coordinator and a planning tool kit adapted to fit the local community process, data on which to base a sports tourism marketing strategy is gathered.

With this data, Soar International facilitates a workshop which provides sufficient information to prepare a strategic business plan. Using a locally facilitated process, this plan is presented to all the key groups in the community with an interest to ensuring its successful implementation. Soar International then assists the community to refine and implement the strategic plan on an ongoing basis.

By the end of 1999 the regions of Kelowna, Cranbrook, Edmonton, London, Kingston, Hamilton, Moncton, St. John's, Gatineau and Western Newfoundland/Cornerbrook had all undertaken the sports tourism planning process. (Canadian Tourism Commission; Swart 1998)

South Africa

In May 1996 the South African Department of Environmental Affairs and Tourism released a white paper on the development and promotion of tourism in South Africa. The sports tourism sector was specifically identified within this policy document. The intent was both to encourage the development of sports tourism and to encourage the provision of facilities, training, marketing and promotion to give emphasis to the development of this segment of the industry.

Following the release of the white paper, and in order to capitalise on South Africa's sporting successes and re-entry into the world tourism scene, South Africa Sports Tourism (SAST) was launched jointly by the Ministry of Environmental Affairs and Tourism, and the Ministry of Sport and Recreation in October 1997. (Swart, 1998; Standeven and DeKnop, 1999). The success of SAST in developing the international market for sport tourism in South Africa is yet to be established.

Appendix I
Sports Related Terms, Acronyms and Definitions

Word	*Sport*	*Definition*
Abadaca	BMX	Where a rider goes straight up the ramp, touches the back tire to the coping, then goes down the ramp fakie.
Abec	SKT	The tolerance rating system for bearing that designates the level for stress resistance of the bushing. The lower the rating the looser the bearing, the higher the rating the tighter the bearing.
Abec 1	SKT	The standard rating for Chinese and Russian bearings.
Abec 3	SKT	The standard rating for German and Swiss bearing, with Swiss considered the best. This is due to the fact that a skater has the options to rebuild these bearings, because they have a C-ring that allows the bearing to be taken apart.
Abs (acrylonitrile butadien)	SNB	A hard tough lightweight plastic that remains flexible and maintains a shape memory when heated. Used in contraction for a tip-tail sidewalls and any area which needs reinforcement.
Acid	INL	Street term, when a skater has his front foot outside of grindplate, with his back foot on soul.
Acid drop	SKT	To ride straight off of something and freefall to the ground.
Aerials	ETC	With specialised big air ramps and landings, original moves were upright moves; spread eagles and back scratches and helicopters. Later complicated inverted maneuvers began to dominate, quadruple flips and multiple front and back flips with twists.
Air to fakie	SNB	Any trick where the wall is approached riding forwards, no rotation is made, and the snowboarder lands riding backwards.

Word	*Sport*	*Definition*
Alley-oop (2)	SNB	A term used to describe any maneuver in the halfpipe where one rotates 180 or more degrees in the uphill direction; that is, rotating backside on the frontside wall or rotating frontside on the backside wall.
Alley-oop	SKT	When a trick is performed in the opposite direction of which the skater is moving.
Alley-oop soul	INL	A backwards soul grind in which the skater turns his body in the air hopping on the rail.
Andrecht	SNB	A rear handed backside handplant with a front-handed grab.
Axle	SKT	The metal rod running through the hanger, with the ends being where the wheels are screwed on.
Back Flip	BMX	Done in the air with the rider still on the bike. In vert, and occasionally in street, the rider will land in fakie position on the same ramp. In dirt and street, the rider will do a back flip from jump to jump.
Backside	MULTI	When a turn or trick is executed in a direction that the back of the body is facing the arc of the trick.
Backside air	SNB	Any air performed on the backside wall of halfpipe.
Backside rodeo	SNB	Coming off a jump and turning your back down the hill, flipping 540 and landing fakie or rotating a total of 720 and landing regular.
Backside rotation	MULTI	Rotating clockwise for a regular footer and rotating counter-clockwise for a goofy-footer. When riding switchstance the exact reverse applies and a regular footer will rotate counter-clockwise and a goofy footer will rotate clockwise.
Backside wall	SNB	When standing at the top of the halfpipe and looking down towards the bottom, the backside wall is the left wall for regular footers and the right wall for goofy footers. If you ride straight down the centre of the halfpipe, your backside wall is behind.
Backslide	INL	A soul grind variation in which the skater has front foot grabbed, back foot on outside plate.
Bar spin	BMX	While a rider is in the air, he spins the handlebars a full rotation or more, grabbing them again before landing. Bar spins are thrown in combination with other tricks, such as back flips, to make them more difficult and earn more points with the judges.

Word	Sport	Definition
Base plate	SKT	The flat part of the truck that fixes to the board via four drilled holes for truck bolts.
Bearings	SKT	Bearings have an inner and outer part, which the balls ride on, allowing the wheel to turn.
Bevel	SNB	The degree of angle to which the edges of a board can be tuned. Snowboards used for racing and carving should have a greater bevel than say a board used in the halfpipe.
Bi-axial fiberglass	SNB	A reinforcing cloth used in the production of snowboards. It provides excellent torsional stiffness compared to regular fiberglass weaves.
Bio grab	INL	To grab the outside of the skate with the hand of the same side.
Blindside	MULTI	A term given to any rotation where the rider has oriented him/herself "blind" to his/her takeoff or landing and must stretch to look over their shoulder. Such a technique usually increases the difficulty.
Blunt	SKT	When a trick is performed, the contact spot of the board with the obstacle is the area of the tail behind the back trucks. The wheels are also on top of the object.
Board	SKT	Also called a deck. The platform that the hardware is mounted to, usually maple laminate.
Board length	SNB	The measurement from the tip to the tail.
Boardslide/railslide	SKT	To slide on an obstacle or lip with the contact point being the underside of the board.
Boned out	MULTI	A term used to explain the emphasis of style in a trick. In other words, if someone "boned out a indy" they would grab hard and create an emphasis of the maneuver such that his/her legs may appear extended or stretched to a maximum degree.
Bonk	SNB	The act of hitting an object with the snowboard.
Box jump	BMX	Jump used in street competitions consisting of two ramps on either side of an approximately 10-foot deck.
Brainless	INL	A backflip with 540 degree turn on a ramp.
Budget variation	INL	A variation where only the position of one skate changes during the trick.

Word	*Sport*	*Definition*
Bushing	SKT	Urethane spacers found in between the base plate and truck that cushions the sleeve of the truck when it is turning.
Butter slide	MULTI	Rider approaches wake or snow, then hops the board and lands on the edge of the wake or on the snow with the board sideways (perpendicular to the direction of travel) and slides the board on top.
Cab	INL	Short for Caballerial.
Camber	SNB	The arched shape that is designed into the boards construction, creating a high point that lies on or near the midpoint of the boards running surface. To create spring or rebound in the flex of a board.
Camber	ETC	The arch built into a ski so that the ski can distribute the skier's weight over the entire length of the ski.
Camel	INL	A toe-tap upon re-entry onto a ramp or obstacle.
Can-Can	BMX	When a rider takes one foot off a pedal and stretches their leg over the frame between his legs so both legs are on the same side of the bike, then returns the foot to the pedal before landing.
Canting	ETC	Wedges placed underneath ski boots to properly position skier's knees over the ski at the proper angle.
Canyon	BMX	The sunken area between ramps in dirt and the empty space between two ramps in street. The big danger in dirt and street is when a rider may not go far enough or may have trouble with a maneuver and doesn't make the second ramp, landing in the canyon.
Cap construction	SNB	A form of integrated structural design that used the outermost material or skin to bear the load of strength of an object. Much like the shell of crab. To reduce weight and enhance torsional rigidity and edge responsiveness and eliminate the need for sepa.
Carbon fiber material	SNB	A fiber woven material produced from the mineral carbon. To stiffen and strengthen a board with a minimum of added weight.
Carve	SKT	To make a long, curving arc while skating.
Carved turn	ETC	A turned arc by a skier with little or no slipping or skidding.
Cased	MULTI	To land short or miss a landing.

Word	*Sport*	*Definition*
Chatter	SKI	The tendency of skis not to grip on snow or ice when pout on edge, caused either by the inability of the ski to dampen vibration or by the skier not weighting the ski properly and sufficiently.
Chicken salad air	SNB	The rear hand reaches behind the front leg, grabs the heel side between the bindings while the front leg is boned. Also, the wrist is rotated inwards to complete the grab.
Cliffhanger	MTX	Rider hooks his feet under the bars and raises his hands in the air.
Closed mold	SNB	A mold that holds all the pre-shaped components of a board in a sealed chamber which eliminates additional shaping after pressing. To mass producer snowboards more rapidly by containing the board shape and minimising finishing and shaping steps.
Concave	SKT	The contour given to decks. The concave will dip down from the left to right and should be asymmetrical. Provides strength to the board and aids the skater when performing tricks.
Construct flex	SNB	Q uniform flex pattern from nose to centre to tail. To balance the overall flex patter of the board from the tip and tail to the centre.
Continuous edge	SKT	Edges designed without small "cracks" in the outmost contact area. To add strength and at times, stiffness to the edges.
Coping	MULTI	A rounded lip at the top of a ramp or obstacle, usually made of metal, cement, or PVC pipe.
Corkscrew 540	SNB	Sideways backside 540, also called a barrel roll.
Cowboy	INL	Skater has front foot on outside plate, back foot on outside plate. Trick is also known as the Cab Driver and it resembles a mix of a Torque and a Backside. The Cowboy comes from the bowed shape of the legs when doing this trick.
Crail air	SNB	The rear hand grabs the toe edge in the front of the front foot while the rear leg is behind.
Crippler	SNB	An inverted aerial where the rider performs a 180 degree flip. The athlete approaches the wall riding forward, becomes airborne, rotates 90 degrees, flips over in the air, rotates another 90 degrees, and lands riding forward.
Crooked cop air	SNB	Tuck kneed backside grab.

Word	*Sport*	*Definition*
Crooked grind	SKT	Nosegrind with nose sliding at the same time.
Crossed	INL	A grab with the opposite hand of the skate.
Crossed up	INL	When the skater's legs are crossed while performing a trick.
Curb grind	INL	A grind performed on a sidewalk curb.
Dampening	ETC	The quality in a ski which absorbs vibration.
Dampening	SKT	To control and minimise the amount of resonance of vibration created by the energy separated by board flex and surface of the snow. Any material like rubber sheer, built into the edges, or core that keep the board quiet and more responsive.
Directional board and flex	SNB	A board designed to provide excellent characteristics when being ridden forward as opposed to backwards. Bindings are usually mounted farther back and the flex and sidecuts are altered accordingly, with the tail being a little stiffer.
Directional twin	SNB	A board that features designs of directions and twin tips to allow for a wider range of use, for example freeriding and halfpipe.
Disaster	SNB	A lip trick where one gets "hung up" on the coping, most often with the board perpendicular to the coping.
Double Can Can	MTX	Rider moves one leg to other side of bike, then brings other leg up to meet it, elevating his butt off the seat.
Double grab	SNB	Basically, doing two separate tricks while in the air. One goes off of a jump, grabs the board one way, then grabs it in another way, then lands.
Downhill ski	SKI	The lower ski or the one that will become the lower ski in any ski turn.
Drop in	MULTI	To enter the ramp or obstacle from the top.
Duck foot	SNB	A term used to describe stance angles with toes pointing outward.
Durometer	MULTI	A measurement of the resiliency, or hardness, of a urethane wheel.
Edges	MULTI	The strips of metal usually made hard steel, on the outer edges of the running surface of skis or snowboards.
Effective edge	SNB	The length of metal edge on the snowboards which touches the ground; it is the effective part which is used to make a turn. It does not include the edge of the tip and tail.

Word	Sport	Definition
Effective edge	SKT	The difference between the two contact areas beneath the tip and tail when the camber is depressed. A measurement used to define the actual length of the surface area that comes into contact on a perfectly flat surface.
Eggflip	SNB	An eggplant where the rider chooses to flip over in order to re-enter the pipe instead or rotating 180 degrees. This trick is performed forward to fakie or switchstance (fakie to forward).
Eggplant	SNB	A one-handed 180 degree invert in which the front hand is planted on the lip of the wall and the rotation is backside.
Electra base	SNB	An extremely hard sintered base material contracted with graphite to reduce friction. Generally black in colour. Used on high-speed boards on colder snow/ice conditions.
Elgeurial (bfm)	SNB	An invert where the halfpipe wall is approached fakie, the rear hand is planted, a 360 degree backside rotation is made, and the rider lands going forward. Named after Eddie Elguera.
Elliptical flex	SNB	A flex pattern which is softer towards tip and tail. To create a smoother flex pattern than the mid-section of the board.
Enduro	MTX	Long distance, cross-country motocross race. Example: Baja 1,000.
Eurocarve	SNB	A term used to describe a certain mode of riding in which the rider makes large and hard cutting turns; usually getting way up on the edge and leaning the body parallel to the ground.
Extruded base	SNB	Particles of base materials are compressed and pushed out through a flat form to create a sheet of base material. This quality of base material is used for average temperature snow conditions and for easy base repair.
Fall line	MULTI	The path of least resistance down and given slope.
Farfernugan	INL	See Torque.
Farside	INL	When a trick is performed on the outside or away edge of a ramp or obstacle.
Fast slide	INL	A grind on one skate on which the skater rides the front foot on the inside of the grindplate and the back foot is grabbed.
Feeble grind	SKT	The back truck is grinding, front of body facing edge with toe-side rail grinding edge also.

Word	*Sport*	*Definition*
Fiberglass	SKT	A fabric of woven glass fibers which is available in different weave patterns and weights for a variety of applications. To strengthen board construction and control the flex attributes in a board.
Fifty fifty	SKT	A double axle grind (on both trucks).
Flat bottom	MULTI	The area in a halfpipe between the two opposing transitional walls.
Flat spin	INL	The trick that turned heads in 1997/98. A skater gets air, turns the axis of his body nearly horizontal to the ground or ramp, spins, rights himself and lands.
Flatland	SNB	Term used to describe tricks performed on the flat slope with obstacles (e.g. nose slide, blunt slide, tail wheelie).
Flex pattern	SNB	The relative softness and stiffness of a board along its length. To allow for the proper distribution of energy to be transferred to the board in the proper location also its running length for more effective edge control.
Floating edge	SKT	When a board is constructed with a rubber strip separating the edge material and core material. To act as a shock absorber to smooth out the ride and a board to enhance its responsiveness.
Foam	SKT	Polyurethane (PU) A synthetic resin material which is comprised of a base and a catalyst. When combined, expand to fill the cavity of a closed mold and bond. Used as a core and sometimes a bonding material in the construction of a snowboard.
Frame	INL	The component that attaches to the base of the skate and holds the wheels.
Free skiing	ETC	Skiing for fun, not competing or training.
Freeriding	SNB	Snowboarding on all types of terrain for fun, no contest, no halfpipe, no gates, no rules.
Freestyle	SNB	The kind of snowboarding which is mostly associated with riding the halfpipe, but may also be used to describe any type of snowboarding which includes tricks and maneuvers.
Freestyle	MTX	Expression contest in which riders are given a time allotment to hit a variety of jumps, performing aerial maneuvers for a judged score. Have also been called Freeride Competitions.
Fresh fish air	SNB	The backside version of the Stale Fish.

Word	Sport	Definition
Front foot	SNB	The foot mounted closet to the nose. A regular footers left foot and a goofy footers right foot.
Front hand	SNB	The hand closet to the nose of the snowboards. The left hand for regular footers and the right hand for goofy footers.
Frontside	MULTI	When a turn or trick is executed in a direction that the front of the body is facing toward the outside of the arc of the trick.
Frontside air	SNB	The trick is best described for its grab. The frontside grab is with the rear hand between the bindings on the toe edge; in this particular maneuver the front leg is boned. It can also be any air performed on the frontside wall of the halfpipe.
Frontside turn	SNB	A turn where the toe edge faces to the outside of the turn while the snowboard is riding on the heel edge. A left for a regular footer and right turn for a goofy footer.
Fun box	BMX	A four-sided box jump (ramp on every side) that is included in street courses.
Gap	MULTI	The space between ramps or obstacles. Separates obstacles and is often jumped over from one obstacle to the other, making for more creative airs. (also called the Canyon)
Gay twist	SKT	While riding fakie, usually at the lip of a ramp, to complete a 360 in the air while grabbing and head back down the ramp forwards.
Gay twist	SNB	Halfpipe fakie to regular 360 spin with a grab.
Giant slalom	MULTI	A form of Alpine racing in which the racer passes through a series of gates, similar to slalom but faster and more open.
Grasser	SNB	A variation on the method air performed with the front hand grabbing the heel edge and twisting the board so it faces down hill. The back leg is also boned out. Named after a group of riders from Grass Valley in CA.
Grind plate	INL	A piece of metal or plastic that attaches to the frame and creates a better grind spot than the frame alone.
Grip tape	SKT	Adhesive backed sandpaper material fixed to the top of the board to provide traction.

Word	*Sport*	*Definition*
Haakon flip	SNB	A halfpipe trick named after freestyle legend Teje Haakonsen of Norway. Haakon flip is like a switch rodeo performed in a halfpipe.
Half cab	SKT	A 180 degree Caballerial.
Half cab	SNB	It is the freeriding version of the Caballerial in which one rotates 180 degrees from fakie to forward off of a straight jump.
Half pipe	MULTI	A type of ramp that is shaped like a "U" and used for vert skating.
Half pipe	MULTI	A snow structure that consists of opposing radial transition walls of the same height and size. Used to catch air and perform tricks by travelling back and forth from wall to wall while moving do.
Hand plant	MULTI	A type of trick where one hand grabs the skate while doing a one handed handstand on a ramp, or obstacle.
Handplant (backside)	MULTI	A 180 degree handplant in which both hands or the rear hand may be planted on the lip of the wall and the rotation is backside.
Handplant (frontside)	MULTI	A 180 degree handplant in which the front hand is planted on the lip of the wall and the rotation is frontside.
Handplant (layback)	SNB	A 180 degree handplant in which the rear hand is planted on the lip of the wall and the rotation is frontside.
Hang up	SKT	When either the back or front truck catches on an obstacle, usually causing a fall.
Hang up	INL	To catch one or both skates on the lip of a ramp or obstacle during re-entry.
Hanger	SKT	Part of the truck that gets the most abuse. When grinding it is done along the top of the hanger. Contained inside the hanger is the axle.
Heel clicker	MTX	Rider brings both feet off the pegs and touches them together over the handlebars.
Heel out	INL	A skater grinds with front foot on heel, back foot on outside plate toes turned out. Known as the "Tom Fry trick" and can only be done backside. Somewhat like a Royale but front foot is on the heel.
Heelflip	SKT	While performing on Ollie, the heel pushed down on the edge of the board causing it to flip over.

Word	Sport	Definition
Hip	MULTI	The spot where a ramp or obstacle comes to a point. Tricks are done while flying over or off of it.
Ho ho	MULTI	A general term given to any two handed handplant.
Horizontal lamination	SNB	Layers a component, most commonly wood, that are bonded together on top of each other to form a strong material from otherwise weak elements. Used as either the full deck material or the core in the construction of a board.
Hucker	SNB	One who throws himself/herself wildly through the air and does not land on his/her feet.
Iguana air	SNB	The rear hand grabs the toe edge near the tail.
Indy air	SNB	A true "Indy Air" is performed backside with the rear hand grabbing between the bindings on the toe edge while the rear leg is boned. The term "Indy" may also be used to simply describe the location of the grab.
Insert	SNB	A small cylinder, which is threaded on the inside, that is install reinforcement to attach bindings to. Used to reinforce the area of a snowboard where the screws for attaching the bindings go into the board.
Inside ski	SKI	The ski which is on the inside of the turn will become the inside ski in any turn.
Interlock system	SNB	The tip and tail sections, usually made of plastic, are mechanically locked to the core using a jigsaw puzzle type arrangement. Spreads out the stress at the junctions of these materials.
Invert	MULTI	Another name for a hand plant.
Inverted 180	MULTI	To get upside down while performing a 180.
Inverted 540	SNB	To get upside down while spinning a 540.
Inverted 720	SNB	An inverted aerial where the rider performs a 720 degree rotational flip. The rider approaches the wall riding forward, becomes airborne, rotates 720 degree in a backside direction while performing a front flip, and lands riding fakie.
Inverted aerial	SNB	A maneuver where the rider becomes airborne and upside down at any given moment.
Japan	MULTI	The front hand grabs the toe edge, the front knee is tucked and the board is pulled up and the back is arched.

Word	Sport	Definition
Jib	SNB	Riding which closely resembles street skating. "Jibbers" commonly slide rails, bonk trees and perform flatland tricks.
Jump ramp	SKT	A small ramp used to give the skater some air to perform a trick.
Kevlar	SNB	A man-made fibrous material that has a high strength to weight ratio. To strengthen a snowboard without adding weight and to enhance the performance of the flex action.
Kick turn	SKT	When pressure is applied to the tail of the board, lifting the front and turning it in another direction.
Kicker	MULTI	A name for a jump ramp. Kickers usually have the property of throwing you up into the air rather than giving you distance.
Kickflip	SKT	The same as a Heelflip except the toe pushes down to flip the board.
Kingpin	SKT	The bolt that holds the hanger and base plate together.
Knee pad	MULTI	A type of protective padding worn on the knees.
Knee slide	MULTI	A way of controlling a fall by sliding on plastic caps on the knee pads.
Late	MULTI	A term used to describe incorporating something into a trick just before its completion and landing.
Lazy boy	MTX	Rider hooks his feet underneath the bars and lies back on the seat with his hands in the air.
Leash	SNB	A retention device used to attach the snowboard to the front foot so that it doesn't run away-completely useless.
Lien air	MULTI	The front hand grabs the heel edge and the body leans out over the nose. Essentially a method on the frontside wall. Named after Neil Blender.
Lip	MULTI	The top edge portion of the halfpipe wall.
Lip trick	MULTI	Any trick performed on or near the lip of the wall of the halfpipe.
Lipslide	MULTI	To force the tail over the lip and slide on the surface before re-entry.
Look Back	BMX	Where the rider in the air turns the handlebars and his body backwards, looking to the back of his bike.

Word	*Sport*	*Definition*
Makio	INL	Skater riders with front foot soul, back foot grabbed. Created by a Japanese skater name Makio. The topside variation is called Fishbrain, created in 1995 by Tom Fry.
Manual	BMX	Where a rider does a wheelie across the top deck before returning to the ramp.
Manual	SKT	Another name for wheelie.
Mcegg	SNB	An invert where the rider plants the front hand on the wall, rotated 540 degrees in a backside direction and lands riding forward.
McMetz	MTX	Double, simultaneous Saran wraps. Both legs pass through the arms simultaneously and both arms release at the same time to allow the legs to pass back through to the foot pegs.
Mctwist	SKT	A 540 degree turn performed on a ramp. Named after Mike McGill.
Mctwist	SNB	An inverted aerial where the rider performs a 540 degree rotational flip. The rider approaches the halfpipe wall riding forward, becomes airborne, rotates 540 degrees in a backside direction while performing a front flip and lands riding forward.
Melonchollie	SNB	The front hand reaches behind the front leg and grabs the heel edge in-between the bindings while the front leg is boned.
Method	SNB	The front hand grabs the heel edge, both knees are bent, and the board is pulled up behind the rider. In the halfpipe, the rider's body can become almost parallel with the ground.
Michalchuk	SNB	Mike Michalchuk's signature halfpipe trick, self-described as my backside flip—sort of like an inverted backside 540 or a backflip backside 540". Essentially a backside rodeo.
Miller flip	SNB	An invert where the halfpipe wall is approached riding forward, the front hand is planted, a 360 degree frontside rotation is made, and the rider lands riding fakie.
Miller flip	INL	A backflip with 360 turn degree turn.
Mistrial	INL	A skater rides with the front foot soul, back foot on the outside plate with toes turning out. The topside variation is called an Overpuss for the exposure it gives to the skaters pelvic area, the reverse topside variation is called Misfit.

Word	Sport	Definition
Misty	SNB	Can also be used as an adjective to describe a spin that gets a bit sideways (somewhere between upright and inverted).
Misty flip	SNB	Partially inverted backside spin. Named by Ali Goulet.
Misty flip	INL	A move first popularised by Ryan Jacklone. The move involves a front somersault with a 540 spin.
Miszou	INL	A grind with the front skate in the soul position, and the back skate perpendicular to the rail or obstacle. A few years ago, the Miszou was the trick of choice for transferring from one rail to another, usually to frontside. Miszou is Japanese for water.
Moguls	ETC	Skiers are judged on how they ski a mogul run, including two mandatory air offs which skiers perform tricks. Pro mogul competitions have racers competing head to head in an elimination format.
Monocoque	SNB	A form of integrated structural design that used the outermost material or skin to bear the load of strength of an object. To reduce weight and enhance torsional rigidity and edge responsiveness and eliminate the need for separate sidewall material.
Mute	SNB	The front hand grabs the toe edge either between the toes, and front leg is boned out.
Mute	INL	A crossed-grab air.
Nac Nac	MTX	Rider brings one leg over the rear fender to the other side of the bike, as if he's dismounting in mid-air.
Natural	INL	The direction that the skater feels best performing a trick, right skate forward or left skate forward.
No Hander Lander	MTX	Landing a jump with no hands on the bars.
No-Footer/No-Hander	BMX	Any air pulled without feet/hands touching the bike.
Nollie	MULTI	Much like an Ollie only you spring off of your nose instead of your tail.
Nollie frontflip	SNB	Springing off of the nose while going off a jump and leaning forward, allows you to do a frontflip.
Nose bonk	SNB	To hit an object with the nose of the board.
Nose grab	SNB	The front hand grabs the nose of the board.

Word	Sport	Definition
Nose poke	SNB	Any maneuver where you bone your front leg and "poke" the nose of the board in a direction away from your body. Usually while grabbing.
Nose slide	MULTI	Sliding on the nose of board on the edge of an obstacle like a handrail, ledge, or ramp lip.
Nose wheelie	BMX	Where a rider rides the front wheel while the back wheel is in the air.
Nosegrind	SKT	Just the front truck is grinding.
Nothing	BMX	When a rider fully lets go of his bike with his hands and feet in the air so that no part of his body is touching the bike.
Nuclear air	SNB	The rear hand reaches across the front of the body and grabs the heel edge in front of the front foot.
Ole	ETC	A rider rotates with the handle over head.
Ollie	SNB	A method to obtain air by first lifting the front foot then lifting the rear foot as you spring off of the tail.
Ollie	SKT	A no handed air performed by tapping the tail of the board on the ground or ramp surface. Named after Alan Gelfend.
One-Footer/One-Hander	BMX	Any air pulled with one foot/hand off of the bike.
One-Handed Superman	MTX	Superman with one hand off the handlebars and grabbing the rear fender.
Open mold	SNB	A form that is used to assemble and hold the parts of a snowboard during the pressing process that allows the expansion and bleeding of the bonding.
Palmer	SNB	A kind of method where the grab is near the nose, the board is pulled across the front of the body, and the nose is pointed downward. Named after Shaun Palmer.
Parabolic	ETC	A super sidecut ski intended to make skiing easier for beginners.
Phillips 66	SNB	An invert where the rider approaches the halfpipe wall riding fakie, plants the rear hand on the lip of the wall while doing a "front flip" and lands on the transition riding forward.
Pick	BMX	Where a rider balances one part of his bike on their coping, stalling for a moment before returning to the ramp. Usually involves stalling on the front tire (Nose) or either front or back or both pegs.

Word	Sport	Definition
Ply	SNB	Short for plywood. The most commonly used material for the deck. Usually seven layer ply.
Poptart	SNB	Airing from fakie to forward in the halfpipe without rotation.
Pornstar	INL	Skater riders with the front foot soul, back foot on outside of grindplate with toes pointing in. This trick was purportedly named by Brooke Howard Smith and is probably the only trick that Brooke has not named after a Mortal Kombat character.
Pre-jump	ETC	A maneuver in which the skier jumps before reaching the crest of a bump so that his trajectory follows the contour of the bump, resulting in less air and more speed.
Pre-peg fiberglass	SNB	A stiff sheet of fiberglass previously treated with epoxy resin. Used as an alternative to fiberglass. Generally a matter of manufacturer's production progress.
Ptex	SNB	One of several names for the plastic base material used on boards.
Quadratic sidecut	SKT	To soften the transition from the entrance to the exit of a turn and provide a more forgiving feel.
Rail	SKT	The edge of the board. Also refers to plastic strips attached to the underside of the board.
Rail	SNB	There are two rails on a snowboard; each comprised of a sidewall and an edge.
Railslide	MULTI	Also called boardslide. To slide on an obstacle or lip with the contact point being the underside of the board.
Ramp boards	SKT	Large deck and firm wheels mounted on wide trucks to make the board as stable as possible.
Rear foot	SNB	The foot mounted closest to the rail.
Rear hand	SNB	The hand closet to the tail of the board.
Regular foot	MULTI	To ride with the left foot forward.
Retainer	SKT	Keep the ball bearings spaced correctly.
Revert	SNB	To switch from riding fakie to forward, or from forward to fakie, usually while the board is still touching the ground.
Rewind	SNB	A term used to describe any maneuver where a rotation is initiated, stopped and its momentum reversed.

Word	Sport	Definition
Rewind	INL	To complete the arc that a skater begins when coming off a grind or stall by spinning.
Rippey flip	SNB	Straight back flipping frontside 360, with a method grab (Jim Rippey).
Riser	SKT	Plastic piece under the base of the truck to raise it for better wheel clearance. Often used with larger wheels.
Roast beef	SNB	The rear hand reaches between the legs and grabs the heel edge between the bindings while the front leg is boned. Also, the wrist is rotated inward to complete the grab.
Rock and roll	MULTI	A trick where the underside of the board and wheels are tapped on the lip before a kickturn to reenter.
Rocket Air	INL	A trick where you grab both skates with both hands, while skates are straight in front of the skater.
Rocket Air	BMX	When a rider takes both feet off the pedals in the air and places them on the back pegs, then returns them to the pedals before landing. Can be landed in this position also.
Rodeo	SNB	Turning frontside 180 while completing an inverted 360 rotation for a total of 540. A rodeo 720 is when you would turn frontside 360 while completing an inverted 360 rotation for a total 720.
Rodeo flip	SNB	Partially inverted 360 with a back flip.
Roll-in	BMX	A portion at the top of a ramp that riders can use to roll into the ramp rather than dropping in over the vertical section of the ramp. Often used to gain more speed entering the ramp and as a gap to air over depending on where it lies on the ramp.
Rolling down the windows	SNB	A phrase used to describe when someone is caught off balance, and they rotate their arms wildly in the air to try and recover.
Royale	INL	Skater riders with the front foot on inside plate, back foot on the outside plate, toes pointed in. Brooke Howard Smith was the founder of the Royale. He 'royaled' the big rail on the first X Games.
Rubber dampening systems	SNB	Incorporating rubber into the construction of the board to dampen vibrations and provide certain performance characteristics.
Run	MULTI	A series of tricks in a sequence.
Sad plant	SNB	A term used to describe any handplant where the front leg is boned for style.

Word	Sport	Definition
Sandwich construction	SNB	Layers of materials, on top of each other, with additional components for sidewall strength and torisional flex patterning. Used to construct a board with different layers of materials on top of each other.
Saran Wrap	MTX	Rider passes one foot between his hands and back to the peg, removing one hand from the bars to let it pass through.
Sato flip	SNB	Halfpipe trick done by Rob Kingwill (Sato—Japanese for "sugar"). Kind of like a frontside McTwist. Rider drops in fast, riders up the transition as if doing frontside 540, pops in the air and grabs frontside, then throws head, shoulders, and hips downs.
Seabelt	SNB	The frontside reaches across the body and grabs the tail while the front leg is boned.
S-bend	ETC	A rider performs an air relay while rotating his body 360 degrees while inverted.
Session	MULTI	A period of skating.
Shifty	SNB	A grabless trick where the upper torso and lower body are twisted in opposite directions and then returned to normal.
Shove it	SKT	A trick performed by spinning the board beneath the feet.
Shovel	SKT	The front of the board that rises up off the snow. Design is usually a result of boards intended use, powder boards have lots of shovel, race boards have very little.
Shovel	ETC	Area near the tip of the ski.
Shovel	SNB	The lifted or upward curved sections of a snowboard at the tip and tail.
Side cut	SNB	The curve built into the sidewalls and edges of a board to enhance turning characteristics. To create a curve on the turning surface that is characteristic of the boards riding style.
Sidewall	SNB	The area between the topsheet and the base, and above the edges on a snowboard. Holds the core and other materials from shifting during the manufacturing process, and to protect them as a finished product.
Sidewall	ETC	Refers to the side of the ski.
Sintered base	SNB	A form of polymer plastic that is compress into a long shape, set on a roller and sliced into sheets of base material. A slightly harder more porous form of base material used on performance snowboards.

Word	*Sport*	*Definition*
Slalom	MULTI	A form of Alpine racing in which the racer must run a course designated by a series of gates set in various combinations as to test technique, speed, and agility. Failure to pass through the gate properly results in disqualification.
Slick	SKT	A board that has a layer of slippery plastic bonded to the bottom for extra slide/strength. They are usually heavier than plain wood boards. Most serious skaters prefer wood.
Slob air	SNB	The frontside air where the front hand grabs mute, the back leg is boned and the board is kept parallel with the ground.
Smith grind	SKT	A type of grind trick where the back truck is grinding, while the rail of the board is also grinding the lip of the ramp or obstacle. Frontside Smith Grind: the toe-side edge is involved; Backside Smith Grind: the heel-side edge is involved.
Soul grind	INL	A grind where the leading skate is parallel with the rail or obstacle and the rear skate is perpendicular to it.
Spaghetti air	SNB	The front hand reaches between the legs and behind the front legs to grab the toe edge in front of the front foot while the back leg is boned.
Spine ramp	MULTI	Two half pipes placed back to back creating a double U shape.
Stain	SKT	Normal deck without a slick bottom.
Stale	INL	Any trick in which the skater reaches behind his body to grab the wheels or frame.
Stale egg	SNB	An eggplant with a stalefish grab.
Stalefish air	SKT	The frontside trick where the rear hand grabs the heel edge behind the rear between the bindings while the front leg is boned.
Stalemasky air	SNB	When a maneuver is performed such that the point of emphasis in the maneuver is held or "stalled" for an extended period of time.
Stall	INL	To land on a lip and stop for a second and then re-enter.
Stall	BMX	When a rider pauses briefly on the coping before dropping back into the ramp.
Stance	SNB	The position of one's feet on the ground.
Stiffy air	SNB	Any maneuver in which both legs are boned and a grab is incorporated.

Word	*Sport*	*Definition*
Stinky	SNB	Riding with the legs spread open.
Street	BMX	An event consisting of different types and styles of ramps positioined so that they can be approached in many different ways. Competitors plan out their runs through these ramps according to individual style.
Street boards	SKT	Shorter and narrower than ramp boards. Usually has a shorter wheelbase than a ramp board.
Sub box	BMX	Street course jump consisting of two ramps, one on either side of a platform that is topped by an approximately 3-foot high box, with a 2-foot deck on top. The height and small surface of the box make it easy for a rider to clip a back wheel.
Sublimated top sheet	SNB	Topsheets that have had the graphics added through the sublimation process. Provides very durable graphics because they are cooked right into the plastic.
Superg	ETC	A faster more open version of the giant slalom, kind of a cross between GS and downhill.
Superman	BMX	Where a rider takes both feet off the pedals in the air and stretches his legs as far behind the bike as possible. Looks like Superman flying holding on the handlebars, hence the name.
Superman	MTX	Rider releases both legs from pegs and throws his legs back, elevating himself over the bike.
Swing weight	SKT	The distribution of weight from the tip and tail to the centre of the board. To balance a board and control its ability to initiate rotation or to stop rotation in relationship to its overall weight.
Swiss cheese air	SNB	The rear hand reaches between the legs and grabs the heel edge in front of the front foot while the back left is boned.
Switch stance	SKT	When the feet are placed in the opposite of the normal stance and you are going forward with a slightly different balance point than in your normal stance. Not the same as fakie where you ride backwards with your normal balance and stance.
Switch take off	SNB	Going into a jump backwards.
Symmetrical design	SNB	When all the design components of the side cut and shape are parallel in design. The opposite of Asymmetrical. To position a rider on a board when less angulation or opposing angulation is necessary.
Table top	BMX	When a rider flattens his bike out into the horizontal plane in the air, then straightens it back out to land.

Word	*Sport*	*Definition*
Table top	MULTI	Type of jump—with a ramp going up, flat on top, and a landing ramp on the far side.
Tail	MULTI	The rear tip of the board or ski.
Tail bonk	SNB	To hit an object with the tail of the snowboard.
Tail grab	SNB	The rear hand grabs the tail of the snowboard.
Tail poke	SNB	Any maneuver where you bone your rear leg and "poke" the tail of the snowboard in a direction away from your body usually while grabbing.
Tail protector/tip protector	SNB	Usually a metal plate built into the tail or tip of the board. To protect the tail or tip from damage and to control swing weight.
Tail slide	SKT	Sliding on the tail of the board.
Tail slide	SNB	To slide along the ground or an object solely on the tail of the snowboard.
Tail tap	SNB	See Tail Bonk.
Tail wheelie	SNB	To ride solely on the tail of the snowboard with the nose in the air.
Tailwhip	BMX	Where a rider whips his bike around the axis of the handlebars, while keeping the handlebars and his body stationary, and landing back on the bike before hitting the ground. Double Tailwhips (two bike rotations) are also popular, but extremely difficult.
Taipan air	SNB	The front hand reaches behind the front foot and grabs the toe edge between the bindings. The front knee is then bent to touch the board tuck knee style.
T-bolt	SNB	A small metal inside threaded cylinder with a disk attached to the bottom, to prevent it from pulling up and out of the board. To repair or substitute the area of binding attachment to a board.
Tip	SKT	Top end of the ski.
Tire tap	BMX	Where a rider's back wheel is on the deck and the front wheel is in the air, balancing for a moment before dropping back in to the ramp.
Toe edge	SNB	A snowboard has two different edges. The toe edge is the one at which the toes rest.
Toeside	SNB	The frontside of the board is the side where the toes rest. And the frontside of the board is the side to which his/her chest faces.
Toeside rotation	SNB	Rotating counter-clockwise for a regular footer, and rotating clockwise for a goofy footer.

Word	Sport	Definition
Tombstone	BMX	A vertical portion of a ramp that rises above the rest of the top of the ramp to add more vert. Resembles a rectangular tombstone on top of the ramp.
Top sheet	SNB	Usually a form of flexible plastic that sits on top of the laminated or foam core. Also the material that is used as the cap in Monocoque Construction. To protect the core materials of the boards, and to act as a material for graphics applications.
Torque	INL	Skater rides with the front foot on the outside of the grindplate, toes turned in, back foot on inside of grindplate. Also called Farfernugan.
Torque slide	INL	Skater rides with front foot on the outside of grindplate, back foot grabbed. This is one of the toughest grinds to master. Some people call it a Suicide because of its difficulty.
Torsion box construction	SNB	When the core material is fully wrapped with a strength enhancing material like fiberglass. To manipulate the flex and torsional rigidity of a snowboard from the core construction.
Torsional flex	SNB	The actual resistance to twisting a board from side to side. To define the flex of a board from side to side. Its resistance to twisting and its responsiveness to initiating a turn and hold an edge.
Traditional skis	ETC	Describes skis with shapes typical of all skis of the past 50 years, these skis have a straighter shape than modern skis.
Transition	MULTI	The curved part of the terrain between 0 and 90 degrees.
Transition	BMX	The point where a ramp or jump goes from the horizontal plane to the vertical plane.
Transition (tranny)	SNB	The radial curved section of a halfpipe wall between the flat bottom and the vertical. A snowboarder pumps and rides the transition to gain speed, catch air, and land.
Traverse	MULTI	Skiing across the slope at an angle to fall line
Traverse	SNB	To ride perpendicular to the fall line. Halfpipe rider traverses from wall to wall in the halfpipe.
Truck	SKT	The hardware that is comprised of the axle and base plate mounted to the underside of the board.
Truck driver	BMX	A regular 360 while simultaneously spinning the handlebars 360 degrees. A double Truck Driver would be spinning the bars 720 degrees.

Word	Sport	Definition
Tuck knee	SNB	A technique where one knee is bent, and the ankle is bent sideways in order to touch the knee to the snowboard between the bindings.
Turndown	BMX	Where a rider turns the handlebars and his body down towards the ground while the rest of the bike stays facing straight up.
Tweaked	SNB	A term used to describe the emphasis of style in a trick.
Twin tip	SNB	A type of snowboard designed for freestyle snowboarding. It has an identical tip and tail so that the board may be ridden similarly in both directions.
Unity	INL	Skater rides with front foot on outside of grindplate and places foot in the front of back foot which is on outside of its grindplate. When skater performs a Unity, it looks as though they're sitting Indian style.
Uphill ski	ETC	The ski higher on the fall, or the one that will become the upper ski in any ski turn.
Variable flex	SNB	When the tip, tail and middle of a board each has varying degrees of flex. To vary the overall flex of a board from the tip to the middle to the tail.
Variable radius	SNB	A side cut design that incorporates a changing radius size along the length of the board. To adjust a side cut design of a board by using many intersecting radius sizes, to enhance its turning characteristics.
Varial	SKT	An aerial where the board is spun from backwards to forwards beneath the feet.
Variation	INL	To change from one type of grind or grab to another while doing long trick such a handrail.
Vert	INL	Short for vertical, meaning a 90 degree ramp, pool, or wall.
Vert	BMX	The half-pipe event. A half-pipe is like a big "U" with two transition areas at either end that extend to vertical stands, separated by the flat bottom in between.
Vertical	SNB	The vertical top portion of a wall in a halfpipe which allows the snowboarder to fly straight up into the air and not out of the pipe or into the pipe.
Vertically laminated wood core	SNB	Pretty much the industry standard. Strips of wood ranging from 1/8" to 3/4" are bonded together side to side with the joints running vertical. This allows for several different woods to be used in each core to optimise performance characteristics.
Waist	SNB	The width measurement taken at the narrowest part of the board which is near the middle of its length.

Word	*Sport*	*Definition*
Wall	MULTI	Any bank that is at or above 90 degrees.
Wallride	MULTI	To ride on a wall that has no transition.
Wax	INL	The substance skaters spread on the curbs and obstacles to make them more slippery.
Wheels	SKT	Attached to the truck-rolling devices which are usually made of urethane. In addition to the standard wheels, there are now those which have a nylon or high-tech plastic on the interior part of the wheel.
Whip	MTX	Classic Motocross move where rider turns and lays the machine flat in mid air.
Wood core	MULTI	Various type of wood used to provide the shape and thickness of a board.
World cup	ETC	An annual series featuring the best freestyle and alpine skiers.
X-Up	BMX	While in the air a rider turns the handlebars as far as they will go in one direction without releasing the grip, then turns them back in the other direction before landing.

Glossary

ABTA: Association of British Travel Agents. Represents the interests of the larger UK tour operators and travel agents (with around 670 members as of 2000), and operates a bonding scheme whereby customers booking with ABTA members have their holidays protected should the operator/agent in question collapse.

Accommodation capacity: The measure of accommodation stock at a defined destination. May be given by various different measures: *e.g.* number of establishments; number of main units within an establishment (*e.g.* rooms, caravan stances); capacity in terms of residents (*e.g.* bedspaces).

Accounting period: Normally one year, the period for which accounts are drawn up.

AITO: Association of Independent Tour Operators. Performs a similar function to ABTA, although its membership (and therefore its agenda) differs in comprising some 160 of the smaller UK tour operators.

All-inclusive hotels: Resort facilities that offer all meals, activities and entertainments on site. All holiday expenses at these hotels are covered by one pre-paid price. Caribbean destinations are noted for their high profile brands of all—inclusive hotels which offer unlimited alcoholic drinks, snacks between meals and motorised sports all included in one price.

All-inclusive: A form of package holiday where the majority of services offered at the destination are included in the price paid prior to departure (*e.g.* refreshments, excursions, amenities, gratuities, etc.).

Allocentric: Of a minority of tourists—adventurous, outgoing, self-confident, independent, needing little tourist infrastructure. Enjoys high contact with locals.

Alternative tourism: In essence, tourism activities or development that are viewed as non-traditional. It is often defined in opposition to large-scale mass tourism to represent small-scale sustainable tourism developments. AT is also presented as an 'ideal type', that is, an improved model of tourism development that redresses the ills of traditional, mass tourism.

Artefact: An object; an item of material culture.

Assets: Something of value that will provide future benefit or utility, can be used to generate revenue. Usually owned, so simply described as 'things we own'.

ATOL: Air Travel Organiser's License. A requirement of the Civil Aviation Authority for all UK tour operators wishing to sell air seats on chartered or scheduled services. Necessitates a financial 'health check' and the putting up of a bond to cover the expense of reimbursing/repatriating tourists in the event of operator failure.

Average room rate achieved: The average of the room rates resulting in room sales which a hotel has experienced for a given time period.

Balance of payments: Record of one country's financial transactions with the rest of the world.

Benchmarking: Measuring your performance against that of best in class companies, determining how the best-in-class achieve those performance levels and using this information as a basis for your own company's targets, strategies and implementation (Pryor, 1989).

Benchmarks: Points of reference or comparison, which may include standards, critical success factors, indicators, metrics.

Bureaucracy: An organisation typified by formal processes, standardisation, hierarchic procedures, and written communication.

Business travel: Travel for a purpose and to a destination determined by a business, and where all costs are met by that business.

Capacity management: A process that seeks to ensure that their organisations operate at optimum capacity whilst maintaining customer satisfaction levels.

Capital expenditure: The cost of long-term assets, such as computer equipment, vehicles and premises. Importantly these are bought to use over several years and not to resell.

Carrying-capacity analysis: Originally a term applied in ecology referring to the maximum number of animals of a given species that a particular habitat could support. In the context of tourism, it refers to the maximum number of tourists a destination can support.

Case: A case describes a dispute taken to court, and specific cases set legal precedents—a legal principle, created by a court decision, which provides an example or authority for judges deciding similar issues later.

Chain of distribution: The means by which products (package holidays in this instance) are distributed from producers (principals) to consumers (tourists), often via wholesalers and retailers (tour operators and travel agents).

Chaos theory: Views organisations/businesses as complex, dynamic, non-linear, co-creative and far-from-equilibrium systems the future performance of which cannot be decided alone by past and present events and actions. In a state of chaos, organisations behave in ways which are simultaneously both unpredictable (chaotic) and patterned (orderly).

Charter: A legal contract between an owner and an organisation for the hire of a means of transport for a particular purpose. An individual traveller will use an intermediary to arrange to be carried on the transport. Often applied to a flight which is the result of a charter.

Class action: A lawsuit filed by a number of people in a similar situation, *e.g.* participants in a particular package holiday might file a class action against the tour operator rather than take action individually.

Code of conduct: Guidelines advising a tourism stakeholder, including tourists, on how to behave in an environmentally responsible manner.

Collaboration: The process of working together in pursuit of common objectives.

Competitive strategies: Offensive or defensive strategies that aim at providing strategic competitive advantage and at increasing the competitiveness of an organisation.

Computer reservation systems (CRS): Computerised Reservation Systems used for inventory management by airlines, hotels and other facilities. CRSs can allow direct access through terminals for intermediaries to check availability, make reservations and print tickets.

Conservation: Can be broadly interpreted as action taken to protect and preserve the natural world from harmful features of tourism, including pollution and overexploitation of resources.

Contract: A legal agreement entered into by two or more parties.

Control: Monitoring and if necessary adjusting the performance of the organisation and its members.

Cost-benefit analysis: Full analysis of public and private costs and benefits of project.

Cost-plus pricing: A method of pricing where an amount, to cover profit, is added to costs to establish the selling price, this is an internally orientated pricing method.

Critical incident point (CIP): A critical incident point or 'moment of truth' is any event which occurs when the customer has (or even perceives that he has) contact with a service organisation.

Cultural: See 'culture'.

Culture: A set of shared norms and values which establish a sense of identity for those who share them. Typically applied at the level of nation and/or race.

Customer: "An organisation or a person that receives a product" (ISO, 2000a: 10).

Decision-making unit (DMU): The combination of inputs to a purchasing decision.

Delegation: The assignment to others of the authority for particular functions, tasks, and decisions.

Dependency theory: This theory maintains that developing countries are kept in a position of dependency and underdevelopment due to existing economic and institutional power structures sustained by leading Western nations. Dependency theorists argue that the policies and activities of multinational corporations, national bilateral and multinational aid agencies such as the World Bank and the International Monetary Fund (IMF) tend to widen the gap between rich and poor countries and perpetuate the dependency of developing nations.

Designation: The act of conferring a legal status on a building which requires compliance with specific legislation on conservation and preservation.

Discretionary income: Money received from employment or other sources which can be freely spent on leisure pursuits (such as travel and tourism) after general living costs, taxation etc. are taken into consideration.

Discrimination: Unequal treatment of persons on grounds which are not justifiable in law, *e.g.* in the UK, discrimination on the grounds of sex or race.

Disintermediation: A process by which the consumer 'bypasses' the services of an intermediary or intermediaries in the chain of distribution, in order to purchase products direct from those who supply them. In the travel industry, examples of disintermediation include airlines selling tickets direct to the public over the internet, thus cutting out the travel agent in the selling process.

Distribution: The process employed to provide customers access to the product. For travel products distribution focuses largely on the ways in which the customer can reserve or purchase the product.

Diversification: The process of developing new products for new markets, in order to achieve business growth.

Due diligence: Taking what is considered in law to be reasonable care.

eCommerce: Internet facilitated commerce, using electronic means for promoting, selling, distributing, and servicing products.

Economic growth: An increase in real output per capita.

e-mediaries: Electronic booking systems (usually web-based) which combine commerce and the traditional intermediary role of travel agents. Products and services are usually sourced from a range of other product providers allowing customers to book a range of different tourism and travel services from one website, and may enable price/product comparisons between competing suppliers.

Employee relations: Covers communications, employee participation in management decisions, conflict and grievance resolution, trade unions and collective bargaining.

Environmental auditing: Inspection of a tourism organisation to assess the environmental impact of its activities.

Environmental management systems: Systems established by tourism organisations with the aim of mitigating negative environmental impacts.

Environmental scanning: The process of collecting information to carry out a systematic analysis of the forces effecting the organisation and identifying potential threats and opportunities with a view to generating future strategies.

Evolutionary theories: Theories of tourism which see destinations evolving, in the sense that the types of tourists change, or evolve, over time.

Exclusion clause: This is a term in a contract that tries to exclude or limit the liability of one of the parties if there is a breach. Such clauses often take the form of "small print" in the standard terms and conditions of the dominant partner in the contract *e.g.* tour operators.

Externalities: Those costs or benefits arising from production or consumption of goods and services which are not reflected in market prices.

Familiarisation trips: (Fam trips) Visits to tourism destinations made in order to experience and learn more about the destination. Such trips are usually organised either by tour operators or by destination managers to improve knowledge of the destination. When travel agents are taken on such trips it is expected that their increased knowledge will lead to greater level of sales of holidays to that destination.

Force majeure: This is an unforeseeable or uncontrollable situation or train of events that would excuse a breach of contract.

Global Distribution System (GDS): The reservation network which links bookers such as travel agencies to travel suppliers' booking systems.

Globalisation: Generally defined as the network of connections of organisations and peoples are across national, geographic and cultural borders and boundaries. These global networks are creating a shrinking world where local differences and national boundaries are being subsumed into global identities. Within the field of tourism, globalisation is also viewed in terms of the revolutions in telecommunications, finance and transport that are key factors currently influencing the nature and pace of growth of tourism in developing nations.

Group norms: Informal standards of behaviour and performance that develop from the interaction of the group.

Heritage: Today's perception of a pattern of events in the past.

History: A pattern of events in the past.

HRM: Human Resource Management, concerned with the strategic management of human resources to achieve a competitive advantage.

Impacts: Effects, which may be either positive or negative, felt as a result of tourism-associated activity. Tourists have at least three kinds of impacts on a destination: economic, sociocultural and environmental. Tourism also has effects on tourists, in terms of possible attitude and behaviour changes.

Industry structure: An explanation of the functions, form and interrelationships of individual elements, organisations and activities within a defined industrial sector (such as tourism).

info-mediaries: Organisations which provide websites/electronic guides as an information resource, sharing other resources such as web links to organisations that sell tourism/travel. The infomediary may be an organisation or company in its own right, or may form part of an individual company's or organisation's customer service.

Information systems: Systems that use information technology to capture, transmit, store, retrieve, manipulate, or display information.

Infrastructure: Construction needed to support economic development.

Inseparability: The characteristic of service consumption being inseparable from its production, meaning that any errors made in production are seen by the consumer.

Institutions: Institutions are 'an established law, custom, usage, practice, organisation, or other element in the political or social life of people; a regulative principle or convention subservient to the needs of an organised community or the general needs of civilisation' (Scrutton 1982: 225, in Hall and Jenkins 1995).

Intangibility: The characteristic of not being touchable—a good is tangible whereas a service is intangible.

Integration: The linking (through changes of ownership such as mergers, acquisitions and takeovers) of different stages of the chain of distribution to form larger, more powerful organisations. Integration can be vertical (where links are developed with suppliers and distributors) or horizontal (where links are at the same stage of the distribution chain).

Intermediary: An organisation within the chain of distribution whose function is to facilitate the supply of a given product from producers to consumers. In the travel industry examples are travel agencies and tourism information offices.

Interpretation: An educational process that is intended to stimulate and facilitate people's understanding of place, so that empathy towards, conservation, heritage, culture and landscape is developed.

Invisible trade: Trade in services.

Labour market: The pool of employees from which an employer can fill vacancies.

Leadership: Influencing and directing the performance of group members towards the achievement of organisational goals.

Leisure travel: Travel undertaken for pleasure and unrelated to paid work time.

Liabilities: An obligation to pay money or provide service in the future. Simply described as 'things we owe'.

Lifecycle: The particular pattern through which a destination evolves.

Limits of acceptable change: Environmental indicators that can monitor changes over time as a consequence of tourism.

Litigation: Legal action to resolve an issue before a court.

Luxury sports tourism: Active or passive sports tourism serviced by high quality facilities and luxuriant accommodation and attendant services.

Marginal or contribution pricing: A method of cost plus pricing which focuses on the variable or marginal cost only and thus establishes the lowest possible selling price.

Market orientated pricing: A method of pricing that benchmarks prices against competitors when deciding on price.

Market segmentation: Market segmentation is a marketing approach that encompasses the identification of different groups of customers with different needs or responses to marketing activity. The market segmentation process also considers which of these segments to target.

Mass tourism: Traditional, large scale tourism commonly, but loosely used to refer to popular forms of leisure tourism pioneered in southern Europe, the Caribbean, and North America in the 1960s and 1970s.

Mature market: A market in which a wide range of substitutable products or services are available to consumers who exhibit a sophisticated approach to consumer decision making.

MAVERICS: Characterisation of tourists of the future as multi-holidaying, autonomous, variegated, energised, restless, irresponsible, constrained and segmented.

Mediation: An attempt to settle a dispute using a neutral third party.

Merit good: One with public as well as private benefits.

Midcentric: Of the majority of tourists—displaying a mix of allocentric and psychcentric characteristics. Prefers to be cushioned from contact with locals.

Mode of travel: The type of transport used to make a journey between an origin and a destination, and can include walking and cycling as well as all forms of mechanical transport.

Modernisation theory: The socioeconomic development and process that evolves from a traditional society to modern economies such as the United States and Western Europe. Harrison (1992) argues that modernisation is a process of westernisation where developing countries emulate Western development patterns.

Motivation: Internal and external forces and influences that drive an individual to achieving certain goals.

Mystery shoppers: These researchers investigate companies through using their services, whilst pretending to be customers (or potential customers). They usually monitor such areas as the level of customer service and product knowledge.

National income: A measure of the total level of economic activity which takes place in an economy over a year.

Negligence: Failing to exercise what is legally considered to be reasonable care.

Net worth/Total net assets: The net value of all operational assets and liabilities, shows the amount of money invested in operational capacity of the business. Calculated by deducting current and long-term liabilities from the value of Fixed assets and Current assets.

Niche tourism: Small specialised sector of tourism which appeals to a correspondingly tightly-defined market segment.

No-frills: A low-cost scheduled travel package based on minimising operator service and costs, which are passed to the consumer as a low price.

Non-profit: Non-profit organisations are those which are driven by non-financial organisational objectives, *i.e.* other than for profit or shareholder return.

Occupancy rate: The measure of capacity utilised within an accommodation unit for a given time period (*e.g.* day, week, month or year).

Online agency: Travel agencies who operate using the World Wide Web to provide information to potential customers as well as allowing the customer to book travel and related products without the necessity of speaking to a salesperson.

Operations management: "The ongoing activities of designing, reviewing and using the operating system, to achieve service outputs as determined by the organisation for customers" (Wright, 1999).

OPODO: A web based booking site linking the reservation systems of co-operating airlines, allowing bookers to compare times and prices for particular journeys.

Organisation: A deliberate arrangement of people to achieve a particular purpose.

Other recruitment difficulties: Includes poor recruitment/retention practices, poor image, low remuneration, poor employment conditions which arise despite sufficient skilled individuals.

Owners' equity: Combines the original investment and any retained profit to show the total value of the owners' interest in the business.

Package holiday: Also known as an inclusive tour. Defined in law as 'the pre-arranged combination of at least two of the following components when sold or offered for sale at an inclusive price and when the service covers a period of more than 24 hours or includes overnight accommodation: (*a*) transport; (*b*) accommodation; and (*c*) other tourist services not ancillary to transport or accommodation', as set out in Section 2(1) of the European Union's Package Travel Regulations, 1992 (cited in Sharpley 2002: 72-3).

Perishability: The characteristic of being perishable. In tourism the term is used to describe, for example, a particular hotel room on a specific night or a particular seat on a specific flight—they cannot be 'stored' and sold later, so they are perishable.

Personal disposable income: The amount an individual has left over for personal expenditure on goods and services, after payment of personal direct taxes, national insurance and pension contributions.

Personnel: Concerned with the practical management and administration of people at work.

PESTEL analysis: Examines the political, economic, socio-cultural, technological, (physical) environmental and legal forces within which businesses operate and which act on them.

Physical evidence: The tangible evidence of a service, including everything which can be seen, touched, smelt and heard.

Politics: Politics has been defined in many ways. According to Heywood, politics is 'The activity through which people make, preserve and amend the general rules under which they live' (Heywood 1997: 410). According to Davis *et al.*, 'Politics is the process by which the structure, process and institutions are brought to a decision [including non-decisions] or outcome. It is an endless activity; while politics operates, all decisions [and non-decisions and actions] are provisional' (Davis *et al.*, 1988: 61). So politics means no decision or action is final. All decisions and actions of a government or institution of the state is open to question and is up for debate and argument and is, ultimately, subject to change.

Pollution: Harmful effects on the environment as a by-product of tourism activity. Types include: air; noise; water; and aesthetic.

Porter's forces: A model which suggests that the profit potential for companies is influenced by the interaction of five competitive forces: rivalry in the marketplace; the threat of substitutes; buyer power; supplier power; and barriers to entry into the market for new players.

Positioning: The process of ensuring potential customers has a desired perception of a product or service, relative to the competition.

Price elasticity of demand: A relationship between the changes in prices charged for a good or service (here taken as hotel rooms) and the change in the amount demanded.

Price elasticity of demand: A measure of the variability that can be expected in sales when prices are changed. Unity elasticity would see equal increase in sales to in reaction to a decrease in price. Inelastic demand would not change when prices went down or up.

Principal: A term that encompasses accommodation providers, carriers, ground handlers and any other provider of services to tourists, except for those whose primary function is to package and distribute tourism products (*i.e.* tour operators and travel agents).

Process control: A systematic use of tools to identify significant variations in operational performance and output quality, determine root causes, make corrections and verify results (Evans and Lindsay, 1999: 345).

Process design: Involves specifying all practices needed, flowcharting, rationalisation and error prevention (Rao *et al.*, 1996: 540-541).

Process improvement: A proactive task of management aimed at continual monitoring of a process and its outcome and developing ways to enhance its future performance (James, 1996: 359).

Process management: Planning and administering the activities necessary to achieve a high level of performance in a process and identifying opportunities for improving quality, operational performance and ultimately customer satisfaction. It involves design, control and improvement of key business processes (Evans and Lindsay, 1999: 340).

Process: "A set of interrelated or interacting activities which transforms inputs into outputs" (ISO, 2000a:7).

Product: "The result of a process" (*i.e.* output), which may be either a service, or a good (hardware or processed materials) or software (*e.g.* information) or their combination (ISO, 2000a:7).

Profit: The excess of revenue over expenses, if expenses exceed revenues in a given period the organisation will make a loss.

Psychocentric: Of a minority of tourists—preferring 'away' to be like 'home'; requiring appropriate tourism infrastructure.

Public policy: Is whatever governments choose to do or not to do (Thomas Dye 1992: 2). Such a definition covers government action, inaction, decisions and non-decisions as it implies a very deliberate choice between alternatives (see Hall and Jenkins 1995).

Quality: The degree to which a set of inherent characteristics of a product fulfils customer requirements (ISO, 2000a).

Regulation: Control through formalised processes.

Relationship marketing: Relationship marketing is a business philosophy which aims to develop strong relationships with a range of stakeholders, such as suppliers, media, intermediaries and public organisations, as well as with customers.

Requirements: Stated, generally implied (as a custom or common practice for the organisation, its customers and other interested parties) or obligatory needs (ISO, 2000a).

Responsible tourism: Type of tourism which is practised by tourists who make responsible choices when choosing their holidays. These choices reflect reponsible attitudes to the limiting of the extent of the sociological and environmental impacts their holiday may cause.

Retained profit: The profit left in the business at the end of the accounting period after all deductions and appropriations have been made.

Revenue expenditure: The cost of resources consumed or used up in the process of generating revenue, generally referred to as expenses.

Revenue management: Revenue management is a management approach to optimising revenue, often based on managing revenues around capacity and timing (yield management), for different market segments or from different sources of funding.

Sales: Revenue from ordinary activities—not necessarily cash.

Seasonality: A phenomenon created by either tourism supply or demand (or both) changing according to the time of the year.

Service encounter: The moments of interface between customer and supplier.

Service marketing mix: The addition of People, Physical Evidence and Process to the four areas of activity more usually associated with marketing products,—Price, Place, Promotion and Product.

Servicescape: The location in which the service encounter takes place.

Skills gaps: Employers perceive existing employees have lower skill levels than needed to achieve business objectives, or where new, apparently trained and qualified for specific occupations, entrants still lack requisite skills.

Skills shortages: Lack of adequately skilled individuals in the labour market due to low unemployment, sufficiently skilled people in the labour market but not easily geographically accessible or insufficient appropriately-skilled individuals.

Small business: A small business is one which has a small number of employees, profit and/or revenue. Often these are owner-managed, with few specialist managers. Some definitions of small businesses distinguish between businesses with under 10 employees, which are micro-businesses, and those with 10-49 employees, which are classified as small businesses.

Social: Relating to human society and interaction between its members.

Sports event tourism: Tourism where the prime purpose of the trip is to take part in sports events as either a participant or spectator.

Sports participation tourism: Active participation in sports that is the prime purpose of the tourism trip.

Sports tourism: A social, cultural and economic phenomenon arising from the unique interaction of activity, people and place.

Sports training tourism: Sports tourism trips where the prime purpose is sports instruction or training.

Sport-tourism link: Not just sports holidays, but all areas in which a link between sport and tourism might be of mutual benefit (*e.g.* joint facility development, marketing and information provision).

Stakeholder: Any person, group or organisation with an interest in, or who may be affected by, the activities of another organisation.

'The State': 'The state' is a set of officials with their own preferences and capacities to effect public policy, or in more structural terms a relatively permanent set of political institutions operating in relation to civil society' (Nordlinger 1981, in Hall and Jenkins 1995). The state includes elected politicians, interest or pressure groups, law enforcement agencies, the bureaucracy, and a plethora of rules, regulations, laws, conventions and policies.

Statute: The law as made by parliament, *e.g.* in the UK, the Disability Discrimination Act (1995). A statute is made up of many parts called 'sections' or 'provisions'.

Statutory instrument: The vast majority of delegated legislation in the UK is in the form of statutory instruments governed by the Statutory Instruments Act 1946.

Strategic information systems: Systems designed to support the strategic management decision processes and implementation.

Strategy pyramid: A visual way of representing the different levels of the strategy conceptualisation and implementation process. The most general assumptions are shown at the apex and the practical, implementation actions are at the base.

Suppliers: Individuals, companies or other organisations which provide goods or services to a recognisable customer or consumer.

Sustainable tourism: Tourism that is economically, socioculturally and environmentally sustainable. With sustainable tourism, sociocultural and environmental impacts are neither permanent nor irreversible.

SWOT analysis: Brings together the internal and external environmental scanning to identify the business's internal strengths and weaknesses and external opportunities and threats.

Tort: A civil wrong.

Tour operator: An individual or organisation in the business of (bulk) buying, and subsequently bundling, the various components that make up a package holiday (see above), for sale via a travel agent or direct to the consumer.

Tourism flows: The major movements of tourists from specific home areas to destinations.

Tourism income multiplier (TIM): Exaggerated effect of a change in tourism expenditure on an area's income.

Tourism satellite account: System of accounting at national or regional level which reveals the total direct impact of tourism on the economy.

Tourism system: A framework that identifies tourism as being made up of a number of components, often taken to include the tourist, the tourist generating region, the transit route region, the tourist destination and the tourism industry (Leiper, 1990).

Tourism with sports content: Tourism products that include participation in sport that is not the prime purpose of the trip.

Tourist attractions: Tourist attractions are defined as being destinations for visitors' excursions which are routinely accessible to visitors during opening hours. Visitors can include local residents, day-trippers or people who are travelling for business or leisure purposes. Formal definitions exclude shops, sports stadia, theatres and cinemas, as these meet a wider purpose, although in practice tourists may consider the excluded categories to be tourist attractions.

TOWS matrix: Uses a SWOT analysis to develop strategies by matching strengths with opportunities, using opportunities to reduce weaknesses, using strengths to overcome threats, and reducing weaknesses and avoiding threats.

Travel agent: The retailer of travel and related products. Whilst this refers to the sales person employed to sell travel products, the term is often applied in reference to the business that is established to sell travel products (the travel agency).

Variability: Because the production and the consumption of a tourism experience are inseparable and because differing circumstances and people will affect each experience, those experiences are prone to variance and create a challenge for tourism managers to achieve consistency of standards.

Virtual organisation: Organisation in which major processes are outsourced to partners.

Working capital: Operational assets and liabilities needed for everyday operation, *e.g.* cash or bank overdraft, stock and trade creditors, known as net current assets/liabilities.

Yield management: "A revenue maximisation technique which aims to increase net yield through the predicted allocation of available capacity to predetermined market segments at optimal price" (Donaghy *et al.*, 1997a).

Zoning: Different eco-systems may be zoned in terms of their robustness to pressures from tourism in an attempt to mitigate environmental damage.

Bibliography

"A Short History of Lacrosse in Canada". Canadian Lacrosse Association. Retrieved on 2008-07-14.

"About Finland: General information: Sports". Embassy of Finland, Washington (2007-06-11). Retrieved on 2008-07-21. the national sport, "pesäpallo."

"About Ireland: Culture and Sport". Government of Ireland. Retrieved on 2008-07-21. "Gaelic Football and Hurling, as Ireland's native sports are the most popular."

"Antiguans and Barbudans". everyculture.com. Retrieved on 2008-07-10. "Cricket, a left-over from the British rule, is the national sport of Antigua and Barbuda."

"Argentina Decree No. 17468 of 16/09/1953". Global Legal Information Network. Retrieved on 2008-07-14.

"Banglapedia: Kabadi". Asiatic Society of Bangladesh. Retrieved on 2008-07-21. "Ha-du-du was given the name kabadi and the status of National Game in 1972."

"Barbados: Sports". Government of Barbados. Retrieved on 2008-07-21. "The national sport of Barbados is cricket."

"Boat Racing Season Officially Opens", *The Anguillian* (2007-03-03). Retrieved on 2008-07-21. "Director of Sports, Alkins Rogers, [..] reported that the Government recognizes boat racing as the national sport of Anguilla and was giving financial resources for its development."

"Buzkashi: the national game of Afghanist [*sic*]". Embassy of Afghanistan, Canberra. Retrieved on 2008-07-21.

"Citizens: Sports: Hockey". *National Portrait of India*. Government of India. Retrieved on 2008-07-22. "Hockey, the National Sport of the Country is one of the most religiously followed games in India."

"Citypaper online". Retrieved on 2007-11-10.

"Colombia Law 613 of 4 September 2000". Global Legal Information Network. Retrieved on 2008-07-14.

"Games". Guyana Tourism Authority. Retrieved on 2008-07-21. "Cricket lovely Cricket! One cannot miss out on Guyana's national sport without participating in a game of cricket while in Guyana."

"History of Jamaica". Jamaican Embassy, Washington. Retrieved on 2008-07-21. "The legacy of Britain also lives on in Jamaica in many ways [..] the game of cricket is the national sport."

"History of Tae Kwon Do". North American Tae Kwon Do Schools. Retrieved on 2008-07-14.

"La Charrería "Nuestro Deporte Nacional"" (in Spanish). Mexican Department of Tourism. Retrieved on 2008-07-14. "El año de 1933 fue muy importante, ya que el general Abelardo L. Rodríguez, emite un decreto presidencial, dando a la Charrería el título de único Deporte Nacional."

"Long-term Prospects: Tourism 2020 Vision". World Tourism (2004).

"Monthly Market Report: Germany". Tourism Australia (February 2008).

"National Sports of Canada Act". Retrieved on 2008-07-09.

"National Symbols". *Bhutan Portal*. Government of Bhutan. Retrieved on 2008-07-21. "National Game: The national sport of Bhutan is archery."

"Number One Tourist Destination is Paris" (01-09-2008).

"Online Etymology Dictionary: tour". Retrieved on 2008-03-01.

"Pak. Hockey Federation Secretary sacked", *Zee news*, United News of India (2008-06-16). Retrieved on 2008-08-05. Sports Minister Najamuddin Khan said [..] "We have been watching with great distress the way hockey which is our national sport has been going downhill".

"Paris Is The Most Visited City In The World" (01-09-2008).

"Paris: Most visited and most expensive city in the world" (01-09-2008).

"Paris—World's Most Visited City—Leisure and Statistics" (01-09-2008). This refers to 2002.

"Puerto Rico Act 64 of 2000, S.B. 1856" (PDF). Office of Legislative Services of Puerto Rico (2000 04-11). Retrieved on 2008-07-14. "In 1966, the Public Parks and Recreation Administration and the Puerto Rico Olympic Committee awarded official recognition of the "paso fino" horse riding sport as the autochthonous sport of Puerto Rico."

"Scientists call for national flowers". *China Daily* (2005-08-09). Retrieved on 2008-07-21. "If you ask a Chinese person what the national wine is, you will no doubt be told it is Moutai. When asked what the national sport is, the answer will be table tennis."

"Some facts about the Dominican Republic". Embassy of the Dominican Republic, Washington. Retrieved on 2008-07-22. "Baseball is the Dominican Republic's national sport."

"Sport, Fitness and Leisure". *New Zealand Official Yearbook*. Statistics New Zealand (2000). etrieved on 2008-07-21. "Traditionally New Zealanders have excelled in rugby union, which is regarded as the national sport, and track and field athletics."

"The Flashpacker: A New Breed of Traveller", *Hotel Travel News* (2006-03-24). Retrieved on 2007-11-07.

"Tokelau FAQ's". Council for the ongoing government of Tokelau. Retrieved on 2008-07-21. "Many Tokelauan men and women regard cricket-island style (kilikiti) as their national sport, which can sometimes involve almost the entire village."

"UNWTO Tourism Highlights, Edition 2007". World Tourism Organization (2007). Retrieved on 2008-03-29.

"UNWTO World Tourism Barometer June 2008". World Tourism Barometer (June 2008). Retrieved on 2008-08-01. Vol. 6, No. 2.

"Uruguay Law 17958 of 21 April 2006". Global Legal Information Network. Retrieved on 2008-07-14.

"Wales – a unique country, a unique culture". British Embassy, Warsaw. Retrieved on 2008-07-21. "Wales is mainly associated with rugby. It is the national sport of Wales." Tourism in India.

"World Tourism Barometer (p. 8)". World Tourism Organization (2007). Retrieved on 2008-03-29.

Adamkus, Valdas (2005-07-28). "Address at Charles University, Prague". President of Lithuania official website. Retrieved on 2008-07-24. "Lithuania is a country that loves basketball. It is our national sport and we are proud to be reigning European Champions."

Aeberhard, Danny; Andrew Benson, Lucy Phillips, *et al.* (2001). *The Rough Guide to Argentina*, p. 198. "displays of traditional gaucho skills (*destrezas criollas*)."

Aidid, S.M. 'Penang (Malaysia) as a Tourism Sport Centre', (online), *Journal of Sport Tourism*, http://www.mcb.co.uk/journals/jst/archive/vol4no1/welcome.htm

Andueza, J.M. 'The Role of Sport in the Tourism Destinations Chosen by Tourists Visiting Spain', (online), *Journal of Sport Tourism*, http://www.mcb.co.uk/journals/jst/archive/vol4no3/jst15.htm

Anon.(1) 'Sport Tourism Consumer Motivation', (online), *Journal of Sport Tourism*, http://www.mcb.co.uk/journals/jst/archive/vol4no3/jst15.htm

Anon.(2) 'Sports Tourism—a Window of Opportunity', (online), *Journal of Sport Tourism*, http://www.mcb.co.uk/services/conferen/feb96/sports_tourism/backgrnd.htm

Anon.(3) 'Sports Tourism in the Barbados—the Development of Sports Facilities and Special Events', (online), *Journal of Sport Tourism*, http://www.mcb.co.uk/journals/jst/archive/vol4no1/welcome.htm

Australian Bureau of Statistics (1999) *More Australians are Going to Aussie Rules*, Australian Bureau of Statistics Media Release, 20 December 1999, 151/99.

Australian Sports Commission (1990) *Hosting an International Sporting Event—A Guide for Australian Sporting Organisations*, Pirie Printers, Canberra.

Australian Travel Research Workshop (1987) *The Impact and Marketing of Special Events*, Australian Standing Committee on Tourism.

Barnard, C.L.P. (1988) *Sport Tourism...For You? a guide to develop a sport tourism strategy*, Recreation and Sport Branch, Ministry of Tourism, Recreation and Culture, British Columbia.

Basra, Sukhwant (2008-03-11). "No national status, except in NCERT textbooks". dnaindia. Retrieved on 2008-07-15. "The status of hockey as the national sport is not enshrined in any official proclamation by the Government of India. The NCERT textbook for Class XI does [..] state that India's national game is hockey and that, in a way, does make for an official take on the issue."

Batting for Grenada. *Grenada Life* p. 38. Grenada Board of Tourism (March 2007). Retrieved on 2008-07-21. "in the first Grenada Cricket Classics [h]eroes such as Sir Viv Richards, Joel Garner and Curtley Ambrose came together to promote what is considered by many to be the national sport in Grenada."

Battisti, G. & Favretto, A. (1997) 'Sporting and Outdoor Activities in the Development of Tourism in Slovenia: The Case of the Triglav National Park', *Tourism Recreation Research*, Vol. 22(2), pp. 29-35.

Berglund, Nina (2006-02-20). "Few cheers for Norway", *Aftenposten*. Retrieved on 2008-07-21. "The scoreboard shows how the Norwegians placed a performance considered much too poor in a country where cross-country skiing is a national sport."

Bramwell, B. (1997) 'A Sport Mega-event as a Sustainable Tourism Development Strategy', *Tourism Recreation Research*, Vol. 22(2), pp. 13-19.

Bull, C. & Weed, M. (1997)(1) 'Influences on Sport-Tourism Relations in Britain: The Effects of Government Policy', *Tourism Recreation Research*, Vol. 22(2), pp. 5-12.

Bull, C. & Weed, M. (1997)(2) 'Integrating Sport & Tourism: A Review of Regional Policies in England', *Progress in Tourism and Hospitality Research*, Vol. 3, pp. 129-148.

Bull, C. & Weed, M. (1998) 'The Search for a Sport-Tourism Policy Network', *Leisure Management: Issues and Applications*, pp. 277-281.

Bull, C. & Weed, M. (1999) 'Niche markets and small island tourism: the development of sports tourism in Malta', *Managing Leisure*, 4, pp. 142-155.

Canada Tourism, 'The Canadian Sports Tourism Initiative', (online).

Caroline Bremner (2007-10-11). "Top 150 City Destinations: London Leads the Way". Euromonitor International. Retrieved on 2008-08-03. This article has the complete list of 150 cities.

Castro, Fidel (1999-08-13). "Speech at a meeting with Pan American Games delegation members". cuba.cu. Retrieved on 2008-07-24. "the game that [..] is [..] our national sport [..] I am talking of baseball."

Chang-Shin, C. 'Benefiting from Mega Events: Olympics 2000, World Cup 2002 and 2005 World Exposition', (online), *Journal of Sport Tourism*, http://www.mcb.co.uk/journals/jst/archive/vol5no3/vol5no3.htm

Chernushenko, D. 'Sports Tourism Goes Sustainable—the Lillehammer Experience', The Delphi Group, Ottawa, Canada.

Cook L. (1999). The 1944 Education Act and outdoor education: from policy to practice. *History of Education*, *28*(2), 157-172.

Craton, Michael; Gail Saunders (1998). *Islanders in the Stream: A History of the Bahamian People*. University of Georgia Press, p. 471.

Crockett, S. (1997) 'Sports Tourism—Bidding for International Events', (online), *Journal of Sport Tourism*, Vol. 3 No. 4, http://www.mch.co.uk/journals/jst/vol 3 no 4/bilding.htm

De Knop, P. (1990) 'Sport for all and active tourism', *World Leisure and Recreation*, Vol. 32, No. 3, Fall 1990, pp. 30-36.

Delpy, L. (1998) 'An overview of sport tourism: Building towards a dimensional framework', *Journal of Vacation Marketing*, Vol. 4, No. 1, January 1998, pp. 91-102.

Delpy, L., Grabijas, M. & Stefanovich, A. (1998) 'Sport Tourism and corporate sponsorship: A winning combination', *Journal of Vacation Marketing*, Vol. 4, No. 1, January 1998, pp. 91-102.

Department for Culture, Media and Sport (1999), 'Media Release—Government Acts to Boost Tourism', (online), 26 February 1999, London, http://195.44.11.137/coi/coipress.nsf

Department of Environment, Sport and Territories (1996) *Expanding Australia's sporting and recreational links with Asia*, Australian Government Publishing Service, Canberra.

Douvis, J., Yusof, A. & Douvis, S. 'An Examination of Demographic and Psychographic Profiles of the Sport Tourist', (online), *The Cyber-Journal of Sport Marketing*, http://www.cjsm.com/vol2/douvisyusof24.htm

Duquette, Jerold J. (1999). *Regulating the National Pastime: Baseball and Antitrust*. Greenwood, p. 104. Retrieved on 2008-07-21. "Baseball justified its privileged legal status by citing the special nature and cultural significance of America's national pastime."

Economic Potential of the Australian Sport and Recreation Industry, (unpublished report).

Embratur (2006). "Anúario Estatístico Volume 33 2006" (in Portuguese). Ministério do Turismo. Retrieved on 2008-06-27.

Encyclopedia of Marine Mammals, editors Perrin, Wursig and Thewissen, In particular the article *Whale watching* by Erich Hoyt.

Faulkner, B. & Tideswell, C. (1998)(1) *Leveraging Tourism Benefits from the Sydney 2000 Olympics* (unpublished paper).

Faulkner, B. (1993) *Evaluating the Tourism Impacts of Hallmark Events,* Occasional Paper No. 16, Bureau of Tourism Research, Canberra.

Faulkner, B., Tideswell, C. & Weston, A. (1999) *Sydney Olympics and the Sports Tourism Nexus,* (unpublished paper) Griffith University Centre for Tourism and Hotel Management Research, and KPMG Management Consultants.

Fernando, Leslie (2005-06-03). "Sponsors President's Gold Cup tourney: Dialog assures future of VB", *Daily News (Sri Lanka).* Retrieved on 2008-07-14. "Way back in 1991 volleyball was declared as the national sport of Sri Lanka but it was only name sake."

Forbes Traveller (2007-04-25). "Top 50 Most Visited Tourist Attractions". Retrieved on 2008-03-29.

Getz, D. (1997) 'Trends and Issues in Sport Event Tourism', *Tourism Recreation Research,* Vol. 22(2), pp. 61-62.

Gibson, H.J. (1998) 'Active Sport Tourism: Who Participates?', *Leisure Studies,* Vol. 17, No. 2, pp. 155-170.

Gibson, H.J. (1998)(2) 'Sport Tourism: A Critical Analysis of Research', *Sport Management Review,* 1, pp. 45-76.

Gibson, H.J. (1998)(3) 'The wide world of sport tourism', *P & R,* September 1998, pp. 108-114.

Gibson, H.J., Attle, S.P. & Yiannakis, A. (1998) 'Segmenting the active sport tourist market: A life-span perspective', *Journal of Vacation Marketing,* Vol. 4, No. 1, 1998, pp. 52-64.

Gonzalez Echevarria, Roberto (1999). "A Cuban *Belle Époque", The Pride of Havana: A History of Cuban Baseball.* Oxford University Press, p. 76. "Baseball is so ingrained in Cuba that it has thrived as the "national sport" through forty years of a bitterly anti-American revolution."

Grabowski, P. (1999) 'Tourism and sport: Parallel tracks for developing tourism in Brunei?', *Tourism Recreation Research,* Vol. 24(2), pp. 99-98.

Green, B.C. & Chalip, L. (1998) 'Sport Tourism as the Celebration of Subculture', *Annals of Tourism Research,* Vol. 25, No. 2, pp. 275-291.

Griffiths, M. (1999) *Positioning the Illawarra & Southern Highlands Region as a Sports Tourism Destination,* (unpublished thesis for Illawarra & Southern Highlands Tourism), University of Technology, Sydney.

Growing Lesbian and Gay Sports Tourism Industry', *Journal of Vacation Marketing,* Vol. 5, No. 1, pp. 31-50.

Grundriss der allgemeinen Fremdenverkehrslehre | author=Werner Hunziker and Kurt | id=OCLC # 69064371 | year = 1942; cf. Hasso Spode in Günther Haehling (ed.): Tourismus-Management, Berlin 1998.

Hagan, J. & Patterson, E. (1991) *Oars Away—Assessing the Impact of the 1990 World Rowing Championships on Tasmania,* Department of Tourism, Sport and Recreation, Hobart.

Hall, C.M. (1997) 'Recent Progress of Sports Tourism in New Zealand', *Tourism Recreation Research,* Vol. 22(2), p. 63.

Harris, John (Summer 2006). "(Re)Presenting Wales: National Identity and Celebrity in the Postmodern Rugby World". *North American Journal of Welsh Studies* 6 (2). North American Association for the Study of Welsh Culture and History. Retrieved on 2008-07-14. "rugby used to be the undisputed national sport of Wales [..] Rugby Union's assumed position as "the national game" has often been questioned on the basis that it is predominantly a game played and followed in South Wales."

Hattie, J.A., Marsh, H.W., Neill, J.T. & Richards, G.E. (1997). Adventure education and Outward Bound: Out-of-class experiences that have a lasting effect. *Review of Educational Research, 67,* 43-87.

Higham, J. (1999) 'Commentary—Sport as an Avenue of Tourism Development: An Analysis of the Positive and Negative Impacts of Sport Tourism', *Current Issues in Tourism,* Vol. 2, No. 1, pp. 82-90.

Industry Policy and Analysis Section (1996) *Sydney 2000 Olympics: Economic Benefits for the ACT Preliminary Estimates,* February 1999, Business and Regional Development Bureau—ACT.

International Association of Scientific Experts in Tourism. "The AIEST, its character and aims". Retrieved on 2008-03-29.

Irwin, R.L. & Sandler, M.A. (1998) 'An analysis of travel behaviour and event-induced.

Jackson, G. & Reeves, M. (1998) 'Evidencing the Sport-Tourism Interrelationship: a Case Study of Elite British Athletes', *Leisure Management: Issues and Applications,* pp. 263-275.

Kirby, David (September 27, 1998). "The Tourist Trap; With All Those Visitors Trampling the Welcome Mat, Can New York Be the Host With the Most for Everyone?" (Web). *News Article.* The New York Times. Retrieved on 2007-03-21.

Kurlantzick, Joshua (Sunday, January 9, 2005). "The True Meaning of the Tourist Trap" (Web). *News article.* The Washington Post. Retrieved on 2007-03-21.

Kurtzman, J. & Zauhar, J. (1995) 'Tourism Sport International Council', *Annals of Tourism Research,* Vol. 22, No. 3, pp. 707-708.

Kurtzman, J. & Zauhar, J. (1998) 'Sport Tourism: a business inherency or an innate compulsion?', *Visions in Leisure and Business,* Vol. 17(2), pp. 21-30.

Kurtzman, J. & Zauhar, J. 'A Wave in Time- The Sports Tourism Phenomena', (online), *Journal of Sport Tourism,* Vol. 3, No. 2, http://www.mcb.co.uk/journals/jst/archive/vol3no2/welcome.htm

Kurtzman, J. 'Sports Tourism Categories', (online), *Journal of Sport Tourism,* Vol. 3, No. 4, http://www.mcb.co.uk/journals/jst/archive/vol3no4/categories.htm

Laysell Pty Ltd., INSTATE Pty Ltd. & Thomas Hogg Consulting (1998) *Examination of the Economic Potential of the Australian Sport and Recreation Industry,* (unpublished report).

Lowell, John (1992). *Ring of Liberation: Deceptive Discourse in Brazilian Capoeira*. University of Chicago Press, p. 61.

Luke, Will (March 2007). "Cricket by association". The Wisden Cricketer. Retrieved on 2008-07-"Bermuda are one of the few sides who count cricket as a national sport."

Lynch, P. (?). *Camping in the Curriculum: A History of Outdoor Education in New Zealand Schools*. PML publications, Lincoln University, Canterbury, New Zealand.

Mckinley, James C., Jr (1999-03-26). "Baseball; Clash of Cultures, Pride and Passion", *The New York Times*. Retrieved on 2008-07-24. "Most Cubans, after all, consider baseball to be their national sport, a game entwined in history with their struggle for independence from Spain and the birth of their nation."

Mølster, Odd (1996). "Skiing and the Creation of a Norwegian Identity—part 2". *News of Norway, issue* 2. Norwegian Embassy, Washington. Retrieved on 2008-07-21. "the national sport could become a fine weapon in time of war. In 1943, Norway's resistance movement won an epochal victory—on skis, of course."

Moreira Recchione, Alberto (December 2007). "La Medialuna: un edificio para Chile" (in Spanish). *Revista de urbanismo* (No. 17). University of Chile. Retrieved on 2008-07-14. "A reconocerse, en 1962, el rodeo como deporte nacional y oficial [10 de enero de 1962, oficio N°269 del Consejo Nacional de Deportes y Comité Olímpico de Chile]."

Mules, T., Burgan, B., Molloy, J., Redman, W. & Hudson, P. (1988) *Financial and Economic Modelling of Major Sporting Events in Australia,* Sport and Recreation Ministers' Council.

Nash, D. (1999) Commentary on 'Sport Tourism as the Celebration of Subculture', *Annals of Tourism Research,* Vol. 26, No. 3, pp. 701-703.

Nicholls, Henry (Wednesday April 19, 2006). "The tourist trap (The Galapagos islands are the world's prime eco-tourism destination. Now the sheer number of visitors is endangering their future)" (Web). *News article*. Guardian. Retrieved on 2007-03-21.

Nogawa, H., Yamaguchi, Y. & Hagi, Y. (1996) 'An Empirical Research Study on Japanese Sport Tourism in Sport-for-All Events: Case Studies of a Single-Night Event and a Multiple-Night Event', *Journal of Travel Research,* Vol. XXXV, No. 2, pp. 46-54.

Pigeassou, C. 'Sport and Tourism: The Emergence of Sport into the Offer of Tourism. Between Passion and Reason. An Overview of the French Situation and Perspectives', (online), *Journal of Sport Tourism,* Vol. 4, No. 2, http://www.mcb.co.uk/journals/jst/archive/vol4no2/welcome.htm

Pitts, B.G. (1999) 'Sports Tourism and Niche Markets: Identification and Analysis of the Growing Lesbian and Gay Sports Tourism Industry', *Journal of Vacation Marketing,* Vol. 5, No. 1, pp. 31-50.

Quintanar Hinojosa, Beatriz (August 2007). "[www.mexicodesconocido.com.mx Oaxaca: jubilo de los sentidos]". *Guía México Desconocido: Oaxaca* 137: 8.

Scarrott, M. (ed)(1999) *Exploring Sports Tourism: Proceedings of a SPRIG Seminar held at the University of Sheffield on 15 April 1999*, Sheffield Hallam University, Sheffield.

Schrag, Myles (2003). "Baseball as National Pastime Revisted: And a Little Town Shall Lead Them", in Peter Carino: *Baseball/literature/culture: Essays, 1995-2001*. McFarland, Chp. 13 p. 140. Retrieved on 2008-07-21. "Tradition—that quality so instrumental in elevating baseball to its century-old status as national pastime— has become less important."

Schwark, J. 'Forms of Supply and Individual Potential in Sport Tourism', (online), *Journal of Sport Tourism*, http://www.mcb.co.uk/journals/jst/archive/vol5no3/vol5no3.htm

Smith, C. & Jenner, P. (1998) 'The Impact of Festivals and Special Events on Tourism', *Travel & Tourism Intelligence*, No. 4, pp. 73-91.

Sport Tourism, Vol. 3 No. 4, http://www.mcb.co.uk/journals/jst/vol3no4/bidding.htm

Stan Hagen—Tourism Minister of British Columbia.

Standeven, J. & De Knop, P. (1999) *Sport Tourism*, Human Kinetics, Champaign, Illinois.

Standeven, J. (1998) 'Sport Tourism: Joint marketing—A starting point for beneficial synergies', *Journal of Vacation Marketing*, Vol. 4, No. 1, pp. 39-51.

STIC Research Unit (1), 'Content Analysis of Tourism Schedules', (online), *Journal of Sport Tourism*, http://www.mcb.co.uk/journals/jst/archive/vol4no1/welcome.htm

STIC Research Unit (2), 'STIX (Sports Tourism Impact Index)', (online), *Journal of Sport Tourism*, http://www.mcb.co.uk/journals/jst/archive/vol4no1/welcome.htm

Swart, K. (1998) 'Visions for South African sport tourism', *Visions in Leisure and Business*, Vol. 17(2), pp. 4-12.

The Development of Social Network Analysis, Vancouver: Empirical Press.

The Equity: "Esprit rafting to be featured in commercial", Wednesday, May 14th, 2008, print edition.

The Hopeful Traveller (2007-07-29). "Forbes Traveller 50 Most Visited Tourist Attractions". Retrieved on 2008-03-29. See the complete Top 50 list at this website.

The Whale Watcher's Guide: Whale-watching Trips in North America, Patricia Corrigan.

Theobald, William F. (1998). *Global Tourism*, p. 10.

Thomas, M. (1987) *Major Events—a descriptive and comparative analysis*, (unpublished thesis), University of New South Wales, Sydney.

Tourism Canada (1993) *Spectator Sporting Activities in Canada—from a tourism perspective,* Department of Industry, Science and Technology.

Tourism Directorate (France) (2007). "Key facts on tourism 2007 Edition".

Tourism in Slovenia: The Case of the Triglav National Park', *Tourism Recreation Research,* Vol. 22(2), pp. 29-35.

Tourism Principles and Practice, C. Cooper, J. Fletcher, A. Fyall, D. Gilbert, S. Wanhill, *Pearson Education,* Third edition, Madrid 2005.

Touristik report. January 2008 (German).

Tow, S. (1997) 'Sports Tourism—the Benefits', (online), *Journal of Sport Tourism,* Vol. 3 No. 4, http://www.mcb.co.uk/journals/jst/vol3no4/benefits.htm

Travel Industry Association of America (1), 'Sporting Events are a Draw for Many Travellers', (online), http://www.tia.org/press/093098sports.stm

Travel Industry Association of America (2), 'TIA Releases Landmark Report on Sports Travel', (online), http://www.tia.org/press/082599sports.stm

Travel Industry Association of America (3), 'Profile of Travellers Who Attend Sports Events', (online), http://www.tia.org/research/summsports.as

Travel Industry Association of America (4), 'Travellers Prefer Golf Over Tennis', (online), http://www.tia.org/press/051199poll.stm

Turco, D. & Eisenhart, H. (1998) 'Exploring the sport-tourism connection', *ICPER=SD,* Winter, pp. 24-27.

Turco, D. 'Are we there yet? Understanding the impacts of competitive vacations', (online), *The Cyber-Journal of Sport Marketing,* http://www.cjsm.com/vol1/turcov14.htm

Vienna University, 'Austrian Sport Tourism Profiles', (online), *Journal of Sport Tourism,* http://www.mcb.co.uk/journals/jst/archive/vol4no1/welcome.htm

Walsh, V., & Golins, G.L. (1976). *The exploration of the Outward Bound process.* Denver, CO: Colorado Outward Bound School.

Whale Watching 2001: Worldwide tourism numbers, expenditures and expanding socioeconomic benefits, Erich Hoyt.

Whale Watching, Discovery Travel Adventures Insight guide.

Whales and Whale Watching in Iceland, Mark Carwardine.

Whitson, D. & Macintosh, D. (1996) 'The Global Circus: International Sport, Tourism and the Marketing of Cities', *Journal of Sport & Social Issues,* August 1996, pp. 278-295.

Index

Able-bodied players, 103
Adventure activities, 316, 325, 362
African Commonwealth, 28
Agassi, Andre, 108, 111, 113-14
Air pollution, 22
Air sports, 48, 67
Air transport, 326
American football, 74, 80
Animal Sports, 68
AQIS, 348
Archaeological Survey of India, 292, 294
Archery, 10, 73, 218-20, 279
Asian Games, 213, 235
Associated Chambers of Commerce and Industry of India, 293-94, 298
Association for Commonwealth Literature and Language Studies, 39
Association of Commonwealth Universities, 35
ATC, 323
Athletics events, 2
Athletics, 2, 10, 77, 78, 85, 169, 173, 178-81, 183, 208-9, 213, 219-20, 234, 239, 279, 296-97
ATP, 105, 111-12
Australian Institute of Sport, 329, 331
Australian Open, 96, 97, 102-3, 110
Australian Tourist Commission, 323, 357, 363
Average room rate, 300, 391
Ayurvedic and Medical Tourism, 295

Baby Sitting, 248-50, 253
Backstroke, 51, 116-19, 122-23
Badminton, 10, 65, 206, 208, 213, 219, 234, 279, 285, 297
Ball Sports, 51
Balloons, hot air, 228, 309
Barbell, 94, 95
Basketball, 4, 10, 49, 61, 74, 181, 183-84, 239, 296, 329
Baton, 142, 188, 222-29
Batonbearer, 223, 227-29
Bench press, 87-89, 91, 92, 94, 283
Bharti, Uma, 205
Board games, 46
Borg, Björn, 108, 114-15
Breaststroke, 51, 116-19, 122-23, 177, 179
Breaststrokers, 122
British Commonwealth Games, 1, 3, 221
British Commonwealth of Nations, 26
British Empire Games, 1-3, 13, 221

Broadcasting Rights, 277-78
BTR, 351-52, 354
Buckingham Palace, 223-25, 227-28
Bungee jumping, 68, 69

Canadian Tourism Commission, 340, 364-65
Canberra Tourism, 345
Catalytic events, 349
Central American and Caribbean Games, 42
Challenger Series, 113
China, 290, 300, 328
Chinese Checkers, 67, 71
Classical fencing, 145, 148-49
Closing Ceremony, 182-83, 186, 199, 200
Club Floors, 246
Commencement ceremonies, 224-25
Commonwealth agencies, 340, 346
Commonwealth Boxing Council, 38
Commonwealth Business Club India, 210
Commonwealth Business Council, 37
Commonwealth Conversation, 40
Commonwealth countries, 1, 27, 35, 37, 39, 175, 305
Commonwealth Day, 188, 224-25
Commonwealth Foundation, 25, 36, 39
Commonwealth fraternity, 210
Commonwealth Games Associations, 260, 270
Commonwealth Games Federation, 1, 4, 12, 15, 169, 186, 188, 200, 213, 260, 269, 271
Commonwealth Games in Delhi, 213, 239, 268, 296
Commonwealth Games in Melbourne, 198, 206, 211
Commonwealth Judo Championships, 38
Commonwealth Lawyers Association, 35
Commonwealth membership, 29, 31, 33, 38, 39
Commonwealth of Nations, 1, 25, 26, 28, 30, 35, 38, 173, 221, 223-25
Commonwealth Sailing Championships, 38
Commonwealth Scholarship, 35
Commonwealth summits, 35
Commonwealth Writers Prize, 39
Commonwealth Youth Games, 13, 14, 166-69, 213, 222
Commonwealth Youth Programme, 34
Connaught Place, 240-41, 244-58, 285
Credit Cards, 245-57, 259-60, 264-65
Cue sports, 71
Cultural diversity, 203-4
Currency Changer, 250
Cyber cafe Food & Beverages, 253
Cycling Road Race, 202
Cycling, 10, 55, 69, 171, 175, 177-78, 181-82, 219-20, 234, 279, 297, 397

Dancesport, 47
Day trips, 330-31, 352, 361
Decolonisation, 28, 29
Delhi baton, 238, 295
Delhi Development Authority, 289
Delhi High Court, 217
Delhi Jal Board, 242
Delhi Metro, 215
Department of Tourism, 244-58, 288, 301, 330

Direct eliminations, 148, 157-58
Diving, 2, 10, 52, 64, 68, 116, 279
Doctor on Call, Services, 248, 253, 255-57
Dodgeball, 54, 74
Domestic
  tourism, 16, 323-24, 328, 330
  travellers, 331
Draft National Sports Tourism Strategy, 316, 321
Dziubak, Oliver, 182

Economic Boom in Indian Capital, 238, 296
Eco-tourism, 290, 302
Egypt, 15, 27, 134-35, 142
Electronic Sports, 69
Elephant polo, 64, 68
E-Mail, 244-58
Empire Games, 12
England, 1, 2, 12-14, 45, 111, 124-25, 134-35, 137, 143-44, 148, 175, 177, 180, 182, 186-87, 224-25
English Tourism Council, 363
Environmental impacts, 19, 22, 394, 400-1
Épée and Sabre events, 145
Equine Sports, 59
ETA, 346-47
Event organisers, 330, 338, 345-49, 355, 357

Federation of Indian Chambers of Commerce and Industry, 210-11
FIE rules, 148, 151, 155, 157
Fire Games, 42
Fireworks, 175, 189
Fitness Centre, 250, 255-56, 260
Flagship Hotel, 259
Flying
  Clubs, 310, 312
  Disc Sports, 60
  Sports Airplane, 60
Flyovers, 211, 214, 238, 240, 242, 292, 296, 302
Food & Beverages, 245-46, 248-50, 252-53, 257, 259
Football, 46, 48
Forehand, 107-8
Foreign exchange, 255-56, 315
Foreign tourist, 216, 288, 291, 293-95, 301, 302, 305
French Open, 96, 97, 102-4, 110
Friendly Games, 15, 37, 221

GAA, 46
Games Family Hotel, 259-61, 286
Games Village, 214, 216, 241-42, 286, 298
Games Volunteers, 199
Gandhi, Indira, 220
Gay Games, 43
Geographical diversity, 308-9
Germany, 20, 78, 134, 143-45, 149, 158, 177
Gleneagles Agreement, 37
GNCTD, 241, 270-71
Gold Coast Indy Car Race, 336
Gold medals, 14, 177-82
Grand Slam, 96, 101, 105, 110-11, 113-14
Greatest Female Players, 115
Greek Olympic Games, 84
GTO, 243, 261, 264-66
Gymnastics, 47, 60, 169, 182, 219, 234, 239, 279, 285, 296

Hammer, 80, 81
Handball games, 61
Handbook for Event Organisers, 346
Harare Declaration, 29, 31, 33
Health club, 246, 248, 260
High jump, 80

High Speed Telegraphy, 65, 69
Himachal Tourism, 313
Historical fencing, 149
Hockey, 137, 139, 169, 182, 206, 208, 219, 234, 279, 285
Hospitality industry, 298-99, 301, 314
Hotel accommodation, 261, 294-95
Hotel Ashok, 286
Human rights, 25, 29, 33, 36, 234
Hurdles events, 82

IAAF, 14, 78, 85, 167
Ice hockey, 49, 50, 62, 70, 75, 138-39
Immigration requirements, 347
India Gate, 238, 279, 295
India Tourism Development Corp, 243
Indian mythology, 268
Indian Olympic Association, 214, 271
Indian performers, 200
Indian Tourism Development Corporation Ltd, 259
Indian Tourism Industry, 292, 297-99
Indian Tourist Transporters Association, 308
Indira Gandhi International Airport, 215, 240-41
Indira Gandhi Sports Complex, 279, 285
Indoor track, 79, 81
Industry coordination, 318, 322, 336
Informal games, 101
Inter-governmental Group, 29
Inter-governmental organisation, 25, 36, 37
International Association of Athletics Federations, 77, 78, 85
International Silent Games, 45
International Sports Federations, 260, 286
International Squash Players Association, 134
International Tennis Federation, 97, 105, 110
International Tourism Receipts, 18
IOC, 14, 65, 97, 118, 124, 167, 260, 271
IPF, 94, 95
Ireland Act, 27, 32
Islamic Games, 43
ISO, 392, 399, 400
Israel, 27, 30
Isthmian Games, 77
ITDC, 243, 259, 286, 289, 304
ITTA, 307-8

Jamaica Tourism Board, 23
Javelin, 80, 81, 84
Jawaharlal Nehru Sports Complex, 279, 285
Jawaharlal Nehru Stadium, 213-14, 220, 223, 227, 229, 239, 242, 282, 285, 297
Johnston, Bill, 108
JTB, 23, 24
Jung, Samaresh, 200

Kalmadi, Suresh, 235, 289
Karni Singh Shooting Range, 285
Kite Sports, 62
Korea Tourism Organization, 16
Kuala Lumpur, 205, 224-26
Kuerten, Gustavo, 113-14

Land pollution, 22
Large-scale mass tourism, 390
Laundry, 244-45, 248-51, 253-57
Laver, Rod, 114-15
Lawn games, 95

Libya, 300
Lindsay, 399
Lipton International Players Championships in Florida, 113
List of Sports, 10
List of Winter Sports, 49
London Declaration, 26-28, 32, 34, 39
London, 2, 13, 27, 35, 36, 38, 96, 111, 125, 143, 223-25, 227, 270, 305, 365
Long Distance Events, 82
Long jump, 80, 84

Majesty Queen Elizabeth, 223-28
Major Dhyan Chand National Stadium, 285
Malaysia, 17, 20, 26, 134-35, 182, 235, 239, 296
Manchester, 13, 214, 224-26, 290
Marathon and Cycling Time Trial events, 203
Mascot competition, 169
Mascot, 168
Mass tourism, 390, 396
Mass transportation, 220
McKay, Heather, 135
Medical tourism, 295, 299, 305
Medical Tourists, 299
Mediterranean, 121, 250, 256-57, 259
Melbourne Commonwealth Games, 307
Melbourne Cricket Ground, 172, 175, 183-84
Melbourne, 11, 12, 37, 170, 172, 184, 186-87, 189, 198-200, 203, 214, 224-26, 290, 299, 333
MGD, 242
Modes of transport, 223, 227-28
Monasteries, 124
Money Changer, 245, 248-50, 253-55, 257
Motor sports, 46, 48, 70
Mountain Bike Cycling Traralgon Traralgon Sports, 184
Multiple event competitions, 84
Multi-sport
  championships, 36
  event, 1, 41, 42, 235
  festivals, 333

National Action Plan for Tourism, 322, 356
National Collegiate Athletic Association, 95
National Sports Tourism Strategy, 316, 322, 356-57
Nemean Games, 77
New Delhi Commonwealth Games, 235, 307
New Zealand, 2, 3, 12, 17, 31, 135, 177-78, 181-82, 221
Newcastle, 333-34
Niche tourism, 397
Non-Competition Venues, 279
Non-competitive events, 362
Non-smoking rooms, 245, 247
Nordic Games, 42

Old Commonwealth, 28
Olympiade, 78
Olympic Games, 1, 3, 41-43, 45, 47, 101-2, 110, 123, 135, 147, 150, 172, 270, 321, 331-33
Olympic Winter Games, 42
Opening ceremony, 175, 187-88, 200, 202, 213, 223-27, 229
Operation Acolyte, 198

Paddle Sports, 63
Pairs, 32, 146, 207-8
Pakistan, 29, 31, 32, 130, 135, 137, 186
Paragliding, 64, 68

Paralympic sport, 45, 88, 148
Parasailing, 64, 68, 309
Para-Sports, 282
Parkland Hotel, 253-54
PARS, 130
Pentathlon, 63, 80, 84
Physical sports, 48, 51
Pigeon sport, 68
Pittman, Jana, 167
Police and Fire Games, 42
Pools, 58, 72, 73, 118, 121-23, 147-48, 157-58, 179-80, 247-48, 250, 255-56, 396
Powerlifting, 71, 87, 88, 89, 94, 283
Prize money, 105, 112-13, 135
Professional players, 135
Promotion of tourism, 334, 365
Pythian Games, 77

Queen's Baton, 188, 222-29, 232

Races, 15, 67, 79-82, 86, 87, 123, 333, 348, 392-93
Racewalking Events, 81
Racing, 52, 53, 79, 121, 314-15
Radiosports, 65
Rafter, Patrick, 113-14
Rafting, 64
Ranking points, 106, 110-11
Rathore, Rajyavardhan Singh, 181
Recreation industry, 317, 342, 357
Recreational players, 96
Referee, 87, 89, 91, 93, 104-5, 130, 132, 152-53, 157
Regional games, 42, 78
Religious tourism, 294, 303
Revenue management, 400
Rhode Island, 97, 98
Rink hockey, 70, 75, 139
Road Transport, 304
Roadshows, 305
Roller hockey, 62, 70, 75, 138-39
Roller sports, 136, 139
Room Rate, 264-65, 391
Royal Commonwealth Society, 40
Royal Highness Prince Edward, 199, 200
Rugby, 38, 46, 219, 234, 279, 285
Rural tourism projects, 304

Safe deposit, 244-45, 247-51, 253, 257
Sampras, Pete, 113-15
Samresh Jung, 183, 206
Scoring systems, 129-30, 150
Scotland, 1, 2, 12, 13, 159, 169, 175, 179-80, 221
Seeded players, 110
Segura, Pancho, 108
Seles, Monica, 108-9, 114
Selja, Kumari, 303, 305
Shooting, 10, 73, 181, 207-9, 213, 219, 234, 239, 279, 285, 296-97
Shopping arcade, 244-46, 248-50
Sierra Leone, 186
Singapore Sports Council, 186
Singapore, 17, 33, 292, 294
Siri Fort Sports Complex, 239, 279, 285, 297
Skating Sports, 70
Sledding events, 49
Snooker, 10, 72, 73, 218
Snowball Association, 50, 71
Snowball fight, 51, 54
Societies Registration Act, 271
Softball, 53, 75, 125-26, 136
South Africa, 2, 3, 28-30, 33, 34, 37, 46, 130, 134, 137, 179, 204, 292, 294, 320, 365
Special Olympics World Games, 45
Special room facilities, 245-47, 249, 251-52, 257-58
Speed skating, 42, 49, 69, 70
Speedcubing, 67, 72

Sport and Recreation Industry, 357
Sport and Recreation Ministers Council, 330
Sport fishing, 59, 68
Sport stacking, 66
Sport Tourist, 362-63
Sport visas, 346
Sporting bodies, 318, 330, 332, 337-38
Sporting weapons, 153-54
Sports Council, 363
Sports industries, 326, 329-30
Sports medicine, 12, 329, 331
Sports Nutrition, 123
Sports tourism, 19-22, 316, 318-24, 327-28, 330-31, 333, 335, 337, 339-42, 344, 351-52, 354, 356-57, 362-65, 401
  article, 361
  definition of, 352, 361
  developing, 320
  domestic, 361
  luxury, 396
  passive, 396
  regional, 342
Sprints, 53, 79, 82, 178-79
Squash balls, 126
Squash court, 126, 128, 134, 136-37
Street hockey, 139
Summer Olympics, 46, 87, 122, 138, 145, 172, 186, 206, 235
Sustainable Tourism, 401
Swimmers, 117, 119-24
Swimming pools, 122, 244, 246-49, 253, 258
SWOT analysis, 402
Sydney Olympic Games, 351, 355
Sydney, 186-87, 317, 321, 323, 347

Table tennis, 10, 65, 72, 173, 207, 209, 213, 219, 239, 279, 283, 285, 296-97
Talkatora Indoor Stadium, 285
Tennis players, 98, 107, 115
Thyagaraj Sports Complex, 285
Tour operators, 292, 294-95, 302, 330, 337, 357, 391-92, 394, 399, 402
Tourism
  adventure, 308-9
  agencies, 323, 345
  associated activities, 395
  destination, 215, 294, 307, 336, 402
  inbound, 16, 321
  monsoon, 303
  outbound, 16
  package, 339, 344
  police, 215, 238
Tourist
  domestic, 216, 288, 291, 294, 361
  hubs, 237, 299, 307
  huge influx of, 214, 288, 298
  police, 215, 237
  trips, 19
Track events, 79, 85, 86
Transport industry, 307
Transportation, 216, 240, 292, 351
Travel agencies, 292, 394-95, 397, 402
Travel services, 251-52, 265, 393
Triathlon events, 178

Underwater hockey, 52, 62, 76
United Kingdom, 1, 2, 27, 28, 30, 33, 95, 96, 221, 320
United States Tennis Association, 96, 110
Uttarakhand, 292-95

Valet services, 251-52
Varpa Catch Games, 54
Video games, 137
Vietnam, 300

Volleyball, 62, 76
Volunteer Programme, 267

Wales, 2, 12, 13, 96, 177, 224-25, 227-28
Weightlifting, 10, 67, 71, 169, 177-78, 183, 207-9, 213, 219-20, 234, 239, 279, 285, 296-97
Wheelchair player, 103
Wimbledon, 96, 97, 102, 104, 110-11, 114
Wind Sports, 76
Winning players, 101
Winter
  Olympics, 138
  Para-Olympic Sport, 50
  sports, 42, 49
World Masters Games, 333
World Tourism Organisation, 15, 17-18, 317, 325
World Travel and Tourism Council, 300, 325
World University Games, 42, 158
Worldwide sporting telecast, 334
Wrestling, 2, 10, 55, 56, 78, 143, 213, 219-20, 239, 279, 285, 296-97

Xingyiquan Cue Sports, 58

Yamuna Sports Complex, 279, 283, 285
Yarra River, 175, 183, 187-88
Yechury, 306
Youth Games, 160, 213

Zimbabwe, 28, 31, 32, 173